LORD METHUEN
AND THE
BRITISH ARMY

LORD METHUEN

AND THE

BRITISH ARMY

Failure and Redemption in South Africa

STEPHEN M. MILLER

University of Rhode Island

FRANK CASS
LONDON • PORTLAND, OR

First published in 1999 in Great Britain by
FRANK CASS PUBLISHERS
Newbury House, 900 Eastern Avenue
London IG2 7HH

and in the United States of America by
FRANK CASS PUBLISHERS
c/o ISBS, 5804 N.E. Hassalo Street
Portland, Oregon 97213-3644

Website http://www.frankcass.com

British Library Cataloguing in Publication Data:

Miller, Stephen M.
  Lord Methuen and the British Army : failure and redemption
in South Africa
  1. Sanford, Paul 2. South African War, 1899–1902
  I. Title
  968'.048

ISBN 0-7146-4904-X (cloth)
ISBN 0-7146-4460-9 (paper)

Library of Congress Cataloging-in-Publication Data:

Miller, Stephen M., 1964–
  Lord Methuen and the British army : failure and redemption in
South Africa / Stephen M. Miller.
    p.   cm.
  Includes bibliographical references and index.
  ISBN 0-7146-4904-X. – ISBN 0-7146-4460-9 (pbk.)
  1. Methuen, Paul Sanford Methuen, Baron, 1845–1932–Military
leadership. 2. Marshals–Great Britain–Biography. 3. South
African War, 1899–1902–Campaigns. 4. Great Britain–History,
Military–19th century. I. Title.
U55.M47M55   1998
968.2'048–dc21   98-24089
                                                                          CIP

Typeset by Vitaset, Paddock Wood, Kent
Printed in Great Britain by
Bookcraft (Bath) Ltd, Midsomer Norton, Somerset

Contents

List of Maps

Acknowledgements

I am grateful to a number of people for their help in the preparation of this book. I would like to thank Edmund S. Wehrle for his invaluable assistance at each stage of this project. I am grateful as well to Peter Bergmann, Amii Omara-Otunnu, Ronald Coons and A. W. Hoglund of the University of Connecticut for their helpful suggestions and criticisms of the work. I would also like to thank the History Department and the Graduate School at the University of Connecticut for their financial assistance. In addition, James Thomas of Blinn College and Fransjohan Pretorius of the University of Pretoria offered insight on aspects of the South African War. I would also like to acknowledge Richard Hull of New York University and Jeanne Penvenne of Tufts University who sparked my interest in the study of the South African War.

I would like to thank the staff of the various libraries and archives used in my research, especially the Wiltshire County Records Office. This project could not have been completed without the kind permission of the late Anthony John, 6th Baron Methuen, to view the papers of his grandfather, Field Marshal Lord Methuen. In addition, many thanks go to P. Boyden at the National Army Museum, S. G. Roberts and J. R. Spain at the Royal Commission of Historical Manuscripts, Claire Brown at the Rhodes House Library, and C. P. Smith at the Hove Central Library. A very special thanks to Robert Vrecenak and the staff at Interlibrary Loan at the University of Connecticut for their assistance. I would like to thank the South African National Museum of Military History for permission to reprint portions of an article published in the *Military History Journal*. Hilary Hewitt, in-house editor at Frank Cass Publishers, and Margaret Wallis, copy-editor, were especially helpful in preparing the manuscript for publication.

Finally, I would like to thank my family for their emotional and financial support. This work could not have been accomplished without them. Above all, I owe a special debt of gratitude to my wife, Jessica Prata Miller, for her scholarly and emotional support. Her advice has shaped the direction of my arguments and helped me at crucial points throughout the project.

List of Abbreviations

AAG	Assistant Adjutant-General
ADC	Aide-de-Camp
CSO	Chief Staff Officer
DSO	Divisional Signalling Officer
GOC	General Officer Commanding
GOCC	General Officer Commanding-in-Chief
IY	Imperial Yeomanry
KOYLI	King's Own Yorkshire Light Infantry
LI	Light Infantry
LNL	Loyal North Lancashires
MI	Mounted Infantry
RAMC	Royal Army Medical Corps
RE	Royal Engineers
RFA	Royal Field Artillery
RHA	Royal Horse Artillery
SSW	Secretary of State for War

1

Introduction

As the centennial of the South African War (1899–1902) approaches, the need to revisit its battles and assess their impact becomes more apparent. The war tells not only the story of a three-year struggle between the British and the Boers, it also tells of a clash between modern technology and the strategy and tactics held by a conservative British War Office and officer class, stagnated by 30 years of successful campaigning in Africa and Asia. The late Victorian British army was not prepared to meet the demands of a modern war. This work focuses on the British army in the South African War, in particular, the failure of its leadership to recognize the changing demands of modern war and its ability to adapt to these circumstances. In this analysis of the British officer class, the career of Field Marshal Lord Methuen, who served as a divisional commander in the South African War, will serve as a case study.

Although well known during his own lifetime, Methuen has fallen into the shadows and has not enjoyed the eminence which many of his peers such as Herbert Kitchener, Garnet Wolseley, Frederick Roberts and Ian Hamilton hold today. Methuen's career deserves more scholarly attention. Very little has been written on his wartime experiences and no biography has yet been published. The existing primary literature which concentrates solely on his command in South Africa is riddled with inaccuracies, relying as it does on contemporary and mostly journalistic accounts.[1] The best secondary sources which examine Methuen's experiences as a field commander, although more reliable, also have their problems.[2] For example, Maurice and Grant's *(Official) History of the War in South Africa*, published by the British Government, was careful not to point any incriminating fingers, and thereby it failed to address some very important issues. Leo Amery's *The Times History of the War in South Africa*, on the other hand, was overly opinionated and relied on informants who had axes to grind with their commanders or the War Office.[3]

Several good scholarly and non-scholarly accounts of the South African War have come out since the late 1950s.[4] However, only two authors have used the extensive collection of Methuen Papers housed in the Trowbridge Records Office, a few miles from the Methuens' baronial Corsham home. The first to do so was W. Baring Pemberton in his authoritative *Battles of the Boer War*.[5] In 1979, Thomas Pakenham drew from Lord Methuen's correspondences with Lady Methuen to support several of the chapters in his book *The Boer War*.[6]

More recently, many historians of the South African War have moved away from battlefield narratives and have researched topics ranging from the role of Africans in the war to the workings of the concentration camps. In addition, biographies continue to be published, most notably Roy Macnab's *The French Colonel: Villebois-Mareuil and the Boers 1899–1900* and Johannes Meintjes' *De la Rey*.[7] In 1985 Jay C. Stone finished his dissertation, 'The Boer War and its Effects on British Military Reform', in which he was able to synthesize a great amount of data and analyse the effect of the war on postwar military reform.[8] However, the need remains to find answers to explain British failures in the initial stages of the South African War and to describe the capability of some British officers to adjust to new circumstances and overcome a mindset which was the product of several decades of colonial training. An analysis of Methuen's experiences in South Africa provides a ready means of understanding British failures and successes in the South African War.

In many ways Lord Methuen was a typical officer of the late Victorian army. His experiences, both administrative and in the field, were gained in Africa, Asia and Europe as well as at home. His military career began in 1858 when he purchased a commission in the Scots Fusilier Guards. This was a period when the British army was stagnating under the conservative leadership of its Commander-in-Chief, the Duke of Cambridge, and the Cardwellian reforms had yet to be enacted. The Commander-in-Chief did little to reform the army after the disasters of the Crimean War (1854–55). Shortly afterwards, as a captain, Methuen, at the age of 28, received his first combat assignment in the British protectorate over the Gold Coast (modern-day Ghana), where he commanded a brigade of local Fante in the Ashanti War (1873–74). He commanded a post north of the Prah River and took part in the decisive battle at Amoaful.

The Ashanti War typified Great Britain's numerous colonial expeditions during the Victorian age. A handful of British officers and a few battalions, armed with the latest in military hardware and accompanied by a larger number of colonial troops, were sent to subdue the Ashanti. British troops moved quickly into the interior of Ashanteland. The opposing force, although determined and courageous, was no match for the modern technology of the British. The war was short, inexpensive, and few British lives were lost in combat.

Following the Ashanti War, Methuen served brief administrative stints in Ireland as an assistant military attaché, in Berlin as military attaché to the British embassy, and in England as Assistant Adjutant-General and Quarter Master General of the Home District. On special service appointment in 1882, he joined the expedition to Egypt to crush the Arabi rebellion. Supposedly, the Egyptian nationalists threatened to take the Suez Canal, thereby cutting British trade, shipping and investment. General Sir Garnet Wolseley, the commander of the British forces in the Ashanti War, was called to conduct British operations. Methuen, serving as Commandant of Wolseley's headquarters, was present at both Mahuta and Tel-el-Kebir, the major engagements of the war. The British assembled 35,000 men for the expedition to Egypt, by far the largest of Wolseley's campaigns, but still a relatively insignificant force compared to that required for the South African War, which was 12 times as great.

In 1884 Methuen sailed to South Africa for the first time. During the expedition to Bechuanaland (modern-day Botswana) under General Sir Charles Warren, Methuen raised and commanded a volunteer regiment known as Methuen's Horse. Bechuanaland, situated north of the Cape Colony in South Africa, had become a trouble spot for the British. After declaring Bechuanaland a protectorate in October 1884, the British found it necessary to send troops to the area to defend their interests. The British force was to block the attempts by Boer mercenaries from neighbouring republics to extend their influence over British territory. This successful but limited engagement lasted less than a year and required fewer then 5,000 troops, more than half of which were volunteers. It would be over ten years before Methuen would see combat again.

Methuen served again in South Africa as Deputy Adjutant-General in the Cape Colony from 1888–90. Among his many duties, he oversaw the inspection and training of Cecil Rhodes' Pioneer Column, the volunteer force in search of gold and glory used to invade Matabeleland (modern-day Zimbabwe). This experience, along with his 1884–85 tour in Bechuanaland, gave Methuen a good understanding of the Boers and the terrain and climate of South Africa. Of the many British officers who would later serve in the South African War, Methuen was one of the few to truly understand the enemy and the roots of the conflict.

For most of the 1890s Methuen held administrative positions in Great

Britain. In 1891 he accepted the command of the Home District. Answering only to Sir Redvers Buller, the Adjutant-General, he attempted to strengthen British defences against the threat of an amphibious invasion. His most important work was to conduct the largest peace-time manœuvres of volunteer forces in England in the nineteenth century. In 1897, to keep his mind alert and his knowledge of combat fresh, Methuen voluntarily travelled to India on special service with General Sir William Lockhart's staff. Lockhart led a punitive expedition to Tirah on India's northwest frontier. Tirah exposed Methuen to the realities of modern firepower in combat. However, this brief conflict did not significantly alter his understanding of modern warfare.

Methuen's service between 1870 and 1897 provided the training and experience for his first field command in 1899: the relief of Kimberley in the South African War. This event proved to be the most pivotal in his career. It also proved to be an event for which he was entirely unprepared.

In tracing the career of Methuen between 1858 and 1902 as it relates to the evolution of the techniques of war, there is a certain logic in the following three-part division. Part One deals with Methuen's career prior to the South African War. Chapter 2 considers his earliest influences and his decision to devote his life to the army and empire, while Chapter 3 shows the development of his thought, the advancement of his career and his role in army administration.

Part Two investigates the South African War and Methuen's initial failure to defeat the Boers on the battlefield. Chapter 4 serves as an introductory chapter, reviewing Britain's decision for war and the War Office's failure to prepare for it in 1899. Chapter 5 discusses Methuen's advance to the Modder River, while Chapter 6 analyses Methuen's failure at the Battle of Magersfontein.

Part Three examines Methuen's struggle to retain his command and his ability to improvise in the later stages of the war. Chapter 7 considers the War Office's treatment of Methuen after his failure at the Battle of Magersfontein and the arrival of Lord Roberts in South Africa. It also explores Methuen's relationship with his men. Chapter 8 examines how Methuen endured and how he changed to meet the demands of guerrilla warfare. Chapter 9 examines the lessons of the war and its impact both on the British army and Methuen himself. Finally, Chapter 10 concludes with some general remarks on Methuen and the British army.

When Methuen died in 1932, at the age of 87, he was mourned in Great Britain as the last of Queen Victoria's great generals: the last vestige of 'the old school'.[9] This work is an attempt to better understand Methuen, a product of the old school, and to demonstrate that the late Victorian age was not just a period of individual small colonial wars but a period of great transition to modern war. It is also an attempt to return Methuen to his proper place in British military history.

NOTES

1. Ernest C. Bennett, *With Methuen's Column on an Ambulance Train* (London: Sonnenschein, 1900); H. S. Gaskell, *With Lord Methuen in South Africa* (London: Henry J. Drane, 1906); Herbert M. Guest, *With Lord Methuen from Belmont to Hartebeestfontein* (Klerksdorp: H. M. Guest, 1901); Alfred Kinnear, *To Modder River with Methuen* (Bristol: J. W. Arrowsmith, 1900); and, Karl B. Spurgin, *On Active Service with the Northumberland and Durham Yeomanry under Lord Methuen* (London: Walter Scott Publishing, 1901).
2. Frederick Maurice and M. H. Grant, (*Official) History of the War in South Africa, 1899–1902* (London: Hurst & Blackwood, 1906–1910); *The War in South Africa: A German Official Account* W. H. Walters (trans.) (New York: E. P. Dutton, 1904); and, L. S. Amery (ed.), *The Times History of the War in South Africa 1899–1902* (London: Sampson Low, Marston & Co., Ltd., 1907).
3. Some like Henry Colvile, who supplied Amery with most of his information on Methuen's relief of Kimberley, denied responsibility for their actions. Others attempted to vindicate themselves by stressing their successes.
4. Eversley Belfield, *The Boer War* (Hamden, CT: Anchon Books, 1975); Byron Farwell, *The Great Anglo-Boer War* (New York: W. W. Norton & Co., 1976); Edgar Holt, *The Boer War* (London: Putnam, 1958); Rayne Kruger, *Good-Bye Dolly Gray* (New York: J. B. Lippincott Co., 1960); and Peter Warwick (ed.), *The South African War* (Harlow: Longman, 1980).
5. W. Baring Pemberton, *Battles of the Boer War* (Philadelphia: Dufour Editions, 1964).
6. Thomas Pakenham, *The Boer War* (New York: Random House, 1979).
7. Roy Macnab, *The French Colonel: Villebois-Mareuil and the Boers 1899–1900* (London: Oxford University Press, 1975) and Johannes Meintjes, *De la Rey* (Johannesburg: Hugh Keartland, 1966).
8. Jay C. Stone, 'The Boer War and Its Effects on British Military Reform' (PhD thesis, City University of New York, 1985).
9. *The New York Times*, 31 Oct. 1932.

PART ONE

The Making of an Officer

2

The Baron's Son Joins the Guards (1864–81)

Paul Sanford Methuen was born on 1 September 1845, at the home of his father's family in Corsham, Wiltshire. His mother, Anna Horatia Caroline Sanford, was the only child of John Sanford, a clergyman from Nynehead in nearby Somerset. His father, Frederick Henry Paul Methuen (1818–91), was the eldest living son of Paul, 1st Baron Methuen. Frederick would inherit the title in 1849 and later serve as Lord-in-waiting to Queen Victoria.[1] The Methuen family had dedicated itself to state service for several generations. They had served mostly as politicians and diplomats, a tradition started by the ardent Whig MP John Methuen, in the seventeenth century.[2] As appreciation for their commitment to public service, they had been granted a barony by Queen Victoria in 1838. As the eldest of ten children, Paul stood first in line to inherit his father's title as well as his lands. For Paul, following in his father's footsteps should have meant a short political career and a life of luxury at his ancestral home in Wiltshire, but he chose a different path.

Although very active in local affairs, the young Methuen's interest in political issues was limited. Like most educated men of means, he kept up on the current events, fraternized with many of the leading politicians of his day, and often debated issues with friends and family, especially his father, with whom he had a close relationship. However, his interest in politics was never more than conversational and rarely stretched beyond military concerns.

In line with the family's long tradition, Methuen became a Whig at an early age. However, he gradually moved to the right over the years, and, like many of the Whigs who defected over the issue of Irish Home Rule, could best be described as a Liberal Unionist by the mid 1890s. Throughout his life, he abhorred public pressure and the manipulation of the media by politicians for limited gain, believing that change should come from those best suited to rule. Methuen thought that William Ewart Gladstone, the adept leader of the Liberal Party, was 'making a fool of himself travelling third class and talking to fiddlers and fishermen' to win support from the lower classes.[3] As a Whig, Methuen saw himself a defender of liberty and religious freedom, but did not champion equality.[4] Although he accepted the importance of merit as a determinant for positions of power, either in politics or in the military, he never disregarded class entirely. A combination of merit and class connections determined his advancement through the ranks, and he was rewarded with appointments by Conservative and Liberal Governments alike.

Shunning a life of politics, Methuen chose a career in the army instead. On leaving Eton, 'the chief nursery of the peerage',[5] and becoming a cornet in the local Wilts Yeomanry, he purchased a commission from Sandhurst in 1864. Thus he became the first real soldier in the Methuen family, subsequently dedicating nearly 70 years of his life to military service. None of his ancestors, his father included, seems to have taken a career in the military very seriously. After a very short military service with the Royal Horse Guards and the 71st Foot, Frederick Methuen retired before his 24th birthday to represent a Wiltshire constituency in the House of Commons, as his father and his grandfather had done before him. However, his son Paul always felt more comfortable discussing war or sport than debating politics, and he preferred the company of his fellow officers to the company of his fellow Peers.

THE STATE OF THE BRITISH ARMY

The British army, which Methuen entered in 1864, was an institution sorely in need of repair. The problems of incompetent leadership, faulty supply, transport and medicine, lack of reserves, and poor strategic planning, which the failures of the Crimean War (1854–56) had demonstrated, had yet to be addressed. Although both the British Government and people had demanded change in the war's aftermath, the combination of a resistant Commander-in-Chief, a frugal parliament and a fickle electorate led to the matter being temporarily shelved. The successful defeat of the Sepoy mutineers in 1857 in India further distracted all but the most determined reformers from the true state of the British army.

One of the features of the British army which troubled reformers most was the system of purchase. Purchase, which valued money above merit, was a problem which had plagued the army for years. It often allowed incompetent but wealthy officers rapid promotion. William III had halted it temporarily in the late seventeenth century; in the eighteenth century, George I was against it, but yet it continued.[6] The British Officer Corps on the eve of the Crimean War remained an élite group of landed men. If nothing else, the Crimean War demonstrated the failure of this group.

Upon the conclusion of the war, a Royal Commission published a scathing report on the subject. The problem for the Commission and for most reformers, oddly enough, was not that the purchase system prevented men of lesser means from entering the officer corps and ensured the advancement of less qualified but wealthier officers. The problem, as they saw it, was the inability of the government to control the actual price of commission. Over-regulation payments, which included the government price and an additional personal fee which served to persuade older officers to retire, cost an increasing amount and the cost of commissions was also skyrocketing. Still, no action was taken to regulate the system, until Gladstone's first ministry convinced the Queen to issue a royal warrant to abolish the system in 1871.[7] At that time, there were 6,938 officers with vested rights, and the value of their commissions was nearly £14,000,000.[8]

THE SCOTS GUARDS

In the waning years of the purchase system Methuen took full advantage of his wealth and connections. There is no indication that he ever believed that what he was doing was wrong. As an aristocrat he believed that the system of purchase prevented the development of an independent military which could threaten the 'patrician governing class'.[9] In November 1864 he purchased the double rank of ensign and lieutenant in the Scots Fusilier Guards, and in December 1867 he purchased the double rank of lieutenant and captain.[10]

Methuen's choice of regiment was not surprising. The Guards was amongst the élite brigades of the British army, and the price of its commissions one of the highest. Boys from the better-known public schools such as Eton and Harrow flocked to the Guards.[11] Attending Eton during the Crimean War and at the time of the Sepoy Mutiny, doubtless filled Methuen and his classmates with overwhelming patriotic zeal. One could not escape William Howard Russell's reports of the charge of the Light Brigade and the battles of the Crimean War in Great Britain's first journalistic war.[12]

His lineage and his father's connections to the Stephenson family, a well-known military clan, made the Scots regiment the likely choice for young Methuen. Frederick Charles Arthur Stephenson, a veteran of Crimea and China, was his first battalion commander (the 2nd battalion), and later his regiment commander. He loved Methuen as a son and carefully watched over him.[13] 'Ben' remained one of his closest confidants throughout Methuen's career. The Baron's connections at the court and in the army helped in Methuen's rapid advancement in the Guards. Merit counted, but being one of the queen's 'favourites' and a personal friend of the Prince of Wales certainly did not impede his progress.

EARLY INFLUENCES

The Scots Guards, as it has been known since 1877, has an illustrious history that goes back to Charles I and to the Irish Rebellion of 1642.[14] The second oldest of the Guards Regiments, it had fought in the War of the League of Augsburg, the War of the Spanish Succession, the War of the Austrian Succession, and the Seven Years War. It had also served in the War of American Independence and in the Napoleonic Wars. In the Crimean War, it had held the centre in the attack at Alma, and had taken part in the actions at Inkerman and Sevastopol.

The men responsible for shaping Methuen's thinking in the earliest years of his service, his commanding officers in the Scots Guards, were all veterans of the Crimea. It was they who encouraged him to continue with his career through the 1880s and 1890s when most men of his station would have retired and returned to their comfortable family estates. George H. Moncrieff, Reginald Gipps, F. W. E. Forestier-Walker and Ben Stephenson all taught Methuen much about being an officer and remained close friends throughout his life. William Frederick, 3rd Baron Abinger, served as Methuen's battalion commander and later his regiment commander. Abinger's praise for his general, as well as military and theoretical, knowledge, his hard-working and trustworthy attitude, and his excellent horsemanship, helped to develop Methuen's confidence in his own ability.[15]

More than any other commander, Colonel H. C. Fletcher was the greatest influence on Methuen during his formative years in the army. Fletcher impressed upon him the importance of duty and honour. 'He moulded [Methuen and his other junior officers] in the form of knights.'[16] He convinced Methuen that because of his upbringing and his social position, he was suited to command and he was obliged to fulfil his responsibility to his Queen and country. At a period when the middle class was beginning to infiltrate the higher ranks of the army, Methuen clung to his caste. Fletcher reinforced Methuen's belief in the aristocracy's inherent ability to govern. This belief, along with Fletcher's influence, is demonstrated in a paper Methuen wrote on discipline. Drawing an example from the American Civil War, an event in which Fletcher served as an official observer, Methuen wrote that although the Southern side was half as strong as its opponent and lacked equipment,

> the difference between the two armies was however at once shown in the stamp of officer. The Southern officers were chosen from its aristocracy, men accustomed to command, to field sport and out of doors exercise, as contrasted with the Northerners who remained indoors looking to the money bags. The wealthy southern planters, the owners of many slaves, all dependent on them for food, clothing, and discipline, acquired habits of command and organization highly valuable to the officers. A man capable of managing the affairs of a large plantation and ruling his servants with orders and regularity, has advanced far in the qualities necessary to make a good colonel of the regiment.[17]

Methuen already possessed the qualities of a commander; Fletcher reinforced them and strengthened his calling.

Methuen's commanders instilled in him an ideal of responsibility to his men and to his nation and they impressed upon him the importance of his new career. He worked very hard at becoming a good officer. Scrawled upon the first page of his earliest military diary is a short entry entitled 'The Commander'.

> No army, however good its organization, or the quality of its personnel and material, can be relied upon at the moment of trial unless it has implicit confidence and faith in the man who gives impulse to it – its commander. Experience shows that exercise of command demands the combination of force of character with an intimate acquaintance with the art of war. Men otherwise good become [confused] when they cannot see the enemy, in consequence of their not having made a study beforehand of the principles which give certainty to military combinations. All great soldiers have devoted hours daily to study [the] art of war. 'Will, character, application and boldness have made me what I am', Napoleon. In wars genius is shown by the aptitude for discerning and knowing to account favourable moments.[18]

No soldier in the British army in the nineteenth century could escape the ghosts of Napoleon and Wellington: all his life Methuen dedicated himself to becoming a great commander in their likeness.

In 1871 Methuen had his first opportunity to observe warfare and meet a 'great commander'. During the Franco-Prussian War he served as a runner for Lord Lyons, the British Ambassador to France, carrying dispatches between Paris and Bordeaux, and on an errand to Versailles, Methuen met the great German general, Count von Moltke. The meeting, albeit short, indelibly marked the young British officer's life. Methuen set himself to read everything he could about Moltke's campaigns and life, writing: 'To soldiers he set the example of how to work through and for others, not to play for our own hand, and not to seek to enhance our own interest by means of self-advertisement.'[19] Interestingly, it is perhaps Methuen's concurrence with Moltke's work ethic which explains his own relative obscurity.[20] Never in Methuen's lengthy career did he act for his own gain, ask for praise, or deny responsibility in failure. 'One does not come into the world to look after one's own comfort', he once wrote to a close friend.[21]

In addition to meeting Moltke at Versailles, Methuen was able to witness the strength of Europe's finest fighting force – the Prussian army. Intoxicated by its sheer strength and ability, he wrote: 'The Prussian officers are the finest built, best looking, most intelligent men I have ever seen. I saw their manual and platoon squad drill, very perfect, very stiff and quite as good as I expected; if you were to tell me they were Frederick the Great's army, I might say "yes".'[22]

Methuen later served as Military Attaché to Lord Odo Russell, British Ambassador to Germany, and became an expert on the German army. His infatuation with the Prussian military led to him trying always when in positions of administration to make the British army more like the German army.

THE SECOND ASHANTI WAR

The army which Methuen had entered in the 1860s was used almost exclusively for colonial combat. Between the years 1857 and 1899, the War Office listed some 17 entries as 'principal British wars'.[23] In Byron Farwell's examination of Queen Victoria's reign (1837–1901), he states that there was not one year during this period in which soldiers employed by the British empire were not fighting somewhere.[24] Some of these campaigns, such as the Zulu War in South Africa, Kitchener's reconquest of the Sudan and the Boxer rebellion in China, are well known. However, others, such as the 1864 Bhutan expedition, the Lushai campaign and the Nikki expedition on the Indian and Afghan frontiers, are now long forgotten remnants of the British imperial record. There were at least a hundred expeditions sent to Africa, Asia and to the rest of the world to extend, consolidate and pacify the overseas empire during Methuen's active service.[25] This was the era of European expansion into the non-western world. Informal empire gradually became formal, and it was the British army's role to maintain and expand the British empire.

Britain led the way in the European race to secure territory. Protectorates and colonies were designated and founded from southern Africa to the Afghan frontier, and from the Sudan to the South Pacific. The causes were both economic and strategic. The question of whether the flag followed commerce or commerce followed the flag is debatable. What is not debatable, however, is that where the flag went, the army followed. Often, troops raised in Britain made up only a minority of an expeditionary force. For example, of the 10,000 men employed in the Persian campaign in 1857 only 33 per cent were British. Only 25 per cent of the 71,700 troops needed to pacify Afghanistan in the late 1870s were British. And perhaps most surprisingly, in the Sepoy Mutiny of 1857 which threatened their 'jewel in the crown', 67 per cent of the troops sent to India were not from the British Isles.[26] Although British soldiers did not often make up the majority of the expedition, British officers were used almost exclusively to command both regiments of the line and regiments raised overseas in these engagements.

While the Franco-Prussian War offered Methuen an opportunity to see war firsthand, his first actual taste of combat came a few years later. On 26 February 1873, the Ashanti, a powerful kingdom situated in the interior of the Gold Coast, crossed the Prah River and invaded the coast, an area proclaimed a protectorate by the British in 1844. After a considerable delay, the government reluctantly agreed to send an expeditionary force under Colonel Garnet Wolseley to punish the Ashanti and exact retribution. In November 1873, when Wolseley asked for European troops, he was flooded by the requests of young British officers who hoped to make names for themselves. With the abolition of purchase, and merit the only means of promotion (at least in theory), there was fierce competition for special service opportunities. Only in Victoria's small wars could an officer prove himself on the battlefield. One of these requests came from Captain Methuen, who was serving in London as Brigade Major on the staff of Prince Edward of Saxe-Weimar. Wolseley accepted Methuen's offer.

On 19 December 1873, Captain Paul Methuen disembarked at the Cape Coast from the *Sarmatian* along with Brigadier General Archibald

Alison, Colonel George Greaves, Captain Arthur Paget, also from the Scots Guards, and the 42nd regiment.[27] Methuen, one of the three captains Wolseley specifically requested, was appointed a brigade major in H. Evelyn Wood's native regiment.[28]

This was the not the first time the Ashanti had come to blows with the British. The conflict centred around the coastal trade, the interior trade and control of the Fante, a weak confederation of coastal peoples. To extend their authority over the coast, the British played the Fante off against their much stronger rival, the Ashanti. In 1806 the Ashanti had attacked the British fort at Annamboo. After two more conflicts erupted in 1816 and 1817, a British embassy on the Gold Coast was established to prevent any further problems.[29] It did little good, however, and peace was not long lasting. In 1824 the Ashanti executed a sergeant in the British service for speaking disrespectfully toward the *asantahene* (the king), Osei Bonsu, and in retaliation, Governor Charles Macarthy organized a small expedition to punish the Ashanti. The expedition failed miserably and British forts were saved only by their rockets and an outbreak of fever in the Ashanti camp. In 1863, when Kwaku Dua I, the *asantehene*, insisted that a runaway slave be returned to him, the tentative peace was broken again. Governor Richard Pine's refusal to comply led to an Ashanti show of force, which produced a strong British reaction. Torrential rains eventually put an end to the conflict.

The Second Ashanti War (1873–74) was fought over trade routes to the interior and control of the fort at Elmina on the Gold Coast.[30] The Ashanti wanted what they believed to be rightfully theirs: this was not an attempt to subjugate the Fante or throw the British into the sea. David Kimble called the Second Ashanti War the 'first war inspired by anti-European sentiment' in Africa.[31] The Ashanti, finding themselves caught in an attempt by the British to consolidate their administration and extend their control over the Gold Coast, exemplified by the transfer of the Dutch fort at Elmina to the British in February 1872, refused to have their fate decided by outside forces. Kofi Karikari, the *asantehene*, claimed the fort as his own. Fearing that he would be cut out of the lucrative trade both on the coast by the expanding and increasingly hostile British and in the interior by the Fante middlemen, the king mobilized his forces. When the inhabitants of Elmina requested aid to prevent British interference, he responded, sending on 22 January 48,000 warriors to the coast.[32]

At first, the British simply watched as the Ashanti invaded. The Fante were capable of rallying over 70,000 troops, and the British expected their ally to put up a lively defence. To their surprise, the King of the Fante failed

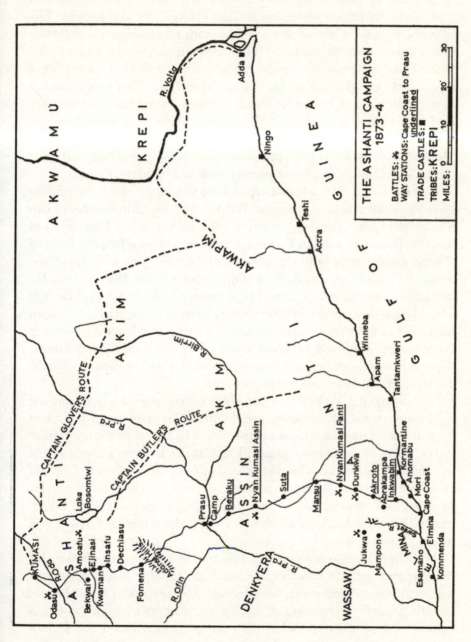

Map 1: The Ashanti Campaign, 1873–74. Map reproduced from Brian Bond (ed.), *Victorian Military Campaigns*, London, Hutchinson, 1967.

to rally his forces and the Fante Confederation fell apart.[33] By June, the Ashanti had smashed through the Fante defences and thousands of fugitives were fleeing for British protection at Cape Coast Castle and Elmina. The forts, the possession of which was of primary importance to the British Government, were threatened.[34] The 100-man garrison at Cape Coast Castle could not possibly stop the Ashanti; thus more Fante police were raised and detachments of Hausas were sent out from neighbouring protectorates. On 9 June, Lieutenant-Colonel Festing and 104 marines landed at Elmina to strengthen the garrison there. Four days later, the Ashanti struck. Although casualties were high, the British held the fort. More reinforcements and supplies were sent to the coast, and in August Gladstone's Cabinet finally committed itself to a military offensive.[35]

Colonel Garnet Wolseley was appointed to command the expedition. Wolseley, a veteran of the Second Burma War, the Crimea, the Indian Mutiny, the China War, and most recently, the Red River Expedition to quell the Fenian invasion of Canada, was an important adviser to Edward Cardwell. Adored by both the queen and the public, he was one of the most talented and reform-minded young officers in the British army. He was Gilbert and Sullivan's 'model of a modern major-general'.[36] He was a 'stately little gentleman of proud military bearing, quick bright eye, broad high forehead, ardent temperament, a sparking intelligence animating every feature', according to Henry Stanley, the famous explorer and newspaper reporter on assignment in the Ashanti War for the *New York Herald*. To Methuen, Wolseley *was* the British army.

Accompanying Wolseley to the Gold Coast were the best and the brightest men the British army had to offer. The 'Wolseley Ring', as it became known, included Lieutenant-Colonel H. Evelyn Wood and Major Baker C. Russell, regiment commanders, Captain Redvers Buller, chief of intelligence, Lieutenant-Colonel John McNeill, chief of staff, Captain Henry Brackenbury, assistant military secretary, Lieutenant Frederick Maurice, Wolseley's private secretary, as well as Captain William Butler, Major Thomas Baker, Captain Robert Home, Major George Greaves and Major George Colley.[37]

Wolseley's 'Ring' was a clique of officers who accompanied him on his many campaigns and who became very influential in building the late Victorian army. A great rivalry later developed between Wolseley's followers and the protégés of 'Britain's other General', Frederick Sleigh Roberts, a commander of great prestige who served primarily on the Indian subcontinent.[38] Methuen was able to walk a fine line between both cliques during his entire career, enjoying service with both, although never really finding his niche in either. He preferred the company of other aristocratic officers.

On his arrival at the Gold Coast, Wolseley assessed the situation as desperate. He had too few men to attempt an invasion of the interior. Of the 70,000 Fante available for service, only 12,000 were mustered. Wolseley believed them to be quite worthless as fighting men but considered them excellent porters.[39] Methuen concurred: 'The Fante are wretched and fools but wonderful men to carry weight. A Fante woman carried my things from Mannak to Anocoomassie with an 18 month child on her back and a 50th month child on her head.'[40] Wolseley demanded that the War Office dispatch reinforcements, and the Treasury was forced to loosen its purse-strings, dispatching three battalions of British regulars at the end of 1872. As Wolseley awaited the arrival of the reinforcements he prepared his stores, built roads leading to the interior and forced the Ashanti to recross the Prah River.

Captain Methuen, dispatched with these reinforcements, was anxious to start on his mission. Unfortunately, the first couple of weeks after his arrival were spent on the coast preparing for the inland journey and attempting to fight off local diseases. He failed in his attempt, as did many of the British soldiers, to stay healthy. Towards the end of December, as the temperatures rose, he felt so depleted by headaches that he could neither eat nor work. After recovery, his enthusiasm turned to boredom. 'It is now a life of inaction here, nothing to do until we move', he wrote his father. 'It is very stupid work, and I will be glad when we move. I am afraid it will be a slow monotonous war. We are to move three miles a day on the other side of the Prah, and I doubt the Ashantis shall fight.'[41]

Sharing Methuen's belief that the Ashanti would avoid battle, Henry Brackenbury wrote, 'Every native of Africa [has] a superstitious awe and dread of the white man that prevents the negro from daring to meet us face to face in combat.'[42] While not as overtly racist in his assessment of the enemy, Charles Callwell, one of the most important military historians of the Victorian age, agreed that the Ashanti would avoid a decisive confrontation.[43] John Fortescue, another contemporary soldier and critic, wrote:

> Speaking generally the sound principle of savage warfare is this – to equip yourself with a good service for transport and supply, march up to your enemy, sit down and fortify yourself in a strong position. Your enemy must do one of three things: attack you, in which case he is sure to be defeated, move on or starve. He is not likely to attempt attack after a lesson or two,

and therefore as a rule he will move on. You then move after him and sit down again.[44]

Methuen was one of 16 officers on special service assigned to Lieutenant Colonel H. Evelyn Wood's native regiment. Wood had only just begun a remarkable career in the military. He had served in the Crimea as a naval officer and returned as a cavalry officer. In the Ashanti War he held a commission in the infantry. One of the best minds in the military, he was never fully utilized by Wolseley.[45] Wood had no more respect for the talents of the local Fante than had Wolseley or Methuen. 'It would be difficult to imagine a more cowardly, useless lot of men', he wrote.[46] Nevertheless, it was his job to raise a local regiment and whip them into fighting shape.[47]

Methuen's main job in Wood's regiment was to keep the local levies, mostly Fante and Hausa, from deserting. He did not blame his men directly for their actions. His diary is filled with concern for the conduct and treatment of his men. '[There is] no system of transport, if they had organized the carriers with regular Regiments under European officers, or had given each regiment permanent transport, like the Regular troops, I do not think there would have been as much desertion. As it is the poor devils have no one to look after them, to see they get paid and rationed.'[48] Methuen attributed the poor conduct of his native troops to their prior organization and treatment. He believed that had discipline been imposed, the Fante would have performed their duties and transport would not have suffered. As it was, it did suffer. Methuen learned a valuable lesson about the care of his men from this experience.

Wood's regiment made up the advanced column of the British expedition. Wolseley's plan was to march straight for Kumasi, the most important city in the kingdom. 'In planning a war against an uncivilized nation who has, perhaps, no capital', Wolseley wrote, 'your first objective should be the capture of whatever they prize most and the destruction or deprivation of which will probably bring the war most rapidly to a conclusion.'[49] Wolseley believed this to be Kumasi, the site of the *asantehene*'s throne, the Golden Stool.

The Second Ashanti War was in many ways a typical British conflict in the age of Imperialism. Firstly, the British force was small, 3,500 men, only half of which were from line regiments. Two regiments from West India and locally raised Hausas made up the rest of the force. Secondly, the war was short. Wolseley landed in October and departed the following March. Thirdly, the cost was minimal. Adding Colonial Office and Admiralty expenses to the War Office's cost of £257,093, the total price of the expedition was only £815,000.[50] Finally, the goal of the expedition was limited. The *asantahene*, Kofi Karikari, was to be reminded that the coast was under British control. He would be punished for disrupting its commerce and for threatening the Fante who lived there.

The main problems the British army faced were logistical: overcoming transportation, supply, and communication problems, battling climate and preventing disease. These were problems common to all expeditions sent overseas. The west coast of Africa was particularly inhospitable to Europeans. Due to the risks of contracting diseases ranging from malaria to trypanosomiasis, it was regarded as 'the white man's grave'.[51] As a result, Wolseley described this campaign as 'the most horrible war [he] ever took part in'.[52] To minimize the risk of his men falling ill, he issued warnings to them on arrival. Quinine was issued with every cup of tea as a preventive measure. To allay the risk of heat stroke, it was permissible to remove patrol jackets when marching during the day. Hats were to be worn at all times to protect the soldiers' heads. Soldiers were told to sleep a few inches above the ground for protection against moisture and shrub life. And, most importantly, to prevent dysentery and malaria only filtered drinking water was to be used.[53]

Wolseley issued special orders to prepare the men for battle against terrain as well as against the climate. Because of the thickness of the bush, visibility was very limited and the risk of ambush was great. This was identified by Callwell, in his influential work *Small Wars: Their Principles and Practice*, as the greatest problem faced when fighting an enemy in this type of terrain. As a precaution, units were kept as small as possible and the men were made to march in extended order, separated by as many as four paces. Fighting would have to take place in skirmishing order rather than in the traditional square, since the bush could interrupt the integrity of the formation. Procedure allowed the men to drop behind trees and fire individually.[54]

The breakdown of larger and more rigid formations, like the square, considerably increased the responsibilities placed on Methuen and other junior officers. Not only was it more difficult to transmit orders and keep control over the men over a wide or irregular front, but soldiers fighting in battalions or even companies could not see their commander because of the dense bush and were subject to confusion and panic. Therefore, troops had to be broken down into sections of no more than 20, each section supplied with an officer.[55] The possibility of the isolation of an individual soldier or unit grew considerably – a factor which could destroy morale. In addition, because of the problems of supply and transport, junior officers had to make sure that their men were not shooting freely, but that they were taking care to conserve their ammunition.

On 14 January, nearly a year after the Ashanti had invaded the coast, the British reprisal began. The *asantehene* would not accept the British demands – the release of his captives, handing over his mother and heirs to tributary kings as hostages, and the payment of 50,000 ounces of gold, worth £200,000, to the British – and would now have to pay the price.[56] Several delays caused by the difficulties in stockpiling necessary supplies, such as water, meat, and medicine, and the construction of a railway and telegraph line into the interior delayed the British advance until the height of the rainy season. Temperatures were well into the 80s and the rains were constant in the New Year. Wolseley put his faith in God and Lieutenant-Colonel George Colley,[57] the staff member in charge of transport, that the weather would not interrupt his operation, but this did not prevent him from tumbling out of bed in the middle of the night in fear.[58]

The first major encounter occurred north of the Prah at Amoaful on 31 January. The Ashanti force had concentrated in the village amid the dense forest. The trees were thick, mostly 40–50 feet high, the undergrowth was dense, and looming high in the skies, perhaps 300 feet, were the tops of the giant cotton trees.[59] The British attacked in four columns: Wood's regiment was on the right, Baker Russell's on the left, Alison and the 42nd Highlanders in the middle, and Charles Warren and the Rifle Brigade in reserve. The artillery laid down barrages as the infantry advanced in very loose square formations. By noon, due to the fire power of the two 7-pr guns and the continuous volleys of the British infantry, the Ashanti were forced to abandon the village. Rather than retreat, 5,000–15,000 Ashanti warriors launched a determined counter-attack on the British right wing (Wood's regiment).[60] Carrying nothing but muskets and rudimentarily fashioned weapons, the extremely mobile attackers were able to break into many of the loose squares and cause confusion. A cool-headed Wood, assisted by Methuen and other junior officers, held the regiment together and, with reinforcements, threw back the enemy. As Methuen described, the Ashanti then 'ran like rabbits'. British casualties were light,[61] but Ashanti casualties were very heavy: probably more than 2,000 were killed, including Ammon Kwatria, the General-in-Chief, and King Aboo, an allied ruler. After the battle, Methuen wrote, 'We had our big fight and it has amply repaid me for coming out. I had such a dose of work to do from Wood that I gave in for one day and unfortunately neither Conger or myself could eat anything, or close our eyes the night before we had to start. Conger was suffering from sickness and bowels, and [I was] sick in the middle of the night.'[62] Thus even sickness could not detract from the thrill of his first encounter with the enemy. The more effort he put into his work, the greater satisfaction he received.

After the British repulsed a small attack two days later near Fomanah, the march to Kumasi continued. On 4 February Kumasi fell with virtually no resistance and the *asantehene* was forced to accept Wolseley's demands. The British expedition returned to the coast and the war was over. On 5 March Methuen boarded the *Himalaya* and sailed home.

The Ashanti campaign not only gave Methuen his first battle experience but it taught him some valuable lessons. He learned that transport, ordnance and medical departments all played major roles in the success of a campaign and could not be overlooked. Terrain and climate could significantly alter the course of the war and had to be addressed when determining strategy. Watching Wood, Methuen was impressed with the impact that an individual commander could have on the outcome of a battle. Wood's strong character, he believed, kept the regiment from breaking at Amoaful and brought victory to the British. Under Wood's command, Methuen felt comfortable and safe surrounded by fellow soldiers even in a potentially dangerous situation.

The Ashanti campaign also gave Methuen some important military contacts. On his arrival home, he joined the 'Ashanti Club' which kept his contacts fresh with Wolseley's Ring. Members included Maurice, Colley, Wood and, most importantly, Redvers Buller. Methuen later served directly under Buller during most of the 1890s when Buller was Adjutant-General and Methuen commanded the Home District, as well as in the South African War, when Buller was Commander-in-Chief of the forces in South Africa and Methuen was a divisional commander. The two officers had a good, although not close, relationship. Methuen greatly admired Buller, writing:

> If there was one man, besides [Henry] Brackenbury, whom I had made up my mind to like, Buller was the man. A splendid soldier, entirely without fear, and a dear practised head, he has the reputation of saying the hardest things behind a man's back or to his face, it doesn't matter which. From the moment we came together I found he was determined to like me, and I think he's just perfect for a soldier.[63]

THE STAFF COLLEGE

Returning to his regiment in 1874 Methuen began preparing for the Staff College entrance examinations. The Staff College, an institution which trained army officers for administrative and advisory work, was undergoing a period of transition in the 1870s. The 1870s, in fact, was a period of transition for the entire British military structure. The Cardwell reforms which had reorganized the War Office, abolished the purchase of commissions, and created the linked battalion system stimulated several controversies regarding military practice. One such controversy concerned the Staff College. This was not a popular institution and it often failed to attract the officers best suited for staff work.[64] Some indeed joined in order to avoid potentially hazardous regimental duty.[65] Nor were those officers who joined for better motives always well served, since courses were often impractical, graduation did not guarantee a staff position, and any prolonged absence from one's regiment (which was impossible to avoid when enrolled) was usually discouraged.

Under the able leadership of Sir Edward Hamley, the Staff College was gradually reformed during the 1870s. Hamley's goal, as Commandant from 1870–77, was to create an effective staff based on the Prussian model. Greater emphasis was placed on practical duties, such as constructing fortifications, sending out reconnaissance, and solving problems of transportation, and less emphasis was placed on academic subjects such as the study of Latin and Greek which traditional British education stressed. New courses, including field engineering, road-making, military drawing, field sketching and military administration, were offered to the students to create an officer corps capable of carrying out staff duties. Despite changes in curriculum, the improvement of instructors, and the general acceptance of the institution, problems still existed until well after this period. Indeed in the 1870s many still had serious doubts about the quality of the Staff College.

In 1875 Methuen received an appointment to the Staff College, but he had a difficult time deciding whether or not he should attend. He worried incessantly about making the right decision. Many of the Wolseley Ring, including Colley, Wood, Buller and Maurice, had attended and probably encouraged him to do so. However, some of his older friends believed that attending the Staff College was not a ticket to advancement and discouraged him. It seems that Methuen's correspondence with E. Primrose, one of his closest friends and advisers, prompted his final decision: he chose not to attend.[66]

During this period of soul-searching, Methuen committed himself to lifelong military service. As we have noted, it was natural for many sons of the landed gentry to join the army, but for most, the military was a temporary call to state service, an interlude awaiting a political life or full-time attendance to the estate. Methuen was different. His early years in the army, highlighted by the Ashanti War, drove him onward in the military profession. He enjoyed the hard work and the rigid lifestyle, and he accepted with delight the responsibilities. In time, he came to believe in the importance of what he was doing. After getting a taste of command, he could no longer devote his life to sitting idly at Corsham or entertaining in London.

THE MILITARY ATTACHÉ

After passing his Staff College appointment and finishing his term on Prince Edward's staff, Methuen headed to Dublin and served as Assistant Military Secretary to Sir John Michel, the Commander-in-Chief in Ireland. Thanks to recommendations from the Prince and Lord Abinger, which stressed his fitness for advancement and his fondness for the profession,[67] Methuen went to Ireland with the rank of captain (and brevet-major in the Scots Guards).[68] Wolseley wholeheartedly endorsed the promotion.[69] Life in Ireland consisted mainly of practising manœuvres at Curragh, drilling cavalry, artillery and infantry, and performing simulated reconnaissance missions. Except for the occasional evening spent with a guest visiting Dublin, such as Gladstone or the Marlboroughs, life was routine. Escorting Lady Randolph Churchill to the Guinness factory was not the type of 'expedition' Methuen wished to undertake. To alleviate the boredom he read military history, particularly on Moltke's campaigns, kept up on the current conflict between Russia and Turkey, and awaited his next assignment. Fortunately for him, his stay in Ireland was brief: within a month of his arrival in May 1877 he was already preparing for his departure.[70]

In January 1878 Methuen was sent to Berlin to replace General Beauchamp Walker as military attaché to Lord Odo Russell, British Ambassador to Germany. Lord Russell, along with Lord Lyons, was one of Britain's most respected ambassadors. As military attaché, Methuen was required to observe the German army, advise Russell on military affairs and represent the British crown at social functions. Methuen was initially nervous about performing all of his duties. Replacing Walker, he wrote to his father, was going to be difficult:

> First of all Walker held an exceptional position here – he was father of all attachés, a great personal friend of the King's beside being *beloved* and *respected* by *everyone*. Make no mistake, he has left his mark, as an able, good man and

soldier. His dispatches told me as much ... I know he had the advantage of being brought up in Germany, he spoke French badly, but German as well as English.

How I stand in this position – I am the youngest attaché here, I speak French, fairly, not so well as any of my colleagues. I am the only one with a slight knowledge of German. I am a 'persona grata' to Lord and Lady Odo, who are simply charming. I *never* met two such people.[71]

In time, however, despite his worries, Methuen proved to himself and to those around him that he could do the job.

Methuen arrived in Berlin in the midst of a European crisis. Russian forces were driving deep into the Ottoman empire. British Mediterranean interests were threatened and Prime Minister Disraeli, supported by the queen, was ready to send British forces to defend the Straits and, if necessary, bring Britain into the war. 'It is a question of Russian or British supremacy in the world', wrote Queen Victoria.[72] In Methuen's assessment, the British people wanted war and the Government was foolishly capitulating to public opinion. Methuen opposed intervention: 'I can't agree with you about fighting the Russians at Plevna. It appears a most cowardly policy to seize the moment a brave enemy is falling to give him a hit. I detest the Turk, and though the Russian deserves now to be licked, they had done nothing more ... [at] Plevna, than they had when they went to war.'[73]

Lord Derby, Benjamin Disraeli's Foreign Minister, also opposed intervention. When Derby resigned at the end of March, Methuen was certain that nothing could hold back public sentiment and that Disraeli would respond to their demand.[74] 'It is a good change', he wrote to his father, 'but I will always maintain that had the Ministry backed [Derby] up he might have saved us from a war; he has been in a false position for a long time ... It is Dizzy who has spoiled our chances of peace.'[75] Great Britain did, in fact, remain out of the conflict and peace was eventually restored in the Near East. What kept the conflict localized, according to Methuen, was the ability of Bismarck to withstand German public pressure, and, strangely enough, France's objection to a war which would interrupt her Exhibition.[76] Germany and France were able to persuade Russia to give in to British demands and pull out of the Ottoman empire. Despite this, Methuen believed, peace in Europe would be temporary. 'I find the opinion in the [German] army in favour of war. My belief is that before three years are past or even in a shorter time [Germany] will have to fight Russia, perhaps Italy, and if Gambetta gets the power, France also. I should take very long odds on [Germany].'[77]

Methuen believed that he had played an important role in the British Government's decision. In the spring and summer of 1878, he advised several British representatives including Hereford, Stanley, the Prince of Wales, the Duke of Cambridge and both Derby and his replacement, Lord Salisbury, on military matters. He got on quite well with Salisbury, which proved important for his later career.[78] '[Salisbury] looked me straight in the face', Methuen wrote, 'and asked me sensible questions. He told me plenty and said, "you will be an important part, for all the supplies will come from Prussia for the Russians". He is a jolly fellow, too. Lord Derby was not.'[79] Methuen appreciated Salisbury's candour. Not all the politicians he met to discuss the crisis were receptive to his views. On a meeting in London with the Earl of Kimberley, Gladstone's Colonial Secretary, Methuen wrote, 'Kimberley came to see me to ask my opinion on affairs in Russia, before I could open my mouth he sat down and said, "let me say what I think". He spoke for half an hour, and then said, "Goodbye, I am glad to find we agree on every single point." Then he vanished.'[80] Methuen could also advise Russell and these ministers of the impending Dual Alliance, signed between Germany and Austria-Hungary, when his friend Prince Lichtenstein confided in him as to its terms.[81]

MARRIAGE

Although very busy with work, Methuen found time in Berlin for other things. He learned how to play the violin, he read Tennyson and he got married. On 18 June 1878 Methuen married Evelyn, the daughter of Clare Emily and Sir Frederick Hutchinson Hervey-Bathurst, 3rd Baronet. The marriage was passionate but tragically short, 'Evy' dying of tuberculosis only a year later while convalescing at the Hotel Bellevue in Cannes. The sudden loss of his first wife was the greatest personal tragedy in Methuen's life. He mourned her passing for several years, becoming uncommunicative for a brief period and corresponding only with his father and a few close friends. He contemplated giving up his military career and went so far as to send his resignation to Russell, who refused to accept it.[82] His decision to recover and get on with his life prompted him to greater service. Written on the opening page of the diary which he started after Evy's death was the short poem,

Ah God, for a man with heart, head, hand,
Like some of the simple great ones gone
For ever and ever by.
One still strong man in a blatant land,
Whatever they call him, what case I.
Aristocrat, democrat, autocrat – one
Who can rule and dare not lie.

And ah for a man to arise in me,
That the man I am may cease to be![83]

Methuen resumed his career in order to propel himself out of this crisis and become whole again.

Thus it was that Methuen returned in sombre mood to Berlin in July 1879. He had a host of tasks to complete for the War Office and Foreign Office, but his primary assignment as military attaché was to acquaint himself with the complexities of the German military system and to make evaluations. The War Office demanded 'full detail' of the size, organization and training of the German infantry and cavalry. Specifically, they wanted Methuen to gather information on its equipment, tools and arms, its use of telephones and carrier pigeons in war, and the organization of its non-commissioned officer schools. He studied the German system of infantry attack, the use of railways in military manœuvres, and all sales of arms, especially those of Krupps. Also while in Germany, he maintained a running bibliography of all printed books and articles related to military and naval service. This list included all papers issued to schools and colleges and information as to their access. He acquired information on German coastal defences, especially on the Baltic coast east of Kiel, for which the British had no recent intelligence. Methuen witnessed Krupps' experiments, observed manœuvres and toured German fortifications in Cologne, Koblenz and Strasbourg. He studied the effects of the growth of 'Pan-Slavism' on the relations of Germany and Austria, and he also assessed Germany's view on the maintenance of Austria as a state.[84] And, surreptitiously, Methuen kept his eyes open for French, Russian and Austrian war plans which the War Office believed to be floating around Berlin, and German mobilization plans.[85] He also reported to the War Office on the terms of conscription and its effect on the prosperity and natural progress of the German state. The issue of conscription always interested Methuen, who was a firm believer in volunteerism as opposed to national service.[86]

SHORT SERVICE VERSUS CONSCRIPTION

The issue of conscription also interested military reformers back in England. At this time the British army was too small and it could not compete with European powers, nor could it handle more than one serious threat at a time to its empire. One of the problems which Cardwell attempted to solve during his tenure as Secretary of State for War was to increase the size of the army without resorting to conscription – a policy he knew the public would never accept. To increase the size of the army, therefore, he initiated the Army Enlistment Act of 1870, which shortened the length of military service. Cardwell believed that if service with the colours was reduced from 12 to six years, there would be increased incentive to enlist. As a result, men would not be giving up all of the best years of their lives. It was expected that more and better-qualified men would enlist. At the same time, an effective reserve would be built at a low cost, by requiring those who had finished their shortened service to enter the reserve for an additional six years.

The results of Cardwell's reforms were a constant source of debate in the last few decades of the nineteenth century. The South African War proved that the reforms had fallen far short in preparing Great Britain for a national emergency. An effective reserve had not been created. The normal establishment for the regular reserve was 90,000. However, by 1901–2 the effective establishment was down to just over 5,000, due to the drain of the war when the reserves were sent to fill the holes in the regiments left by casualties.[87] At that point it became necessary to fill these holes and create new brigades out of the volunteers, the militia and the yeomanry. As for increasing the size of the army, Major John Adye, an intelligence officer, asserted that enlistment did increase with the introduction of short service. Enlistment in the British army went from 24,594 in 1870 to 28,325 in 1878.[88] Yet the increase had not kept pace with the growth of the empire, and, in his opinion, could not meet the demands of minor emergencies, let alone a war with a great power. Only 0.8 per cent of eligible British men joined the army, whereas in Germany, where they had a system of conscription, nearly 5 per cent of all men served at any given time.[89] Also, Adye insisted that the age of the recruits, which averaged over 20, remained much higher than was desirable.

Although Adye's enthusiasm for conscription led him to accentuate the flaws in the Cardwellian system, he was not alone in thinking that the Army Enlistment Act had failed. Patrick MacDougall, an influential military reformer, put forward a number of ideas for improving the army. He wanted to reduce the age allowance for new recruits, to enable sergeants to remain on active duty while receiving their pensions, to allow the re-enlistment of soldiers, and to increase the size and function of the militia reserve.[90] J. L. A. Simmons argued that the Cardwellian system had failed as early as 1882, when the British sent an expeditionary force to Egypt (a campaign in which Methuen took part). Of the 32,000 men sent by the British, the home army struggled to send 20,000, half of which came from the reserves. Had there been another emergency elsewhere in the empire, the government could not have dealt with it. Short service, Simmons argued, had failed. There was still a great deal of wastage as a result of desertion, bad physique, poor character and purchase of discharge. He believed that the only way to increase the size of the army and to get a better and younger soldier was to increase the pay.[91]

Methuen agreed with the monetary incentive; parliament, however, did not. Like Wolseley, who was a strong supporter of Cardwell, Methuen also agreed in theory with the short service system, arguing that long service was detrimental. 'The best man', Methuen believed, 'is he who has served three or four years in the army goes into the Reserves and can in time of war fill the ranks. If only we made Reserves' men available for all active service as the standard suggests. We have the chance of the finest army we ever had.'[92]

THE HOME DISTRICT

Studying German conscription, however, could not maintain Methuen's interest for long.[93] By 1880 he had done everything he could do to advance the army's knowledge of the German military system and, driven by his newly found enthusiasm and by his desire to put behind him bitter-sweet memories of his wife, he wanted to leave Berlin. From London, Wolseley wrote that Aldershot needed a new Quartermaster-General. Methuen persuaded Ben Stephenson to talk to the Duke of Cambridge about the opening, but as he awaited his friend's word, he was offered the position of Assistant Adjutant and Quartermaster-General of the Home District instead. Methuen, preferring the Aldershot position, tried to buy time, but he was persuaded eventually by Wolseley to accept the job in London. So, after giving Crown Princess Victoria her last military history lesson, attending Prince Wilhelm's wedding to Augusta Victoria of Schleswig–Holstein and receiving the 2nd Class of the Order of the Red Eagle and the Silver Medal for Saving Life from the Emperor,[94] Methuen packed his bags and sailed for England.

As Assistant Adjutant and Quartermaster-General of the Home District, under the command of Sir Arthur Herbert, Methuen attempted to incorporate some principles of the German military system into the British army. The first issue he tackled at his new post was the role of the junior officer in military drill. In Germany, Methuen saw that junior officers drilled their battalions during peace-time. He felt it kept them interested in their work, it gave them more responsibility for their men, it freed up time for senior officers, who were customarily responsible for drill, and it brought the rank and file into a closer working relationship with the often distant lieutenant or captain.[95] Methuen wanted to introduce this practice into the British army,[96] believing it to be a necessary step towards modernization. In an age in which the intensity of firepower grew by leaps and bounds, traditional formations were breaking down. The 'square' might, and did, still work against irregular and ill-armed troops, but it could not withstand modern firepower. Close formations proved disastrous against quick-firing weapons. As the battlefield grew in size and battle formation became more extended, the responsibilities of the junior officer increased. The senior officer could no longer do everything himself. Napoleon's dictum was rapidly becoming obsolete:

> The Commander-in-Chief is the head; he is everything to an army. It was not the Roman Army which conquered Gaul, but Caesar. It was not the Carthaginian army which made Rome tremble at her gates, but Hannibal. It was not the Macedonian army which marched to the Indus, but Alexander. It was not the Prussian army which defended Prussia for 7 years against the three most powerful states of Europe, but Frederick.[97]

In this age of transition, the Commander-in-Chief was still very important; Wolseley could still defeat the Ashanti, Roberts could still defeat the Afghans and Kitchener could still defeat the Mahdists. Yet, the role of the junior officer was expanding and, as Methuen knew, he had to gain the necessary experience to be effective on the battleground.

After encountering a great deal of resistance from his superiors over his proposed changes in drill and failing to convince them that these methods were sound, Methuen moved on to another cause – musketry. In May 1881 Methuen presented evidence to the Committee of Musketry Instruction in the Army, presided over by General Sir Daniel Lysons. He testified as an experienced marksman in the Scots Guards, where he held an Extra First Class Certificate in Musketry, as a witness to the effectiveness of the British soldier in the Ashanti War, and as an observer of the German system. Thoroughly impressed by the German system, Methuen implored the

Committee to modernize musketry instruction. Unlike the British soldier, who received very limited training, the German soldier received three years of training; reserves continued to train twice a year for 28-day periods. The German musketry drill included firing at moving targets and targets of unknown distances, as well as firing individually, in small groups, and in large volleys. Training sessions, unlike the British system, took place throughout the year in order to add seasonal variations. The German army also practised firing from several stances and from behind cover. The German soldier had at his disposal much more ammunition for practice and more and better training grounds than his British counterpart. Methuen advocated that the British army follow the lead of the Germans. If they wanted to compete with Europe's leading army, he believed, they would have to spend the money for more and better instruction. In musketry instruction, as in drill, Methuen also stressed the importance of the junior officer in carrying out the instruction. He believed that all junior officers should be thoroughly trained in musketry, continue to practise under the guidance of senior officers, and train their own companies.

As it turned out, Methuen did not have much time to address the problem of musketry instruction or drill as Assistant Adjutant. On 4 August 1882 Lieutenant-General Garnet Wolseley was appointed to command the British expedition to Egypt to crush the Arabi Rebellion. Methuen was selected by Wolseley as a member of his staff. A few weeks later, after only a year London, Methuen joined Wolseley and his Ring and headed for Cairo.

In his first ten years of service in the army Methuen had gained a wealth of experience. He had travelled to France, Germany, Ireland and the Gold Coast. He had reported on war, participated in battle and observed in the manœuvres. Aided by personal and professional contacts, he gradually rose through the ranks, receiving attractive administrative and command positions. By 1881 the baron's son had become a capable soldier and a thoughtful and skilful officer. He was destined for a long and noteworthy career in the British army.

NOTES

1. Frederick Henry Paul, 2nd Baron Methuen, served as Queen Victoria's Lord-in-waiting during the Palmerston and Gladstone governments, 1859–66, 1868–74, 1880–85 and 1886. He resigned in 1886 over Gladstone's position on Home Rule. He, like many of his fellow Whigs, including his friend and neighbour Lord Lansdowne, clung to the Union.

2. John Methuen (1610–1706) served as Lord Chancellor of Ireland in 1697 under King William III. Later in 1703, as ambassador to Portugal under Queen Anne, he and his son, Paul, successfully negotiated the Methuen Treaty which brought Portuguese wines to England at low prices. Today, the name Methuen is synonymous with port. Paul Sanford, 3rd Baron Methuen, was descended from Anthony Methuen, the younger brother of John Methuen's father, who was also named Anthony. Bernard Burke, *A Genealogical and Heraldic History of the Peerage and Baronetage* (London: Harrison & Sons, 1915).

3. P. S. Methuen to F. H. P. Methuen, 27 Oct. 1877, Methuen Papers, Wiltshire Records Office, Trowbridge.

4. David Cannadine, *The Decline and Fall of the British Aristocracy* (New York: Anchor Books, 1990), p. 506.

5. Old Etonians who would influence Methuen's career were Lord Lansdowne, Herbert Gladstone, Frederick Roberts, Redvers Buller, Henry Colvile, and Francis Rhodes. Lionel H. Cust, *History of Eton College* (New York: Scribner's, 1899), p. 281.

6. H. Biddulph, 'The Era of Army Purchase', *Journal of the Society for Army Historical Research* 12 (1933): 229.

7. Edward Cardwell, the Secretary of State for War in Gladstone's first government, after failing to secure the House of Lords' approval to end purchase, received a royal warrant to abolish the system on 20 July 1871. Purchase was abolished on 1 November 1871. 'Report on Abolition of Purchase', WO 32/6928, Public Records Office, Kew.

8. Ibid.

9. Cannadine, *The Decline and Fall of the British Aristocracy*, p. 265.

10. Cardwell would also end this system of double ranks in the Foot Guard regiments in 1871, although officers who had purchased their commissions continued to hold one rank in their regiment and a higher substantive rank in the army.

11. W. E. Cairns, *Social Life in the British Army* (London: Long, 1900), p. 5.

12. P. Knightly, *The First Casualty* (New York: Harcourt Brace Jovanovich, 1975), p. 4.

13. Frederick Charles Arthur Stephenson, *At Home and on the Battlefield*, comp. Mrs Frank Pownall (London: Murray, 1915), p. 53.

14. Frederick B. Maurice, *The History of the Scots Guards* (London: Chatto & Windus, 1934), p. 1.

15. 'Supervisor Report', WO 27/489, 14 May 1873, Public Records Office.

16. A. Methuen to G. Aston, 16 Nov. 1932, Aston Papers, Liddell Hart Centre for Military Archives, Kings College, London University, London.

17. Paul Methuen, 'Discipline: Its Importance to an Armed Force, and the Best Means of Promoting and of Maintaining It', unpublished essay, 1887, Methuen Papers, Wiltshire Records Office.

18. P. S. Methuen, 1870 Diary, Methuen Papers, Wiltshire Records Office.

19. Friedrich August Dressler, *Moltke in his Home*, with an introduction by Lord Methuen (London: John Murray, 1907), Introduction.

20. Methuen met Moltke in 1881 in Berlin. After being honoured with the Gold Medal for Saving Life by Wilhelm I, Moltke congratulated the heroic Methuen. Methuen wrote, 'I hardly think anything could make me prouder than to have the finest soldier in the world [congratulate] me.' Dressler, *Moltke in his Home*, Introduction.

21. George Aston, Diary entry, 4 June 1909, Aston Collection, Liddell Hart Centre for Military Studies, King's College, London.

22. P. S. Methuen to F. H. P. Methuen, 5 Feb. 1871, Methuen Papers, Wiltshire Records Office.

23. 'Costs of Principal British Wars', WO 33/256, Public Records Office.

24. Byron Farwell, *Queen Victoria's Little Wars* (New York: Harper & Row, 1972), p. 1.

25. Ibid., pp. 364–71.

26. 'Costs of Principal British Wars', WO 33/256, Public Records Office.
27. Frederick Boyle, *Through Fanteeland to Coomassie* (London: Chapman & Hall, 1874), p. 226.
28. 'Confidential Report', WO 33/26/0561, Public Records Office.
29. Henry Brackenbury, *The Ashantee War of 1873–74* (London and Edinburgh: William Blackwood & Sons, 1874), p. 7.
30. F. Agbodeka, *African Politics and British Policy in the Gold Coast 1869–1900* (Evanston, ILL: Northwestern University Press, 1971), p. 45.
31. D. Kimble, *A Political History of Ghana: The Rise of Gold Coast Nationalism 1850–1928* (Oxford: Clarendon Press, 1963), pp. 270–1.
32. Agbodeka, *African Politics*, p. 47.
33. Brackenbury, *The Ashantee War*, p. 64.
34. Telegram No. 18, Kimberley, Secretary of the Colonies, to Colonel Harley, 12 May 1873, CO 879/4/30, Public Records Office.
35. Cabinet minute, 2 Aug. 1873, CAB 41/5/33, Public Records Office.
36. Henry M. Stanley, *Coomassie: The Story of the Campaign in Africa 1873–4* (London: Sampson, Low, Marston & Co., 1896), p. 16.
37. William F. Butler wrote a fitting tribute to his former ring in *An Autobiography* (London: Constable & Co., 1911), p. 148:

    It was in the habit in later years to call these men, and a few others, 'The Wolseley Gang'. I see in the dictionary that the word is derived from the Danish, and that it means, in its primitive sense, 'to go', but I don't think that was the meaning its users attached to it. I see, too, that its modern signification is sometimes 'a number of persons associated for a certain purpose, usually a bad one'. I look back now over nigh forty years, and I don't think there was any bad purpose individually or collectively in that little group of men. I accept with pleasure the Danish definition of the word, 'to go'. We, for I was a humble member, certainly did go: some dropped on the road early, and others fell out later; a few struggled on to the end. They rest in many places: one at Prah-su, another under Majuba, another in the middle of the Desert of Bayuda, another at Spion Kop, another under the sea near St Helena, another in the sands at Tel-el-Kebir, another in the veldt at Magersfontein. Poor old 'Gang'! They kept going as long as they could go, and now they are nearly all gone. May they rest in peace!

38. The Roberts 'Ring' included Horatio Herbert Kitchener, Ian Hamilton, Douglas Haig and Reginald Pole-Carew. The rivalry of the two rings was often bitter. Hamilton wrote in 1944, 'Sixty years ago I would gladly have given away all my belongings provided thereby Roberts could be hoisted up and Wolseley brought low.' I. Hamilton, *Listening for the Drums* (London: Faber & Faber, 1944), p. 150.
39. 'Precis of the Ashanti Expedition', War Office Intelligence Department report 13 April 1874, p. 27, Public Records Office.
40. P. S. Methuen to F. H. P. Methuen, 18 Jan. 1874, Methuen Papers, Wiltshire Records Office.
41. P. S. Methuen to F. H. P. Methuen, 5 Jan. 1874, Methuen Papers, Wiltshire Records Office.
42. Brackenbury, *The Ashantee War*, p. 211.
43. Charles Edward Callwell, *Small Wars: Their Principles and Practice*, rev. edn (London: HMSO, 1899), p. 304.
44. John Fortescue, *Military History* (Cambridge: Cambridge University Press, 1914), p. 100.
45. Wolseley never forgave Wood for making the peace with the Boers which ended the First Anglo-Boer War. Wolseley would have preferred to see him resign rather than to

commit such an act. Wolseley later described Wood as 'the vainest [*sic*] but by no means the ablest of men' (Farwell, *Eminent Victorian Soldiers*, pp. 252–6).

46. Brackenbury, *The Ashantee War*, p. 249.
47. The regiment consisted of 16 British officers, five native officers and 431 fighting men, as well as 206 carriers to carry medical supplies, mess supplies and personal effects.
48. P. S. Methuen to F. H. P. Methuen, 18 Jan. 1874, Methuen Papers, Wiltshire Records Office.
49. Callwell, *Small Wars*, p. 19.
50. 'Precis of the Ashanti Expedition', WO 33/26/0561, Public Records Office.
51. Farwell, *Queen Victoria's Little Wars*, p. 191.
52. Farwell, *Eminent Victorian Soldiers*, p. 216.
53. *The Ashantee War* (London: H. S. King, 1874), pp. 205–12.
54. Ibid., p. 208.
55. Callwell, *Small Wars*, p. 304.
56. 'Precis of the Ashanti Expedition', War Office Intelligence Department Report, 13 April 1874, p. 49, Public Records Office.
57. George Pomeroy Colley, one of the most prominent members of the 'Wolseley Ring' and one of Wolseley's closest friends, was killed in the First Boer War in 1881 at Majuba Hill.
58. 'Wolseley Diary', 6 Jan. 1874, WO 147/4, Public Records Office.
59. Archibald Forbes, *et al.*, *Battles of the Nineteenth Century* (London: Cassell & Co., 1901), I, 215.
60. P. S. Methuen to F. H. P. Methuen, 30 Jan. 1874, Methuen Papers, Wiltshire Records Office.
61. One officer was killed and 21 were wounded, including Wood. Three soldiers were killed and 173 were wounded.
62. P. S. Methuen to F. H. P. Methuen, 30 Jan. 1874, Methuen Papers, Wiltshire Records Office.
63. P. S. Methuen to F. H. P. Methuen, 7 Sept. 1882, Methuen Papers, Wiltshire Records Office.
64. A. R. Godwin-Austen, *The Staff and the Staff College* (London: Constable, 1927), p. 156.
65. 'Report of the Committee in the Working of the Staff College', March 1880, WO 33/34, Public Records Office.
66. After a dinner in Berlin with General Villiers, Lord Dufferin and Wolseley in 1880, Wolseley told Methuen that he had acted quite wrongly giving up the Staff College for an appointment on Sir John Michel's staff. When Methuen explained to Sir Garnet that the appointment he had accepted fulfilled certain staff service requirements, the General nodded his approval. Wolseley told him to finish his staff duty and in the event of any war erupting, 'go to it'. Upon its conclusion, Wolseley advised Methuen to ask for the Quartermaster General job at Aldershot, the job which Buller was planning to give up (P. S. Methuen to F. H. P. Methuen, 15 Sept. 1880, Methuen Papers, Wiltshire Records Office).
67. 'Supervisor Report', WO 27/489, 18 Feb. 1874, Public Records Office.
68. The Scots Fusilier Guards became the Scots Guards in 1877.
69. Wolseley to Abinger, 20 June 1874, Methuen Papers, Wiltshire Records Office.
70. P. S. Methuen to F. H. P. Methuen, 28 June 1877, Methuen Papers, Wiltshire Records Office.
71. P. S. Methuen to F. H. P. Methuen, 9 Jan. 1878, Methuen Papers, Wiltshire Records Office.
72. Queen Victoria to B. Disraeli, W. F. Monypenny and G. E. Buckle, *The Life of Benjamin Disraeli*, rev. edn (New York: Macmillan, 1929.), VI, 132–3. As cited in William L. Langer, *European Alliances & Alignments*, 2nd edn (New York: Vintage, 1964.), p. 122.

73. P. S. Methuen to F. H. P. Methuen, 13 Feb. 1878, Methuen Papers, Wiltshire Records Office.
74. P. S. Methuen to F. H. P. Methuen, 25 March 1878, Methuen Papers, Wiltshire Records Office.
75. P. S. Methuen to F. H. P. Methuen, 30 March 1878, Methuen Papers, Wiltshire Records Office.
76. P. S. Methuen to F. H. P. Methuen, 2 April 1878, Methuen Papers, Wiltshire Records Office.
77. Berlin Diary, October 1879, Methuen Papers, Wiltshire Records Office.
78. Lord Salisbury was prime minister of Great Britain during the South African War, 1899–1902.
79. P. S. Methuen to F. H. P. Methuen, 4 April 1878, Methuen Papers, Wiltshire Records Office.
80. Berlin Diary, n.d., Methuen Papers, Wiltshire Records Office.
81. Winifred Taffs, *Ambassador to Bismarck: Lord Odo Russell* (London: Frederick Muller Ltd, 1938), p. 350.
82. P. S. Methuen to O. Russell, 2 June 1879, Russell Papers, Public Records Office.
83. Berlin Diary, 13 Oct. 1879, Methuen Papers, Wiltshire Records Office.
84. Unknown source to P. S. Methuen, Methuen Papers, Wiltshire Records Office.
85. FO to P. S. Methuen, 2 Feb. 1878, Methuen Papers.
86. After the South African War, Methuen realized that the British army could not match the continental armies and needed serious reform. He advocated an overhaul of the volunteer forces and, later, supported the creation of the Territorial Army.
87. 'Army Estimates for 1901–2', 1900: XXXVIII, 1.
88. John Adye, 'The British Army', *Nineteenth Century* 6 (1879): 349.
89. John Adye, 'Has Our Army Grown with Our Empire?', *Nineteenth Century* 39 (1896): 1017.
90. Patrick MacDougall, 'Have We an Army?', *Nineteenth Century* 15 (1883): 501–16.
91. J. L. A. Simmons, 'The Weakness of the Army', *Nineteenth Century* 13 (1883): 529–44.
92. P. S. Methuen to F. H. P. Methuen, 18 Feb., 1881, Methuen Papers, Wiltshire Records Office.
93. Nor could entertaining British and foreign dignitaries maintain Methuen's interest for long. Joseph Chamberlain paid a visit to Berlin in the winter of 1879–80. 'The Great Chamberlain', Methuen wrote to his father, 'joined in a supper with some actresses at a restaurant in the town. … The actresses and the Chamberlain stripped, and danced around the table.' Methuen did not witness this event, but read about it in a German newspaper. P. S. Methuen to F. H. P. Methuen, 17 Jan. 1880, Methuen Papers, Wiltshire Records Office.
94. On 2 Feb. 1881, while crossing the bridge over the canal near Charlottenburg in Berlin, Methuen saw a man fall into the iced-over Spree River. As a crowd gathered, Methuen jumped in and attempted a rescue. The man was eventually saved although Methuen was not able to get close enough to him. 'I eventually ascended the ladder, having quite forgotten to take off my high hat all the time!!' Methuen then escaped into the crowd and walked home alone. The newspapers later discovered his identity. Moltke came to his home and said: 'You must have the order for saving life – *it is the only order*, when you wear that you can wear no other.' P. S. Methuen to F. H. P. Methuen, 2 Feb. 1881, Methuen Papers, Wiltshire Records Office.
95. Memo, 20 Dec. 1881, Methuen Papers, Wiltshire Records Office.
96. More than ten years later, the military reformer Stewart Murray picked this idea up. Stewart Murray, *Discipline: Its Reason and Battle-Value* (London: Gale & Polden, 1894).
97. Cited in Patrick L. MacDougall, *Theory of War*, 2nd edn (London: Longman, 1858), p. 61.

3

Establishing a Name: From Egypt to India (1882–99)

Thus it was that in the summer of 1882 Methuen boarded the *Orient*, bound for Alexandria to serve with Wolseley's expedition. Now 36, he had during the last few years acquired an air of authority: he was no longer the young officer of a decade ago. He was sharp-minded enough to be receptive to the ideas and opinions of his fellow officers, yet his deeply paternal instincts led him always to put his men first, never gambling with their lives for the sake of dubious glory or personal advancement. John Masefield described him as one of those 'wonderful men', against whom 'no enemy could stand', and fulsome though this might have been, Methuen was certainly an officer to be reckoned with.[1]

THE ARABI REBELLION

British interest in Egypt had reached new heights when Disraeli purchased Khedive Ismail's share of the Suez Canal Company in 1875, making the British Government the owner of nearly half of the company's stock. The Khedive's attempts to reform Egypt, by building infrastructure, encouraging the use of irrigation and developing a more progressive educational system, left the country in a state of bankruptcy when French and British financiers demanded payment for their loans. In 1878 the Khedive, under great pressure, accepted one French and one British administrator to reform (i.e. control) the Egyptian economy. When the administrators tried to initiate political reform, the Khedive adamantly resisted. Frustrated, Great Britain and France pressured the Ottoman Sultan, the nominal ruler of Egypt, to depose Ismail and replace him with his son Tewfiq. In response to European interference, Egyptian nationalism grew.[2] Colonel Ahmed Arabi, an army officer and the Minister of War, became the centre of the movement. When the new Khedive attempted to force his resignation, nationalist sentiment exploded.[3]

In a country where the government and army were dominated by Turkish influence, the Muslim religious leaders felt increasingly threatened by the growing Christian presence, and the landowners resented the artificially high tax rate created by the European administrators, the cry of 'Egypt for the Egyptians' was extremely popular. Two mutinies, led by Arabi, in February and September of 1881, made it clear to the British and French governments that the Khedive had lost his authority and some officials feared that the Suez Canal could no longer be safeguarded. The Joint Note, delivered in January by the French premier, Leon Gambetta, further undercut the Khedive's position. With his inability to block Arabi's reinstatement as Minister of War, and the growing panic among Egypt's 90,000–100,000 European residents, the British and French threatened a naval demonstration to reassert their support for the Khedive. Undaunted, Arabi and his followers strengthened the fortifications along Alexandria's harbour.

On 11 June 1882 a confrontation between a Maltese and an Egyptian over a donkey fare precipitated the Alexandria Massacre which left at least 50 dead and the European quarter in complete disarray.[4] Arabi's refusal to surrender his weapons, coupled with the failure of the Khedive to protect foreign investment, compelled the British to take action and provided them with an opportunity to reassert their position. Abandoned by their French partner, they bombarded Alexandria on 11 July. Forced by his 'men on the spot' and Arabi's proclamation stating that 'irreconcilable war existed between the Egyptians and the English',[5] Gladstone issued orders 'to uphold the authority of the Khedive and seize his person from danger'.[6] Sir Garnet Wolseley began his preparations for a military expedition to Egypt and the first troops arrived in Port Said with General Archibald Alison within the week.

Wolseley's expedition to Egypt in 1882 was the largest British operation since the Sepoy Mutiny of 1857. Britain and the Mediterranean garrisons provided 24,000 troops and 7,000 were sent from India.[7] It was one of Britain's most expensive expeditions, costing over £4.5 million,[8] and, in addition to this, it was necessary from 1882 onwards to maintain a large occupation force in Egypt.

Accompanying Wolseley to Egypt were the familiar faces of his ring: Wood, Alison, Russell, McNeill, Butler, Maurice, Hugh McCalmont and Redvers Buller. Methuen served as the Commandant of the Headquarters Camp as well as Press Censor. Lieutenant-Colonel Francis Grenfell was selected by Wolseley as Assistant Adjutant. Grenfell was a veteran of the 5th Kaffir War, the Boer War and the Zulu War,[9] and later Sirdar of the Anglo-

Egyptian army. He and Methuen became close friends and remained so thereafter.[10]

The expedition to Egypt was quite different from Wolseley's expedition to the Gold Coast in 1873. Although the heat was similarly unbearable, the climate offered few deadly challenges and the health of the British soldiers remained good throughout. Transportation problems, which had hindered the march to Kumasi, were overcome with relative ease in Egypt. Canals and railroads provided short lines of communication and access to supply depots – a luxury denied to Wolseley in the Gold Coast expedition. The general plan, however, to defeat the Ashanti and to defeat the Egyptians was similar. Wolseley's strategy called for one swift knockout blow of the enemy's army. He predicted, correctly, that this would occur along the advance to Cairo.

The advance to Cairo was very rapid. The first troops from Britain arrived on 10 August 1882. Alexandria was reinforced and a trap was set to convince Arabi that the main advance would come from there. It worked. Some 15,000 men, roughly 25 per cent of Arabi's forces, were diverted to Kafr-ed-Dowar to defend against an advance from Alexandria. The main British force, meanwhile, slipped through the Suez and Maritime Canals, and landed at Ismailia on 21 August. Marching west, Wolseley planned to move on Tel-el-Kebir, where Arabi had entrenched at an old military station, and then continue on toward Cairo. A railroad was constructed as the British advanced to provide access to supply and a secure line of communications. The British met minor resistance at Mahuta on 24–25 August. Three days later, they engaged a larger Egyptian force at Kassassin. Although the Egyptian army was forced to retreat, the British could advance no farther, having pushed too far ahead of their transport and supply lines. Thus Wolseley ordered a temporary halt to the advance.

During the advance, Methuen had little time to himself. In addition to his duties as HQ Commandant, which included supervising the base camp, assisting in the inspection and drill of the men, and providing Wolseley with any necessary information or resources, he acted as press censor.[11] The official military position on the nature of the press was that it was 'an evil of modern warfare which can not be avoided'.[12] In 1878, when Lieutenant John Ross of Bladensburg wrote that statement, he was well aware that the press had entered a new age. 'The public', he wrote, 'will not consent to be shut out from the news of the theatre of war; nor is it wise that they should be.'[13] It was the job of the press censor to weigh the fragile balance between information which was harmless and that which, if it fell into the wrong hands, could be potentially hazardous to the success of an operation.

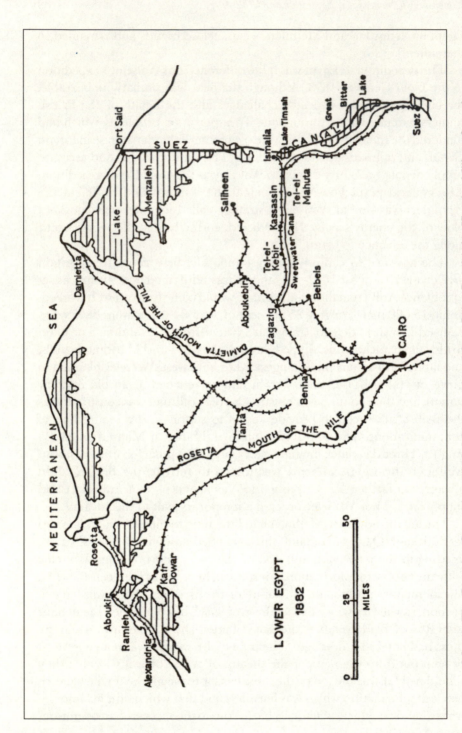

Map 2: The Egyptian Campaign, 1882. Map reproduced from Brian Bond (ed.), *Victorian Military Campaigns*, London, Hutchinson, 1967.

As the first to inaugurate a definite system of press in the camp, Wolseley took the responsibilities of the press censor very seriously. Methuen executed 'this most delicate duty … with great tact and judgement, and to my entire satisfaction', Wolseley wrote in his dispatch on the operation.[14] As his guideline, Methuen carried with him at all times a copy of the *Revised Rules for Newspaper Correspondents at the Seat of War*, a short rule book for journalists, which he had completed as Assistant Adjutant-General just prior to leaving Great Britain. As press censor, he supervised all press matters, including furnishing licences to all newspaper correspondents, enforcing all censorship rules, such as prohibiting the use of a cipher or a foreign language other than French or German, funnelling all acceptable non-classified information from the Commander-in-Chief to the journalists, and examining every newspaper issued for violations of the censorship rules. Violators were subject to the Mutiny Act.

As Wolseley's liaison to the press corps, Methuen was the staff officer most in demand. Under any conditions, it would have been difficult for a journalist to get five minutes alone with the army press censor. However, in this case it was even worse, since 'The special officer selected happened to be the very busiest man in the camp.'[15] Phil Robinson, a respected reporter for the *Daily Chronicle* (London), infuriated with the censorship rules and with his inability to meet with the press censor, wrote a pamphlet of his experiences in Egypt whimsically entitled, 'How I Found Methuen'. Overall, the job ran smoothly and Methuen satisfied most of the reporters. There was one exception, however. One reporter, Mr Bernard, who claimed to work for the *New York Herald* and the *Standard* (London), failed to adhere to the press rules and wrote whatever he saw fit. The *Standard*, although they denied employing him, printed his articles. The War Office was forced to take action against both the newspaper and the journalist.

On 8 September Methuen shifted his attention to the advance. After the problems of transport and supply had been overcome, Wolseley's force began moving again. The next day, the British artillery bombarded the Egyptian defences at Kassassin and recaptured the position. On 12 September the advance guard first sighted Arabi's main army at Tel-el-Kebir. Wolseley prepared for the attack. One hundred rounds of ammunition, a day's rations, and enough tea to fill a water bottle were distributed to each man. After a night advance, four brigades of infantry, one division of cavalry, 60 guns and about 17,000 men, attacked Arabi and his 20,000 infantry, 2,500 cavalry, and 6,000 bedouins and irregulars.[16]

The battle of Tel-el-Kebir lasted only two hours and was a decisive victory for the British. Alison's night march of the Highlanders took the

Egyptians completely by surprise. Nearly 2,000 of Arabi's troops fell, mostly from bayonet wounds.[17] Demoralized by the shock and pummelled by the British artillery, Arabi's inner defences were shattered in a second charge led by Major-General Gerald Graham's 2nd Brigade. The night march had worked exceedingly well. Taking the Egyptians by surprise was not its intended goal but was an added bonus. Wolseley's strategy was focused on protecting his men from both the forces of nature, i.e. the heat and the lack of water, and from Egyptian firepower. Marching at night was not only less tiring, but also allowed the British to advance right up to the Egyptian entrenchments with little risk. The success of the night march had a great impact on Methuen and he later employed it during the South African War.[18]

After Tel-el-Kebir, all that remained for Wolseley was the formality of capturing Cairo. Meeting little resistance, he and his staff entered the capital city on 15 September, the same day that Arabi surrendered to the Major-General Drury Drury-Lowe, the British cavalry commander. Within a month the British had defeated a much larger Egyptian force and restored the Khedive's nominal authority. Wolseley returned home a hero, while Methuen, for his part, was honoured with the Third Class of the Order of Osmanieh and a CB (Companion of the Order of the Bath).

In 1882 after returning from Egypt, Methuen became involved with the volunteer movement. Following in his father's footsteps, who was the Honorary Colonel of the 3rd Militia Battalion of the Duke of Edinburgh (Wiltshire) Regiment, Methuen accepted the title of Honorary Colonel of the 2nd Volunteer Battalion.[19] Later in his life, as a representative of the crown and as a friend and associate of Jan Smuts and Louis Botha, he strongly advocated the development of a citizen's army in the newly created Union of South Africa. Methuen served as a member and sometimes acting president of the National Defence Association, an organization founded in 1907 to support the development of Lord Haldane's volunteer Territorial Army.

In the 1880s Methuen became active in advocating much-needed reform for the volunteer forces. Unlike many of his fellow aristocrats who jealously guarded their local militias as their exclusive reserves, Methuen, influenced by his father who had served as the Queen's Militia aide-de-camp, called for universal change. He became friends with Henry Spenser Wilkinson, one of the leading advocates of military reform, who believed that, if properly trained, the volunteer army could become an effective fighting force. Methuen, always a keen student of his profession, was very ready to listen to Wilkinson's or any other layman's suggestions.[20] In March

1883, back in London as Assistant Adjutant-General, Methuen directed volunteer marches and several war games. Wilkinson, observing the volunteers on manœuvres, wrote to Methuen, 'that was the first sham fight I ever saw that was not a specimen of "how not to do it"'.[21]

Methuen made another friend in the 1880s, Mary Ethel Sanford. 'Ettie', as she was known, was the daughter of Methuen's cousin, William Ayshford Sanford. He married her on 9 January 1884 after a brief courtship. With Ettie, he had five children, three daughters and two sons, the eldest of whom, Paul, was born in the autumn of 1886. Throughout their lives, Methuen and his wife were seldom together for any length of time (Methuen's career kept him busy in London and abroad and usually away from his home in Corsham), but the arrangement seems to have suited them well. Ettie was always there for him when he needed her, and over the course of their marriage he wrote her hundreds of letters. She was his closest adviser and confidante. Methuen's second marriage, although not as passionate as his first, endured. They were still together when he died in 1932.

WARREN'S EXPEDITION TO BECHUANALAND

In the later years of the nineteenth century Britain's relationship with its South African colonies underwent a period of great tension (see Chapter 4). In 1867 diamonds had been discovered outside Kimberley, a giant reef located outside Johannesburg in the Transvaal. To maximize output, the mine owners exploited neighbouring Bechuanaland for its food, fuel and manpower. Burghers from the Transvaal, impassioned by greed, instigated rebellion against British authority in Bechuanaland by supporting minor chiefs against the British-recognized paramount chiefs. In return for their support, the Boers were able to secure more territory and eventually, in 1882, shortly after the end of the First Anglo-Boer War, establish two new republics: Goshen and Stellaland. Increasingly, they monopolized Bechuanaland's resources.

British merchants such as Cecil Rhodes jealously guarded their interests in Bechuanaland and on the Rand. Pressured by their demands, Sir Hercules Robinson, the Cape Governor and High Commissioner, established a British protectorate over Bechuanaland in March 1884 to prevent further penetration by the Boer burghers. Although humanitarians such as the Revd John Mackenzie, the Deputy Commissioner of Bechuanaland, pressured Robinson to take more decisive action in defending native interests, he refused. The First Anglo-Boer War had just ended and the peace between Great Britain and the Transvaal was precarious at best. A forceful action against the Stellalanders and Goshenites could have led to the renewal of general hostilities, something the British Cabinet wished to avoid at all costs.[22] In May 1884 stability in the protectorate further weakened when Goshenites, led by Gey van Pittius, attacked and defeated the British-recognized paramount chief of the Baralongs, Montshiwa, and proclaimed the merger of an enlarged Goshen with the Transvaal. When Pittius refused to discuss the situation with Cecil Rhodes, the new Deputy Commissioner, the British ran out of options. As Robinson maintained, the 'freebooters' would not listen to peacemakers.[23]

Gladstone's Cabinet decided to force the freebooters from Bechuana-land and strengthen the British hold over its protectorate. In doing so, they would protect British trade routes to the interior, control the fuel and native labour supplies in Bechuanaland, and prevent the enlargement of the Transvaal.[24] In Mackenzie's opinion, 'A higher and clearer conception was now entertained than ever before of our duty and obligation in Native Territories, as well for the sake of the colonists as for the protection of the natives and the progress of civilization and commerce.'[25] Clearly, however, British action was motivated by strategic and economic interest. Sir Charles Warren, a veteran of the Gaika War who knew the territory well,[26] was chosen to drive the Goshenites from Bechuanaland (the Stellalanders had accepted British rule) and re-establish order.[27]

Warren's Bechuanaland Field Force consisted mostly of irregular troops. Carrington's Horse, the 2nd Mounted Rifles, comprised mainly of colonials from the Cape Colony. Gough's Horse, the 3rd Mounted Rifles, was raised in the Kimberley Diamond Fields. Colonel C. E. Knox commanded the 4th Pioneer Rifles, made up of volunteers from Griqua-land West and the Cape Colony. And, Colonel F. J. Kempster raised a native corps from South Africa. The regular troops consisted of the 1st Battalion Royal Scots from the West Indies, the 6th (Inniskilling) Dragoons from Natal, and a battery of Royal Artillery. In addition, engineers, the medical staff and other specialized troops were dispatched from Great Britain. In all, the Bechuanaland Field Force numbered about 4,000 men, at a cost of £750,000.[28] The Goshen freebooters were thought to number only 450. However, the Colonial Office believed that the freebooters could get the assistance of as many as 1,000 Transvaal burghers, and if the Transvaal Government decided to intervene, another 2,000 more men would join them. The Colonial Office wanted to send a force with Warren large enough to prevent any disaster.

Part of Warren's force consisted of volunteers raised by Methuen in London's Leicester Square. Methuen personally inspected and enrolled 600 British volunteers and accompanied them to Bechuanaland.[29] Named the 1st Mounted Rifles, the regiment was referred to as Methuen's Horse. The volunteers, for the most part, were 'young men of good family – briefless barristers, yeomen out of luck – in short, all that nondescript class who, although decently if not well educated, cannot find in these days of depression the right sort of work and are "ashamed to beg"'.[30] The volunteers, in general, were patriotic, enthusiastic and happy that Methuen led them. The *Swashbuckler's Gazette*, a short circular written by the volunteers of the 1st Mounted Rifles, wrote about Methuen:

> All who know him testify to his genuine qualities of head and heart; and we have every confidence in these qualities, together with the admirable tact and personal magnetism which he has displayed in dealing with Volunteers and in attracting all who come under his influence. We will serve him in good stead as Leader of the Irregular Horse which he is to command in South Africa.[31]

In the Cape Colony, Methuen and his junior officers drilled the volunteer regiment into an efficient fighting force. 'Colonel Methuen says we know all he can teach us', a volunteer wrote, 'that we show great aptitude at our work, and that the way we handle our horses after only six months' training is highly creditable. Such an opinion is valuable, for he is the last man in the world to praise when undeserved.'[32] Methuen, throughout his long career, rarely praised his men. During the South African War, some of his junior officers criticized him for not helping in their personal advancement. But his attitude is entirely understandable, since he himself was one of the hardest working officers in the British army.[33] H. C. Fletcher, his regimental colonel, wrote, 'with all the temptations of a life of pleasure, [Methuen] lives entirely for his duty, works hard and [does] far more for others than for himself'.[34] A man so committed to his work and duty would not often praise a soldier for simply doing his job. Thus when praise did come, it was indeed well deserved.

The Bechuanaland expedition made few headlines in Great Britain. There, the public was much more concerned with Charles Gordon and Wolseley's relief of Khartoum. Methuen, as well, was more interested in these events. He would have preferred to be part of the relief force. General Sir Arthur Herbert, the Quartermaster-General, and General Sir George Harmon, later Military Secretary, recommended Methuen for a position, but Wolseley unaccountably passed him over. 'I am at a loss to know what happened', Methuen wrote to his wife, 'as Wolseley has asked all kinds of officers but has left me out.'[35] He began to doubt the future of his career: 'The [Ashanti] club are not certain whether I am to be KCB [Knight Commander of the Bath] or General.'[36] He continued, 'There's so little between my career being nothing or a really fine one, and it's so hard to see the chance gone.'[37] Apparently, someone had invented a rumour that his health was in doubt, having never fully recovered from a previous operation. (In fact, Methuen was quite healthy.) When he discovered this, he accepted the decision but still blamed Wolseley for overlooking 'an old friend'. Trying to impress his father, Methuen made no mention of Wolseley's concern for his health. He wrote only that he had asked for the command of the Camel Corps, and that the job had gone to Herbert Stewart because of the latter's seniority.[38]

Even with the news of Gordon's death, Methuen remained hopeful about getting to the Sudan, and in late February he telegraphed Wolseley offering the services of his entire regiment. He proposed riding overland from the Cape to Cairo. Methuen had 330 men at this time, and every one of them volunteered for the duty. In addition, he planned on enlarging his regiment by enlisting 1,250 Bechuanaland Boers, who were valued as good riders and crack marksmen. At the Colonial Office, A. W. L. Hemming noted that 'this would seem to be an excellent way of getting rid of some of the restless and dangerous spirits among the Boers, and they would no doubt be a valuable addition to the Soudan [*sic*] force'.[39] With the approval of Lord Hartington, Gladstone's War Secretary, Wolseley accepted Methuen's offer providing his regiment was no longer needed in Bechuanaland.[40] Warren, however, refused to allow Methuen to leave until the operation was finished. By 5 May, when British forces were retiring from the Sudan, Methuen remained in Bechuanaland. Feeling worse for his men than for himself, he wrote, 'The game is up, and we are no longer counted here. It is a very bitter disappointment ... for the others who have never seen service.'[41]

The situation in Bechuanaland was tedious; not a shot was fired in the entire expedition. Methuen rode back and forth every day along the Bechuanaland border with the Boer republics – an area which he would administer from 1900–2. The weather in the summer was unbearably hot in the day and constant dust storms left his troops blinded and dry. Methuen found that many of the older soldiers were useless and often drunk. Although he enjoyed the companionship of his troops and his junior officers, whom he constantly tried to keep happy through entertainment,

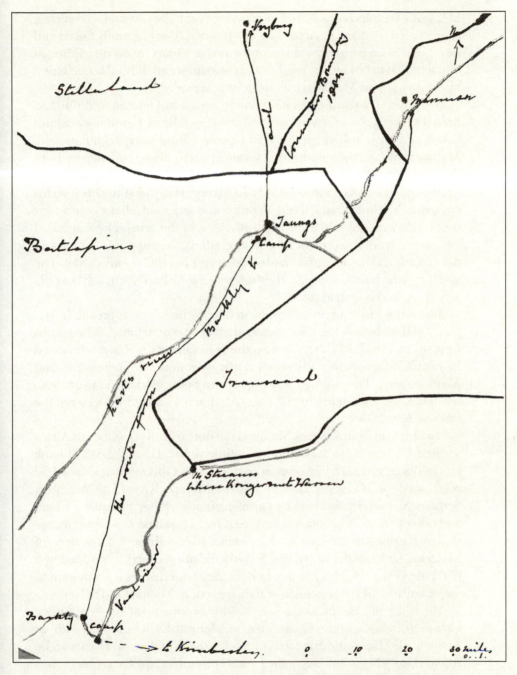

Map 3: Methuen's Sketch of Bechuanaland, 1884–85. Map reproduced with
the permission of the Wiltshire and Swindon Record Office.

high jinks, steeplechases and other sporting events, he often felt completely exasperated by Warren. According to Methuen, Warren rarely talked and he refused to keep his subordinates informed as to current events. Although Warren tried to be kind, he was not a likeable man and showed no feelings.[42] He in turn found Methuen over-zealous and pushy.[43]

The Bechuanaland expedition finally ended in October 1885. It had been a success: the area was pacified, the Republic of Goshen was eliminated and Britain had reinforced its protectorate over Bechuanaland. Methuen thought the volunteers in general proved to be good soldiers, both shooting and riding admirably. As he wrote: 'All did his [*sic*] duty well, rich gentlemen as well as poor workers.'[44] In his report to the War Office on his regiment, Methuen made a very detailed assessment of all the equipment used on the expedition, finding fault with many of the items. These included cartridges (which were sticking in the rifles), stirrups (too small and dangerous) and mauls, putties and wooden tent pegs (all poorly made). The uniform, which he found to be the most sensible he had worn, was the only article for which he had praise.[45]

It was not just equipment that incurred Methuen's disapproval. In late January 1885 he met Cecil Rhodes, and 'did not take to him'.[46] Their paths were to cross again in 1890, when Methuen inspected the Rhodes-financed Pioneer Column before it headed north to conquer Matabeleland and Mashonaland. The two met also during the South African War in 1900, when following the relief of the siege, Methuen's 1st Division entered the town of Kimberley.

Taking a tip from Rhodes, Methuen did not go home from South Africa without attempting to make himself a little richer. He and Lord Elibank received a territorial concession from the British Government situated 50 miles north of Mafeking, just south of the Molopo River. The 'Methuen Settlement' had rich fertile soil for growing maize, millet, pumpkins, wheat and other cereals. The scheme, endorsed by Mackenzie as well as George Baden-Powell (the brother of Methuen's friend Robert, later hero of Mafeking and founder of the Boy Scouts), did not succeed. Thus Methuen had little to show for his journey to Bechuanaland besides a promotion to major and a CMG (Companion of the Order of St Michael and St George).

For most of the following year (1886) Methuen sat on War Office Committees, such as the Committee on Medical Establishments with an Army in the Field and the Committee on the Number of Horses to be Allowed to Officers Serving in the Field. The empire, for the moment, was relatively quiet with few opportunities available for special service appointments. Methuen was asked to renew his term as Assistant Adjutant and Quartermaster-General at the Home District, but he rejected the offer. He wanted a position with new responsibilities and new challenges.

For lack of something better to do, Methuen enrolled in some courses at the Staff College, where he studied military engineering, field fortifications and military sketching. For assignments, he constructed mock defences of Sandhurst, entrenchments at Hartford Bridge Flats and attacks of Newbury. He learned, among other things, how to utilize railways, cross rivers, bivouac and set up outposts, and participated in the war games at Aldershot as a battalion commander. At this time he also read a great deal of military history and studied the campaigns of Napoleon, the American Civil War, the Austro-Prussian War and the Franco-Prussian War. For his essay entitled 'What Have We Learnt Regarding Modern Warfare', J. F. Maurice, a well-respected professor at the college and a veteran of Ashanti and Egypt, presented Methuen with an 'A'. The essay emphasized the importance of discipline, aggressive defence, and flank attacks in the age of modern firepower.

Of all his work at the Staff College, Methuen was most proud of an essay he wrote, entitled 'Discipline: Its Importance to an Armed Force, and the Best Means of Promoting and of Maintaining It'. In this essay, he examined the effects of discipline on the outcome of certain battles. Borrowing from the thesis of the Prussian-influenced, French military reformer Colonel Georges Stoffel, Methuen argued that discipline among the ranks was not determined by drill or by the conduct of any individual officer, but rather was created by the nation's perception of its army. Methuen used the Franco-Prussian War as his example. In Germany, he wrote, 'the army takes its moral tone from the character of its country. … All other professions give way to the military careers. The honours, all the advantages, all the rewards in Germany are for those serving or for those who have served.'[47] Methuen argued that while the Prussian model was dedicated to building a strong bond between the army and the nation, in the French case, the opposite existed. The French nation had little respect for its army, considering it useless. As a result, French soldiers looked elsewhere for spiritual and emotional guidance and did not submit themselves to an army in which military discipline was virtually non-existent.[48]

Methuen believed that the officer played an integral role in initiating and developing the bond between army and nation. The officer reinforced the values of the army in the nation. A well-educated and 'zealous' officer could both train his men to fight and indoctrinate them to love and honour their country. This, he believed, would make them better soldiers on the battlefield and better citizens later on in life.

> By kindness, by taking interest in their new men the first day they join, by treating them like educated, responsible beings, the officers and n[on] c[ommissioned] o[fficer]s gain the confidence of these lads. When later as they leave the service as trained soldiers to take up their work in civil life they carry with them the confidence in and respect for their commanders and instructors. This feeling of confidence and respect spreads itself through the nation.[49]

To understand these words is to understand at once both Methuen the citizen and Methuen the officer. Just as it was not the role of an aristocrat, he believed, merely to stroll about the estate, trailed by an obedient pack of hounds, it was not the job of an officer simply to give an order and then watch the results from some distant hill while squinting through a spyglass. The job of the officer started long before his regiment recruited its first soldier. The job of the officer was to spread the values of the army through the nation.

Methuen's essay on discipline broached another topic – military education. He believed that the army placed too much importance on military education. No doubt, Methuen was dissatisfied with his classes at the Staff College. In this essay, his rarely expressed beliefs about the ability of the landed gentry to rule are apparent.

> I venture to think, there is a danger in believing that examinations will give you the kind of interest and knowledge you require from an officer, and perhaps there is some truth in [the] remark that the system in some cases tends to discourage an honest desire to study. ... Enthusiasm is created by placing the utmost amount of responsibility possible within the grasp of each officer, giving him every chance of making use of his education and of showing the stuff of which he is made.
>
> ... It is not necessary for me to say that in tone and social position we stand as high, perhaps higher, than any European army. We recruit from the same material as the German Officer Corps and those mainly independent qualities that are the outcome of English Public School life combined with the out of door sports and pursuits that form part of most of our lives. ... I fear sometimes in our desire, I might say mania, for education, we perhaps run the risk of passing over those common sense practical qualities that in truth link man and man together, and are the causes that promote discipline. ...
>
> No amount of theoretical knowledge, no examination tests can ever ensure an officer in possessing those ... attributes that make the leader of

men. Common sense, tact, practical experience, a determined character, are qualities which are at once recognized by all ranks in a regiment.[50]

Methuen believed that men either had the qualities to be good officers or did not, and no amount of schooling could change this. These qualities were either innate or developed from the proper social upbringing.

RETURN TO SOUTH AFRICA

In 1888, after finishing his courses at the Staff College, Methuen was promoted to the rank of Colonel and appointed Deputy Adjutant-General of South Africa. He sailed to Cape Town where his stay was short and uneventful. He found himself in the company of men for whom he had little fondness. The General Officer Commanding, Sir W. Cameroon, was 'an old martinet'; Methuen did not care for Cecil Rhodes; and, Graham Bower, the Imperial Secretary, was 'a friend, but in political life would apparently give his country to anyone in want of it'.[51] Methuen also spent a great deal of time among Boers such as Francis Reitz, the president of the Orange Free State, and Chief Justice Sir Henry de Villiers.

In South Africa Methuen quickly came to an understanding of the Boer and British relationship and formed some general predictions about its future. 'There is not the faintest chance of the Transvaal ever belonging to England again', he wrote to his father.[52] He continued:

> … a broadminded policy is required. England should do her utmost to win the sympathy of the future English Republic in the Transvaal, that she should have an agent in Pretoria, not a touchy querulous man, but a genial friendly person, whose aim it should be to bring the mother country and the Republic together.
>
> [Britain] should encourage any scheme of amalgamation, as long as [the] English flag is paramount and must act in a broadminded liberal spirit, not as Jingoes [*sic*] for ever harping upon disasters and errors, which should now be forgotten by Dutch [and] English alike.[53]

In Methuen's opinion, the chief obstacle to reconciliation was the native question. The British interfered with the Boers' exploitation of Zulu labour. By sacrificing the Zulus, Methuen believed, the gap between Boer and Englishman could be bridged. Although he admired the Zulu as 'a race of men pure, simple and noble',[54] and, later as Governor of Natal, fought to protect their limited rights, he believed the interests of the empire outweighed humanitarian concern. On this issue it is fair to say that his position was determined by a mixture of political rationale and racist assumptions. A clear demonstration of the latter is found in the following statement:

> We say the native is our equal; that though inferior in education he can be made like to ourselves through the means of civilization. The Dutchman says the native is an inferior being, never intended by Nature or the Creator to be our equal. That he is and must always remain, subject to the white man. That it is a fatal mistake to let him think for a moment he is the white man's equal in anything. Personally I believe the Dutchman's views to be practical and sound, the Englishman's philanthropic and rotten.[55]

Methuen believed that unless his view was accepted by the British, peace with the Boers would remain out of reach. In theory, it was accepted in 1910 and peace was made.[56]

In the 1890s, while they were preventing the Boers from exploiting the Zulu, the British ironically were assisting in the subjugation of the Shona and the Ndebele. In 1888 Cecil Rhodes and his British South Africa Company fraudulently acquired from King Lobengula the exclusive rights to exploit the minerals of Mashonaland. This arrangement was known as the Rudd Concession.[57] To secure the minerals safely, to prevent Portuguese interference and to prevent the possible expansion of the Transvaal, Rhodes decided to raise an armed force and send it to Mashonaland. Sir Henry Loch, the Governor and High Commissioner of the Cape Colony, and Lord Knutsford, the Colonial Secretary, gave their blessings to the expedition. Loch ordered Methuen to Bechuanaland, where the force was assembling. The force, known as the Pioneer Column, was a rag-tag assortment of ill-trained, poorly disciplined and undersupplied freebooters. Methuen's task was to drill and mould them into a cohesive body. He drilled them in close and extended order, musketry and artillery fire, signalling, and setting up piquets and vedettes. Although the men proved quite unsatisfactory, Methuen did his best to improve them in the short time he had, and this he did almost single-handedly.[58] Many of his criticisms regarding equipment were acted upon immediately by Bower and Colonel Sir F. Carrington, but he had virtually no help in conditioning the men.[59] Since little resistance was expected from the Shona, the three-week inspection was not taken seriously by anyone. Even Methuen, who spent much of his time in Bechuanaland riding and hunting on the veldt, had little patience for his work once it became clear that no one else seemed to care. The following amusing exchange between Methuen and officers of the Pioneer Column illustrates how little preparation was made for the expedition.

> 'Gentlemen, have you got maps?'
> 'Yes, sir.'
> 'And pencils?'
> 'Yes, sir.'
> 'Well, gentlemen, your destination is Mount Hampden. You go to a place called Siboutsi. I do not know whether Siboutsi is a man or a mountain. Mr Selous, I understand, is of the opinion that it is a man; but we will pass that by. Then you get to Mount Hampden. Mr Selous is of the opinion that Mount Hampden is placed ten miles too far to the west. You had better correct that; but perhaps, on second thoughts, better not. Because you might possibly be placing it ten miles too far to the east. Now good morning gentlemen.'[60]

Despite the poor troops and the limited preparation, the Pioneer Column's expedition into Mashonaland (and later Matabeleland) was successful. Loch was thoroughly satisfied with Methuen's work.[61]

COMMANDER OF THE HOME DISTRICT

After finishing his work with Rhodes' force and being promoted to Major-General, Methuen returned to England. In September 1891, his father Frederick, 2nd Baron of Corsham, fell ill and died. Methuen inherited his father's estate and title, as well as his seat in the House of Lords. Many expected him to retire and live out his days as a gentleman; however, he never once considered that as an option, and his decision to dedicate his life to the army remained unaltered. In April 1892 he was appointed the Commander of the Home District.

The British army underwent an important change shortly after Methuen received this appointment. The Duke of Cambridge, who had served as Commander-in-Chief of the British army for nearly 40 years, retired in 1895, leading to a brief power struggle between Wolseley and Buller, in which Wolseley emerged victorious. In the 25 years since the Cardwell reforms, the reactionary Duke had ignored the pleas of military reformers. At last, Wolseley, their man, was in charge. Unsure of where to begin and what role he should play, Wolseley hesitated, and the War Office was temporarily paralysed.

Methuen's years commanding the Home District (1892–97) were uneventful. Wolseley's appointment had failed to produce the anticipated revolution and business continued as usual. Methuen's work in London was very routine, and his immediate superior, General Redvers Buller, the Adjutant General, gave him few responsibilities. Much of his work was ceremonial, such as the inspection of the Bulgarian army in 1894, which he described somewhat ungraciously as nothing more than a 'great nuisance'. He also organized all of the armed forces in the procession for Queen Victoria's Diamond Jubilee in 1897. The Diamond Jubilee, an event which 'celebrated not only sixty years of the Victorian era, but the final assembly of the forces and satisfactions of imperialism', as Jan Morris noted, was for Methuen nothing more than a tedious exercise in arrangement.[62] During the procession itself, he personally accompanied the queen on her inspection of the colonial troops.[63] In fact, it appears that the most exciting event during these years was the disappearance of his dog, when he had all of London's police searching the streets for the chow!

As Commander of the Home District, Methuen was responsible for defending England against any amphibious invasion. With the demands of the empire stretching the resources of the army dangerously thin, England's safety was becoming harder and harder to ensure. The War Office had proposed strengthening home defence by increasing the size of the Guards Brigade. This was to be accomplished by adding a third battalion to each regiment. No sooner had this been done, than Wolseley and Lord Lansdowne, the War Secretary, decided to rotate a Guards battalion to the Mediterranean garrisons, where it could be employed in Africa or in Asia if the need arose. Methuen, however, opposed this moved strenuously and fought desperately to keep the Guards in England.[64] He pleaded his case before the Prince of Wales, Wolseley and Lansdowne (his friend and neighbour), believing that two battalions of Guards could not adequately defend England in the event of an invasion. Methuen also argued that the volunteers and the militia needed dramatic reform and were in no condition to support the Guards. To his dismay, his worries were brushed aside: Wolseley sent the Guards to Gibraltar, and Buller, for fear of the political ramifications, refused to touch the volunteers and militia.[65] In addition, Methuen's attempt to abolish the costly Cavalry Guard was rejected by the Prince of Wales.[66]

During these years, Methuen was occupied with manœuvres, mobilization exercises and other preparations for home defence. The most noteworthy of these exercises was a series of mock attacks on the English coast near Brighton. On two occasions Methuen carried out the defence and Major-General Lord William Seymour conducted the offence. The first action, which Buller deemed successful, occurred between 21 and 26 June 1895.[67] After watching the second action on 6 September 1896, H. Spenser Wilkinson heralded Methuen as a 'skilful tactician'.[68] Methuen himself was proud of his performance. '[Wolseley's] only two criticisms on myself', he wrote, 'were so palpably wrong that I deferred to accept either. Hale congratulated me on having answered and for having shown him wrong.'[69] Four days later, Methuen, commanding some militia and four batteries, masterfully succeeded in repulsing four divisions and 15 batteries. In August 1895 he commanded a unique operation – the first peace-time mobilization of a force consisting entirely of reserves under service conditions.[70] This too was a great success. Most of the reserve troops fared very well and were found 'equal to the colours'.[71] Some of the more specialized troops, such as the Bearer Companies, needed work. After watching the manœuvres, Methuen was convinced that the reserves, although still a small force, could be counted on in an emergency to fill some gaps in the army.

By the autumn of 1896 Methuen was ready to move on to a new position. He searched for one, safe from the interference of Wolseley and Buller, where he could leave his mark. Rumours circulated that he was a candidate to replace his friend Francis Grenfell as the Chief of Staff of the Militia. Methuen wrote of that position: 'Except Aldershot, it is the only berth that gives me a field for original work. I have said I will take it if Lord Wolseley offers it to me. I have strong views regarding the militia, and shall be Boss. ...'[72] Despite his confidence and enthusiasm, however, he was passed over, and the position went elsewhere.

THE TIRAH EXPEDITION

In September 1897, after receiving the KCVO (Knight Commander of the Victorian Order), Methuen headed for India to join Lockhart's punitive expedition to Tirah. Longing for action and running out of career options, he joined the expedition as an observer. His service in India illustrates his ability to work within both Wolseley's Ring and Roberts' Ring. (This was an accomplishment that very few could claim. Ian Hamilton, who accompanied Methuen, was a Roberts man through and through. After fighting his enemies, Hamilton spent his remaining energy fighting for Roberts against Wolseley as he could not bring himself to serve under Wolseley.)[73]

Methuen's decision to go to India was a strange and rather sudden one. Throughout the summer of 1897 he had been questioning his future in the army. He had served for over 30 years and felt that his achievements had gone largely unrecognized. He was also troubled by his failure to secure a post at Aldershot or to succeed Grenfell. In the autumn of 1896 he had dissuaded his eldest son Paul from joining the army.[74] He even discussed his retirement with his wife.[75] And then, without warning and without an appointment, he crossed the Channel, took a train to the Adriatic, and then boarded a ship for Port Said, Aden and Bombay. In all likelihood, Methuen seriously considered retiring at this time and he saw the expedition to Tirah as his last hurrah. In his diary, he wrote that he was only seeking experience.[76] But there is little doubt that Methuen, who had not participated in a war since 1882, wanted to see battle one last time.

The battle was to be waged on India's northwest frontier. Under Lord Lytton's viceroyship in the mid 1870s, Britain had established a 'forward policy' in India to countermine Russian advances. This policy was continued under Lansdowne and Lord Elgin in the 1890s. To keep their position in India secure, the Government felt that it had to extend India's borders outward toward Afghanistan and Tibet. In doing so, they disrupted the various indigenes of the frontiers and expeditions were launched almost yearly to maintain peace. The Tirah expedition was directed against two indigenous groups: the Orakzais and the Afridis.

In the summer of 1897 the frontier erupted. Plagues, earthquakes, famines and floods had driven many to desperation. In June Mr Gee (a political officer) and his escort were murdered in Maizar when they tried to settle some fines. News spread quickly and a revolt began. Up the River Swat, the Swatis and Bunerwals attacked the British garrisons at Malakand and Chakdarra. The Mohmunds rebelled, attacking the forts at Shankargarh and Shebkadar in the Peshawar Valley. In August the Orakzais, led by Mullah Sayyid Akbar (a holy man who the people believed could feed them all with a handful of rice and turn stones into bullets) and the Afridis, led by Aka Khel Afridi, joined the uprisings and seized the Khyber Pass.[77] The British Government decided to punish the tribes and to retake the strategic pass. Lieutenant-General Sir William Lockhart and 30,000 troops were mobilized. In addition, the Indian Government sent two reserve brigades under Major-General Yeatmann-Biggs and Brigadier-General Westmacott to the frontier. The Simla Memorandum authorized Lockhart to 'exact reparation for unprovoked aggression' from the Orakzais and the Afridis.[78]

Tirah was a unique campaign and a harbinger of the South African

War. It was the first example in British history of a regular army facing an irregular force armed with modern weapons.[79] As a result, the casualties were higher, the battlefields were larger, and sniping became a greater threat to transport and communication. The enemy was able to place fewer men in the field to defend a larger piece of ground. Also, the regular forces were forced to send pickets farther and farther away to protect the main body from an attack. As the pickets were pushed out, they became increasingly isolated and endangered.

Tirah was also Methuen's first introduction to hill warfare. It was a land of rocks, chasms, hidden valleys, and sharp rises which made supply and communication lines very long and subject to disturbance, and transport prone to ambush. Because of the great likelihood of an ambush, rear-guards and outposts had to be strengthened. Due to the nature of the terrain, the British were forced to march in single file, making it more difficult to attack *en masse*. There was also the problem of attacking an enemy which inevitably chose the high ground: crowning the heights was rarely a simple task.

Methuen's role in the expedition was extremely limited, and he served only in the capacity of press censor. Lockhart respected Methuen's ability and wanted to employ him, but General George White, the Commander-in-Chief in India, worried that doing so would create a bad precedent since technically Methuen was just an observer. Methuen himself agreed with White's decision and did not hold it against him.[80]

Methuen enjoyed good relations with his commander, writing of Lockhart:

> He is very different to Sir George [White], being quite quiet, very determined and as simple minded as a child. There are a few men like Ben Stephenson and Buller who all men at once devote themselves to, and Sir William compares favourably with either, for he has Ben Stephenson's charm and Buller's firmness. Sir George is a handsome, cold, unsympathetic man, who is no doubt, an equally fine character, but not a man one would take to at once.[81]

For Methuen, the most interesting event of the campaign was the battle at Dargai. First, he witnessed on 18 October, the 'futility of attempting to carry an almost impregnable position by rushes of only driblets of men'. Then on the 20th, he witnessed one of the greatest charges in British military history, in which the Gordon Highlanders *en masse* successfully stormed the enemy's position, suffering relatively few casualties in the process.[82] Methuen wrote:

The Gordons gave fresh proof that the only way to carry a position in these days of quick firing arms of precision, is to push forward at close intervals line after line of men in extended order and under perfect control.

The enemy can not shoot down more than a small fraction of the attacking force, and the moral effect of the onward rush of so large a number of men is certain to demoralize the defenders.[83]

This lesson, which reaffirmed over 20 years of colonial experience, seemed to prove that even in the age of modern firepower, the will of the British soldier could overcome all obstacles. It was a belief that Methuen held to firmly when he travelled to South Africa a few years later to command the 1st Division in the South African War.

RETURN TO ENGLAND

In early 1898 Methuen returned to England and was promoted to Lieutenant-General, making him the youngest high-ranking officer in the British army. Still questioning his future, he enjoyed a year and a half of hunting, fishing and travelling. Although talk of a possible war in South Africa excited the public, Methuen remained sanguine. Unlike the periods before the Ashanti War and the Arabi Rebellion, no flood of letters came from Corsham begging for a special service appointment. He was convinced that the British public would turn against a pro-war Cabinet and that the troubles in South Africa would, temporarily at least, go away.[84]

He was of course wrong. On 11 October 1899 the war in South Africa began, and ten days later Methuen set sail for Capetown as the Commander of the 1st Division. Strangely enough, his heart was not in this expedition, and in a letter to his wife he expressed regret at the prospect of a long period of absence: 'Darling Ettie, It was sadder by far leaving you this time, because with Methuen's horse we had the excitement, and in the Tirah, I knew we should soon meet again in India, whereas this time, I fear six months may be the minimum ... .'[85] In fact he was not to return from South Africa for two-and-a-half years.

Paul Methuen had entered the British army to serve his country, to experience combat, to become a great commander, and to leave his mark. His early career, although aided in advancement by personal contacts, had been somewhat typical of the late Victorian army officer. He served in colonial expeditions, in administrative positions and on regimental staffs.

He saw action in Africa and Asia. And he observed the British army undergo a major transition. With his knowledge of the German army and his experience with volunteers, he tried to guide this transition, but was frustrated by superiors who caved in to political issues or feared change. In his 35 years of service Methuen had become a respected and decorated officer but so far had not had the opportunity to make his mark. Little did he know, as he sailed somewhat reluctantly for South Africa in 1899, that his time had come and he would finally be given that chance.

NOTES

1. Denis Winter, *Haig's Command: A Reassessment* (New York: Viking, 1991), p. 12. Winter was comparing Douglas Haig to Methuen and Ian Hamilton.
2. There has been a great deal written on the causes of the Arabi Rebellion. For some of the more traditional British sources, see: Earl of Cromer, *Modern Egypt* (London: Macmillan, 1911), Wilfrid S. Blunt, *Secret History of the English Occupation of Egypt* (London: T. Fisher Unwin, 1907), Edward Malet, *Egypt, 1879–1883* (London: John Murray, 1909), and, Ronald Robinson and John Gallagher with A. Denny, *Africa and the Victorians*, 2nd edn (London: Macmillan, 1981). For sources which use the Egyptian archives, see: Juan Ricardo Cole, *Colonialism and Revolution in the Middle East* (Princeton, NJ: University Press, 1993), and Alexander Schölch, *Egypt for the Egyptians* (London: Ithaca, 1981).
3. Malet to Granville, 25 July 1882, FO 407/21, Public Records Office, Kew.
4. M. E. Chamberlain, 'The Alexandria Massacre of 11 June 1882 and the British Occupation of Egypt', *Middle Eastern Studies* 13 (1977): 14.
5. Cromer, *Modern Egypt*, p. 300. In Robert T. Harrison's *Gladstone's Imperialism in Egypt* (Westport, CT: Greenwood Press, 1995), the author argues that Great Britain's intervention in Egypt was not caused by the decisions of 'the men on the spot', but was part of Gladstone's strategic policy to ensure the safety of the Indian trade route.
6. Cabinet Report, 27 July 1882, CAB 41/16/40, Public Records Office.
7. 'Costs of Principal British Wars', WO 33/256, Public Records Office.
8. Ibid.
9. Grenfell was perhaps the last British officer to see Louis Napoleon, the Prince Imperial, alive.
10. When Grenfell died in 1925, Methuen became Britain's senior Field Marshal.
11. Grenfell praised Methuen for his forethought in hiring a cook in Malta for the staff mess. General Dormer, Colonel Butler, Colonel Buller, Colonel Ardagh, and Major Sandwith were also very thankful. F. W. Grenfell, *Memoirs of Field Marshal Lord Grenfell* (London: Hodder & Stoughton, 1925).
12. 'Newspaper Correspondents with an Army in the Field, and Military Attachés of Foreign Powers at Headquarters', 28 Feb. 1878, WO 33/32, Public Records Office.
13. Ibid.
14. Wolseley's dispatch on the expedition to Egypt, 2 Nov. 1882, ZJ 1/406, Public Records Office.
15. Phil Robinson, 'The Army, the Volunteers, and the Press', *Contemporary Review* 42 (1882): 977.
16. G. Wolseley to Hugh Childers, Secretary of State for War, 13 Sept. 1882, WO 32/6096, and WO 33/41/0938, Public Records Office.

17. Charles Royle, *The Egyptian Campaigns 1882 to 1885*, rev. edn (London: Hurst & Blackett, 1900), p. 176.
18. While assisting the casualties, Methuen counted only 68 dead and 369 wounded, a rather small figure considering Arabi had placed over 28,000 men in the field. The low casualty numbers are certainly a reflection of Wolseley's strategy. Miscellaneous note, Methuen Papers, Wiltshire Records Office.
19. Methuen held this position until the death of his father in 1892. He then held his father's rank in the 3rd Battalion.
20. H. Spenser Wilkinson, *Thirty-Five Years* (London: Constable, 1933), p. 223.
21. H. Spenser Wilkinson to P. S. Methuen, 23 Dec. 1886, Methuen Papers, Wiltshire Records Office.
22. Robinson and Gallagher, *Africa and the Victorians*, p. 203.
23. 'Correspondence relative to the Bechuanaland Expedition 1884–5', H. Robinson to Lord Derby, 17 Oct. 1884, WO 33/45, Public Records Office.
24. For more on British interests in Bechuanaland, see Joseph Chamberlain's Cabinet minute of 1 October 1884, as cited in J. L. Garvin, *The Life of Joseph Chamberlain* (London: Macmillan & Co., 1932–34), I, 492.
25. John Mackenzie, *Austral Africa. Losing it or Ruling it* (London: Sampson, Low, Marston, Searle & Rivington, 1887), p. 24.
26. 'Correspondence relative to the Bechuanaland Expedition 1884–5', H. Robinson to Lord Derby, 23 Oct. 1884, WO 33/45, Public Records Office.
27. Participants in the Bechuanaland Field Force included Colonel F. W. E. Forestier-Walker, Warren's second-in-command and a close friend of Methuen; Sir Bartle Frere, the son of Henry Bartle Frere, the former British Governor and High Commissioner of the Cape Colony; Colonels F. Carrington and C. E. Knox, both later generals in the South African War; and, Lord Clandesboy, the son of Lord Dufferin, the British Ambassador to Russia. Dufferin personally asked Methuen to watch out for his son. 'Diary of the Bechuanaland Expedition', 26 Jan. 1885, Methuen Papers, Wiltshire Records Office.
28. CO 23/301, Public Records Office.
29. Because of an Act of Parliament, the volunteers could not legally be enrolled in England. Discipline, therefore, was a potential problem on the high seas, since the men were not yet soldiers. With the exception of one man's mysterious disappearance, the voyage, however, went smoothly, and the force was enrolled in Cape Town.
30. *St Stephen's Review*, 13 Dec. 1884.
31. *Swashbuckler's Gazette*, 7 Dec. 1884.
32. Dudley Pullin, *A Devonshire Volunteer with Methuen's Horse in Bechuanaland under Sir Charles Warren* (Sidmouth: Frank Carter, 1886), p. 7.
33. 'Supervisor Report', 20 July 1875, WO 27/489, Public Records Office.
34. 'Supervisor Report', 4 Aug. 1876, WO 27/489, Public Records Office.
35. P. S. Methuen to M. E. Methuen, 16 Sept. 1884, Methuen Papers, Wiltshire Records Office.
36. Ibid.
37. P. S. Methuen to M. E. Methuen, 17 Sept. 1884, Methuen Papers, Wiltshire Records Office.
38. Stewart was mortally wounded in January 1885. P. S. Methuen to F. H. P. Methuen, 21 Sept. 1884, Methuen Papers, Wiltshire Records Office.
39. CO 417/8, Minute by A. W. L. Hemming, 4 March 1885, Public Records Office.
40. 'Diary of the Suakin Expedition 1885', letter no. 324, G. Wolseley to Lord Hartington, 28 Feb. 1885, WO 33/44, Public Records Office.
41. P. S. Methuen to F. H. P. Methuen, 16 March 1885, Methuen Papers, Wiltshire Records Office.

42. P. S. Methuen to F. H. P. Methuen, 3 Feb. 1885, Methuen Papers, Wiltshire Records Office.
43. P. S. Methuen to F. H. P. Methuen, 14 Feb. 1885, Methuen Papers.
44. 'Report from Col. Methuen on the Organization and Recruitment, 1st Mounted Rifles, 20 June 1885 from Sitlagoli', WO 106/264, Public Records Office.
45. 'Report of the Proceedings of the Bechuanaland Field Force', appendix, 12 June 1885, WO 106/264, Public Records Office.
46. 'Diary of the Bechuanaland Expedition', 26 Jan. 1885, Methuen Papers, Wiltshire Records Office.
47. Paul Methuen, 'Discipline: Its Importance to an Armed Force, and the Best Means of Promoting and of Maintaining It', unpublished essay, 1887, Methuen Papers, Wiltshire Records Office.
48. For a discussion on discipline and morale in the Franco-Prussian War, see Michael Howard, *The Franco-Prussian War* (London: Rupert Hart-Davis, Ltd, 1961; reprinted, New York: Routledge, 1989).
49. Methuen, 'Discipline'.
50. Ibid.
51. P. S. Methuen to F. H. P. Methuen, 15 Jan. 1890, Methuen Papers, Wiltshire Records Office.
52. Ibid.
53. Ibid.
54. P. S. Methuen to M. E. Methuen, 29 April 1890, Methuen Papers, Wiltshire Records Office.
55. P. S. Methuen to F. H. P. Methuen, 15 Jan. 1890, Methuen Papers, Wiltshire Records Office.
56. Many years later, Methuen's letter to his father was given to Lord Haldane, the Liberal War Minister (1906–15). Haldane was very impressed with his foresight. Upon his recommendation, the letter was donated to the Institute of Historical Research.
57. For a brief summary of the Rudd concession and Rhodes' acquisition of Mashonaland and Matabeleland, see Richard W. Hull, *Southern Africa: Civilization in Turmoil* (New York: New York University Press, 1981), pp. 74–7.
58. CO 879/32/392, 'Inspection Report on the Bechuanaland Border Police', 'Report on the British South African Company's Force', and 'Inspection of Pioneer Force at Pioneer Camp, Macloutsi River', Public Records Office.
59. Carrington served in Bechuanaland with Methuen in 1884–5 and commanded the Rhodesian Field Force in the South African War.
60. J. G. Lockhart and C. M. Woodhouse, *Cecil Rhodes. The Colossus of Southern Africa* (New York: Macmillan Co., 1963), p. 178.
61. CO 879/32/392, H. Loch to Lord Knutsford, 24 Sept. 1890, No. 323, Public Records Office.
62. James Morris, *Pax Britannica* (New York: Harcourt, Brace & Jovanovich, 1968), p. 26.
63. George E. Buckle (ed.), *The Letters of Queen Victoria* (London: John Murray, 1932) III, 2nd series, p. 186.
64. P. S. Methuen to North Dalrymple Hamilton, 12 Dec. 1896, Methuen Papers, Wiltshire Records Office.
65. R. Buller to P. S. Methuen, 2 Jan. 1896, Methuen Papers, Wiltshire Records Office.
66. P. S. Methuen to R. Buller, 5 Jan. 1895, Methuen Papers, Wiltshire Records Office.
67. *Record of the Proceedings During a Staff Ride Between Brighton and Red Hill 1895*, HMSO, 1895.
68. H. Spenser Wilkinson, *Lessons of the War* (Philadelphia: J. B. Lippincott Co., 1900), p. 67.
69. P. S. Methuen to M. E. Methuen, 6 Sept. 1896, Methuen Papers, Wiltshire Records Office.

70. 'Report of the Mobilization of the 1st Brigade, 1st Division, I Army Corps, 1895', Public Records Office.
71. 'Report on the Efficiency of Men of the Army Reserve', 1897, WO 33/57, Public Records Office.
72. P. S. Methuen to F. Grenfell, 13 Nov. 1896, Methuen Papers, Wiltshire Records Office.
73. Farwell, *Eminent Victorian Soldiers*, p. 178.
74. P. S. Methuen to M. E. Methuen, 18 Sept. 1896, Methuen Papers, Wiltshire Records Office.
75. P. S. Methuen to M. E. Methuen, 19 Sept. 1897, Methuen Papers, Wiltshire Records Office.
76. 'Tirah Diary', 13 Sept. 1897, Methuen Papers.
77. C. Collin Davies, *The Problem of the North-West Frontier 1890–1908* (Cambridge: Cambridge University Press, 1932; repr. New York: Barnes & Noble, 1974), p. 96.
78. Charles Edward Callwell, *Tirah, 1897* (London: Constable & Co., 1911), p. 9.
79. Ibid.
80. P. S. Methuen to M. E. Methuen, 2 Oct. 1897, Methuen Papers, Wiltshire Records Office.
81. P. S. Methuen to M. E. Methuen, 17 Sept. 1897, Methuen Papers, Wiltshire Records Office.
82. The British suffered only 200 casualties. Lionel James, *The Indian Frontier War* (New York: Chas. Scribner's Sons, 1898), p. 123.
83. 'Report of the Dargai Attack', 6 Jan. 1898, Methuen Papers, Wiltshire Records Office.
84. P. S. Methuen to M. E. Methuen, 22 Sept. 1899, Methuen Papers, Wiltshire Records Office.
85. P. S. Methuen to M. E. Methuen, 22 Oct. 1899, Methuen Papers, Wiltshire Records Office.

PART TWO

The Army's Scapegoat

4

The British Army and the
Outbreak of War in South Africa

Methuen had correctly anticipated that the situation in South Africa would deteriorate further if the British did not make some concessions to gain the loyalty of the Boer republics. Contrary to his thinking, an aggressive British administration, led by Sir Alfred Milner, the British High Commissioner in South Africa and Governor of the Cape Colony, and Joseph Chamberlain, Salisbury's Colonial Secretary, and an assertive colonial administration, led by Cecil Rhodes, the Cape prime minister, refused to compromise. Instead, Milner, Chamberlain and Rhodes attempted to extend their influence over what the Boers considered to be solely domestic concerns.

When these attempts failed and the differences between Boer and Briton seemed more irreconcilable than ever, Salisbury's Cabinet prepared to launch a colonial expedition. In June 1899 Lord Lansdowne, the Secretary of State for War, approached General Sir Redvers Buller and informed him that he was to command British operations.[1] For over two months, Buller was mystified as the Cabinet, uneasy with its decision, stalled: no council of war was held, no plan of campaign was adopted and no military preparations were made.[2] Preparations between August and late September remained negligible. On 10 October 1899 the Transvaal delivered an ultimatum to the British Government – the 'most egregious document ever addressed to a great Power by a petty state'.[3] The following day, the unanswered ultimatum expired. Ready or not, Britain had to accept that a state of war existed.

ORIGINS OF THE SOUTH AFRICAN WAR

The events leading up to the South African War are well known and do not need to be reviewed in detail. The conflict between Boer and Briton originated in the early decades of the nineteenth century and reached its first climax with the Great Trek of 1832, an event which started the migration of thousands of Boers from the Cape into the interior of South Africa. British policy, for the time being, tolerated their separate existence and eventually recognized their independence through the Sand River Convention of 1852.

During this period, British interest concentrated on the security of the Cape Colony. Prior to the construction of the Suez Canal in 1869, possession of the Cape ensured the integrity of Britain's most vital trade route to India. Therefore, the Cape Colony had to be protected from external threat. With the exception of the Zulus, the majority of the Bantu-speaking peoples of South Africa were subjugated and 'pacified' by either the British or the Voortrekkers, the Boer migrants. In addition, the British expanded their control over the South African coast by establishing a colony in Natal. Neither the two poor Boer states, the Transvaal (South African Republic) and the Orange Free State, nor the Portuguese, with their colony in East Africa (modern-day Mozambique), gave the British cause for concern.

In the early 1870s British interest in South Africa changed. To the west of Bloemfontein, diamonds were discovered. Within five years, 50,000 migrant workers had converged on the area to seek their fortunes.[4] This migration was accompanied by large capital investment and a tremendous growth in trade. The new-found wealth of the South African interior altered the relationship of Boer and Briton. For the time being, the British could control the trade and, to a degree, the influx of investment and immigration, because they controlled all transportation and communication which ran into the interior. However, they grew increasingly fearful that the Boers would circumvent this monopoly and escape their commercial dependence by trading through the Portuguese colony situated on Delagoa Bay.

Lord Carnarvon, Disraeli's Colonial Minister, planned to thwart the emerging economic independence of the Boer states by forcing them into a political federation with the two British South African colonies. Under normal circumstances, the Boers would have adamantly rejected this plan. However, the wealth generated in the republics by the diamond trade led to grandiose schemes of internal reform and expansion. Attempts at 'westernization', much like the attempts of Khedive Ismail in Egypt, failed and the Transvaal headed toward bankruptcy. In addition, Carnarvon believed that the Transvaal, left increasingly vulnerable to a Zulu attack, would eagerly accept British protection.[5]

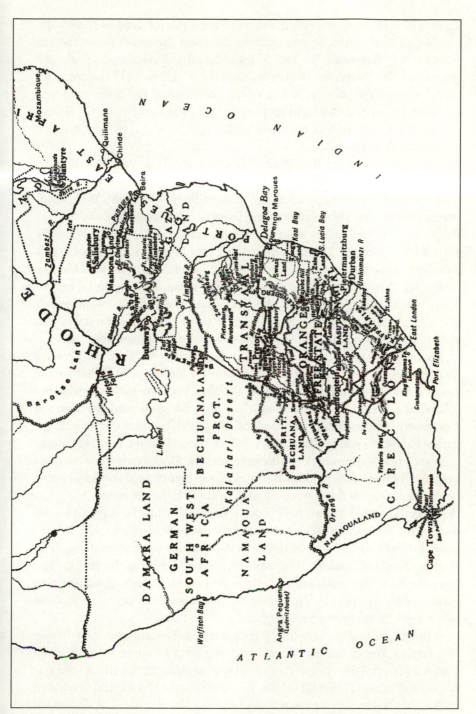

Map 4: South Africa, 1899. Map reproduced from Mordechai Tamarkin, *Cecil Rhodes and the Cape Afrikaners: The Imperial Colossus and the Colonial Parish Pump*, London, Frank Cass, 1996.

In 1877 Disraeli accepted his minister's advice and annexed the republic. The decision proved catastrophic, and the annexation failed to stabilize the Transvaal. To satisfy their Natal colonists and to win the support of the Boers, the British crushed the Zulus in 1879. In doing so, they destroyed the primary threat to the existence of the Boer states and the Boers found that they no longer needed the protection which the British offered. The more radical burghers in the Transvaal, led by Paul Kruger, asserted their independence.

The outcome of the British annexation of the Transvaal was the First Anglo-Boer War of 1880–81. The British Government had disastrously underestimated their opponents' skill and willingness to fight. With insufficient manpower, poor military intelligence and limited resources, the British were bested by the Boers in almost every battle. On 27 February 1881 a small force of burghers drove over 500 British regulars from their seemingly impenetrable position atop Majuba Hill. Major-General George Colley, the expedition's commander and one of the key men in Wolseley's Ring, was killed. Over half of the British force was killed, wounded or taken prisoner. The Boers lost one man.[6] Rather than raise the stakes and send reinforcements, the British made peace shortly afterwards.

Peace negotiations after the war produced two treaties: the Pretoria Convention of 1881 and the London Convention of 1884. Whether the London Convention was a revision of the Pretoria Convention or whether it was an addendum to it is debatable. The Boers viewed the London Convention as the final word; the British agreed, but also recognized the earlier Convention as binding. As a result of these differing interpretations, the exact relationship between Britain and the Boer republics remained unclear. Terms such as paramountcy, sovereignty, self-autonomy and suzerainty continued to be tossed back and forth for the next 15 years to describe that relationship. Both sides recognized that the republics were autonomous, but the British refused to concede independence. Did Britain have the right to interfere in the external policies of the republics? The Boers argued no, insisting they were sovereign republics; the British, yes, asserting their imperial authority. It is certain that the second war was caused at least in part by the failure of these treaties to do no more than bring a quick end to this first conflict.[7]

The question of paramountcy grew more important over time due to two factors: the discovery of gold and the establishment of a German colony in South West Africa (modern-day Namibia). In the 1880s gold was discovered in the Transvaal on the Witwatersrand. The capital generated by the gold boom far surpassed that of the diamond trade. The Transvaal economy recovered from bankruptcy and began growing by leaps and bounds. Great Britain feared that its colonies, the Cape Colony and Natal, would become economically dependent on the Boer republic. To prevent further growth of the republic, the British encircled it by seizing Bechuana-land and Rhodesia and tightened their grasp over the Boer state's trade routes to the coast.

The second factor complicating the British–Boer relationship was the arrival of the Germans in South West Africa in the 1890s. German presence in South West Africa, a small and underdeveloped colony, posed a direct threat to British interests in South Africa. A German invasion, though unlikely, remained a concern of every British defence scheme after 1890. Far more likely than an invasion was the possibility that the Germans would offer the Boer republics an outlet for their trade. Even after the path to German South West Africa was cut off by the British establishment of a protectorate over Bechuanaland, they still feared German interference. To the east, they carefully watched the colony at Delagoa Bay and pressured the Portuguese to hold it. Clearly, German presence in southern Africa endangered the security of the Cape Colony and Natal, as well as the British protectorates in South Africa. This fear had to be lessened and the Transvaal's economic domination of the British colonies had to be prevented.

In 1895 Cecil Rhodes conceived of a plan to assuage Britain's concern over its South African possessions by reasserting its control over the Transvaal. The plan was simple. Rhodes' agent, Dr Leander Starr Jameson, was to lead a small armed force across the Bechuanaland border into the Transvaal and stimulate an insurrection. The Boer regime would be overthrown, and the British would compel the destabilized territory to join a South African federation.

Rhodes' plan rested its hopes of success on the Uitlanders, the large immigrant population, who had come to Johannesburg to work the Rand. Rhodes believed that the Uitlanders, the majority of who were British or from British colonies, were unhappy with their social and political conditions. Among their alleged grievances was the inability to vote and to use their language in the courts and schools. As it turned out, Rhodes overestimated the value of the Uitlanders as allies. The result was the disastrous Jameson Raid,[8] in which Jameson and his men were arrested, Rhodes was toppled as Cape prime minister, and Joseph Chamberlain and the British Government were implicated. For many, the discord created by the Jameson Raid made future conflict between Briton and Boer inevitable.

Rhodes was not alone in putting his faith in the Uitlanders. Sir Alfred

Milner, the British High Commissioner in South Africa and Governor of the Cape Colony, also believed that they could be used to gain control of the Transvaal. However, rather then rely on insurrection, Milner, with Chamberlain's blessing, championed a British victory through democratic election. By 1899, the Uitlanders made up the majority of the Transvaal population. However, oppressive electoral laws prevented their proportionate representation in the Volksraad, the Transvaal's legislative assembly. Milner believed that if these laws were changed and the Uitlanders gained control of the Volksraad, the Transvaal could be forced into a federation. The issue of Uitlander civil liberties, whether or not a legitimate concern of the British Government, became the keystone of Milner's policy to gain political – and thus economic – control of the Transvaal and to manipulate popular support for an aggressive British policy in South Africa. In his meetings at Bloemfontein with Paul Kruger, the president of the Transvaal, Milner put the question of the Uitlanders' grievances in the foreground.[9] He believed that a 'big concession of the franchise question would be such a score that we could afford to let other concessions drop quietly into the background or settle them by compromise'.[10] In fact the Bloemfontein Conference in June proved unsuccessful as neither side was willing to grant any significant concessions.

When negotiations deteriorated between Milner and Kruger after the Conference, the Boers wisely prepared themselves for the worst by stockpiling foreign weapons and ammunition. Milner, with his hands tied, did nothing. Firmly in control of British policy in South Africa, he had little recourse to the resources of the empire outside of the Cape Colony and Natal. He could hope to achieve little without the full backing of the Cabinet. The Cabinet, however, refused to accept the inevitability of a war. Chamberlain informed Milner that the Government's desire was to reach a 'satisfactory settlement'.[11] British preparations were delayed until the autumn when the true nature of the situation was finally exposed by the Boer ultimatum.

In anticipation of an expected British ultimatum, the Boers issued one of their own on 9 October. Referring to the London Convention of 1884, they reasserted their sovereignty. They blamed Britain for creating the existing tension and preventing further discussion. The Transvaal Government demanded arbitration to settle their differences and assess British violations of interference in their domestic affairs. It demanded that all British troops on its borders be withdrawn, that all troops which had arrived in South Africa since 1 June leave immediately and that no further reinforcements be permitted to land. The British were given 48 hours to accept the conditions of the ultimatum.[12] On 12 October Chamberlain informed Milner that he could issue a proclamation of war.[13]

Ronald Robinson and John Gallagher, in their *Africa and the Victorians*, argue that in 1899 the British risked war in South Africa because they had no other conflicts in the empire that required immediate attention.[14] Kitchener's expedition to the Sudan, culminating in an encounter with the French at Fashoda, had been resolved. India, after the punitive Chitral and Tirah expeditions, was quiet. British colonies in West Africa were also safe for the time being. Therefore, 1899, Robinson and Gallagher claim, proved to be the moment to strike.

However, if the British Government was actively supporting an aggressive and belligerent policy in South Africa, it was unconcerned with its ability to enforce that policy. From the summer of 1899 until the outbreak of the war in October, British policy can be described as nothing short of indecisive. Talk of an ultimatum was discussed in the Cabinet as early as 13 June, yet no ultimatum was delivered.[15] By early autumn, the people of Britain had been sufficiently prepared for war by an enthusiastic, jingoistic press, 'the most successful recruiting officers of the Queen's army'.[16] A clear majority in parliament also favoured action. Yet, Salisbury and Lansdowne ordered few preparations.

THE GOVERNMENT'S FAILURE TO PREPARE FOR WAR

At the beginning of the year British forces in South Africa numbered only about 10,000. These included six and a half battalions of infantry, two regiments of cavalry, four field artillery batteries, one mounted battery and some additional volunteer levies from South African possessions. In August these troops were reinforced by two battalions of infantry, four field artillery batteries and three companies of Royal Engineers. This was hardly a sufficient force to launch an offensive against either the Transvaal or the Orange Free State, or even to establish adequate protection for Natal, the Cape Colony, or any British protectorates or colonies in South Africa.[17] In September, just a month before hostilities erupted, the British mobilized an additional 10,000 more troops – a force large enough to protect Cape Town, Port Elizabeth and Durban, yet still inadequate to defend their colonies' frontiers. If the British Government was bluffing by sending these forces, the bluff failed. Less than a week before the war began, the British seemed, at last, to take the problem seriously and mobilized at Salisbury Plain the 1st Army Corps – 40,000 men.

The failure of the British Government to prepare adequately for war in South Africa was the product of political and economic calculations. During the summer, Lord Wolseley, the Commander-in-Chief of the British army, had urged that an army corps be mobilized to prepare for possible conflict. The plan was rejected. Believing that peace was still possible, Lansdowne did not want to provoke the Boers. In Wolseley's opinion, timing prevented any immediate conflict. With the limited grazing of South Africa's winter months, Wolseley knew that the mounted burghers would oppose armed conflict. Not until early October, he believed, would they risk war.[18] However, the Government refused to sanction any military preparations. In early September, it aborted a plan to send a brigade of Guards to Natal,[19] and as late as 22 September, had failed to obtain supplies, raise men or take any necessary steps to prepare adequately for war.[20] Not until war was actually declared did the Government finally agree to loosen its purse-strings. As a result of this delay, the British army was in no position to launch an effective offensive until 15 November – a month after the war had begun.

Not only did considerations of cost prevent the early mobilization of the British forces, they also obstructed the efforts of military intelligence. As of the autumn of 1899 the British had not even prepared maps of the vast interior regions of South Africa. As described in the *German Official Account of the War in South Africa*, the size of the Transvaal was roughly that of southern and central Germany, including Alsace-Lorraine; while the Orange Free State approximated to an area the size of northern Germany, excluding Prussia and Silesia.[21] It was a country of plains, steep mountains, rugged tablelands (or *karoos*), endless hills (or kopjes), and few roads. A multitude of rivers snaked through the colonies, often lined by steep banks which made crossing all but impossible. It was also a country with few large population centres to serve as targets for an invading force. Proof of the Boer disdain for centralized authority, the population of the republics was diffuse. Whereas the density in Germany at the turn of the century was roughly 270 persons per square mile, the density in the Transvaal was less than eight; the Orange Free State, five.[22]

Because of insufficient funds, military intelligence failed to supply the British army with the maps it needed. Throughout the South African War, commanding officers bitterly complained about the poor maps with which they were supplied. After the Battle of Modder River in November 1899, Methuen too complained of the uselessness of his maps.[23] But despite the inaccuracies which led him to believe that the Modder could be forded at will, the battle was won. As General Archibald Hunter bluntly put it, 'Our maps are worse than useless, they are a positive danger and delusion'.[24] At the beginning of the war, the best map of the Transvaal was Jeppe's map, the result of a Boer farm survey conducted in the 1850s. This map, although not suited for military purposes, did at least accurately locate towns and farms by name. Fortunately for the British, Jeppe's map fell into their hands at the beginning of the war and was widely distributed.

Since the Jameson Raid, military intelligence reports had emphasized the need for preparing maps of South Africa. In 1896 the War Office sent Lieutenant Colonel S. C. N. Grant to map Natal, but due to insufficient funding and tensions caused by the raid he produced only a useless sketch.[25] Grant observed that it would have been impossible to create an adequate map of South Africa after the Jameson Raid, due to the alert watch of the Boers.

In addition to improving maps, the military intelligence department recommended strengthening the British garrisons in South Africa. As early as April 1897, Major-General John Ardagh, the Director of Military Intelligence, urged the War Office to send more British soldiers to South Africa. Well aware that it would take at least two months after mobilization for reinforcements to land, he encouraged the immediate reinforcement of Natal and the Cape Colony.[26] Ardagh knew that even with reinforcements, the British would still be forced on the defensive at the start of a war. A year and a half later, military intelligence was still pressing the War Office to act. Major E. A. Altham, one of Ardagh's assistants in the small intelligence department, believed that a show of force would reduce the number of disloyal colonists in Natal and the Cape Colony and would strengthen the British garrison as well. Ardagh warned in his reports to the War Office of the enemy's numerical superiority, but the Government refused to act.[27]

The climate of South Africa could be as difficult as the terrain, and in this case as well, military intelligence failed to convince the Government and the War Office of the severity of the problems which a British expeditionary army would face. In the summer, the heat was terrible, reaching temperatures above 100° and water was scarce. In the winter, temperatures could fall drastically. At that time of year, the veldt hardened, foliage died, and foraging became increasingly difficult. The British army in 1899 did not possess the uniforms or equipment required to meet these challenges.

In March 1897 Lieutenant-General W. H. Goodenough, General Officer in Command in South Africa, submitted a lengthy report to the War Office raising many of the equipment problems he had in South

Africa. The helmets, for example, were too heavy and offered no protection from the sun. The khaki trousers and jackets were too restricting. The water bottles were unreliable and waterproof sheets were not thick enough to protect the men from the damp ground. Also, Goodenough found it extremely difficult to purchase supplies from local firms. The supplies he could buy were high in price and poor in quality. In the event of a war, he warned, acquiring goods in South Africa would be next to impossible. Britain would have to be prepared to get all of its supplies, particularly grain, from abroad.[28]

The War Office neglected Goodenough's report. During the war, Goodenough's predictions turned out to be correct. The army had to be completely refitted in khaki. Equipment like helmets and boots had to be borrowed from India.[29] Finally, as Goodenough foresaw, goods purchased in South Africa tended to be expensive and of inferior quality.[30]

The Government and the War Office also failed to heed the advice of the 'men on the spot' as to military strategy, although they did rely on local South African sources for intelligence. Various general officers commanding the forces in South Africa drew up defence schemes to help form strategic policy. In December 1898 Major-General Sir William Butler, the Commander-in-Chief in South Africa, was asked to formulate a defence scheme for Natal and the Cape Colony. He believed the best plan in Natal was to pull back from the frontier.[31] Knowing that his forces would be outnumbered, he wanted to conduct a defensive campaign by guarding the mountain passes, sending out scouting parties, destroying bridges, and, if necessary, retiring across the Tugela River to Estcourt. He also wanted the garrison in Ladysmith to retreat. In the Cape Colony the plan was similar.[32] Butler's plans were ignored in the autumn of 1899. He wrote, 'The thing that puzzled me most was that, while the work of making up the diplomatic case against the Transvaal had the apparent support of some powerful men, not one word of preparation or warning, not even a query, was coming to me from my own chiefs at the War Office.'[33]

Lord Milner had wanted to appoint Methuen, a fellow Unionist, as the Commander-in-Chief of the planned expedition, but Lansdowne chose the more senior Buller.[34] From the moment of his appointment, Buller remained in the dark as to the Government's intentions and its war preparations. As late as 15 August, Lansdowne's door was still closed to him. Even after this date, the Secretary of State for War did little to assist his General. Buller's plan to attack the Transvaal through the Orange Free State was not accepted by the Cabinet until 29 September, less than a week before the declarations of war.[35] It was only then that military preparations for the expedition began in earnest. Lansdowne, however, rejecting Milner's policy, believed that mobilization was 'a dangerous risk' and refused to allow it. Finally, on 7 October, only days before the war started, mobilization was approved. This delay ensured that the British would begin the war on the defensive.

As mentioned above, Buller's role in the preparations for the war was negligible. He never once met with Salisbury, Chamberlain or anyone else in the Cabinet except for Lansdowne, and Lansdowne refused to discuss strategy.[36] Lansdowne felt that Buller's role was to obey orders and nothing more. 'His [Lansdowne's] view was that a Commander-in-Chief was a mere title and that a military board and secretary of state was a better arrangement.'[37] Even though Buller pressed him to prepare for the war, Lansdowne stalled. Eventually, in early September, Buller went directly to Salisbury and asked for 50,000 troops.[38] This only further embittered Lansdowne. Buller knew nothing of Milner's negotiations with Kruger. He never attended a meeting of either the Defence Committee or Army Board. He did occasionally meet with Wolseley, but because of their differing beliefs on strategy, these meetings were unproductive. Their discussions were kept strictly private and produced no formal decisions.[39] Frustrated, Buller wrote, 'I am in the tightest place I have ever been in and the worst of it is that it is, I think, none of my creating. I don't know if I [can] get out of it ... .'[40]

As late as 14 October, when Buller set sail for Capetown, Lansdowne had yet to inform him of the purpose of the mission or give him any general instructions.[41] Nor were there any instructions awaiting him when he arrived in South Africa two weeks later.[42] Ironically, Buller was informed by a newspaper and not by his own government that the Orange Free State had joined the Transvaal in their pronouncement of war against Britain. 'I was in a position of a man', Buller testified after the war, 'who had never been consulted at all, and whose advice had virtually been rather curtly, not very politely, refused.'[43] Clearly the Government's failure to transfer information hindered Buller's preparations for conducting a campaign.

When operations finally commenced, Buller was given little freedom and was not allowed to choose his own staff. Whereas Wolseley had had almost complete control over the appointments in his expeditions, Buller had little or no say. He inherited, so to speak, Lieutenant-General Sir George White, his commander in Natal.[44] In September Lansdowne had appointed White to replace Major-General Sir William Penn Symons, whom he considered too inexperienced for the position, but did not consult Buller. Lansdowne had no liking for either Wolseley or Buller, whom he considered too close to Wolseley and too much to the liking of the Liberals. He specifically chose White because he was a member of Roberts' Ring. Lansdowne also chose Major-General John French, without consulting Buller, to direct the cavalry.[45] None of the expedition's three divisional commanders, Major-General Sir C. Francis Clery,[46] Major-General Sir William F. Gatacre,[47] or Methuen,[48] were appointed by Buller.[49] Of all the senior officers appointed to commands in South Africa, only two, Major-Generals Henry Hildyard and Neville Lyttelton, were given the assignments requested by Buller.[50]

DEPLOYMENT

The initial deployment of Buller's force in South Africa was hindered by political considerations and delayed decisions. Buller had proposed massing his forces and making a beeline for Pretoria, the capital of the Transvaal, through Bloemfontein and the Orange Free State. This strategy was not unlike Wolseley's marches on Kumasi in 1874 and Cairo in 1882. However, the state of affairs in South Africa at the start of the war forced Buller to abandon his plan. In the three weeks since the war had begun, the Boers had laid siege to Mafeking, Ladysmith and Kimberley, and had captured all but one of the bridges across the Orange River. Buller was forced on the defensive.

London had failed to heed Butler's warning to abandon the frontiers and concentrate British forces in more secure positions closer to the coast. Mafeking was the first town to pay the price. Remotely located in northern Cape Colony, just south of Bechuanaland and west of the Transvaal, Mafeking was completely isolated from the outside world only a day after hostilities began. The small British garrison, commanded by Colonel Robert Baden-Powell, protected a strategically unimportant position and a civilian population of just over 1,000 whites.[51] That Baden-Powell's Chief of Staff was Major Lord Edward Cecil, the prime minister's son, was only one of the reasons that it was imperative for Buller to break the siege. Another was public pressure at home, which grew daily. The siege of Mafeking lasted for 217 days.

On 30 October – the day Buller landed in Cape Town – the first shells fell on Ladysmith. Butler's 1898 report had specifically warned the War Office about the danger of attempting to hold Ladysmith, an important arms depot, situated just north of the Tugela River in Natal. Buller had concurred, warning Lansdowne in the early summer, 'Do not go north of the Tugela, do not go north of the Tugela.'[52] However, their advice was ignored by the 'men on the spot' in Ladysmith, who in this case determined British policy. Sir Walter Hely-Hutchinson, the Governor of Natal, fearing that any British retreat in Natal would stir up its 75,000 Zulus, encouraged White to hold onto Ladysmith.[53] White, who appreciated Ladysmith's forward position from which he could conduct an offensive (and did not see the danger in attempting to hold it), needed little encouragement.

The decision proved fateful. On 11 October, General Piet Joubert and 18,000 Boers entered Natal. Two days later they took General Penn Symons by surprise at Dundee, forty miles north of Ladysmith. Penn Symons was able to rally his forces at Talana Hill and temporarily stop Joubert's offensive, although doing so cost him his life. White, in order to regroup, ordered his forces back to Ladysmith. Once there, they could not get out.

Since the bulk of British forces in Natal were held up in Ladysmith, it became essential for Buller to divert at least a division to protect the colony. Without regard to battle order, troops which had been designated for the Cape Colony and the advance on Bloemfontein were sent to Durban. These included Hildyard's brigade, which was meant to be part of Methuen's division. The 4th, 5th and 6th Brigades were also sent to Natal. Eventually, General Charles Warren and the entire 5th Division would be diverted there as well. Buller, who was forced to abandon his planned march to Bloemfontein, personally took control of operations in Natal. The siege of Ladysmith lasted 118 days.

Buller had more than just the sieges of Ladysmith and Mafeking to contend with. On 14 October Kimberley too was besieged. Situated in the Cape Colony 650 miles north of Cape Town, just west of the Orange Free State, Kimberley was the centre of Rhodes' thriving diamond industry and hence could not be abandoned. Rhodes, although no longer prime minister of the Cape Colony, and tarnished by the fiasco of the Jameson Raid, was still an influential entrepreneur. When the possibility of hostilities became apparent, rather than evacuate the city, Rhodes dug in and fortified the town, knowing that its resources would make it one of the Boers' primary targets. Although by October 1899 Kimberley's population had shrunk by nearly half, there were still over 20,000 civilians in the town. Political exigency demanded its relief. As a result, Salisbury's government, which could ill-afford to risk the political consequence of Kimberley's surrender, was manipulated by Rhodes into sending a relief force. The siege lasted four months.

Fearful of negative public opinion, the Government compelled Buller to divide his forces and simultaneously relieve Kimberley and Ladysmith.

In doing so, the British forfeited their numerical superiority in both theatres of operation.[54] From a report of June 1899 the British believed that the Boers could field as many as 40,000 men against them in battle.[55] These men, it was assumed, would be organized in small commandos spread throughout the Boer republics. Although the British could field only 15,000 men at the outbreak of the war, Buller was confident that a force this size was sufficient to march on Bloemfontein. However, by dividing its forces, Britain lost any opportunity to conduct an immediate offensive, and the potential for conducting a successful campaign became dependent on rapid mobilization and timely reinforcement. One thing was certain – the British could not launch an effective offensive until the overwhelming discrepancy in numbers could be corrected.

Buller was well aware that the shortage of manpower was only one among many serious problems. He realized that this war would not be fought on the European model – a war waged by massed armies, fighting over limited ground, relying on short lines of communications. He also knew that this was not just another imperial expedition, another of 'Queen Victoria's small wars'. Sir Michael Howard was justified in claiming that the South African War did resemble a classic war of imperial expansion in certain respects: a 'tribe' threatened imperial authority and it therefore needed to be subjugated and 'civilized'.[56] However, the deep differences between the South African War and, for example, the Ashanti War, bely the adequacy of such a comparison.

Buller correctly expected the conflict in South Africa to be more like the American War of Independence.[57] It would be a war against a 'civilized' enemy – one equipped with modern armaments, in an 'uncivilized' country – one which possessed a scattered population, no centralized administration and no command centre. It would be a war where civilians could either become 'rebels' or 'loyalists', depending on the way the army treated them. Having been introduced to the enemy's spirit in the First Anglo-Boer War, Buller knew that he would have to conquer not just a city but every man capable of bearing arms. Buller understood, as few at that time did, that success in South Africa would be a long and arduous struggle, requiring all of Britain's resources.

Buller's army began arriving in South Africa at the beginning of November, a month after the war had started. Methuen spent the end of October and the first week of November at sea aboard the *Moor*. He and his travelling companions, Clery and Gatacre, having received no orders from Buller, were completely in the dark regarding future operations. While Gatacre shut himself off in his cabin, Methuen and Clery tried to anticipate the course of the war. Methuen expected to march to Colesberg and then by 'about the middle of December or later start for Bloemfontein, having a little fighting crossing the Orange River and the important fight crossing the Vaal River. ... I feel almost sure we shall see very little fighting, but from the energy displayed, and the amount of writing Gatacre gives himself and his staff you would imagine we are in for a second Peninsular War. I calculate we shall be in England anytime in April ... .[58] Methuen also evaluated his fellow officers: 'Gatacre never ceases working and has energy on the brain. I imagine he is a very capable man, but he keeps much to himself and is seldom seen. Clery tells me Hildyard is very slow. I think he has the two best brigadiers in Wauchope and Lyttleton – Gatacre the worst, and five Irish regiments. I am glad I am not in his division.'[59]

On 8 November, Methuen, Clery and Gatacre arrived in Cape Town where they were met by Forestier-Walker and Hanbury-Williams. As they rode to meet Buller, they were informed of the latest events in South Africa and, most significantly, of White's retreat into Ladysmith. Events in Natal were not going well: 'White was frightened to death, Hamilton was mad, and only French was doing all right.'[60] They were also informed that both the order of battle and their command assignments had been changed. Buller was sending Methuen to Kimberley.[61]

> [I will] take [the] Guards Brigade, a scratch brigade, 9th Lancers, 200 free booters under Rimington, who I swear by, to relieve Kimberley. My other brigade, [the] Highlanders, to protect my rear; when relieved I want to go straight for Bloemfontein, but [Buller] wants me to come here, and go along [the] Orange River but [mine] is the proper strategy, as I shall force the Boers to come back to me. ... I don't imagine I will find 8,000 Boers, but anyhow he has given me a grand job. I hope to start the 18th and relieve Kimberley, 74 miles, the 25th, but it will be a hard job. Can anyone have ever dreamt of commanding a division of Guards and Highlanders?[62]

On 10 November 1899 Lord Methuen received his orders from Buller. Taking the 1st, 3rd and 9th Brigades, he was to march north, cross the Modder River and relieve Kimberley. After evacuating the town of its non-combatants, Methuen was to return to the Modder River and prepare for an advance on Bloemfontein.[63] That same day, Methuen left the Cape for Orange River Station, which he reached two days later. There, he awaited the arrival of the rest of his division. On 15 November, Major-General R. S. R. Fetherstonhaugh, commanding the newly formed 9th Brigade, arrived. General Colvile and the Guards Brigade joined them two days later. In reserve, General Wauchope and the Highland Brigade remained at De Aar. On 18 November Methuen sent a ciphered message to Lieutenant-Colonel Robert Kekewich, the garrison commander at Kimberley: 'General leaves here with small force on 21st November, and will arrive Kimberley on 26th, unless detained at Modder River.'[64]

By the summer of 1899, British foreign policy seemed committed to a war in South Africa. Yet, at the same time, military policy was not fashioned to assist the growing developments. Few troops had been sent to reinforce the colonial garrisons in Natal and the Cape Colony, no general or partial mobilization had been called, and military intelligence had done little to furnish assistance on the relatively unknown interior of South Africa. No plans for war had been drawn up by the Government, which seemed to have no official position regarding the Orange Free State. The Government had done almost nothing to prepare for war, apart from appointing Buller to command an expedition were it required.

This failure to act forced Buller to put aside his plan for a decisive drive on the capitals of the republics, and to divide his forces to relieve the besieged towns of Ladysmith and Kimberley. The Boers had forced a strategy upon the British and now waited for them to come and break the sieges. The result was 'Black Week'.

NOTES

1. Sir Redvers Buller, age 59, came from a wealthy Devonshire family. Joining the service in 1858 as an ensign in the 2nd Battalion 60th Rifles, he progressively rose through the ranks. He served in India just after the mutiny and in the war in China in 1860. During the Red River Expedition to Canada, Buller met Wolseley and became an integral member of his Ring. He later served as Wolseley's Chief of Intelligence in both the Ashanti expedition and the Arabi rebellion. Buller was no stranger to South Africa. He had served with Lord Chelmsford in the Gaika War and in the Zulu War, and with Wood after the First Anglo-Boer War. In 1884 Buller returned to London after the failed attempt to rescue Gordon, and accepted an administrative post at the War Office. He served as Quartermaster-General and, in 1890, succeeded Wolseley as Adjutant-General. As Adjutant-General for seven years, Buller created the Army Service Corps and reformed barracks life. In 1895 Henry Campbell-Bannerman, Lord Rosebery's Secretary of State for War, selected Buller over Wolseley to succeed the Duke of Cambridge as Commander-in-Chief. Buller was extremely reluctant to cross Wolseley. When the Rosebery government fell, Buller lost his chance. In 1898 he was appointed to the Aldershot command, and a year later he was selected to command the expedition to South Africa. See Lewis Butler, *Sir Redvers Buller* (London: Smith, Elder & Co., 1909); Owen Wheeler, *The War Office: Past and Present* (London: Methuen, 1914), and James B. Thomas, *Sir Redvers Buller in the post-Cardwellian Army: A Study of the Rise and Fall of a Military Reputation* (PhD thesis, Texas A&M University, 1993).
2. 'Report of His Majesty's Commissioners appointed to Inquire into the Military

Preparations and Other Matters connected with the War in South Africa', 1904: cd 1790, XL, 14953.

3. Unspecified Blue Book, as cited in Byron Farwell, *The Great Anglo-Boer War* (New York: W. W. Norton & Co., 1976), p. 47.
4. Leonard Thompson, *A History of South Africa* (New Haven, CT: Yale University Press, 1990), p. 115.
5. R. Robinson and J. Gallagher with A. Denny, *Africa and the Victorians*, 2nd edn (London: Macmillan, 1981), p. 61.
6. Byron Farwell, *Queen Victoria's Little Wars* (New York: Harper & Row, 1972), p. 250.
7. Edward Dicey, 'After the Present War', *Nineteenth Century* 46 (1899): 693–707.
8. According to his diary entry of 1 Jan. 1896, Methuen had known about the plan to launch the Jameson Raid at least a month before it occurred.
9. 'Secret Papers related to Affairs in South Africa', CO 879/56/572, J. Chamberlain to A. Milner, 5 May 1899, telegram no. 77, Public Records Office, Kew.
10. 'Secret Papers related to Affairs in South Africa', CO 879/56/572, A. Milner to J. Chamberlain, 4 June 1899, telegram no. 97, Public Records Office.
11. 'Secret Papers related to Affairs in South Africa', CO 879/56/572, J. Chamberlain to A. Milner, 2 Sept. 1899, telegram no. 337, Public Records Office.
12. 'Further Correspondences of the Affairs in the South African Republic', Ultimatum of 9 Oct., CO 879/59/600, Public Records Office.
13. 'Secret Papers related to Affairs in South Africa', CO 879/56/572, J. Chamberlain to A. Milner, 12 Oct. 1899, telegram no. 505, Public Records Office.
14. Robinson and Gallagher, *Africa and the Victorians*, pp. 410–61.
15. Cabinet minute, 13 June 1899, CAB 41/25/12, Public Records Office.
16. Edward M. Spiers, *The Army and Society, 1815–1914* (New York: Longman, 1980), p. 213.
17. *The War in South Africa, A German Official Account*, W. H. Walters, trans. (New York: E. P. Dutton, 1904), p. 1.
18. 'Report of His Majesty's Commissioners appointed to Inquire into the Military Preparations and Other Matters connected with the War in South Africa', cd 1790, 1904: XI, 8778–86.
19. Ibid., 8787.
20. Ibid., 8793.
21. *The War in South Africa, A German Official Account*, p. 2.
22. Ibid., p. 4.
23. P. S. Methuen to R. Buller, 2 Dec. 1899, Buller Papers, WO 132/15, Public Records Office.
24. R. L. Wallace, *The Australians at the Boer War* (Canberra: Australian Government Publishing Service, 1976), p. 31.
25. 'Report of His Majesty's Commissioners appointed to Inquire into the Military Preparations and Other Matters connected with the War in South Africa', 1904: cd 1790, XL, 750.
26. 'Report of His Majesty's Commissioners appointed to Inquire into the Military Preparations and Other Matters connected with the War in South Africa', 1904: cd 1790, XL, 25.
27. Ibid., p. 26.
28. 'Report of a Committee of Officers on the Most Suitable Dress and Accoutrements for Troops Employed on Active Service in South Africa, 1897', WO 33/69, Public Records Office, London.
29. 'Report of His Majesty's Commissioners appointed to Inquire into the Military Preparations and Other Matters connected with the War in South Africa', 1904: cd 1790, XL, 1611–20.

30. 'Evidence Taken by the Committee of Enquiry into Cases of Certain Officers', The case of Ordinance Stores in South Africa, 1902, WO 33/218, Public Records Office, London.
31. W. F. Butler, *An Autobiography* (London: Constable & Co., 1911), p. 417.
32. Ibid., p. 120.
33. Butler, who opposed the war, approved of this policy of inaction. Although he was hard pressed by Milner in 1899 to prepare an offensive, he refused, arguing that the War Office had sent him no orders. Milner believed Butler's decision to 'wait and see' was a product of his 'pro Boer' tendency. Butler was forced to resign in August and was replaced by General Sir F. W. Forestier-Walker, a close associate of Methuen. Forestier-Walker was GOC of the lines of communications during the war (ibid., p. 429).
34. Julian Symons, *Buller's Campaign* (London: Cresset Press, 1963), p. 137.
35. 'Report of His Majesty's Commissioners appointed to Inquire into the Military Preparations and Other Matters connected with the War in South Africa', cd 1790, 1904: XI, 14953.
36. Ibid., p. 15023.
37. R. Buller to Tremayne Buller, 3 Nov. 1899, Buller Papers, WO 132/6, Public Records Office.
38. R. Buller to Lord Salisbury, 5 Sept. 1899, Buller Papers, 7065 M/SS4/17, Devonshire Records Office, Exeter.
39. 'Report of His Majesty's Commissioners appointed to Inquire into the Military Preparations and Other Matters connected with the War in South Africa', cd 1790, 1904: XI, 150046.
40. R. Buller to T. Buller, 3 Nov. 1899, Buller Papers, WO 132/6, Public Records Office.
41. 'Report of His Majesty's Commissioners appointed to Inquire into the Military Preparations and Other Matters connected with the War in South Africa', cd 1790, 1904: XI, 150030.
42. Ibid., 150032.
43. Ibid., 150028
44. White, a former Commander-in-Chief in India, was a veteran of several Indian campaigns, and, prior to his appointment, served as Quartermaster-General at the War Office. Most recently he had been responsible for Lockhart's expedition to Tirah.
45. French had served in Egypt in 1883 and in India in the early 1890s. As Inspector-General of the Cavalry under Buller, French had made his mark at Aldershot where he attempted to modernize the cavalry. Before French, as Sir Baker Russell put it, 'British military leaders essentially believed that the function of cavalry was to look pretty in time of peace and to get killed in time of war.' French changed this view of the cavalry. Probably more than any other British commander, he understood the tactics and strategy which the Boers would employ in the South African War. Jerrold Walter, *Field Marshal Sir John French* (London: Hammond, 1915), pp. 44–5, quoted in George H. Casser, *The Tragedy of Sir John French* (Newark: University of Delaware Press, 1985), p. 29.
46. Clery was primarily known for his work in London. Although he had served in the Zulu War and in the Sudan, he had never held a line command. He had made a name for himself as Commandant of the Staff College and through his book *Minor Tactics*. He commanded the 2nd Division, which originally consisted of the 3rd (Highland) Brigade, commanded by Major-General Andrew Wauchope, and the 4th (Light Infantry) Brigade, commanded by Major-General Hon. Neville G. Lyttelton.
47. Gatacre, commander of the 3rd Division, had served in India and the Sudan, and had most recently held the Eastern District command at home. According to Amery, Gatacre was 'looked upon as the most likely of Sir R. Buller's subordinates to make

his mark on the history of the campaign'. His 3rd Division was composed of the 6th (Fusilier) Brigade, commanded by Major-General Geoffrey Barton, and the 5th (Irish) Brigade, commanded by Major-General Arthur Fitzroy Hart. Leo S. Amery (ed.), *The Times History of The War in South Africa 1899–1902* (London: Sampson Low, Marston & Co., Ltd., 1907), II, 114.

48. Methuen was assigned the command of the 1st Division which included Major-General Sir Henry Colvile's 1st (Guards) Brigade and Major-General Henry Hildyard's 2nd Brigade.

49. Other appointments included Major-General Sir G. H. Marshall, commanding the artillery; Major-General Elliott Wood, commanding the Royal Engineers; Major-General F. W. Forestier-Walker, commanding the lines of communication; Colonel W. D. Richardson, commanding supplies; Colonel C. H. Bridge, commanding transport and remounts; Colonel Sir E. P. C. Girouard, directing the railways; and Surgeon-General Sir W. D. Wilson was in charge of medicine and the hospitals.

50. Jay C. Stone and Erwin A. Schmidl, *The Boer War and Military Reforms* (Lanham, MD: University Press of America, 1988), p. 55.

51. There were also 7,500 Bantu-speaking Black Africans held up in Mafeking. Farwell, *The Great Anglo-Boer War*, p. 274.

52. R. Buller to A. Bigge, 4 Jan. 1900, as cited in Thomas Pakenham, *The Boer War* (New York: Random House, 1979.), p. 115.

53. Ibid., p. 109.

54. The siege of Mafeking did not play a role in the deployment of Buller's forces.

55. The British estimated that there were 22,374 men between the ages of 16 and 60 in the Orange Free State and 31,229 in the Transvaal available for service. *The War in South Africa, a German Official Account*, p. 19.

56. Michael Howard, *The Continental Commitment* (London: Temple Smith, 1972).

57. 'Report of His Majesty's Commissioners appointed to Inquire into the Military Preparations and Other Matters connected with the War in South Africa', 1904: cd 1790, XL, 14953.

58. P. S. Methuen to M. E. Methuen, 24 Oct. 1899, Methuen Papers, Wiltshire Records Office.

59. P. S. Methuen to M. E. Methuen, 29 Oct. 1899, Methuen Papers, Wiltshire Records Office.

60. P. S. Methuen to M. E. Methuen, 8 Nov. 1899, Methuen Papers, Wiltshire Records Office.

61. Methuen's staff included his aides-de-camp, Major H. Streatfield of the Grenadier Guards and Captain J. A. Bell-Smyth, 1st Dragoon Guards; his Assistant Adjutant-General, Colonel R. B. Mainwaring; his Deputy Assistant Adjutant-Generals, Lieutenant-Colonel H. P. Northcott and Major R. H. L. Warner; his divisional signalling officer, Lieutenant Hon. E. D. Loch; his Assistant Provost-Marshal, Captain R. J. Ross; his chaplains, Revd T. F. Faulkner and Revd E. M. Morgan; and his medical officers, Colonel E. Townshend, MD, and Major C. H. Burtchaell, MB.

62. P. S. Methuen to M. E. Methuen, 8 Nov. 1899, Methuen Papers, Wiltshire Records Office.

63. Methuen's complete orders were as follows:

    1. You will take command of the troops at De Aar and Orange River stations, with the object of marching on Kimberley as rapidly as possible.
    2. In addition to the troops now at De Aar, the infantry of which are being formed into the 9th brigade under Colonel Fetherstonhaugh, you will have under your command:
        i. The 1st Infantry Brigade – Major-General Colvile.

    ii.   The Highland Brigade – Major-General Wauchope.

    iii. The 9th Lancers.

    iv. The Brigade Division, Royal Field Artillery, under Colonel Hall.

    v.   The Divisional Troops except Cavalry of the Division.

    vi. Certain Royal Engineers, Army Service Corps and Medical Details which have been collected at the two stations. I wish you to march from the Orange river to the Modder river, communicate with Kimberley, and to hold the line De Aar, Modder river, so that we shall be able to bring up stores and heavy guns and pass them to Kimberley.

3. The half-battalion Loyal North Lancashire regiment, which will form part of the 9th brigade, is to be left in Kimberley.

4. You will afford help to Kimberley, to remove such of the natives as they wish to get rid of, and, generally, you will give such advice and assistance in perfecting the defences as you may be able to afford.

5. You will make the people of Kimberley understand that you have not come to remain charged with its defence, but to afford it better means of maintaining its defence, which will at the same time be assisted by an advance on Bloemfontein.

See Frederick Maurice and M. H. Grant, *(Official) History of the War in South Africa, 1899–1902* (London: Hurst & Blackwood, 1906–1910) I, 14.

64. Walter A. J. O'Meara, *Kekewich in Kimberley* (London: Medici Society, 1926), p. 69.

5

The Advance to Modder River

By early November 1899 British forces in South Africa had positioned themselves to launch a three-pronged attack on the Boers. In the east, Sir Redvers Buller, the General Officer-in-Command, would lead one division to relieve General George White and his besieged troops in Ladysmith and to block further Boer penetration into Natal. In the centre, General William Gatacre was assigned to take his small force to the northern edge of the Cape Colony to prevent any Boer thrust into the Colony and to draw off Boers from the Ladysmith vicinity. In the west, Lord Methuen, commanding the 1st Division, would advance toward Kimberley to relieve the beleaguered garrison. After supplying the garrison with guns, ammunition and food, his plan was to return to the Cape with all non-combatants residing in and around Kimberley, including all Uitlander women and children and the more than 10,000 Africans. Methuen was not expected to meet much resistance. This chapter will examine in particular the false expectations of the British, the decision to advance along the Western Railway, the 1st Division's three encounters with the Boers before the Modder River and Methuen's ability to command his division in set battles.

DEPARTURE FROM ORANGE RIVER STATION

As advised by his superior, General Redvers Buller, Methuen would proceed by the safest and surest route which cut northward along the Western Railway from Orange River station to Kimberley. Methuen believed that it was necessary to stay in close proximity to the railroad for two reasons. First, a lack of fresh water and a lack of supply animals made the railway his only safe and reliable supply line. Second, Buller had ordered the removal of all civilians from Kimberley, and the railway was the only feasible means of moving such a large group.

Methuen was optimistic and anxious to begin the advance toward Kimberley. H. S. Gaskell wrote, 'About only one thing was [Lord Methuen] more anxious than the comfort of his horses and men, and that was, to get into touch with his enemy, and keep there.'[1] Methuen would have liked to have started immediately but Buller told him to wait for the arrival of the Naval Brigade and its 4.7-inch quick-firing guns. With the Brigade's arrival on 21 November, the march of the 1st Division to Kimberley began.

Accompanied by a seemingly sufficient number of infantry,[2] a weak force of cavalry,[3] and a superior number of field batteries,[4] Methuen and the 1st Division departed from the Orange River station on 21 November. His course was well plotted. It was clear to all observers that he was heading to Belmont, marching parallel to the railway line which ran north to Kimberley and from there to Mafeking and into Rhodesia. If Kimberley was to be relieved and its inhabitants were to be brought to safety, the railway had to be safeguarded. In his testimony to the Royal Commission on the War in South Africa, Methuen later stated:

> I had to relieve Kimberley, throw in a large supply of provisions, clear out the non-combatants, and return to the Orange River. To fulfil these conditions it would not have been an easy matter to march through the country with a large force, because of the limited amount of mule transport (I had no ox transport), and the small supply of water in the country I had to traverse.[5]

For these reasons, Methuen had little choice but to take Buller's advice and follow the course of the railway to Kimberley. He was aware that once Kimberley was relieved, it would be impossible to march a large group of civilians across the veldt with little water.

Without viable alternatives, Methuen's decision to advance along the railroad, although often criticized, was the right one. Leo Amery wrote, 'We let the existence of the railroad completely paralyse our movements. [It] induces a mental paralysis on all our generals: it is so simple and obvious to stick to it – to improvise other transport requires thinking out afresh as it was not in the original programme [*sic*] and so it isn't done.'[6] In this instance, however, Amery's criticism is unjust. The safety of the railway had to be ensured to overcome Methuen's lack of supply and to allow him to accomplish the task of returning so many people to the Cape Colony.

Even the Boers realized this. As Charles S. Goldmann has noted, the British did little to deceive their enemy as to the timing and the course of their advances. 'There is nothing more remarkable in the early stages of the campaign than the neglect on our part of any attempt to deceive the enemy as to our intentions. That Lord Methuen proposed to advance upon a certain date towards Kimberley by Belmont was known to the readers of every London paper for some days before he started ... .'[7] Only a few hours after the 1st Division departed from the Orange River Station, newspaper readers in Johannesburg became aware that the march to Kimberley had begun.[8]

Methuen expected the first encounter with the enemy to take place about 19 miles away from the Orange River station just north of Belmont Station where a Boer camp, or laager, of 2,500 men and five guns were waiting. A reconnaissance party led by Colonel B. Gough had spied the Boers in that vicinity in early November. It was clear that a force that size could not be ignored. Had Methuen moved around them to speed the relief of Kimberley, he would have faced a large enemy presence on his flank.

Methuen realized that a substantial Boer force with the advantage of reliable intelligence and time to entrench could not be taken lightly. Although the Boers had proven themselves fierce fighters in Natal at the battles of Glencoe, Elandslaagte, Dundee and Lombard's Kop in October, neither the British press nor the public took them seriously. Methuen had known the Boers for over 15 years and while he respected them as worthy adversaries, he had complete confidence in his force. From his experience at Dargai, Methuen held the British soldier in high esteem and believed him capable of defeating any adversary. This force, he was certain, could carry out its orders. He declared to one staff officer before the attack at Belmont, 'My good fellow, I intend to put the fear of God into these people.'[9]

The Boers knew Methuen was heading towards Belmont. They also knew the size and the composition of the British force.[10] The British knew the Boers were at Belmont but they could determine neither their exact number nor their composition. Methuen's mounted forces were limited in number and unable to carry out an effective reconnaissance of the area. The Boers were free to take defensive positions in the kopjes. The problems of reconnaissance plagued the relief of Kimberley from start to finish.

Meanwhile, the Boers worked out their defensive strategy. The Boer forces were commanded by an inexperienced Free Stater, Jacobus Prinsloo. On 20 November near Belmont, he and his 1,500 burghers joined T. Van der Merwe, a Cape Boer, and 500 others. On the 22nd, when the British began their march, Prinsloo sent out detachments to all of the kopjes surrounding the railway. Veggeneral de la Rey and 800 burghers from the

Western Transvaal hurried to join the Free Staters and arrived on the 23rd, the day of the battle.

Jacobus Herculaas de la Rey, more commonly known as Koos, was 52, two years younger than Methuen. The two men's paths crossed several times between 1899 and 1902. Eventually, they came to respect one another, and after the war became friendly. De la Rey was a veteran of the First Anglo-Boer War, in which he had served as the youngest ever Veldt Coronet. When the war broke out in October 1899 he was appointed as an adviser to General Piet Cronjé, the Commandant for the Western Transvaal. Unable to work with Cronjé, because of their conflicting opinions about how the war should be conducted, de la Rey was sent to the Kimberley area to delay the British by directing guerrilla raids on the railway. When news arrived that the British advance had begun, he and his troops rode for Belmont. To their surprise, Methuen had reached Belmont station sooner than expected.

Throughout the war the mobility of Methuen's troops set an example for the rest of the British army. His men were called the Mobile Marvels, the Mudcrushers and the Salvation Army, because of the speed and endurance they demonstrated in relieving garrisons and pursuing the enemy. In the later stages of the war, during the two great de Wet chases, Methuen alone was able to match the pace set by his adversary. The many campaigns of his earlier years had taught him the importance of mobility. Although Methuen was tied to the course of the railway in the first stage of the war, he still tried to maximize his division's mobility. The field packs of the soldiers carried nothing but essentials: field cap, flannel shirt, canvas shoes, socks, towel, soap, worsted cap, housewife (mending kit), laces and grease-pot.[11] No tents were provided and the men had to sleep in their greatcoats. Methuen saw to it that in his division, officers would get no special treatment. They were subject to this tenet and carried only what was necessary. He himself led by example and slept at night on the veldt in a Mexican poncho.

For the officers it was more than just a question of mobility when determining what they should bring with them or what they should have carried on the march: it was a question of survival. It was a necessity for every officer to appear as if he was just any ordinary soldier. The Boers were known for their excellent marksmanship, which was a required skill for living on the veldt surrounded as they were by potentially hostile African neighbours. They were able to distinguish between officers and men and then hit their selected targets – officers. Before Methuen had reached the Orange River Station to take command of the 1st Division, a British reconnaissance party led by Gough had had a skirmish with a small Boer raiding party. Of the six British casualties, four were officers, and all four were fatally wounded.

Methuen, with Buller's approval, ordered his officers to carry and wear nothing that would distinguish them from the regular troops.[12] Buttons, belts, and other marks of rank, once bright and shining, were dulled with mud or painted brown. Officers were ordered to carry rifles rather than swords. To confuse the Boers further, and to conserve water, shaving was abandoned by most of the officers. Again, Methuen led by example. He wrote 19 November, 'As likely as not, I may have to see no more tents this side of January or my plum pudding. No officer has a sword, all rifles, no marks on their [uniforms], and [look] like the men. I am in a Boer hat, a pair of Norwegian slippers, khaki trousers, and short sleeves, looking the most disreputable man in camp.'[13] Two days later, the 1st Division broke camp and headed toward Kimberley in the direction of Belmont.

Methuen's main force left the Orange River station on 21 November. A reconnaissance party, consisting of 9th Lancers and Rimington's Guides, was ordered in advance to scout the area in the vicinity of Belmont. Heading out from Fincham's Farm, they spied several hundred Boers climbing up a kopje at Belmont. The following day, the British reached Thomas's Farm two miles south of Belmont. The advance party was fired upon. Methuen ordered the artillery forward to return fire and the Boer fire ceased. At midnight, the troops bivouacked and prepared for battle.

On the morning of 22 November, Methuen reconnoitred as far as possible from his position at Thomas's Farm. Because of the strong position held by the Boers at Belmont and the absence of sufficient British cavalry, it was impossible to learn about the area in detail. Therefore, Methuen did not have information on the exact position of his enemy nor details on the topography of their emplacements. This would be the greatest challenge to the success of the night operations which he implemented.

Methuen's plan for driving the Boers from their position in the kopjes was relatively simple. Some two miles to the southeast of Belmont Station, the Boers had positioned themselves in two lines of broken kopjes which ran more or less parallel with the railroad. The Boer position to the west was closer to the railroad; it rose on the average about 100 feet above the plain. Methuen decided to attack this position first and focus on two points: Gun Hill and, just to the north, Table Mountain. Once these positions were taken, the British troops could continue to advance east to the next range of kopjes where Sugar Loaf Hill and Razor Back lay in the south, and where Mount Blanc loomed in the north, another hundred feet above Table Mountain. Mount Blanc was the key to controlling the area since it overlooked all the surrounding kopjes and the railroad.

THE BATTLE OF BELMONT

Methuen had planned to give the 9th Brigade the lion's share of the fighting that day. At 0300 hours, as the Guards Brigade was ordered to advance upon Gun Hill supported by the Naval Brigade, the 9th Brigade was ordered to advance upon Table Mountain. Mounted troops were sent to guard the right flank of the Guards Brigade and the left flank of the 9th Brigade. Batteries would clear the ground before the advance. Then, in the dark of the night, the men were to march across the open plain and arrive at a position close enough to charge the enemy at daybreak. After securing Table Mountain, the 9th Brigade would swing round to the left and would attack the Boer flank on Mount Blanc. The Guards, after seizing Gun Hill, would conform to the advance of the 9th Brigade and would hold the Boers' front. In the meantime, the mounted troops would move to the rear of the enemy to cut off any path of retreat. Methuen watched from the rear as his plan unfolded.[14]

With the Northamptons on the right, the Northumberland Fusiliers on the left and the King's Own Yorkshire Light Infantry (KOYLI) in reserve, the 9th Brigade advanced on the Boer position at Table Mountain in darkness. While the Northumberland Fusiliers temporarily held their ground, the Northamptons, although exposed to a heavy fire from Gun Hill, concentrated volley fire on the Boer flank and after a minor action were able to drive them from the crest of the hill. The Northumberland Fusiliers were then able to continue their advance. By dawn, the 9th Brigade was in a position to seize the last few ridges held by the Boers on Table Mountain and advance upon Mount Blanc.[15]

The advance of the Guards Brigade did not go as well. In the first place, the Grenadier Guards got lost. Secondly, the Guards Brigade had assembled late at 0320 hours – 20 minutes behind schedule.[16] To make up for the lost time, they hastily rushed towards Gun Hill, but their maps were faulty and Gun Hill was some 1,000 yards farther away than they had reckoned. Although Methuen blamed no one in his report, Lieutenant-Colonel Eyre Crabbe, commanding the Grenadiers, mistakenly led his battalion away from the face of Gun Hill and towards the western face of the kopje.[17] As a result of this misdirection, the Grenadier Guards

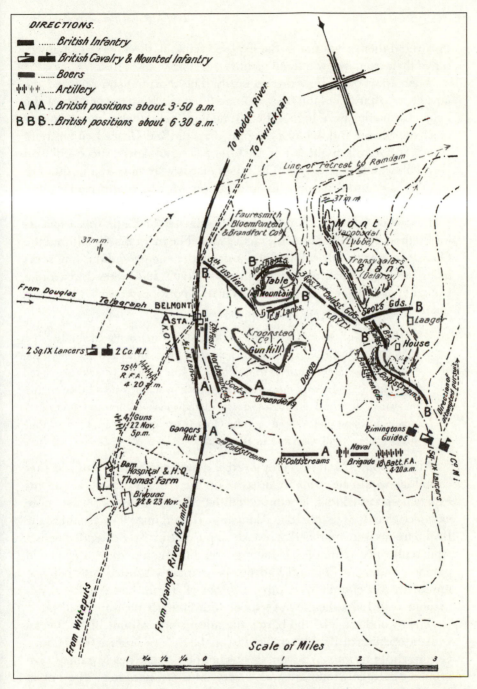

DIRECTIONS.

▬▬ ...... British Infantry
🔲 ◼️ ...British Cavalry & Mounted Infantry
▬▬ ...... Boers
⊹⊹⊹ ⊹⊹ ....Artillery
A A A ..British positions about 3·50 a.m.
B B B ..British positions about 6·30 a.m.

To Modder River
To Zwinckpan

Line of retreat to Ramdam

37.m.m.

From Douglas

Telegraph BELMONT

Fauresmith
Bloemfontein
& Brandfort Co[?]

Mont

Jacobsdal
(Lübbe)

Transvaalers
(Delarey)

Blanc

3ch Fusiliers

Northants
Table
Mountain

Scots Gds.

B

B

3 Coss Z[?]rd Coldst Gds

Laager

KOYLI.

9.N. Lancs.

Kroonstad
Co[?]

Gun Hill

House

A STA.

KOYLI

N.L.Lancs

N[?]rthumberlands

2 Sq.IX Lancers

2 Co. M.I.

75th
R.F.A.
4·20 a.m.

A

A

Scots

Dorga

Grenadiers

2nd Coldstreams

Coldstreams

B

B

B

Direction of attempted pursuit

1 Sq.IX Lancers

1 Co M.I.

4·Guns
22 Nov.
5 p.m.

Gangers
Hut

A

A

1st Coldstreams

A

Rimingtons
Guides

Naval
Brigade 18 Batt.F.A.
4·20 a.m.

Bam
Hospital & H.Q.
Thomas' Farm

Bivouac
22 & 23 Nov.

From Witteputs

From Orange River 18¾ miles

Scale of Miles

1   ¾   ½   ¼   0   1   2   3

Map 5: The Battle of Belmont, 23 November 1899. Map reproduced from Leo
Amery, *The Times History of the War in South Africa*, London, Sampson Low,
Marston and Co., 1907.

discovered themselves not at the exposed flank of the Boers as planned, but at their front below a steep incline.

The earlier delay now proved costly. The morning sun revealed the advancing Guards and the Boers poured fire down from the heights of the kopje. Casualties were high. The Grenadiers, nevertheless, were able to reach the summit and, at bayonet-point, drive the Boers from their position. The Scots Guards, to the left of the Grenadiers, advanced successfully on Gun Hill with little incident. Thus the Guards were now in a position to support the 9th Brigade's advance upon Mount Blanc from Table Mountain.

In spite of Crabbe's blunder, the first stage of the battle was a success for Methuen; he had chosen his tactics well. The night march allowed the Guards to advance to within 350 yards of the enemy without any shots being fired. Methuen, fearing high casualty rates, had wanted to avoid a frontal attack. After considering his current position, however, he chose not to call off the attack.

> ... [Because of the misdirection] the Brigades were leaving each other, the enemy were surprised and firing everywhere, and I was going straight for enormous precipices instead of going to A., [the point of attack chosen for Gun Hill] .... An awful movement, no retreat available, and a brave enemy ready to destroy us. I did not lose my head. I saw I was committed to a frontal attack, and sent one ADC to get the Guards straight, and another to [the] 9th Brigade ...; all was right in 10 minutes.[18]

At this point, Methuen employed a new tactic which ensured that casualties would be limited, in spite of the frontal attack. Using his experiences from India, he conducted the advance in an order far more extended than that practised at Aldershot. To minimize the casualties, the British troops were marched as quickly as possible in three extended lines.[19] Apparently, five years of conducting drill and manœuvres on groomed parade grounds in England had not permanently stunted his ability to improvise. Ian Hamilton, another veteran of Tirah, had employed this manœuvre at Elandslaagte in October with similarly pleasing results.

The second stage of the battle, the advance on Mount Blanc, began with the opening of British artillery fire on the Boer position at 0450 hours. Getting the guns into an advantageous position on the newly gained high ground of Table Mountain was a very difficult operation. The horses needed for the task had not yet recovered from their five-week sea voyage, nor had they had sufficient rations since reaching South Africa.[20] As a result, although the British managed to drag a few field artillery pieces on to the heights, the heavier pieces, such as the horse artillery, could not ascend the steep slopes. Consequently, British firepower could not drive off the Boers.[21] Methuen would later claim that had a battery of horse artillery been able to get to the heights, they could have fired on the Boers as long as they liked.[22] As it was, the artillery played only a small role in this stage of the battle.

The 9th Brigade, now visible to the Boers in the full light of the sun, encountered stiff resistance. The Boers remained on the north and southeast ridges of Table Mountain and supporting fire from Mount Blanc continued to pour down on the advancing British. The British plan to advance by sweeping across from Table Mountain to the northern ridge of Mount Blanc proved unworkable in the face of this crossfire. Major-General R. S. R. Fetherstonhaugh, the brigadier of the 9th, was wounded in the shoulder, forcing Colonel C. G. C. Money of the 5th Fusiliers to take command. Eventually, bayonets drove the Boers from the southern ridge of Table Mountain just before 0600 hours.

Methuen had to change his plan midway through the battle. It had become clear by 0600 hours, that the 9th Brigade was not, in fact, going to get the lion's share of work that day.[23] It was the Guards Brigade which was in the thick of it. The Coldstream Guards were to reinforce the advance on Gun Hill and to support the 9th Brigade's advance. However, because they conformed to the line of the misplaced Grenadier Guards, several companies were too far to the right to aid in the advance of the 9th Brigade. As a further consequence of this shift to the right, the Guards Brigade found themselves the targets of a heavy Boer fire directed from Razor Back and Sugar Loaf hills. Three companies of the 2nd Coldstream Guards, along with the remaining KOYLI and two companies of Mounted Infantry still in reserve, were diverted by Methuen to conform to the Guards' attack on Mount Blanc, but the remainder of the 2nd Battalion and all of the 1st Battalion were needed to seize Razor Back and Sugar Loaf hills. With the 9th Brigade pinned down on Table Mountain and the majority of the Coldstreams attacking the two hills to the south, the Scots and Grenadier Guards were forced to attack the Boer front at Mount Blanc from a dangerous position below the Boer line without the benefit of a strong flanking attack. Methuen threw in the last of his reserves to aid the attack. The Naval Brigade bombarded the heights of Mount Blanc with their large 4.7-inch quick-firing gun. As the Boers began to retreat from their positions on Table Mountain, the 9th Brigade slowly joined the wide advance. By 0600 hours, the heights of Mount Blanc had been cleared and the enemy was seen 'in large numbers galloping into the plains'.[24]

The problems which the British faced in this second phase of battle were primarily the result of poor reconnaissance and the misdirection of the Grenadier Guards in the first phase. In this case, poor reconnaissance was the product of a weak mounted force and a strong, well-covered Boer position at Belmont. It is a problem which beset almost every British operation. One colonel of the Guards commented to a fellow officer, 'It seems to me that our leaders find the strongest position of the enemy, and then attack him on front.' Tellingly, the other officer replied, 'It appears to me that they attack him first and find out his position afterwards.'[25] At Belmont, poor reconnaissance led Methuen and his staff into believing that the 9th Brigade would be able to advance easily past the Boer positions on Table Mountain and on to Mount Blanc. This proved false. Even after the plateau at Table Mountain had been gained, Boer troops were still well fortified on the north and southeast ridges. These positions continued to receive support from Mount Blanc.

The other problem in the second phase of the battle was a result of the Grenadier Guards getting lost and attacking the position upon which the Coldstreams were to have advanced. As a result, the Coldstream Guards were forced to shift further to the right, losing touch with the 9th Brigade. From their new position, they came under the fire of the Boers situated atop the Razor Back and Sugar Loaf hills and could no longer support the 9th Brigade. Clearly, given the Grenadiers' loss of direction, the bulk of the regiment could not conduct a flank attack upon the Boer position at Mount Blanc.

Despite these problems, the Battle of Belmont was a victory of sorts for Methuen and the 1st Division. It was not, however, the decisive victory Methuen had wanted. As a result of these problems, the British had failed to turn their victory into a rout because of a lack of mounted troops. Methuen had only 900 mounted men out of a division which comprised 10,000 men. This force was too small to cut off the Boer retreat protected as it was by the numerous kopjes along the way. Any attempt to conduct a sufficient, bold pursuit of the Boer troops was equally impossible. This was a problem which Methuen well understood and could not have avoided. The inability to achieve a decisive victory at Belmont allowed the orderly retreat of the enemy and gave them the opportunity to return to battle in force two days later at Graspan.

It was at the Battle of Belmont where Lord Methuen first commanded a force larger than a battalion in battle. As an officer schooled in the methods of classic nineteenth century warfare, i.e. colonial combat, Methuen hoped to achieve a decisive victory by relying on the basic tenets of the British commanding officer in 1899. Accordingly, he tried to get his troops close enough to the enemy to conduct a bayonet or 'cold-steel' charge. Tactical writers like Wilkinson Shaw, C. E. Callwell, and General Francis Clery, who was commanding the 2nd Division in Natal, argued that fire action was no longer just a preparation for the bayonet charge but the crux of the attack itself, but most of the British army was trained during an earlier time when rifles did not shoot as far and as accurately, when charges obscured vision, and before magazines increased the rate of fire.[26] Consequently, as their main tactic in battle, it was still common to rely on the bayonet charge preceded by volley fire.[27] Therefore, at the time of the South African War, British officers still used firepower to establish a position close enough to the enemy for a bayonet charge to be launched.[28]

Volley fire had proven very effective in Africa and Asia. It was used against irregular forces especially in defending against the frontal attack. It provided necessary discipline and courage for soldiers who otherwise had received poor training or lacked those qualities. But most military theorists by the outbreak of the South African War had become aware of the dangers of massing troops in close order. Technical changes had made the square anachronistic. Increasingly, military critics advocated the use of independent fire. But independent fire in extended order, to be successful, required properly trained and drilled troops. Officers were less able to command the individual soldier as the firepower of weapons improved and lines extended along wider fronts.

Better training and drill were needed not just to keep up with the handling of modern and more advanced weaponry but to fill the gap left behind by the departure from close order which until now had provided good morale. This improved training was never provided. No drill prepared the British troops to meet the challenge of the Boers and their new tactics.[29] British soldiers through the 1890s, unlike their German counterparts, continued to fire at their rifle ranges standing and kneeling. Targets were stationary. The order for individual fire was given at roughly 485 yards. In Germany, in contrast, the army was being trained at distances of up to 1,050 yards.[30] Therefore, both because of the poor training of the soldiers and because of their own training as instructors, most officers continued to employ volley fire.[31]

Methuen did indeed get his bayonet charge at the Battle of Belmont and, to a certain extent, he got his victory by winning the ground.[32] The operation secured the railway and protected the division's flank. It successfully drove the Boers from their fortified position and allowed the advance toward Kimberley to continue. However, the victory Methuen achieved at Belmont was not the decisive victory he had hoped for. There were two main reasons for this.

The first reason hinged on Methuen's decision to employ a night march. Many years earlier, when he was at Tel-el-Kebir, he watched Wolseley, his commander, conduct a successful night march which caught Arabi's forces by surprise and led to a relatively easy victory over the Egyptian troops. Methuen, always an admirer of Wolseley, had been a good student. This would be the first of his night marches: others would follow at Graspan and Magersfontein.

The advancement of military technology toward the end of the nineteenth century rendered certain tactics anachronistic. Many believed the night march was one of these: Herbert Gall, for example, questioned its reliability. In the dark, on unknown terrain, the march could break down and lead to panic and to unnecessary delays.[33] It could, moreover, limit the individual soldier's ability to continue fighting throughout the rest of the day as fatigue was apt to set in.[34]

However, many argued that the night march was still a valid tactic. In fact, with the increasing devastation of modern firepower, night operations, successfully employed, could bring the advancing force much closer to the enemy at smaller risk. Night operations provided the offence with the opportunity to surprise the enemy. Thus the night march seemed to Methuen and others the best chance to get a large force, in relative safety, close to an entrenched enemy. At close range, the infantry could then attach their bayonets to their rifles and charge. The expectation was that the charge would shock the defenders, crippling their morale and cause their lines to crumble as they lost heart and ran. This would prevent an orderly retreat and allow for a successful rout of the enemy and a decisive victory. As Major A. R. Mead astutely wrote in 1904: 'the British, looking to the assault as the final deciding factor of the contest, and seeing their main difficulty lie in getting their troops into a close position from which to deliver it, were naturally led to attempt night attacks.'[35] Although Methuen was but one of many British officers in the South African War who employed this tactic, he is the one most criticized for it.[36]

The success of Methuen's plan required that the night march get the Guards and 9th Brigades into their assigned positions. The march was undertaken in extended order at intervals of at least five paces, 'a formation more extended than any practised at the same period in broad daylight by continental nations'.[37] Even Leo Amery, the well-known journalist and editor of the *Times History of the War in South Africa*, and a harsh critic of Methuen's tactics, praised Methuen for conducting this radical manœuvre on the battlefield which showed his 'insight into one of the chief features of modern warfare'.[38] Methuen's experiences during the Tirah expedition, a few years earlier, had taught him the dangers of close order in the age of modern firepower.

Two things hampered the effectiveness of Methuen's night march. First, because of individual error, one of the Brigades got lost and did not get to its assigned position. Second, the Boers were alerted as, just before the advance, the artillery conducted a barrage to clear the ground[39] which effectively took away the element of surprise. After weighing the advantages and disadvantages, Methuen decided that the risk of alerting the Boers to the possible night march was not as great as the danger of leaving the enemy's artillery fully functional. As a result of Methuen's decision to open fire, the Boer artillery was forced to retreat from the range of British fire and its role was diminished in the battle the following day.

Although the Boers were alerted to the British preparations, the night march still came very close to providing Methuen with the position he needed to conduct a decisive bayonet charge. In his opinion, it also saved the lives of many his soldiers. He telegraphed to Buller that had he attacked later in the full light of the day he would have incurred far heavier losses.[40] The darkness of the night provided valuable cover for his advancing troops. To a greater extent than any observer could have expected, the operation did succeed in surprising the Boer troops. Methuen wrote, 'The attack was a complete surprise, for they did not know I had moved from Witte Putt to Belmont, and expected an attack in three or four days.'[41]

The second reason why the British did not achieve a decisive victory at Belmont was the shortage of mounted troops.[42] Methuen had approximately 850 mounted troops at the Battle of Belmont, which made up roughly ten per cent of his entire force. Military pundits such as Gall recommended that any force, especially an army which had little intelligence of the surrounding area, should consist of between 12 and 25 per cent mounted troops.[43] Without a sufficient number of cavalry and mounted infantry it proved impossible for Methuen to reconnoitre in any great detail, to cut off the enemy's retreat or to pursue effectively the retiring force.[44]

The shortage of mounted troops in South Africa plagued many British commanders throughout the war. Decisive victories were rendered all but hopeless by the mounted Boers' ability to retire rapidly from the field of battle at any time without great risk. Methuen would learn that heeding Garnet Wolseley's advice of following an infantry success with a cavalry pursuit could no longer secure the decisive victory.[45]

The Battle of Belmont was, as General Henry Colvile described it, 'a soldiers' fight'.[46] In Colvile's opinion, the battle was well planned but because of the circumstances which arose, planning failed and only the 'sheer pluck' of the men brought victory. In his judgement, 'The men did for themselves what no general would have dared ask of them.'[47] However, to take credit away from the commanding officer is unjust. As Methuen pointed out to his wife, 'sheer pluck *and* military knowledge won the day'.[48] The night march succeeded in getting the bulk of Methuen's advancing troops safely up to the enemy's first line. It is also to Methuen's credit that the reserve troops were committed when they were and that the plan was altered to compensate for the misdirection of the Grenadier Guards.

Belmont was a costly victory.[49] The British suffered roughly twice as many casualties as the Boers,[50] with nearly 300 British and perhaps 150 Boers wounded or killed.[51] Throughout the war, Methuen was deeply disturbed by the loss of human life. None of his previous battle experience had prepared him for such high casualty rates. He wrote, 'People congratulate me; the men seem to look on me as their father, but I detest war the more I see of it. I do admire them.'[52]

After the battle, the dead were buried. The wounded and those too ill to continue, including Major-General Fetherstonhaugh, were sent back to Orange River Station. The severely wounded were sent back to Cape Town. Methuen addressed his men and praised them, 'Comrades, I congratulate you on the complete success achieved by you this morning. The ground over which we have to fight presents exceptional difficulties, and we had as an enemy a master in the tactics of mounted infantry. With troops such as you are, a commander can have no fear as to the result.'[53]

Methuen had always admired the courage and the skill of the Boers. As a 'Christian Knight', he put honour, duty and justice above all else, and he believed that the Boers too possessed these traits. He was one of the first of the British officers publicly to praise their courage and tactical skill.[54] This explains why he was so disturbed at unethical acts committed by the Boers on the battlefield. As Methuen put it, 'Their tactics and their courage are indisputable, and it is only to be regretted that they are guilty of acts which a brave enemy should be ashamed of.'[55] In his official report to Buller, Methuen made mention of the fact that while the 9th Brigade was struggling to dislodge the Boers on Table Mountain at the point of bayonet, a Boer had improperly used the white flag, the accepted symbol of surrender. With the appearance of the flag, the British troops ceased fire. A Boer then fired. This was not the last time that the Boers (and later the British also) would be accused of this treacherous act.[56]

The advance to Kimberley continued. Notwithstanding the delay at

Belmont, Methuen expected to relieve Kimberley by 27 November. He believed that the main Boer force was north of the Modder River and expected that this group would attempt to block his division's final advance on Kimberley. On the 24th, he received news that there were 400 Boers and two guns positioned in the kopjes just to the northeast of Graspan Siding.[57] The Boers under Prinsloo had fallen back after the battle some thirteen miles behind the border of the Orange Free State to the town of Ramdam. De la Rey and his Transvaal commando, which had arrived at Belmont late in the morning and played only a small part in the conflict, had retreated eleven miles to the north and had taken up a defensive position at Graspan, knowing that Methuen would continue his advance along the railroad. De la Rey asked Prinsloo for more men. Prinsloo would not commit the bulk of his force. However, he did dispatch T. van der Merwe and 800 Free Staters. The Boers, a force not 400 but 2,000 to 2,500 strong, once again dug in to fortified positions in the kopjes and awaited the British advance.[58]

Methuen could not sweep around these Boers anymore than he could have skirted them at Belmont. They would prevent the safe passage of the railway necessary to transport the non-combatants from Kimberley to the Orange River Station. Indeed, on 24 November Boer forces shelled the British armoured train which had advanced up the line. Methuen knew that there was also a tactical risk in leaving a potentially destructive enemy force on his flank. Adding to his worries was the fact that there was scarcely any water between Belmont and the Modder River, a distance of 32 miles.[59] He did not have the necessary animal transport to abandon the railway,[60] thus he chose to follow Buller's advice and advance along the railroad to meet the Boers at Graspan.

Late in the afternoon on 24 November, Methuen's main force, composed of the 9th Brigade, the Naval Brigade and the artillery, marched toward the Boer position at Graspan in the direction of Swinkpan. The mounted troops guarded their flanks. The 1st Battalion Scots Guards and two companies of Munster Fusiliers remained at Belmont Station to prevent a Boer raid on the lines of communication. The remainder of the Guards Brigade, along with the baggage, marched straight toward Enslin.

Methuen personally accompanied the mounted reconnaissance. He found nothing to suggest that there were more than the originally assumed 400 Boers, and so developed a simple and straightforward plan. Under the cover of darkness, the artillery, accompanied by the infantry, would advance close enough to the Boers to conduct a barrage and drive them from the kopjes. The mounted troops, stretched far on his flanks, would then capture the fleeing Boers, something they had failed to do at Belmont. Only if absolutely necessary would the 9th Brigade and the Naval Brigade be used to assault the enemy's position; otherwise their primary role was to protect the guns.[61] Whereas Methuen's emphasis of the night march at Belmont had been on manœuvring the infantry into a position to implement a bayonet charge, at Graspan he planned a night march to push the artillery forward under the safety of darkness.

THE BATTLE OF GRASPAN

The night march to Enslin began at 0330 hours on 25 November. The artillery came into action by 0630 hours. By 0700 hours, Methuen realized that he had underestimated the Boer strength considerably. Well hidden in the kopjes above Rooilaagte Farm some 150 to 200 feet above the surrounding veld, commanding the approaches to the south, east and west, was de la Rey and his commando.[62] Immediately, Methuen compensated for the larger enemy force. He heliographed Colvile to bring the Guards up to protect his right flank and rear, where Major Rimington had reported the movement of at least 500 more Boers.[63] The artillery continued to fire for over two hours (one battery alone fired off over 500 rounds), before Methuen was satisfied that the ground had been adequately prepared for the assault. The naval guns, brought north by armoured train, joined the fire. Despite this effort, the Boers, thanks to their fortified position, were little affected by the British artillery. To take the kopje and thus to continue the advance along the railway toward Kimberley, Methuen was forced to attack this large force with his infantry.

Methuen's main thrust was made on the Boer flank. Five companies of the Northumberland Fusiliers were ordered to hold the left and the centre. The rest of the 9th Brigade, including the Naval Brigade which had feigned a frontal attack, attacked from the right. The advance was supported by artillery fire. The shrapnel was effective in pinning down many of the Boers, but their mobility and their ability to act independently of their officers allowed the rapid reinforcement of their left flank. The Boer line was extended and, as a result, what had been the Boer left flank was now part of the Boer front. The attack which followed the main thrust degenerated, once again like the Battle of Belmont, into a frontal assault.

Methuen, personally conducting the operation, gave the orders to assault the eastern kopje around 0900 hours. Under the cover of artillery

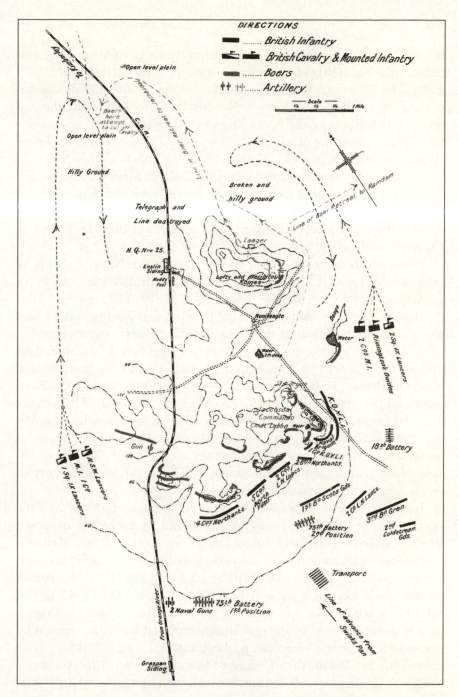

Map 6: The Battle of Enslin (Graspan), 25 November 1899. Map reproduced from Leo Amery, *The Times History of the War in South Africa*, London, Sampson Low, Marston and Co., 1907.

fire and the volley fire of the 2nd Battalion King's Own Yorkshire Light Infantry, the Naval Brigade advanced toward the kopjes in rushes of 50–60 yards. The fire of the Boers was deadly. Among the first to fall was the commander of the Naval Brigade, Captain Prothero, and before the day was out, 44 per cent of the Naval Brigade, sailors and marines, would be lost. Nearly half of the first line fell before it reached the kopje.[64] As Julian Ralph described, there was just 'no room for the bullets to miss'.[65]

According to Methuen and Lieutenant-Colonel Money, the excessive loss was caused by a tactical error. Although ordered to attack in extended order, the Naval Brigade had manœuvred in too close and the impact of modern firepower was clearly displayed.[66] The Naval Brigade indeed 'at last ha[d] a "show" all to herself', and it paid dearly.[67]

While the Boers concentrated their fire on the Naval Brigade, a company of the KOYLI and the 1st Battalion Loyal North Lancashire Regiment, from the left, and the remainder of the KOYLI regiment, from the right, were able to advance upon the Boer position. As they approached to within 25 yards of the top, the Boers abandoned their *sangars*, or breast-works, and fled, leaving the British to capture the ground. Methuen then ordered the artillery to advance up the hill, so it could fire down on the retreating Boers. The Boers, however, were too quick, their mobility allowing a rapid descent from the kopje. As Methuen recorded, 'The heights gained, I found I had taken the whole Boer force in flank, and had entirely cut them off from their line of retreat. My guns played on the masses of horsemen, but my few cavalry, dead beat were powerless, and for the second time I longed for a Cavalry Brigade and a H[eavy] A[rtillery] Battery to let me reap the fruits of a hard fought action.'[68]

For the second time in two consecutive battles, Methuen had his opportunity for a decisive victory taken from him by the lack of mounted troops. The path of the Boer retreat crossed the open veldt and Methuen had positioned his mounted troops so as to intercept them. A large mounted force could have wreaked havoc on the retreating Boers, but the British numbers were just too small and their horses too tired from a full day of reconnaissance to take advantage of the situation. In fact, Methuen's cavalry was threatened by the retreating Boers, and had to be rescued by the mounted infantry. Once again, the Boers fled with light losses. The commando headed northeast, more or less intact, toward Jacobsdal. As Frederick Maurice has pointed out, the operation strengthened the Boers' belief that they could face superior British numbers and, thanks to their mobility, they could avoid any disaster.[69] L. M. Phillips, a reporter who accompanied Methuen's mounted troops, wrote, 'Want of frigates was to be found in Nelson's heart … and I'm sure want of cavalry must be written in poor Methuen's.'[70]

At Belmont, Methuen's advance had turned into a frontal attack due to the misdirection of the Grenadier Guards. At the Battle of Graspan, Methuen again attempted a flanking movement and once again he was forced to fight the Boers' front. This time the alteration was caused by the ability of the Boers to rapidly change their own front. After these experiences, Methuen was well aware of the problem in overcoming the mobility of the Boers.[71] He concluded that with the resources he had, only British firepower could counter its effects.

> There is far too great risk of failure in making flank and front attack in the case of a position such as lay before me at Belmont. The very first element of success is to keep touch between Brigade from the first. Nor is there any question of taking the enemy in flank, as on horses he changes front in fifteen minutes as will be shown in the next fight. Shrapnel does not kill men in these koppies, it only frightens, and I intend to get at my enemy.[72]

Almost everyone, including Methuen, expected the destruction caused by the British artillery fire to be far greater than it was. The effects of shrapnel on the enemy, however, were minimal. To Methuen, the battles of Belmont and Graspan provided proof that a heavy artillery barrage could *not* drive the Boers from well-fortified positions. The lessons of Belmont and Graspan encouraged him, therefore, to rely on the frontal attack.

So as not to give the Boers much time to regroup, Methuen continued the British advance on 27 November after the 23 dead and 165 wounded were dealt with.[73] The scarcity of water also encouraged Methuen to move out as quickly as possible. He wanted to get his men and animals to the Modder River, about twenty miles away. The hurried pace caused one sergeant of the Guards to muse, as the war correspondent Alfred Kinnear overheard, 'Why are we like the early Christians? Because "Paul" gives our feet much to do.'[74]

From Kimberley, the British searchlight signalled to Methuen that the Boers were massing north of the Modder River at Spytfontein. Anticipating the difficulties of breaking through a fortified position located high in the hills before Kimberley, Methuen planned a march via Jacobsdal and Brown's drift which could hit the Boer flank. Despite the fact that leaving his main supply-line (the Western Railway) was a risky strategy, Methuen expected to seize large stocks of supplies in the lightly defended town of

Jacobsdal. He planned on leaving only a small force at the Modder River to hold the bridge and to prevent the Boers from discovering his plan.

The 1st Division marched toward Modder River, and on the 27th, they camped at Wittekop. There the command of the 9th Lancers was transferred to Major M. O. Little,[75] and Major-General R. Pole-Carew (affectionately called 'Polly' by Methuen), who had been a colonel on Buller's Staff, took over the command of the 9th Brigade.[76] Methuen ordered Rimington and Little to reconnoitre the surrounding area while he himself rode to examine the Modder River Bridge. Methuen was unaware that while he inspected the bridge, between 6,000 and 8,000 Boers looked on, the closest being a mere 300 yards away.[77] Not a shot was fired. The Boers held a front approximately five miles long, and Methuen, unaware of their position, returned to the base camp, intending to attack the next day.

The commander of the waiting enemy force at Modder River was General Piet A. Cronjé. An impatient and nervous 65-year-old Transvaaler, Cronjé was an experienced veteran who had led the Boers into battle at Potchefstroom in 1880 during the First Anglo-Boer War.[78] Cronjé had not yet met Methuen in battle, but he knew from talks with Prinsloo and de la Rey that he could expect two things: first, Methuen's advance along the railroad would bring the British to the vicinity of the Modder River railroad bridge; and second, the British would launch a frontal attack. Cronjé ordered his force to deploy around the Modder River Bridge.

De la Rey, who planned the overall deployment of the Boer forces, respected Methuen as a commanding officer, describing him as 'one of the bravest soldiers England ever chose to place against me'.[79] At Belmont and Graspan, where he had witnessed Methuen's artillery shell strong positions in the kopjes with excellent marksmanship, he decided not to give the British gunners easy targets at the next confrontation.

De la Rey convinced Cronjé that where the Modder and Riet Rivers met was the location most suitable to defend. The ground approaching the rivers from the south was flat with a few giant ant hills offering the only available cover. There was no crest of kopjes to provide good targets for the British gunners. With the assistance of German volunteer officers, the Boers constructed trenches on both sides of the river, and dug in, concealing themselves on the slopes of the riverbanks. Lying on the slopes of the riverbanks, the Boers could get the full range out of their Mausers. De la Rey, wanting to make a stand against Methuen, also knew that this position would be very difficult to retreat from or, in the case of Prinsloo and the Free Staters (who de la Rey did not respect), run from. The Boers also constructed bomb-proof shelters for their mounts and dug several gun emplacements, so as to get the most from their few batteries. Their position was well-nigh impregnable.[80]

In the early hours of 28 November, Methuen learned that his own eyes had deceived him at the Modder River. A local English speaker transmitted a message during the night that 'the Boers were in force in the village and were digging themselves in like rabbits'.[81] This confirmed Major Little's earlier report that at least 4,000 Boers were in and around the Modder River village and preparing for its defence.[82] Although Methuen still believed that the bulk of Boer forces were a few miles to the north at Spytfontein, he could not ignore these reports.[83] Fearing that his lines of communication were now threatened, Methuen immediately abandoned his flanking manœuvre toward Jacobsdal and prepared to do battle with the unseen force in front of him.[84]

Limited strategically by his inability to locate the enemy's flanks and by the courses of the rivers, Methuen prepared to conduct a frontal attack.[85] Not only was he ignorant of the Boer position when he drew up his battle plans to cross the Modder River, but he was to remain so after the fighting began. He wrote to his wife,

> My Darling Ettie, I do not suppose a harder fight, or under more trying conditions, ever took place than that on the Rivers. I honestly admit it was a surprise to me, for I thought the enemy had cleared off, as did everyone else, whereas Kronje [*sic*], De la Rey, and 9,000 men were waiting for me in an awful position. I never saw a Boer, but even at 2,000 yards when I rode a horse, I had a hail of bullets round me.[86]

THE BATTLE OF MODDER RIVER

It was exceptionally hot on 28 November, with temperatures reaching 108°. Having marched alongside Wood toward Coomassie in 1874 and ridden with Buller at Ismailia and Kassassin in 1882, Methuen was well aware of the difficulties of fighting in hot weather with little water available. Heat and thirst would put an unbearable strain on his men, many of whom would be pinned down by Boer fire for most of the day. Inevitably, British soldiers would be killed as a result of desperate attempts to get water. In the oft-quoted words of Methuen, the Battle of Modder River 'was one of the hardest and most trying fights in the annals of the British army'.[87]

That, perhaps somewhat exaggerated, view depicts the battle as a

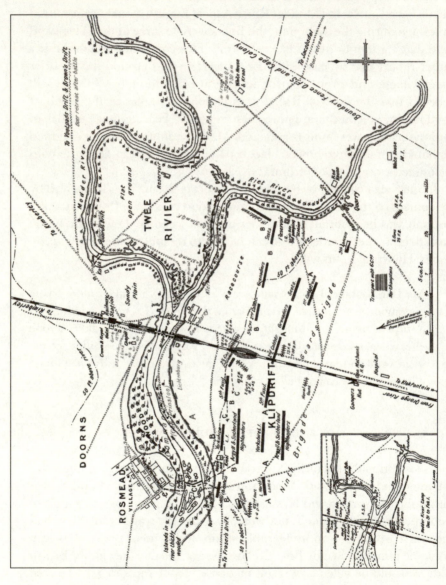

Map 7: The Battle of Modder River, 28 November 1899. Map reproduced from Leo Amery, *The Times History of the War in South Africa*, London, Sampson Low, Marston and Co., 1907.

desperate struggle, fought not just against the Boers but against the climate. W. Baring Pemberton, however, saw it also as a battle between tradition and technology: it was a 'farewell to the 19th Century, Modder River was the Waterloo of the Victorian Age'.[88] The battle clearly demonstrated the use of nineteenth-century military tactics against an enemy armed with twentieth-century weapons. Had Cronjé not lost heart and retired late in the battle, the results would have sounded an alarm. As it was, Methuen and the 1st Division would once again win the ground, and the army did not take on board the implications of new weaponry.

The Battle of Modder River began early on 28 November. Without clear knowledge of the enemy's location Methuen had decided not to commit himself to any specific plan. Thus the British were forced to march forward without a detailed battle plan. To discover the location, the 9th Lancers were sent forward at 0400 hours. At about 0530 hours, they located the Boer position on the right, but were prevented from reconnoitring further by enemy fire. Major Little reported back to Methuen that the Boers held a strong position between the bridge and a group of poplars to the east. The farms on the south bank of the river were well fortified, as were the nearby villages of Modder and Rosmead. While this information helped, it was still incomplete: the mounted troops could not see that west of the bridge as well as further east of the poplars, the riverbanks were also well fortified.

Methuen's maps and intelligence had indicated that the Modder and the Riet Rivers could be forded at any point.[89] This intelligence, inscribed in British maps, was totally erroneous. Since the Modder River Bridge had been dynamited by the Boers, the only places where the British could cross were four miles to the east at Bosman's Drift and six miles to the west at Rosmead's Drift. Unfortunately, the British had no knowledge of either of these places,[90] and there were not enough mounted troops to carry out a thorough reconnaissance of the area. To make matters worse, the course of the Riet had also been improperly drawn. In fact, just about every detail on Captain W. A. O'Meara's roughly drawn map was inaccurate. W. Baring Pemberton was correct about his assessment of the battle: as a result of poor intelligence, the British would pay a huge cost for their victory that day.[91]

Methuen hurriedly ordered the Guards Brigade and 9th Brigade out of camp early in the morning at 0430 hours. Many did not have a chance to drink their coffee or to eat their breakfast. This would prove most unfortunate since the battle would last most of the day. After marching in close order for two hours, at 0630 hours, the two brigades were ordered to extend. By 0700 hours, most of the British regiments had entered the battle. The 9th Brigade advanced on the left, toward Rosmead, to the west of the railway. Rosmead, unbeknown to them, had been fortified by Prinsloo and the Free Staters. The Argyll and Sutherland Highlanders waited in reserve. To the right of the railroad, the Guards Brigade advanced toward the junction of the two rivers, where de la Rey's commando awaited them. There, Methuen believed, the Guards could extend and hit the Boer left flank. Both British flanks were protected by mounted troops. The two field artillery batteries, the 75th and the 18th, as well as the naval guns, stayed in the center along the railway. The 62nd Battery RFA arrived later in the battle from Orange River Station and was deployed on the far left.

General Colvile deployed the Guards in two lines. On the front line, the Scots Guards advanced on the right, the Grenadiers in the middle and the 2nd Battalion Coldstream on the left. The second line, consisting of the 1st Battalion Coldstream, stayed behind in reserve. Although the Guards had not yet located the enemy, they cautiously advanced toward the river in extended order.

About 1,200 yards from the river, the Boers opened fire, sending a hail of bullets over the British force. Had the Boers waited for the British to come in closer, the casualties would have been far greater than they were. As it was, Methuen and his Chief of Staff and close friend, Lieutenant-Colonel H. P. Northcott, who were inspecting the ground trying to locate the Boers, got caught in the deluge – both escaping unscathed. Later in the battle, Northcott's luck deserted him. While riding Methuen's horse, he was mortally wounded in an attempt to deliver a message to Colvile.

The Guards Brigade attempted to advance directly into the Boer fire-zone. Colvile ordered the 1st Battalion Coldstream Guards to move to the right and envelop the enemy's left flank. Lieutenant-Colonel Alfred Codrington, their commander, quickly realized the Boer flank was protected by the Riet River, the course of which had been incorrectly drawn on British maps. In vain, detachments were sent down the river to scout for fords. Since the Coldstream battalion could not get at the Boers, Colvile was forced to make a frontal attack. Heavy Boer fire prevented the force, with the exception of the odd heroic but costly rush, from getting closer than 1,000 yards. From roughly 0700 hours to nightfall, when the battle ended, the Guards remained where they were. Their only cover was provided by friendly artillery fire. Accordingly, their casualties increased and their ammunition decreased.

Commanded by Major-General Pole-Carew, the 9th Brigade was likewise in action all day. Methuen ordered Pole-Carew to advance toward the railway bridge. Pole-Carew soon realized, however, that he could not send the Northumberland Fusiliers to hit the railroad bridge from the east without risking their overlapping the extended Guards. This would create confusion and increase the risk of being caught in close order. The rest of the force – the KOYLI in the centre and the Loyal North Lancashires on the left – were then forced west to make room for the Northumberland Fusiliers. At about 0730 hours, as the Northumberland Fusiliers were crossing the railroad tracks, the Boers opened fire. With the Northumberland Fusiliers pinned down on the right, the other two battalions advanced on Rosmead village. The faulty intelligence reports again resulted in heavy loss as Pole-Carew attempted to ford the river. Luckily, the British located a *donga*, or a small ravine with steep sides, extending into the river toward the Boer trench which they quickly occupied.

Like Wellington at Waterloo, Methuen was seen everywhere that day on the battlefield. He believed that he could do more good on the battlefield raising the morale of his tired men, than he could from a safe distance directing the overall battle with field glasses. As Conan Doyle wrote, 'his own personal gallantry and unflinching resolution set the most stimulating example to his troops. No general could have done more to put heart into his men.'[92] On the left of the railway, Methuen personally led one of the rushes to reinforce the captured *donga*. Safe in the *donga*, a small party of Argyll and Sutherland Highlanders provided covering fire for a detachment of the KOYLI which successfully seized the Boer trench on the south bank of the river. This gave the British their first foothold on the Modder. Rather than rest, Methuen returned immediately to the other end of the battlefield to assist Colvile.

This position proved significant. The British were now able to advance across the river. Pole-Carew led a successful rush across the 300-yard-wide river, in which his men at times had to wade up to their armpits, and seized Rosmead village.[93] As de la Rey feared, Prinsloo and the Free Staters fled. More soldiers of the 9th Brigade were eventually able to cross the river and reach the safety of the northern trench. However, due to heavy Boer artillery fire, they could not get to Pole-Carew and reinforce him. Pole-Carew made one gallant rush to reach the Boer guns, but was forced to retreat and entrench in Rosmead. Although the British artillery fired all day, it could not silence the well-entrenched Boer guns.

By late afternoon, the British troops were tiring. The heat, the weariness from the long day of battle, the fatigue of fighting three battles in less than a week, and the lack of water had sapped their energy. Then, the worst happened. Just before 1630 hours, Methuen was seriously wounded by a bullet. The shrapnel entered his thigh and he was forced to leave the battle-field, taking much of the British morale with him. Command of the division devolved to Colvile, while Colonel Arthur Paget took over the Guards.[94]

At first, Colvile wanted to continue the battle. Although his own Guards Brigade had not been able to advance, Pole-Carew's capture of Rosmead gave the British a strong position on the north bank of the river. But with Methuen injured and the men too tired to attempt another river crossing, Colvile postponed the attack. He decided, with Methuen's approval, that he would continue the attack the next day at dawn.[95]

As it turned out, Colvile's preparations were all for nothing. At 2000 hours that night, Cronjé decided that in view of the departure of Prinsloo and his men, he could not hold his position. The Boers retreated toward Jacobsdal. The next morning, the British crossed the Modder without inter-ference and made camp.[96] There they stayed for the next week. Kimberley would not be relieved according to Methuen's timetable.

The Battle of Modder River was another victory for Methuen and the British, but it was also, relative to the other colonial wars of this era, another extremely costly one. More than 60 British were killed and 300 more were wounded, a casualty rate of seven per cent.[97] Though faulty maps and the insufficient reconnaissance were responsible for much of this loss, these factors alone can not explain everything that happened that day, and Methuen must bear some of the blame.

What went wrong? Clearly, Methuen's underestimation of the situation was a serious error, but his lack of overall direction of the battle was also a problem. Because the location of the enemy was not entirely known, only a general plan was formulated before the advance. He did not send out more reconnaissance parties to obtain this information because he did not want to delay the British advance. Regardless, the troops were laid out in battle order with specific assignments based on the limited information available.

Amery and a few others have criticized Methuen, with some justi-fication, for his role in the battle. Once the fight began, they claim, he failed to take control and issue specific orders. He can, in part, be blamed for some of the miscommunication or lack of communication which resulted during the battle since throughout its course he failed to remain stationary in the rear, where he could have received information and transmitted orders. It is true that his personal conduct was admirable by leading rushes and directing movements on the battlefield. But, taking part as he did in these small actions, it was difficult to contact him at headquarters during the day, and therefore few orders were issued.

However, in Methuen's defence, orders that were issued were not always successfully delivered. As he emphasized in his report, it was very difficult to relay information across the battlefield: 'It seems like "Dante's Inferno", out of which men hope someday to emerge.'[98] Not expecting to face an enemy equipped with powerful modern weapons, the War Office had neglected to supply Methuen's division with runners. This made battlefield communication virtually impossible, since the bulk of both brigades was constantly under heavy fire. Methuen, therefore, had to rely on his aides for transmitting information, but he hesitated to send them into dangerous situations. Northcott was killed in one such attempt and Methuen took the news of his death very hard.[99] As a result of poor communication, Colvile did not become aware that he had assumed command of the division for at least thirty minutes after Methuen's injury. Also, it was not until after dusk that Pole-Carew heard that Colvile had decided to stop the battle. Thus Methuen cannot be held responsible for the communication difficulties on the battlefield.

As Pemberton has pointed out, communication was also hindered by the lack of a signal corps,[100] which the War Office had also failed to provide. Without a signal corps, Methuen could not transmit the position of the Boer artillery to his own artillery. As a result, detachments of the 9th Brigade which successfully crossed the river were often endangered by friendly artillery fire. Pole-Carew had to retreat more than once to escape that hazard and the British penetration was halted. Clearly, it was the ignorance of the War Office with regard to new technology, rather than Methuen's leadership, that was the major cause of communication failure.

One decision of Methuen's which can be justly criticized is the tactical choice he made to conduct a frontal assault at the Battle of Modder River. However, it is much more illuminating, in terms of historical analysis, to place his decision in the context of the Victorian military system rather than indict him personally. Could it be that Methuen's decision was connected to his training and experience of the previous 30 years? The answer is a decisive yes. Battles waged at Amoaful, Tel-el-Kebir, Dargai and elsewhere reinforced the belief that the British soldier was capable of turning the enemy regardless of his position. It is true that Methuen learned valuable lessons at Belmont and Graspan about the changing nature of warfare. He realized the difficulties of trying to conduct a flank attack against the much more mobile Boer, which led him to write, 'Every attack becomes a direct attack unless one has troops enough to contain the enemy while moving to a flank.'[101] He learned that a frontal assault without an accompanied flank attack could be dangerous. He learned too that the frontal assault was the only available tactic to ensure contact with the enemy. But his belief in the invincibility of the British foot soldier remained unshaken. As a result, he thought that the outcome of the battle would still be determined by his tactics and not the enemy's. He felt that his men could bring victory through a frontal attack no matter how heavy the odds.

Had Methuen known the exact number of the Boer forces he still would have had to assault their position, or leave them on his flank. Believing that the force at the Modder River was only a small party attempting to delay the British, and expecting the main Boer force to be busily entrenching further north at Spytfontein, it made sense for Methuen to act as he did. The surest and fastest way to drive the Boers from the Modder River, he believed, was with a frontal attack. He wrote to Buller, describing the situation as he saw it:

> We are terribly handicapped. The maps are of little value, the information obtained still less, and the open country plus Mauser rifles render a reconnaissance impossible – add to all this a march before you come into action of eight miles, a boiling sun, and sand mixed with salt, and I think I have described the situation on the day of the fight here. People talk of making a detour, or sending one brigade round a flank; there is no use talking in that way with 8,000 horsemen in front of you, a river, and a position not to be turned. The job has got to be done, and we have taken an [important] position with less loss than I expected, for many casualties are light, no credit due to me.[102]

Methuen resigned himself to the fact that the final push to Kimberley was going to be extremely difficult.

CONCLUSION

To this point in his career Methuen had demonstrated both good and bad qualities of leadership. His aptitude in commanding 10,000 men can legitimately be questioned. He cannot be blamed for the inaccurate maps, the scarce reconnaissance intelligence, and the inability to transmit information across the battlefield; nevertheless, he did not manage to co-ordinate the movements of his division. And his use of certain tactics, for instance the night march, before each of the encounters at Belmont, Graspan and Modder River, is also open to criticism. With limited military intelligence, partly a result of a weak mounted force and partly a result of poor British preparation prior to the outbreak of hostilities, Methuen chose to enter into three battles without full knowledge of the enemy's whereabouts. At both Belmont and Modder River this led to great confusion. Clearly, however, the greatest fault he had so far demonstrated was his general reluctance to deviate from the lessons he had learned whilst serving in many successful colonial expeditions.

If his adaptability is in question, then his personal courage is not. Methuen had displayed considerable bravery in the three encounters. It took a serious injury to drive him from the battlefield at the Modder River. Likewise he had demonstrated his care and concern for his men. His ability to use the three arms of his division, the infantry, artillery and cavalry, in unison is undeniable. And he was at times able to improvise, for instance in his use of extended order demonstrated at Belmont. Thus his march to Kimberley so far might be judged a qualified success.

By the end of November 1899 Methuen and the 1st Division had encountered the Boers three times *en route* to Kimberley. French and Gatacre slowly advanced in the northern Cape Colony and Buller began his advance from Maritzburg. So far as the British army was concerned, the nature of warfare decisively changed in November. For the first time, British troops in the open had faced the full fire of modern weapons. The devastating effects of this at Modder River should have put an end to the frontal assault as the main tactic for conducting a battle, since even the best British divisions could not withstand modern firepower. However, Methuen's nearly successful employment of traditional tactics served to blunt the impetus for change. The British army could still win following the old methods, and therefore, it did not abandon them.

Methuen had expected to reach Kimberley by 27 November. It was already the 28th, and although he had established contact with the besieged town, it was still 20 miles away. Ahead of him at Magersfontein, the bulk of Cronjé's force was busy entrenching itself in the kopjes. Methuen could no more avoid this force than he could avoid the Boers at Belmont, Graspan and Modder River. He was inevitably committed to the course along the railway which passed directly through Magersfontein. To evacuate Kimberley of all its non-combatants required (as we have noted) that the British control the entire stretch of rail from Orange River station to Kimberley. However, even had the rail not gone through Magersfontein, Methuen would have had to engage the enemy there, for it would have been poor strategy to have allowed so large an enemy force to remain unchecked on his flank.

NOTES

1. H. S. Gaskell, *With Lord Methuen in South Africa* (London: Henry J. Drane, 1906), dedication page.
2. The force consisted of about 7,750 infantry, which Methuen believed was large enough to relieve Kimberley. The Guards Brigade, commanded by Sir Henry Colvile, consisted of the 3rd Battalion Grenadiers, the 1st and 2nd Battalions Coldstream and the 1st Battalion Scots Guards. The 1st Battalion Coldstream Guards arrived at Belmont on 22 November after being relieved from guarding the railway at Orange River Station. Major-General Fetherstonhaugh commanded the newly formed 9th Brigade, which consisted of the 1st Battalion Northumberland Fusiliers, the 2nd Battalion Northamptonshire Regiment, the 2nd Battalion King's Own Yorkshire Light Infantry and half of the 1st Loyal North Lancashires.
3. Although the two infantry brigades seemed sufficient to complete his task, Methuen was well aware of the dangers of advancing with such a small mounted force. He requested more mounted troops, but Buller advised him that no more troops were forthcoming. Methuen's cavalry force, about 850 strong, led by Bloomfield Gough, consisted of the 9th Lancers, two and one half companies of mounted infantry, approximately thirty New South Wales Lancers and Rimington's Guides, also known as the 'Catchem-Alive-Os' and the 'Tigers'.
4. The British throughout the war could claim a numerical superiority in artillery batteries. Lieutenant-Colonel F. H. Hall commanded the 18th and 75th Field Batteries. The 62nd Field Battery joined the division at the Modder River. The division included four companies of Royal Engineers, the Naval Brigade and other divisional troops.
5. 'Report of His Majesty's Commissioners appointed to Inquire into the Military Preparations and Other Matters connected with the War in South Africa', 1904: cd 1790, XL, 14147.
6. L. Amery to V. Chirol, 19 Dec. 1899, John Barnes and David Nicholson (eds), *The Leo Amery Diaries* (London: Hutchinson, 1980).
7. Charles Sydney Goldmann, *With General French and the Cavalry in South Africa* (London: Macmillan, 1902), p. 31.
8. L. S. Amery (ed.), *The Times History of the War in South Africa 1899–1902* (London: Sampson Low, Marston & Co., Ltd., 1907), II, 325.
9. Edgar Holt, *The Boer War* (London: Putnam, 1958), p. 125.
10. Michael Davitt, *The Boer Fight for Freedom* (New York: Funk & Wagnals, 1902), p. 189.
11. Walter Wood, *The Northumberland Fusiliers* (London: G. Richards, 1901), p. 163.
12. R. Buller to G. Wolseley, 30 Nov. 1899, Wolseley Papers, Hove Central Library, Hove.
13. P. S. Methuen to M. E. Methuen, 19 Nov. 1899, Methuen Papers, Wiltshire Records Office.
14. P. S. Methuen to GOC, 26 Nov. 1899, WO 32/1891, Public Records Office.
15. Ibid.
16. Amery, *Times History of the War*, II, 327.
17. Methuen did not blame Lieutenant-Colonel Crabbe. He, in fact, praised the wounded man for his 'conspicuous courage'. See, P. S. Methuen to GOC, 26 Nov. 1899, WO 32/1891, Public Records Office. Major-General Colvile, commander of the Guards Brigade accepted responsibility in his report to the CSO, 1st Division of 23 Nov. 1899. See, WO 32/7891, Public Records Office.
18. P. S. Methuen to M. E. Methuen, 1 Dec. 1899, Methuen Papers, Wiltshire Records Office.
19. Frederick Maurice and M. H. Grant, *(Official) History of the War in South Africa, 1899–1902* (London: Hurst & Blackwood, 1906–10), I, 226.

20. P. S. Methuen to GOC, 26 Nov. 1899, WO 32/1891, Public Records Office.
21. Five horses died from exhaustion. Charles Edward Callwell and John Headlam, *The History of the Royal Artillery* (Woolwich: Royal Artillery Institution, 1940), p. 344.
22. 'Report of His Majesty's Commissioners appointed to Inquire into the Military Preparations and Other Matters connected with the War in South Africa', 1904: cd 1790, XL, 14161.
23. P. S. Methuen to GOC, 26 Nov. 1899, WO 32/1891, Public Records Office.
24. Ibid.
25. Alfred Kinnear, *To Modder River with Methuen* (Bristol: J. W. Arrowsmith, 1900), p. 1.
26. The majority of Methuen's infantry were armed with Lee-Metford Rifles M/95, .303 calibre, a rifle adopted by the British army in 1888. The Lee-Metford was a breech-loading rifle with a bolt lock and detachable magazine capable of firing up to 2,800 yards. The magazine could hold eight to ten cartridges. The improved Lee-Enfield rifle, developed in 1895, made its way to South Africa very late during the war. Unfortunately for the British soldier, it arrived with a faulty sight.

      The British had found that the Mark II bullet, the cartridge used by the Lee-Metford and Lee-Enfield, was too light and had proven insufficient during the campaign to Chitral. Looking for a replacement, they developed the Mark IV, or dum-dum, a soft expanding bullet which disintegrated when it entered a man's body. By March 1899 over 66 million dum-dum cartridges had been produced. The Hague Convention, of which the British had not been signatories, had outlawed all expanding bullets. Although the dum-dum cartridge was still used in other parts of Africa and in Asia, it was deemed unfit to use against white adversaries. Some Mark IV cartridges turned up at the Battle of Glencoe and elsewhere. See Jay C. Stone, *The Boer War and its Effects on British Military Reform* (PhD thesis, City University of New York, 1985), p. 255.

      The real reason for not using the Mark IV in South Africa, however, according to General Sir Henry Brackenbury, the Director-General of Ordnance during the war, was that in hot weather, in an unclean gun, this cartridge left a residue which frequently clogged breeches by the second or third shot. With the excessive heat and the dust of South Africa, that could prove disastrous. Therefore the British infantry was forced to used the understocked Mark II, a brass cartridge containing lead encased in copper nickel which used a smokeless cordite charge. The cavalry were equipped with a similar Lee-Metford carbine. See 'Report of His Majesty's Commissioners appointed to Inquire into the Military Preparations and Other Matters connected with the War in South Africa', cd 1790, 1904: xl, 1602.
27. The lessons of the American Civil War had very little 'material effect' on British military thought. See A. W. Preston, 'British Military Thought, 1856–90', *Army Quarterly and Defence Journal* 89 (1964): 63.
28. Napoleon demonstrated the effectiveness of organization along the greater scale of the corps in his early victories against the Grand Coalitions. Yet the British ignored this and had refused all change since. From Wolseley on down, there was a preference in the British army to organize along a much smaller scale. Arnold-Forster's attempt to reorganize the army after the Boer War, in which Lord Methuen would command the IV Army Corps, was met with such fierce opposition that he was forced to abandon his scheme.

      The battalion was the tactical unit used by the British army. It consisted of eight companies of approximately 100 to 120 men in each. In battle, this force was divided into three lines. The first line would attempt to hold the enemy and secure a position within 800 yards of it. Once established, the second line would advance and aid the assault. The third line would follow in reserve and establish a position where they could successfully pursue the enemy in the event of its retreat or, in the event of its own retreat, could serve as a rear guard. As the first line advanced to within 350 yards, rushes of 30–40 yards would be made under the cover of volley fire. Within 200 to 250 yards the order was given to attach bayonets and a general rush was performed.

Although this tactic was common practice, it was certainly not official policy. Ultimately, the commanding officer was responsible for conducting the tactics on the battlefield. As C. E. Callwell has pointed out, 'To the commander thrown upon his own resources in a distant land, hedged round by dangers and perplexity, outnumbered and perhaps at bay, who sees a great chance open should he risk all on one single throw, the accepted code of strategy and tactics is of no avail and the maxims of the academic school of military thought have small significance. The leader endowed with the gift of command knows instinctively how to act and creates for himself his own rules of conduct.' Nevertheless, British practice up to that point was so uniform, and successful, that an officer who chose to shun traditional tactics for an experimental approach in battle could ill afford to lose. See Colonel Charles Edward Callwell, _Small Wars: Their Principles And Practice_, rev. edn (London: HMSO, 1899), p. 62.

29. Stone, _The Boer War and its Effects_, p. 281.
30. Ibid., pp. 25–29.
31. Volley fire was eventually abandoned by the British army as an effective tactic in 1902. Buller had advised his officers to abandon the traditional tactic of volley fire in favour of slow individual fire. He wanted to make sure that the enemy positions were pinned down and occupied by a continuous fire. 'I think volley fire is a mistake', he wrote to Methuen. Although Methuen did not rely on the use of volley fire, some of his junior officers did employ the tactic. See R. Buller to P. S. Methuen, telegram, 14 Nov. 1899, Methuen Papers, Wiltshire Records Office.
32. Viscount Esher, who served on the Royal Commission on the South African War and who chaired the War Office (Reconstitution) Committee, wrote, 'You see Methuen's first fight only drove back the Boers _six miles_! Hardly further than from O'Lea to Windsor. That is not a very big "victory". When you think of Napoleon riding from Waterloo to Paris!!!' Cited in M. V. Brett (ed.), _Journals and Letters of Reginald Viscount Esher_ (London: Nicholson & Watson, 1934), p. 246.
33. Also, as Hippolyte Langlois pointed out, against an enemy in depth, a night march can only succeed against the front line. Hippolyte Langlois, _Lessons from Two Recent Wars_ (London: HMSO, 1909), p. 79.
34. Herbert R. Gall, _Modern Tactics_ (London: W. H. Allen, 1899), Chapter 4.
35. A. R. Mead, 'Night Attacks in the Transvaal War', _United Services Magazine_ May (1904): 202.
36. Others include Generals Gatacre, Hildyard and White.
37. Maurice and Grant, _(Official) History of the War_, I, 228.
38. Amery, _Times History of The War_, II, 327.
39. The artillery was the arm of the British army which lagged farthest behind the changes dictated by the new technology. British generals remained oblivious to the true impact of artillery until well into the First World War. In the South African War, the 15-pounders of the Royal Field Artillery, the 12-pounders of the Royal Horse Artillery, and the large 4.7-inch quick firing naval guns were still primarily used as a support for the infantry. The artillery had two basic tasks: first to eliminate the enemy's artillery and then to shell all enemy positions in preparation for an infantry charge. It was a maxim of the British army that until 'a considerable effect had been produced by this fire, no position should be assaulted by infantry'. See C. Francis Clery, _Minor Tactics_ (London: Kegan Paul, 1893), p. 170.

As Herbert Gall accurately predicted in early 1899, more entrenchments were built during this war. The 'spade beats the rifle', he wrote, citing examples at Plevna and Shipka Pass. The only way to penetrate the fortified positions of the enemy, Gall believed, was with a substantial artillery barrage. Although this eliminated the opportunity for surprise, it was expected that this would cause the necessary destruction and demoralization of the enemy which could insure the success of the bayonet charge to produce the decisive victory on the battlefield. Gall, *Modern Tactics*, p. 87.

Several different guns were deployed by the British at the outset of the South African War and more were to follow after January 1900. The most common gun used by the Royal Artillery was the 12-pr 6-cwt, a three-inch calibre breech-loader which fired shrapnel at a rate of seven to eight rounds per minutes an average distance of 2,000 yards. Its range increased steadily up to 4,000 yards by the end of the war. The 15-pr 7-cwt, used by the Royal Horse Artillery, was another three-inch calibre breech-loader which also fired shrapnel. Its range was slightly longer than the 12-pr and its ammunition slightly heavier. Shrapnel was primarily an anti-personnel weapon which when detonated unleashed a rain of bullets. The five-inch breech-loading Howitzer was also commonly used at the start of the campaign. The shorter barrelled Howitzer could fire a heavier shell but at a shorter range. One of the advantages of the Howitzer was its higher trajectory which permitted the shell to strike downwards and therefore could hit targets behind cover. The common shells used by the Howitzers which exploded into several large pieces were much more effective against structures than shrapnel. British heavy artillery used 16-pr muzzle-loaders, mountain batteries were 15-pr muzzle-loaders and garrison batteries used both 20-pr and 40-pr breech-loaders. After watching the Boers use them effectively during the early stages of the war, the British purchased several 37-mm Maxim machine guns, more commonly known as Pom-Pom guns, which could fire ten rounds per second, and employed more than 50 after 'Black Week'. The Maxim Gun fired a one-pound iron shell encased in a brass cartridge, 25 to a belt. It was the only gun in South Africa with a protective shield. For a detailed description of the artillery used in the South African War, see Darrel D. Hall's 'Guns in South Africa, 1899–1902', *South African Military History Journal* 2 (June 1971): 7–15; (Dec. 1971): 41–6; (June 1972): 82–7.

The British guns used cordite, a smokeless propellant much stronger than gunpowder, which enabled the firing of heavier shells without major alterations to the guns. The use of cordite and more volatile bursting charges like lyddite, melinite and pertite, revolutionized the artillery. First, smokeless powder allowed the easier locating of targets in the open since vision was not obfuscated by dark clouds of smoke. However, with the removal of this smoke, artillery targets hidden by cover became more difficult to locate. Secondly, not only could guns fire heavier shells, but the effects of the detonation of the shells was far more extensive. As Major Darrell Hall has pointed out in his article 'Guns in South Africa, 1899–1902', it was expected that the new bursting charges like lyddite would cause tremendous damage to enemy fortifications. 'There were exaggerated press reports that the mere concussion of the explosion was enough to kill any enemy in the vicinity.' Methuen's use of the artillery in his early encounters with the Boers at Belmont, Graspan, the Modder River and Magersfontein show clearly that he believed that the Boer troops would be overwhelmed by the new shells. See Hall's 'Guns in South Africa', pp. 9–10. For information on the British use of artillery in the late Victorian age see, Robert H. Scales, *Artillery in Small Wars: The Evolution of British Artillery Doctrine, 1860–1914* (PhD thesis, Duke University, 1976).

40.   Telegram from P. S. Methuen to R. Buller, WO 108/229/No. 1374, Public Records Office citing GOC, Lines of Communication, Natal, to Secretary of State for War,

23 Nov. 1899.

41. P. S. Methuen to GOC, 26 Nov. 1899, WO 32/1891, Public Records Office.
42. As G. F. R. Henderson wrote in 1901, the British cavalry had three basic functions. The first function was to conduct reconnaissance of the enemy's position and to seize tactical points. The second function was to pursue retreating troops in order to capture and demoralize the enemy. The third function was to threaten all potential lines of retreat. George Francis Robert Henderson, *The Science of War* (London: Longman, Green & Co., 1912), pp. 49–78.
43. Gall, *Modern Tactics*, pp. 9–15.
44. The change in the nature of firepower had also affected the cavalry, although many British military theorists refused to accept this. Methuen's commanding officer during his formative years with the 2nd Battalion Scots Guard, H. C. Fletcher, had been influential in encouraging this resistance. Fletcher and J. A. L. Fremantle, among others, had served as observers for the British army during the American Civil War. Their conclusion, that the cavalry on both the Union and the Confederate sides had failed not as a result of increased firepower but due to poor training and discipline, determined British cavalry tactics for the next 35 years. The British refused to accept the change.

    By the South African War, military theorists like G. F. R. Henderson were hotly debating the issue of the cavalry and what its exact role should be. The considerable extension of the fire-zone naturally increased the danger to both the rider and his steed and took away the cavalry's shock value. To many, the days of the heroic cavalry charge across open ground to force a gap in the enemy's front or to dissipate the enemy's morale were all but gone. By 1899 few cavalry officers remained that dared to risk this type of manœuvre against the overwhelming force of modern firearms. See Stone, *The Boer War and Its Effects on British Military Reform*, p. 354.

    However, this did not altogether eliminate the value of the cavalry. In a limited action on the battlefield a cavalry charge could still be effective, for example, in hitting the enemy's flank when speed was of the essence. When it was necessary to reach a strategic position before the enemy, the cavalry again was very effective, such as in French's race to Klip Drift to open up the road to Kimberley. The cavalry could still perform other useful functions like threatening the enemy's lines of retreat and communication or pursuing and harassing the defeated enemy with the goal of capture or demoralization. But more important than ever was the cavalry's role in reconnaissance.

    Reconnaissance, as Henderson argued, was the first job of the cavalry. In South Africa, where British maps were often hindrances to operations, where knowledge and familiarity of the ground was limited, and where the enemy was mounted, reconnoitring became a prerequisite for knowing the whereabouts of the enemy and thus for preventing ambushes. As the difficulties of reconnoitring open ground increased, the need for mobility also increased. During the South African War, it became quite clear to the War Office that a mounted force was still necessary and that the original dispatched force was sorely inadequate. To fight the Boer mounted troops across the seemingly endless karoo of South Africa required a much larger mounted force but it also required a mounted force which could work effectively when dismounted, unlike the traditional cavalry, and thus take advantage of the available ground for cover. By the end of the war, this need would be met by mounted infantry. This conversion of sections of infantry to mounted infantry and the sudden disdain for the cavalry started a whole new series of debates. See Henderson, *The Science of War*, pp. 49–78.

    The tactical unit of the cavalry was the squadron. Four squadrons made up one regiment. A regiment consisted of 32 officers and 634 men, of which approximately

80 acted as drivers or remained behind during combat to guard the base, giving the regiment a field strength of just over 550. A brigade of cavalry consisted of three regiments, two machine guns, and various departmental troops adding up to just over 2,280 men. They were armed initially with carbines and swords. However most of the carbines were abandoned late in the war for the more accurate rifle and swords were often dropped altogether. See Wilkinson J. Shaw, *Elements of Modern Tactics* (London: Kegan Paul, 1894), pp. 20–30.

45. Garnet Wolseley, *The Soldier's Pocket Book*, 4th edn (London: Macmillan, 1882), pp. 124–40.
46. H. E. Colvile, *The Works of the Ninth Division in South Africa in 1900* (London: Arnold, 1901), p. 2.
47. Amery, *Times History of the War*, II, 332.
48. P. S. Methuen to M. E. Methuen, 1 Dec. 1899, Methuen Papers, Wiltshire Records Office.
49. GOCC to SSW, 28 Nov. 1899, No. 1466, WO 108, South Africa Telegrams, Public Records Office.

Emended list of casualties at Belmont, 23 November 1899

	officers/men killed	officers/men wounded	men missing
staff	–	1/0	–
9th Lancers	–	0/4	–
18th Battery RFA	–	0/1	–
3rd Bn. Grenadier Guards	2/19	7/98	0/2
1st Bn. Coldstream Guards	0/7	1/20	–
2nd Bn. Coldstream Guards	–	2/6	–
1st Bn. Scots Guards	0/9	3/35	–
1st Bn. Northumberland Fusiliers	2/10	4/36	–
2nd Bn. King's Own Yorkshire L.I.	–	0/5	–
2nd Bn. Northamptonshire Regiment	–	1/14	–
South African Reserve	0/1	0/3	–

50. Some writers do consider the Battle of Belmont to be a 'brilliant success'. See Louis Creswicke, *South Africa and the Transvaal War* (Edinburgh: T. C. & E. C. Jack, 1901), p. 87.
51. In addition to the Boer casualties, the British captured more than 50 prisoners and 100 horses, destroyed 64 wagons and blew up four large cylinders of gunpowder, along with 5,000 rounds of ammunition. P. S. Methuen to GOC, 26 Nov. 1899, WO 32/1891, Public Records Office.
52. P. S. Methuen to M. E. Methuen, 1 Dec. 1899, Methuen Papers, Wiltshire Records Office.
53. Wood, *The Northumberland Fusiliers*, p. 167.
54. Rayne Kruger cites Methuen as the first British general to publicly acknowledge the technical skill and courage of the Boers. Kruger, *Good-Bye Dolly Gray* (New York: J. B. Lippincott Co., 1960), p. 113.
55. P. S. Methuen to GOC, 26 Nov. 1899, WO 32/1891, Public Records Office.
56. Several sources also accused the Boers of firing Mark IV bullets. There is no mention of this in the Methuen papers, although Rayne Kruger states that Methuen wrote Prinsloo a letter regarding the use of 'dum-dums' at the battle. Cited in *Good-Bye Dolly Gray*, 112.
57. P. S. Methuen to GOC, 26 Nov. 1899, WO 32/1891, Public Records Office.
58. Estimations vary. Maurice puts the number at no less than 2,300. Maurice and Grant (Official) History of the War, p. 234. Hall suggests as many as 3,000. Colonel John

Hall, *The Coldstream Guards 1885–1914* (Oxford: Clarendon Press, 1929), p. 44. Louis Creswicke, in an often jingoistic book, gives 2,500. Creswicke, *South Africa and the Transvaal War*, p. 93. J. Meintjes, a source sympathetic to the Boers, estimated the number at only 2,000. Johannes Meintjes, *De la Rey* (Johannesburg: Hugh Keartland, 1966), p. 115. In his official report to Buller, Methuen estimated 2,500. P. S. Methuen to GOC, 26 Nov. 1899, WO 32/1891, Public Records Office.

59. P. S. Methuen to M. E. Methuen, 15 Nov. 1899, Methuen Papers, Wiltshire Records Office.

60. 'Report of His Majesty's Commissioners appointed to Inquire into the Military Preparations and Other Matters connected with the War in South Africa', 1904: cd 1790, XL, 14147.

61. P. S. Methuen to GOC, 26 Nov. 1899, WO 32/1891, Public Records Office.

62. Maurice and Grant, *(Official) History of the War*, p. 230.

63. P. S. Methuen to GOC, 26 Nov. 1899, WO 32/1891, Public Records Office.

64. Amery, *Times History of the War*, II, 338.

65. Julian Ralph, *Towards Pretoria* (New York: Frederick A. Stokes, 1900), pp. 135–75.

66. Lieutenant-Colonel Money to CSO, 1st Division, 26 Nov. 1899, WO 7890, Public Records Office.

67. Surgeon T. T. Jeans (ed.), *Naval Brigades in the South African War, 1899–1900* (London: Sampson, Low, Marston & Co., 1901), p. 22.

68. P. S. Methuen to GOC, 26 Nov. 1899, WO 32/1891, Public Records Office.

69. Maurice and Grant, *(Official) History of the War*, p. 242.

70. L. March Phillipps, *With Rimington* (London: Arnold, 1901), p. 15.

71. Major-General C. E. Webber wrote in a letter to *The Times* that because of the lack of mounted troops, 'Our Generals are forced to attack almost impregnable positions because they cannot mask, turn, or ignore, them. And these are positions which the mobility of the Boer enables him to occupy, change his front, or abandon, at his pleasure.' Until a balance in mobility was achieved in both armed troops and transport, Webber believed, the British offensive would be paralysed. *The Times* (London, 18 Dec. 1899).

72. P. S. Methuen to GOC, 26 Nov. 1899, WO 32/1891, Public Records Office.

73. GOCC to SSW, 27 Nov. 1899, No. 1449, WO 108, South Africa Telegrams, Public Records Office.

List of Casualties at Graspan, 25 November 1899

	officers/men killed	officers/men wounded	men missing
2nd Bn. KOYLI	0/7	3/37	6
9th Lancers	0/1	0/8	–
75th Battery RFA	–	0/1	–
1st Bn. Northumberland Fusiliers	–	0/3	–
1st Bn. Loyal N. Lancashire Regiment	0/1	1/19	–
2nd Bn. Northampton Regiment	0/1	0/4	1
Naval Brigade	3/2	0/13	–
Royal Marine Artillery	1/5	0/55	–
Royal Marine L.I.	2/0	0/22	–

74. Kinnear, *To Modder River with Methuen*, p. 106.

75. Methuen dismissed Lieutenant-Colonel B. Gough on no specific charge. In his reply to a letter from Gough, Methuen wrote that although he believed Gough had done everything he could, he had lost confidence in him. Gough committed suicide in early 1900. Cited in P. Methuen to B. Gough, 4 Dec. 1899, Methuen Papers, Wiltshire

Records Office.

76. Lieutenant-Colonel Money was wounded and sent to Simonstown by ambulance train. Major-General Reginald Pole-Carew took command of the 9th Brigade. At the Battle of Modder River, Pole-Carew became the 9th Brigade's third commander in its third battle of the campaign.

77. Herbert Wrigley Wilson, *With the Flag to Pretoria* (London: Harmsworth Bros., 1901), p. 155.

78. See Frederick Rompel, *Heroes of the Boer War* (London: Review of Reviews Office, 1903), for descriptions of Cronjé and other Boer commanders.

79. Meintjes, *De la Rey*, p. 118.

80. W. Baring Pemberton, *Battles of the Boer War* (Philadelphia: Dufour Editions, 1964), pp. 59–60.

81. Maurice and Grant, *(Official) History of the War*, p. 246.

82. Estimates of the number of Boers range from 3,000–4,000 to as many as 9,000.

83. P. S. Methuen to CSO, Modder River, 1 Dec. 1899, WO 32/7893, Public Records Office.

84. 'Report of His Majesty's Commissioners appointed to Inquire into the Military Preparations and Other Matters connected with the War in South Africa', 1904: cd 1790, XL, 14380.

85. *The Times* (London), 5 Dec. 1899: 9.

86. P. S. Methuen to M. E. Methuen, 1 Dec. 1899, Methuen Papers, Wiltshire Records Office.

87. Creswicke, *South Africa and the Transvaal War*, p. 97.

88. Pemberton, *Battles of the Boer War*, p. 76.

89. P. S. Methuen to F. C. A. Stephenson, 4 Dec. 1899, Methuen Papers, Wiltshire Records Office. Thomas G. Fergusson writes that although military intelligence, due to limited resources, failed the British army often in the South African War, the most notable occasion was at the Modder River. *British Military Intelligence 1870–1914* (Frederick, MD: University Publications of America, 1984), p. 114.

90. Thomas Pakenham, *The Boer War* (New York: Random House, 1979), p. 199.

91. Pemberton, *Battles of the Boer War*, p. 58.

92. Arthur Conan Doyle, *The Great Boer War* (London: Smith, Elder & Co., 1900), p. 147. Lord Methuen took none of the praise when he telegraphed Queen Victoria, 'the victory was entirely due to the gallant conduct of the troops'. Cited in George E. Buckle (ed.), *The Letters of Queen Victoria* (London: John Murray, 1932), III, 2nd series, 424.

93. Maurice and Grant, *(Official) History of the War*, p. 255.

94. Paget had served in Methuen's battalion and had accompanied him to West Africa in 1873 to fight the Ashanti. He later was involved in the Curragh Mutiny in 1914.

95. P. S. Methuen to CSO, Modder River, 1 Dec. 1899, WO 32/ 7893, Public Records Office.

96. De la Rey, who had left during the battle to care for his mortally wounded son, Adaan, was furious when he heard the news. See Byron Farwell, The *Great Anglo-Boer War* (New York: W. W. Norton & Co., 1976), p. 100.

97. GOCC to SSW, 2 Dec. 1899, No. 1527, WO 108, South Africa Telegrams, Public Records Office.

List of Casualties at Modder River, 28 November 1899

	officers/men killed	officers/men wounded	men missing
staff	1/0	1/0	–
9th Lancers	–	0/1	–
18th Battery RFA	–	1/19	–

List of Casualties at Modder River, 28 November 1899 cont.

62nd Battery RFA	0/1	0/4	–
75th Battery RFA	0/2	3/11	–
7th Co. RE	–	1/2	–
3rd Bn. Grenadier Guards	0/8	3/41	0/4
1st Bn. Coldstream Guards	–	0/21	–
2nd Bn. Coldstream Guards	2/10	1/56	–
1st Bn. Scots Guards	0/10	2/37	0/1
1st Bn. Northumberland Fusiliers	0/11	0/34	–
1st Bn. Loyal N. Lancashire Regiment	0/3	1/16	–
1st Bn. Argyll/ Sutherland	0/15	2/98	0/2
RAMC	–	1/1	–
South African Reserve	–	0/1	–
Rimington's Guides	–	0/3	–

Another account lists 71 killed and approximately 400 wounded. See George R. Duxbury, *The Battle of Magersfontein*, Battles of the Anglo-Boer War, 1899–1902, no. 9 (Johannesburg: National Museum of Military History, 1979), p. 7. Boer casualties amounted to about 50 killed, 25 taken prisoner and an unrecorded number of wounded.

98. P. S. Methuen to M. E. Methuen, 1 Dec. 1899, Methuen Papers, Wiltshire Records Office.
99. Methuen wrote to his wife, 'My *only* staff officer, my one companion has gone in Northcott; I shall never get over his death. I am to blame, for each day he prayed me not to impose myself, and had I remained away from the firing line neither of us need have been hit.' P. S. Methuen to M. E. Methuen, 1 Dec. 1899, Methuen Papers, Wiltshire Records Office.
100. Pemberton, *Battles of the Boer War*, pp. 72–6.
101. Note jotted in the margin of 'C. of S. Circular Memorandum No. 5, Notes for Guidance in South African Warfare', issued by Lord Kitchener 26 Jan. 1900, Wiltshire Records Office.
102. P. S. Methuen to R. Buller, 2 Dec. 1899, WO 132/15, Public Records Office.

6

Failure at Magersfontein

In three successive battles, Belmont, Graspan and Modder River, Lord Methuen's 1st Division successfully drove the Boers from their fortified positions. However, the British were unable to claim a decisive victory in any of these encounters and the enemy force easily slipped away. After outpacing the British, the Boers headed north, regrouped and received reinforcements. Anticipating Methuen's next move, they repositioned themselves enfilading the course of the railway. As a result, Methuen and his plodding division faced an awaiting Boer force as they advanced up the rail-line and arrived at the next station. In order to preserve the integrity of their line of communication, the British reluctantly engaged the enemy at each encounter. At the heights of Magersfontein, six miles to the north of Modder River and fifteen miles south of Kimberley, the Boers again entrenched and awaited Methuen's advance. At his camp on the banks of the Modder River, Methuen prepared for one last battle at Magersfontein which he hoped would open up the railway to Kimberley and allow for its relief. This chapter focuses on Methuen's advance from the Modder River to Kimberley in December 1899, providing a narrative and analysis of the Battle of Magersfontein and its effects on Methuen and the British army.

Through the closing months of 1899 the British army in South Africa was advancing slowly and determinedly towards the Orange Free State. In the east, Sir Redvers Buller, the General Officer in Command, continued to move toward Ladysmith to relieve Lieutenant-General George White and his beleaguered troops. Reaching Frere on 5 December, Buller prepared his force to drive the Boers from Colenso where they blocked his route to Ladysmith. In the centre, Lieutenant-General William Gatacre and his small force inched toward the northern Cape Colony, drawing off Boer forces from Natal and the western Cape Colony and easing the pressure on Ladysmith and Kimberley. They reached Putter's Kraal on 27 November, some 20 miles south of Stormberg Junction. Also in the northern Cape

Colony, Major-General John French and his division of cavalry moved north out of Naauwpoort toward Arundel. And in the west, advancing along the Western Railway line, Methuen continued his march toward Kimberley.

The slowness of the advance of the British army into the interior of South Africa was of some concern to Buller. As the sieges of Kimberley, Ladysmith and Mafeking continued, pressure from the Government and from the British public mounted. However, Buller lacked the forces necessary to bring about the quick victory demanded by those back at home. Already constricted by manpower shortages, he had been forced to break up the First Army Corps, which had been earmarked for an advance upon Bloemfontein, into its several weaker divisions to quell the crisis created by White's entrapment at Ladysmith. Buller's hands were tied for the moment. A fifth division had been mobilized in mid November under the command of Lieutenant-General Sir Charles Warren, Methuen's former commander in the Bechuanaland expedition, but it would not arrive in South Africa for at least another month. It was not until late November, after the unexpectedly heavy losses at Modder River, that the mobilization of a sixth division in Britain was announced.[1] More reinforcements were to follow and before the new year, the War Office had announced the mobilization of a seventh division and the calling up of the first-class reserves. In addition, the Government accepted offers from Canada, Australia and New Zealand for more colonial contingents, as well as the volunteer service of the Yeomanry, Militia and City of London Imperial Volunteers.

Aware that more troops were *en route* to South Africa, thus guaranteeing the safety of the coast, Buller freed the (3rd) Highland Brigade, which had been guarding the 1st Division's lines of communication, for the relief of Kimberley. They were ordered north to join Methuen and by 10 December the entire Brigade had arrived at his base camp at the Modder River. Major-General Andrew G. Wauchope, a much-decorated and well-respected veteran of several colonial campaigns, commanded the Highlanders.[2] The Brigade was made up of the 2nd Battalion Royal Highlanders (the Black Watch), the 2nd Battalion Seaforths, the 1st Battalion Highland Light Infantry, and the 1st Battalion Argyll and Sutherland Highlanders.

With the Guards and the Highlanders, Methuen, like the Duke of Cambridge in the Crimean campaign, was in command of the two brigades in the British army with perhaps the richest history. He was familiar with both brigades, having served in the Guards and having just witnessed the Highlanders in action in India. In addition, the 12th Lancers, commanded by Major-General J. M. Babington, the 1st Battalion Gordons, G. Battery RHA, the 65th (Howitzer) Battery RFA, some detachments of mounted infantry, and a reinforcement of the Naval Brigade, were dispatched to Methuen at the Modder River, as well. The fighting strength of Methuen's force thus consisted of 10,200 rifles, 800 sabres and 33 guns.[3] As Methuen described it, his new force was indeed a 'beautiful command'.

As the reinforcements arrived between 29 November and 9 December, Methuen and most of his units remained in and around the British camp at Modder River. Because of his own health and the overall fatigue of his men, Methuen decided to remain at Modder River and await reinforcement rather than to continue his advance immediately. Of his 350 officers, nearly 60 were dead or wounded; a casualty rate of over 16 per cent. In addition, Methuen's own wound sustained at the Battle of Modder River prevented his participation in any impending battle. Had they advanced right away, Methuen saw that in the next encounter (which he expected to occur at Spytfontein, just nine miles to the north) he would have had to hand over his command to one of his brigadiers. As it was, when Methuen did meet the enemy next at Magersfontein, his movement was still greatly restricted by bandages.[4] Few officers would have willingly parted with their own command in this situation. To make matters worse, command would have devolved once again to General Henry Colvile, who Methuen considered to be 'a most peculiar fellow'.[5]

Methuen's decision to rest at Modder River rather than to continue his advance has been severely criticized by analysts,[6] some of whom have branded him a 'breakfast strategist' – one who can make crucial decisions only after digesting dozens of subordinate opinions and considering even the smallest details.[7] They argue that by the time such consultations are completed, all initiative has been lost. In this case, Methuen's opponents insisted that had he taken advantage of the Boer flight and immediately continued with his advance, he would have gained two advantages: first, the enemy, already shaken by defeat at Modder River, would not have had an opportunity to regain composure or learn any lessons from this latest encounter; and second, the enemy would not have had the chance to entrench at Magersfontein. An immediate British advance would have kept the path to Kimberley virtually unobstructed. As Leo Amery argued: '[Methuen] sacrificed the moral and strategical advantages he had gained by his rapid advance and his hard fought victories. The indefinable psychological impression produced on an enemy by an army in motion, the paralysing sense of uncertainty as to whither the next move will be, or where the next blow will fall, are assets in strategy that are thrown away the moment that army comes to a prolonged standstill.'[8] These sentiments were echoed by many other critics.

However, such criticisms miss the mark. Amery's assumption, for example, that Methuen possessed great psychological advantages is erroneous. As shown earlier, the moral advantage which the British possessed was slim. While it is true that the Boers were in retreat, this was only because the failure of the British to pursue them successfully at the conclusions of the battles of Belmont and Enslin had taught them that they could retreat with very little risk. Besides, even had Methuen advanced immediately after the Battle of Modder River, the Boers, due to their mobility, would still have had time to retreat and regroup. What is more, the Boers were well aware that the British possessed no strategical advantage in determining the course of their operations to relieve Kimberley as a result of their dependency on the railroad. In sum, Boer mobility neutralized any advantages that might have been gained by hastening the British timetable.

Further, it is only with hindsight that one can actually conclude that the failure of Methuen to continue his advance allowed the Boers to recover their composure.[9] There was no knowledge of Boer morale immediately after the Battle of Modder River. Methuen, injured early in the day, could not have known the reason for the Boer retreat, and he ventured no suppositions in any of his detailed reports or personal papers. Neither is there any reason to believe that either Colvile or Pole-Carew could have known Cronjé's reasons for retreating. At a range of only 850 yards, Colvile's Guards Brigade was pinned down for 12 hours by the Boer fire. No reconnaissance was possible. Further evidence that Colvile had no knowledge of Cronjé's retreat lies in the fact that, when he took command from the wounded Methuen, he decided to continue the battle the next day. Pole-Carew, commanding the 9th Brigade, to the west of the railway, did witness the retreat of Prinsloo and his Free State Commandos, but he was cut off from the rest of his brigade with a small detachment. What he observed was a strong Boer position covering any further British advance. He, too, could not have been aware that Cronjé's retreat was caused in part by the weakness of the Free Staters.

In addition to this lack of information about the disposition of the enemy, Methuen also had positive reasons for staying at Modder River. First, as Foster Cunliffe pointed out, his men, having fought three battles in one week, and having suffered nearly a thousand casualties, were just too tired to continue the advance.[10] Also, Methuen expected an enemy force at Spytfontein numbering somewhere around 16,000. Even if this force had withdrawn and had chosen not to attack, as some critics suggest would have been the result of an immediate British advance, Methuen's present command, without reinforcements, was not large enough to ensure the integrity of a 75-mile long railway and at the same time defend against this undiscovered force.

Second, the critics seem to have forgotten to take into account Methuen's original orders: to evacuate Kimberley of its non-combatants and to resupply the garrison. Pole-Carew, in his testimony before the Royal Commission on the War in South Africa, admitted that the 1st Division could have left the Modder River within 48 hours of the battle and could have easily relieved Kimberley; however, it could not have also evacuated the civilians. Accordingly, Methuen used the delay to construct a temporary railroad bridge, spanning the Modder River, to make the evacuation of the beleaguered city's inhabitants possible as they withdrew via the Western Railway. The bridge was finished by 10 December, complete with redoubts on both sides of the river which would enable a small garrison better to defend the bridge once the 1st Division had continued its advance. Although protecting the line and defeating the Boer force at Magersfontein were central to holding the railway, repairing the Modder River bridge was also one crucial part of Methuen's task. Attention to the fact that Methuen was ordered not just to reach Kimberley but to evacuate it, sheds considerable light on his decision to remain at Modder River.[11]

Finally, it is important to note that Methuen believed Kimberley to be in no immediate danger. Lieutenant-Colonel R. G. Kekewich,[12] the commander of the British garrison in Kimberley, had signalled on 4 December, that the town could hold out for 30 or 40 more days.[13] Thus Methuen instructed Kekewich to strengthen his defences and prepare for the brief delay.

While at the Modder River, Methuen also ordered Kekewich to use this time to reinforce his own authority as garrison commander, which was being challenged by the non-combatants held up in Kimberley, and in particular by Cecil Rhodes. Rhodes was a thorn in Kekewich's side, constantly harassing him with complaints and annoying him with endless suggestions on how to better his command over Kimberley. Methuen refused to allow Rhodes' interference in what he considered strictly a military issue. Unlike Roberts (later in the war) who was sensitive to political issues, Methuen flatly refused to negotiate with Rhodes about anything. Like many others, Methuen believed that the British army was sent to Kimberley not to rescue the Uitlanders but to save Cecil Rhodes. Thus he saw Rhodes as a major cause of the war and always treated him with contempt.[14] After the Battle of Magersfontein, Methuen wrote to his wife, 'Our Presbyterian Minister was with the wounded … and they asked him for some whiskey. He said they could have some if they would drink the

Queen's health. They took the whiskey, and said: God save the Queen and d-m Rhodes. That represents the feeling of the country.'[15]

With the arrival of the last reinforcements, Methuen made plans for the advance. He wrote, 'The longer I remained inactive, the stronger would the enemy become. Therefore, on the day my last reinforcement arrived, I decided to continue my advance.'[16] His plans were influenced by the reconnaissance operations conducted daily from 30 November through 8 December. During this time, balloons were launched to survey the neighbouring area. Major George Elliott Benson, one of Methuen's staff officers, also conducted a reconnaissance operation toward Spytfontein. The cavalry, a force which Leo Amery accurately noted 'cannot take the place of trained scouts or spies, especially against a watchful mounted enemy',[17] carried out most of the preliminary operations. Too much was expected of the Rimington Guides, Methuen's only veteran scouts. They were needed not just to reconnoitre in the direction of Kimberley, but also to watch the flanks of the 1st Division and the course of the railway south to Enslin which otherwise would have been vulnerable to attack.

As a result, the reconnaissance was not as successful as Methuen had hoped. However, it did carry out several useful missions. One of these was to Magersfontein Kop, the site of the next encounter with the Boers, which was discovered to be,

> ... a wide perfectly level plain with a ridge straight across it like a great railway embankment, but with arms at each end curving towards the front as the arms of a trench are curved; behind the ridge, and higher, two or three kopjes which command it; behind the kopjes another like the first, with more kopjes to command it; the same thing repeated half a dozen times, without another eminence within fifteen miles.[18]

After 4 December, with the arrival of a small Boer force, the British could not get within 1,000 metres of Magersfontein without severe risk.[19] Reconnaissance did show that Boer forces stretched some five miles from Langeberg Farm, three miles northwest of Merton Siding, to Magersfontein Hill, while other information obtained by reconnaissance showed that farther east up the Modder River the Boers controlled Moss Drift. However, with few properly trained scouts, Methuen was not able to gather all of the information he needed, and he knew little about the positions which the Boers held at Magersfontein. Also, he had no information about the trenches which the Boers constructed at the base of the hill, and he was ignorant of the gaps in the Boer defences to the east and to the west of Magersfontein.[20]

By far the most significant failure in Methuen's reconnaissance was its inability to ascertain the size of the enemy force. Methuen could not determine the exact number of Cronjé's force in the region nor the numbers that he would have to fight at Magersfontein. Best guesses by Methuen and his staff ranged between 12,000 and 13,000. To this day, the exact number of the Boer forces impeding Methuen's advance to Kimberley remains unknown. However, it is indisputable that the force was much smaller in number than the British anticipated, certainly no more than 8,500.[21] Filson Young, a reporter who accompanied the Kimberley Relief force, wrote: 'No one could tell us whether or not the twelve miles to Jacobsdal were free from the enemy; people thought so, but they were not quite sure.'[22]

Methuen believed that a strike at Magersfontein was his only option for the successful relief of Kimberley. From their position atop the heights of Magersfontein, the Boers could shell any train *en route* to or from Kimberley, thus threatening the British line of communications and making the evacuation of the city too great a risk to undertake. Had Methuen attempted to bypass this large force on his flank and break the siege of Kimberley, the risk, contrary to his critics' claims, would have been enormous. Heading east along the Modder River and then north around Magersfontein, would have involved risking continued harassment from the forces atop Magersfontein to Methuen's communications and transport and an encounter with an entrenched force of Boers at Moss Drift. A wider flanking move to the east, avoiding Moss Drift, would have only brought the British closer to Jacobsdal where an estimated 16,000 Boers were situated.

Methuen's only other alternative was to advance along the railway, avoid Boer fire, and strike directly at Spytfontein. Information about the Boer forces at Spytfontein was sparse: Methuen believed that the forces occupying Spytfontein had been fortifying their position since the Battle of Modder River, whereas reconnaissance had shown, as noted above, that Boer movement to Magersfontein was recent. He assumed that a Boer force at Magersfontein would be smaller and in a weaker defensive position then a force at Spytfontein. The British artillery could fire freely at Spytfontein only once the occupation of the Magersfontein Heights was achieved.

The factor which most influenced Methuen's decision to advance against the Boers at Magersfontein was the lack of water in the vicinity. Had he chosen to circumvent the enemy's left flank and avoid a confrontation at Magersfontein altogether, his troops would have had to carry at least five days' provisions.[23] He had available transport to carry a sufficient supply, but his lines of communication would have been threatened by the Boer force at Magersfontein. Since reconnaissance had not discovered any sources of water within 20 miles of the Modder River, Methuen felt that he could not risk being cut off from his supply line for more than two days.[24] He knew the hazards of such a situation to his men and, as an expert on horsemanship, he knew the hazards to his cavalry and mounted infantry.[25] Thus he concluded that the dangers of an advance toward Kimberley on any but the most direct route far outweighed any potential gains.[26] Sir Redvers Buller agreed with this decision.[27]

As the division prepared to leave camp on 9 December, Methuen ordered that the 4.7-inch quick-firing naval gun be moved three miles up the railway line toward Merton Landing, a few miles south of Magersfontein. From there, he experimented with lyddite, a new explosive, shelling Magersfontein Hill at a range of 5,000 yards. Once the target had been successfully ranged, Methuen ordered the firing to halt.

On Monday, 10 December, at approximately 1500 hours, Methuen renewed the British advance. His expectations are evident in a letter to his wife:

> Darling, My reinforcements were complete this morning, so I began firing this afternoon, and anticipate three days hard work and then the relief of Kimberley a gigantic job. I have said that any civilians who remain in Kimberley unless he [*sic*] has some valid reason will be turned out by me, and have to find food and transport, which means death. I have now 13,000 men and thirty guns, so the Boers must suffer. I fired a long navy gun with lyddite at their position *four miles* off at day break yesterday.
>
> I anticipate having to fight 10,000 to 12,000, because the Transvaal have sent help from Natal, and they are determined to destroy my force; however I am in a stronger position than I have been in yet, and hope to deal a heavy blow on Wednesday.[28]

Methuen steadily pressed forward. Wauchope and the Highland Brigade proceeded toward Magersfontein to a slight rise, later known as Headquarter Hill, just to the left of the Kimberley road. This position, along a ridge, could not be seen from Magersfontein Hill.[29] Cavalry and mounted infantry, attached to the brigade, carried out reconnaissance and covered the advance. After being greeted by a short burst of Boer fire, they fell back and protected the Highland Brigade's right flank. The 2nd Battalion KOYLI advanced along the Modder River to Voetpads Drift, where they entrenched. From this position, they defended the far right flank of the 1st Division and prevented any Boer movement across the Modder River.

Major-General Reginald Pole-Carew, accompanied by the 1st Battalion Northumberland Fusiliers, three companies of the 2nd Battalion Northamptonshire Regiment, and the naval gun, proceeded north along the railway. From this position, the artillery could co-operate in a bombardment of Magersfontein Hill and the infantry could protect the left flank of the division. Rimington's Guides extended on Pole-Carew's left.

Major-General Henry Colvile commanded the Guards Brigade in reserve.[30] Shortly after 1900 hours, he left camp and followed Wauchope's route. The Gordon Highlanders were ordered to accompany the supply column along the same route at 0400 hours, the following day. The remaining forces – a half battalion of the Loyal North Lancashires, five companies of the Northamptonshire Regiment, two companies of the Royal Munster Fusiliers and most of the Naval Brigade – were left to defend the camp at Modder River. They also protected the rear of the advancing units.

PREPARATIONS FOR THE BATTLE OF MAGERSFONTEIN

On 10 December, at 1600 hours, Methuen ordered the British guns to open fire on the Boer position. The guns targeted the southwestern face of the Magersfontein kopje, the sight chosen for the next day's offensive. The bombardment of the kopjes lasted nearly three hours, ceasing at 1845 hours.[31]

Military analysts and historians alike have severely criticized Methuen's decision to bombard the enemy's position before the attack. They point out that by shelling the enemy position, Methuen alerted the Boers to the likelihood of an attack, thus reducing British hopes for a successful surprise the following morning. However, this criticism is significantly blunted when Methuen's reasons are understood. Foremost amongst these was the psychological factor.[32] Methuen anticipated that the sheer visual and aural magnitude of the bombardment would greatly disrupt the enemy's morale. The bayonet advance that was planned immediately to follow the shelling would weaken the Boer resolve to continue the fight.[33]

Also, Methuen's believed that his artillery would wreak havoc on the enemy's defences, allowing for an easier infantry advance the following morning. Neither he nor his officers, nor indeed anyone in South Africa, were fully aware of the effects of lyddite. Both demonstrations in England and exaggerated rumours had led most, including Methuen, to expect its results to be far more devastating than those produced from any other charge they had ever seen. Without lyddite shells at the battles at Belmont and Graspan, the artillery had failed to drive the Boers from their positions. However, it had successfully targeted the Boer positions during those encounters. Methuen now believed that his artillery could combine accuracy with increased destructiveness. He assumed that the destruction would be so great that nothing could live in the trenches after the artillery attack.[34] This would increase the likelihood of a successful British advance.

Further, Methuen hoped that the Boers would respond to the British fire with the traditional response – the return of their own artillery fire – thus enabling the British better to pinpoint the enemy position. Also, this would allow Methuen's superior artillery to neutralize the Boers' in an artillery duel, and would thereby foreclose the possibility of the use of the Boer artillery against the British infantry advance.[35] And, finally, Methuen's similar decision at Belmont to shell the enemy positions before the start of the battle had driven the Boer artillery from the field and had rendered them virtually inoperative during the battle. Buller, the General Officer in Command, fully supported Methuen's decision.[36]

The critics are right that Methuen's strategy was flawed. However, his mistake lay not in firing on the Boer position before the infantry advance, but rather in waiting nearly 11 hours after the bombardment to strike with his infantry. As G. R. Duxbury has so accurately pointed out: 'Tactically, the purpose of a bombardment is to inflict as many casualties as possible, demoralize the enemy by the weight of fire and follow up with an infantry bayonet attack before he has time to recover and organize his defence.'[37] Yet, any ill effect on Boer morale was neutralized by the long delay before the advance. As Duxbury has suggested, this delay, coupled with the British artillery's inability to hit the Boer trenches and cause the anticipated 'great loss of life', actually served to strengthen Boer morale.

Indeed, far from causing great devastation, the heavy preliminary fire managed to wound only three Boers. There are two reasons for the ineffectiveness of the shelling. First, although the lyddite shells did hit the ridge where the Boers had taken up position they were far less powerful than had been supposed. Second, and more importantly, the Boers, under General Koos de la Rey's guidance, had constructed deep, narrow and well-disguised trenches. So effective were these trenches that the Boers had only to keep their heads down to avoid the onslaught of shrapnel. Thus, it is fair to conclude that while Methuen's calculations proved disastrously wrong, they were not wrong-headed. Methuen should not be blamed, rather de la Rey should be credited.

Immediately after the Battle of Modder River, General P. A. Cronjé had ordered a retreat toward Jacobsdal. Pressured by de la Rey and others, he agreed to engage Methuen and the British once more before they could reach Kimberley. Cronjé was certain that the British would continue to advance along the railway in their attempt to relieve Kimberley. He therefore believed the best place to stop the British advance was at Spytfontein. Just to the south of Spytfontein Station, Scholtz Kop commanded the southern and eastern approaches. Across the rail, Langeberg farm overlooked the western approach. Cronjé anticipated that a Boer force of 8,000 men, well entrenched and holding the high ground, notwithstanding their weak artillery, could successfully block the passage of 10,000 British. On 29 November he ordered his men to begin their movement toward Spytfontein. After circling north, the bulk of the Boer force arrived at Spytfontein and immediately began to dig in along the summits of the surrounding heights. In anticipation of Methuen's march, trenches and *sangars* were built on both sides of the railway. As a precaution, their laagers were positioned roughly ten miles east of Methuen's probable line of advance. The Boer ammunition depots were left in Jacobsdal, practically undefended.[38]

The position which the Boers held at Spytfontein was subject to one weakness: it was vulnerable to long-range artillery fire from Magersfontein. As pointed out earlier, Methuen was well aware of this fact. After a reconnaissance of Magersfontein, de la Rey concluded that taking a position at that point would not only eliminate this weakness, but at this site the British would be forced to attack across open ground. Supported by the president of the Orange Free State, Marthinus Theunis Steyn, and a *krygsraad*, or a Council of War, de la Rey convinced Cronjé to make their stand at Magersfontein. The first Boers arrived there on 4 December,[39] and de la Rey was put in charge of planning the defence.[40]

The Boer position at Magersfontein was virtually impregnable. Although only 60 yards above the surrounding ground, Magersfontein commanded the area for miles.[41] To the south lay an open field containing only a few patches of bushes and scrub. Ant hills, three feet high, offered the only additional potential cover for a force advancing from that direction; hence a frontal attack, in daylight, could only be made at great risk. To guard the right flank, a single line of trenches was built from Langeberg farm to the railway, just north of Merton Siding, and trenches were to have been built to protect the left flank, stretching east to the river, as well. However, the British attacked before these were ready. The main line of trenches was situated in the centre at Magersfontein Hill. In addition to this line, rifle pits and trenches were constructed on the upper slopes of the hill.

At Magersfontein, the Boers dug trenches 150–200 yards in front of the hill rather than at its base, on its face or on its crest. This was done for several reasons. First, as at the Battle of Modder River, the Boers would not offer themselves as easy targets for the British gunners. It is much easier for artillery to sight a target if it is clearly marked by its surrounding landscape. Second, because the hill was only slightly higher than the surrounding ground, the range and destructiveness of the Boer firepower would be increased through 'grazing fire', or firing parallel to the plane of the battlefield rather than firing down from the heights. Third, as Duxbury suggests, had the Boers occupied the top of the ridge, the British could have advanced under the cover of night to the base of the hill, and, in daylight, rushed the Boer position with bayonets from a distance of only a few hundred yards.[42] The risk taken by this course of action would have been minimal for the British. Finally, and most importantly for morale, by building the trenches in front of rather than on the hill, retreat would not be possible. To emerge from the trench and then run up the hill toward safety would be suicidal. In this way, de la Rey ensured that there would be no repetition of Prinsloo's retreat at Modder River.

As Leo Amery stated, the Boer fieldworks at Magersfontein were of 'one of the boldest and most original conception[s] in the history of war'.[43] Although the term trench warfare was new in 1914, the practice of using trenches was not. British soldiers had seen trenches in the Crimean War and observers had witnessed those used during the American Civil War, 50 years earlier. However, in 1899 no Englishman had ever come across such an elaborate design of trenches as those constructed at Magersfontein.

The design of the trenches not only minimized the risk to the Boers, but also maximized their firepower. Rather than build their trenches in one long single line, the Boers dug them in such a way that they conformed to one another and to the ground, thereby providing mutual support to the flanks.[44] The trenches, constructed almost perpendicular to the ground, were roughly three to four feet deep and extremely narrow. Their height provided full protection to the lower body from British infantry fire and their width gave exceedingly good cover from British artillery fire. The latter was proven by the ineffectiveness of the British bombardment on 10 December. Low parapets gave further protection to head and shoulders. These were camouflaged with rocks and brushwood, and went unnoticed by British reconnaissance.

Methuen did not know exactly what he was up against but he believed his force was sufficient to drive the Boers from Magersfontein. Once again, reconnaissance supplied him with little information. He knew the Boers were at Magersfontein but he did not know their number or position. Although he still had some time to delay his advance, since Kimberley could hold out for about another month, he could not expect his current situation to change. He had just been joined by the Highland Brigade and his requests for more mounted troops had been denied by Buller. The 5th Division was expected to reach Cape Town shortly, but neither their arrival date nor their mobilization to his theatre of operations could be guaranteed.[45]

British officers had been taught at Sandhurst that when facing an entrenched force, a commander should have at his disposal a force at least three times greater than that of the enemy. Methuen expected the ratio of offence to defence at Magersfontein to be between one to one and three to two.[46] Nevertheless, he decided to attack, putting his faith in the British soldier and not in military theory. The lessons he had drawn from his colonial expeditions as well as from the recent battles at Belmont, Enslin and Modder River, could not have led him to make any other decision which, as we have already noted, was fully supported by his Commanding Officer, Buller.[47]

Methuen's plan of attack was very simple. A heavy bombardment of Magersfontein Hill on 10 December would precede a frontal assault by the Highland Brigade on the southern ridge. As noted above, the bombardment was expected to cause great damage to the Boer entrenchments and to demoralize them as well. The artillery barrage would be followed by a night march – a tactic dear to Methuen's heart, and one which had often brought him success. Just after midnight, the battle-ready Highlanders would advance toward the Boer position (a march of roughly two and a half miles) in close order and under the cover of darkness. After reaching their destination, a few hundred yards from the Boer trenches, the brigade would extend and fix bayonets. The Black Watch would hold the centre, the Seaforths would prolong on the left and the Argyll and Sutherland Highlanders would prolong on the right. The Highland Light Infantry would follow in reserve. At first light of day, Wauchope would give the order to charge. The Guards Brigade, kept at a safe distance behind the rear of the Highlanders, could lend support at Colvile's discretion.[48] The right flank would be protected by the 9th Lancers, the Horse Artillery Battery and mounted infantry. Pole-Carew's column, astride the railway, would protect the left flank and, in addition, would make a diversion against the ridge of Magersfontein facing the railway.

The battle plan showed little imagination on the part of Methuen and his staff, but without better information on the enemy's position and strength there was little else they could do.[49] Once again, night operations would precede a frontal assault. With no available cover for the British, this appeared to be the best way to cross the open plain. A night march would allow his advancing force to get within a few hundred yards of the Boer redoubts in relative safety. From there, the demoralization of the Boer forces which had begun with the artillery bombardment would be completed with the sight of the oncoming British bayonets. With few mounted troops at his disposal, Methuen did not want to risk a flank attack, which although it might succeed in capturing Magersfontein, would also enable a successful Boer retreat. This action would only lead to a reinforcement of Spytfontein.[50] Methuen, therefore, judged it best to meet and destroy the enemy at Magersfontein with cold steel. He was confident that the Highland Brigade, whose battalions he saw defeat the Ashanti at Amoaful and the Egyptians at Tel-el-Kebir, were capable of completing this task. Methuen believed that the Battle of Modder River had proven that a frontal assault was the only sure means of making and keeping contact with the enemy.

There is some controversy surrounding Methuen's battle plan and Wauchope's opinion of it. In attempts to preserve Wauchope's reputation, many historians of the South African War suggest that he disapproved of Methuen's proposed night march. In this way they direct all responsibility for the British failure at Magersfontein toward Methuen and away from Wauchope. They defend their speculations with an oft-mentioned discussion which took place between Wauchope and Colonel Charles Douglas, Methuen's ADC and Chief of Staff.[51] This discussion, according to Frederick Maurice and M. H. Grant in their *(Official) History of the War in South Africa, 1899–1902*, took place after a meeting between Methuen and Wauchope on the afternoon of 9 December. Wauchope, on leaving Methuen, remarked to Douglas, 'I do not like the idea of this night march.'[52] Douglas urged Wauchope to convey his misgivings to Methuen, but Wauchope declined. Leo Amery, in his *Times History of the War in South Africa*, went much further in illustrating the supposed debate than Maurice and Grant. He wrote that Wauchope immediately disapproved of Methuen's plan and did not 'hesitate to express to his commander the doubts that rose up in his mind at the thought of the hazardous venture to which his brigade was being committed'.[53] One source has written that Wauchope told Methuen he was ordering the Highland brigade into a trap and Methuen quickly reminded him who was in charge.[54] Perhaps the most colourful account in this controversy has Wauchope writing to England, 'This is my last letter, for I have been ordered to attempt an impossible task. I have protested, but I must obey or give up my sword … .'[55]

There is no written evidence to substantiate any of these claims that Wauchope resisted Methuen's plan. In his official report to Buller, Methuen stated that Wauchope understood his orders and said nothing more.[56] Methuen wrote home: 'There is a false rumour in a low paper that poor Wauchope asked me for guides, and that I refused saying I command all the division; that he then said: "I will obey your orders." He never said a word, for I remember saying to him, "are my orders quite clear?" and he said: "yes". I looked at him wondering whether we should meet again.'[57]

Two biographies on Wauchope, one by George Douglas and the other by W. Baird, make no claim that there was any debate or confrontation with Methuen regarding the battle plan laid down before Magersfontein. Douglas's research, which relies heavily on Wauchope's correspondence with his wife, suggests that although Wauchope did entertain private reservations about the plan of battle, he offered no public objections to it. Wauchope's last letter home neither raises objections to the plan nor expresses any sense of foreboding disaster.[58] To Major A. G. Duff, 1st Black Watch, a friend of over 20 years, Wauchope simply communicated the orders.[59] Arthur G. Wauchope, a lieutenant in the Black Watch who charged the Boers at Magersfontein alongside his cousin, had perhaps the best sense of General Wauchope's attitude prior to the battle. Yet in his *A Short History of the Black Watch*, he makes no mention of any objections his cousin put forth, nor is there any negative comment on his cousin's relationship with Methuen.[60] Douglas's speculation on Wauchope's opinion of the proposed night march is probably the most accurate assessment: Wauchope was 'too staunch a soldier and too well trained to allow his own feelings to interfere'.[61] The Scottish general, like any good leader, displayed no feelings of doubt or fear the night before the battle.

Wauchope had to carry out the night march under conditions for which no Salisbury Plain training exercise could have adequately prepared British troops. A light drizzle which had begun the afternoon of 10 December had turned into a pouring rain by midnight. Accordingly, there was some question among Methuen's staff of whether the night operation should proceed. Wauchope agreed with Methuen that any delay of the operation would only give the Boers more time to strengthen their position.[62] Although, as we have seen, it is unclear whether Wauchope fully approved of the initial plan, his determinedness to carry out that plan once it had been decided upon is beyond question.

Methuen assigned Major George Elliott Benson the task of guiding the

Highlanders to the foot of Magersfontein Hill. He was assisted by two of Rimington's Guides. Benson, a staff officer, had made a reconnaissance of Magersfontein and had taken accurate readings with his compass. He directed the night march with a compass in each hand. Wauchope accompanied him at the head of the brigade. The Highland Brigade followed in a mass of quarter-columns, company after company. In all, 30 companies marched in 96 successive lines. The close formation of the brigade – six paces between each company and eight paces between each battalion – was necessary to prevent troops from becoming lost. As Frederick Maurice described, 'The ranks were closed up as densely as possible, and each soldier was ordered to grasp the clothing of his neighbour.'[63] In addition, from the front to the back of the formation ropes were run along the left flank.

In the preparations for the night march all the emphasis was on stealth. The men were ordered to extinguish any fires and were prohibited from smoking.[64] The Highlanders donned khaki aprons to hide the fronts of their brightly coloured kilts. They removed their sporrans, so as not to offer the Boers good targets, and their coat buttons were smudged to prevent them reflecting light. Finally, to make the officers indistinguishable from the men, all swords were left behind. Wauchope would be the only officer to carry his claymore into battle.

THE BATTLE OF MAGERSFONTEIN

Shortly after 0030 hours on 11 December, the night march began. It continued until dawn, with few unplanned delays. Periodically, the Brigade was ordered to stop to regroup and to make sure all was going according to plan. The inclement weather increased the likelihood that the advancing column would err in reaching its proposed destination. At approximately 0200 hours, the column shifted slightly to the right to compensate for a misdirection caused by the rain's effects on Benson's compass readings. Other than that, miraculously, the Highland Brigade reached its proper destination before the first light of day, just as the rain began to stop. By all estimates, Benson had fulfilled his task to the letter. The night march was successful. The British had arrived at their destination safely, a mere half hour late, at about 0330 hours, and now needed only to extend and await daybreak. Daybreak was already later than expected; it should have occurred at 0325 hours. Since it would take 15 minutes for the brigade to deploy, it was a pressing concern to give the order.

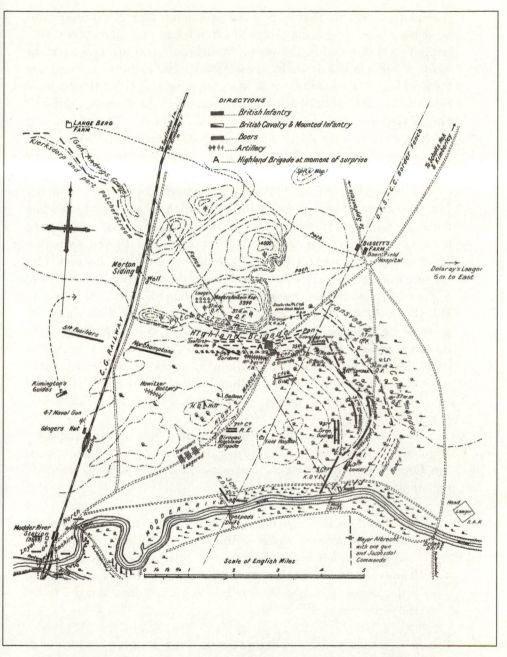

Map 8: The Battle of Magersfontein, 11 December 1899. Map reproduced from Leo Amery, *The Times History of the War in South Africa*, London, Sampson Low, Marston and Co., 1907.

Unfortunately, the Highlanders did not extend. Twice, Benson encouraged Wauchope to give the orders to extend, and twice the commander refused. With the end of the storm, Wauchope could just make out the Magersfontein salient. It was impossible to calculate its distance. Expecting the Boers to be on or at the foot of Magersfontein Hill rather than in front of it, Wauchope believed that his brigade was still too far from the presumed enemy position. 'At all hazards', the *Times* reported, 'Wauchope was resolved that dawn should not find the brigade beyond striking distance of the position.'[65] Frustrated, Benson returned to headquarters as Wauchope ordered his men to advance further.

The advancing brigade continued their march for 15 more minutes. Just as Wauchope was about to order his men to extend, the leading battalion, the Black Watch ran into a dense patch of prickly mimosa. To keep the integrity of the brigade, Wauchope further delayed giving the order to extend to give the Black Watch time to traverse the patch. This they did in single file. The other battalions, at the same time, went around it. Therefore, the advance continued another 300–400 yards.[66] At this point, Wauchope and the Highlanders were within 700 yards of the hill and 400 yards of the hidden Boer trenches. At 0400 hours, Wauchope ordered the Seaforths to move forward on the left of the Black Watch and the Argylls to do the same on the right. The Highland Light Infantry remained in reserve. At last, almost an hour later than Methuen's plan had advised, and a half hour after Benson's urging, Wauchope had ordered the Highlanders to extend.

The order to deploy came too late. The first light of day caught the Highlanders extending into battle formation, and at once, the Boers opened fire. Captain J. H. Bruche, a Victorian Special Service Officer, described the immediate outcome:

> Had the Highlanders been deployed when the Boers opened fire the pipers would have sounded the charge and the impetus of the first rush would have carried the brigade into the Boer trenches before the enemy could stop it. [However, as Wauchope] gave the order to deploy, the Boer fire commenced at that instant. It caught the brigade at its greatest disadvantage – halted and partly deployed.[67]

Bruche's assessment accurately conveys the stark contrast between what Methuen had wanted to happen and what actually did happen. Only minutes from the final preparation for the assault, the Highlanders were caught completely off guard, halted, in close formation and only 400 yards from the Boer trenches. From that range, a single bullet could pass through many men.[68] The results could easily have been disastrous.

As it turned out, however, not all the Boers were yet aware that the British were nearly upon them and only some were able to respond immediately by joining in the first volley. Although the Boers had been anticipating a British strike in the morning, the heavy rain had numbed their bodies as well as their senses,[69] and many had yet to stir. The darkness of the morning, which made it very difficult for the Boers to locate their targets, also saved many British lives. As a result, much of the Boer fire rose above the heads of the Highlanders.

In order to salvage the situation, Wauchope attempted a desperate assault on the Boer trenches. In the confusion of the fire, he was able to rally some of his men to fix their bayonets and charge. He himself fell, heroically, in the first few minutes of the assault, when two bullets pierced his body and one struck his head. His body was found within 200 yards of the Boer position.

Methuen was too magnanimous a gentleman and too honourable a 'Christian knight' to blame a dead man for the failure of the battle. Besides, it is clear from a letter to Buller that Methuen adamantly believed that although a costly error had been made in not deploying the brigade sooner, the battle was not lost. In that letter Methuen wrote: 'The report of Colonel Hughes-Hallett tells its own tale, and collaborates what wounded men of the Black Watch in front and in the trenches say. Namely that if "Forward" had been given instead of "Retire", the trenches and with them, the kopje and position, would have been ours in a few minutes.'[70] The day after the battle, he reiterated Hughes-Hallett's words to his wife: 'I will only say the victory was a matter of minutes, for had the word *forward* been given, not *retire*, the trenches were ours and the field of battle.'[71] Although Methuen questioned Wauchope's reasons for not deploying earlier, he never blamed the fallen general for the outcome of the battle.[72] In fact, he praised his 'military reputation' and his 'grand character'.

Wauchope's death left the Highland Brigade in complete disarray in the field. In attempting to deploy under fire, the three leading battalions, the Black Watch, the Seaforths and the Argyll and Sutherland Highlanders, became hopelessly intermixed in the near darkness. Both individual battalions and companies were confused as troops in the rear attempted to advance forward through the still-tight formations. Some sources suggest that much of the confusion stemmed from one or more fleeing soldiers shouting the order to retire. The evidence is sketchy at best, but certainly many of the Highlanders broke ranks. Many of the Black Watch fell back through the ranks of the Seaforths and Argylls. Others fell back several hundred yards. Some of the Highland Light Infantry in reserve, including Lieutenant-Colonel Henry Kelham, the commanding officer, were trampled by the fleeing soldiers.[73]

The chaos was compounded by the fact that no orders were given to the brigade after Wauchope's death. As Wauchope attempted to rally his men and lead an assault on the trenches, he gave orders to his cousin, Lieutenant Arthur G. Wauchope, to extend the brigade to the right where there appeared to be a gap in the Boer defences. Lieutenant Wauchope, before being wounded, was able to relay this order to Lieutenant-Colonel John Coode, commanding the Black Watch. Coode was killed attempting to carry out Wauchope's order. Lieutenant-Colonel Gerald Goff, commanding the Argyll and Sutherland Highlanders, was also killed when he tried to move his men forward. This left Lieutenant-Colonel J. W. Hughes-Hallett as the highest-ranking officer in the Highland Brigade. Hughes-Hallett, unaware that his fellow battalion commanders had fallen, gave orders only to his own men and to those who were now interspersed among them. For nearly nine hours, from just after 0400 hours until 1300 hours, no orders were given to the brigade.

Thus the Highland Brigade became a confused mass of men desperately searching for what little cover they could find. By 0800 hours, as the summer sun began to pound down on their exposed legs, the majority of the Highlanders had found some sort of temporary cover to shield them from the direct fire of the enemy. Without food or water, many remained in these positions for the rest of the day, fearful that any movement would alert the Boers to their whereabouts. Casualties were high.[74] The brigadier as well as two of the battalion commanders were dead and a third lay wounded, incapable of continuing his command. The remaining battalion commander still did not know that he was in command. Methuen wrote, 'The Highland Brigade was of little use to me, during the remainder of the day, greatly owing to the paucity of officers.'[75] Methuen did note, however, that 'the men were ready enough to rally, when asked to do so by any officer'.[76]

All was not lost, however. The Highland Light Infantry had successfully extended, and their commander, Lieutenant-Colonel Henry Kelham, was attempting to bring them forward on the right. In front of Magersfontein Hill, located between the Boer left and centre, mixed parties of Highlanders had destroyed an outpost manned by Scandinavian volunteers. This resulted in a minor breach of the Boer line of defence. A detachment of the Black Watch was able to advance up the slope of the hill. Small parties of the Seaforths, a battalion still relatively intact, were also able to advance up and around the hill under the leadership of Lieutenants R. S. Wilson and E. Cox, and were threatening the Boer rear.[77] In addition, the majority of the British forces had yet to engage the enemy. The Guards Brigade and the Gordons, still in reserve, had yet to be brought forward and the British artillery, which possessed overwhelming superiority, was just now coming into action.

Methuen's orders during the battle seem to have been limited to the general direction of the troop movements. No contingency plans had been drawn up in case the Highlanders failed to breach the Boer trenches. After balloons were launched to gather information on the Boer movements and reports indicated that reinforcements were arriving from Spytfontein and Abon's Dam,[78] Methuen ordered the Gordons forward to support the Highland Brigade at 1100 hours. Otherwise, still recovering from his leg wound, he did little more than watch the battle unfold from his position atop Headquarters' Hill. His heroic displays at Modder River were not, indeed could not be, duplicated at Magersfontein.

Neither the Guards nor the Gordons were in a position to offer immediate help to the faltering Highland Brigade. The location of the Guards was the only feature in the battle which led Methuen to second guess his plan. Specifically, he questioned his decision to begin the Guards' night march at 0000 hours rather than at 1900 hours, the night before.[79] Had he done this, the Guards would have been in a position to advance immediately to exploit the gap in the Boer line that the Highlanders had temporarily created. As it was, the Guards Brigade could do no more than support the Highlanders. Colvile's only orders to his brigade were to prevent it from getting too seriously involved.[80] After Wauchope's assault had failed, Methuen, with few reserves left, did not want Colvile to become committed to an attack from which he, too, could not withdraw his troops.[81] Therefore when the initial assault had failed, the Guards were sent in to stabilize the Highlander lines rather than to attempt another assault. One critic wrote, 'The idea that an attack might turn the tide of battle seems to have vanished from the minds of the divisional staff, although more than half the force had not yet been in action.'[82] Certainly, Methuen was playing it cautiously.

At 0000 hours, 11 December, as the Highlanders were beginning their night advance, Colvile and the Guards Brigade marched out of camp.[83] Well behind, they moved to protect the right flank and the rear of the Highlanders. As the leading battalions marched on to the battlefield, the Scots Guard, in the rear, encountered the same problems of darkness and rain which the Highland Brigade had faced. Soon they lost direction and were forced to return to headquarters. The remaining battalions succeeded in reaching their positions and extended toward the river. As the day wore on, more Guards in the rear line were ordered forward to join the front line until they covered a front of just over one and one half miles.

The cavalry played a small but important role in the battle. The 12th Lancers, like the Guards Brigade, left camp at midnight. They arrived on the battlefield shortly before the Guards. There they joined the 9th Lancers, the mounted infantry and the Royal Horse Artillery which guarded the right flank. In a controversial move, Major-General J. M. Babington, commanding the cavalry, used the 12th Lancers as mounted infantry by ordering them to dismount and push forward in order to prevent the Boers from threatening the Seaforths' right flank. This was accomplished and the Seaforths were protected from a flanking move. The arrival of the Guards, later in the day, allowed Babington to withdraw the Lancers. To their right, the Horse Battery and the 9th Lancers played an important role in keeping the Boers pinned down. The KOYLI held the drift at the extreme right flank of the British force. The right front remained stationary until 1300 hours.

Pole-Carew's 9th Brigade, Rimington's Guides and some of the artillery were situated on the left flank. They were to demonstrate against the railway, provide artillery support for the main assault, protect the left flank from any possible Boer move from Spytfontein, and guard the camp. Like Colvile, Pole-Carew was given orders not to seriously commit his troops to the battle.

The *Times History of the War in South Africa* suggests that Pole-Carew could have played a decisive role in the battle had it not been for Methuen's cautious stance since they were in a position to assault and seize the lower ridge of Magersfontein Hill, just east of the railway.[84] Once in command of the hill, the 9th Brigade, accompanied by the naval gun, could have fired down on the Boer trenches virtually unhindered. However, it is very difficult to substantiate Amery's claim that Pole-Carew could have easily taken this position. Duxbury's research shows that Pole-Carew's actions, for the most part, had little effect on the Boers since there was never a need to reinforce their right flank during the battle.[85] In addition, even Amery realized that this task would have required reinforcement, but failed to emphasize the fact that none was forthcoming. Methuen knew that if the 9th Brigade had advanced, the camp would have been extremely vulnerable to an attack. He realized that even had the British won the battle, if the camp was destroyed the 1st Division would have been forced to retreat and the advance to Kimberley would have been halted. Since Boer reinforcements did arrive from the direction of Spytfontein, Methuen's decision not to allow Pole-Carew to become fully engaged seems to have been the right one.

At 1100 hours Methuen realized that the Highlander front was weakening, and ordered the Gordons to advance in support. Detached from the battalion guarding the divisional transport, six companies of the Gordons, commanded by Lieutenant-Colonel G. T. F. Downman, crossed the open battlefield in a series of rushes. The lines were extended with five paces between each man in 'Tirah style'.[86] They passed through the rear of the dispersed Highlanders rallying some of that brigade to join them. Methuen wrote, 'I saw, as I saw at Dargai, the grand spirit which animates this Regiment. But the trenches, even after the hardest hammering from lyddite and shrapnel were not to be evacuated in daylight.'[87] The first rush came within 290 paces of the Boers where they were forced to fall and find cover.[88] The following rushes likewise halted and, with the last of the reserves now committed, the battle once again came to a standstill. The spirit of the British soldier alone could not bring victory at Magersfontein.

At around 1300 hours, Boer movements once again threatened the Seaforths' right flank. The movements went unobserved by the Guards who failed to react and fill the gap.[89] Hughes-Hallett ordered his men to pull back their right flank, an act which if successful would prevent the advancing Boers from breaking through their lines. Downman, reading Hughes-Hallett's intentions, rose to direct the Gordons to shift themselves to compensate for the Seaforths' manœuvre;[90] however, he fell immediately, mortally wounded. Other Gordon and Seaforth officers attempted to carry out Hughes-Hallett's orders, but their intentions were misunderstood. Many of the soldiers believed that they were being ordered to withdraw. Hughes-Hallett clearly heard the order to retire sounded by some officer.[91] Major Duff, 1st Black Watch, apparently did not. He later wrote to Methuen, 'The story of a retirement so graphically narrated in the *Morning Post* of 9th January is the purest fiction, and emanated from the imagination of some budding war correspondent.'[92] Regardless, by 1330 hours, most of the Brigade began to fall back and did not regroup until about 1530 hours some 1,500 yards from the trenches. The Scots Guards were sent forward to aid in the Highlander retreat.

From the original assault, perhaps only 200 men still remained at the front by nightfall. Too few to advance, they were ordered to fall back, but for reasons unknown they did not move. Colvile, who hoped to continue the assault the following morning, ordered the Guards Brigade to hold their positions through the night. They were reinforced by the Scots Guards.

The troops on both the extreme flanks were likewise ordered to hold their positions. By 1915 hours, all firing had ceased. Methuen could do nothing but wait and hope that the Boers would retire from their trenches as they had at the Modder River. To his dismay, his personal reconnaissance the next morning found the trenches still occupied. Supported by his senior officers,[93] he gave the orders for the retreat.[94] He telegraphed a brief message to Kekewich in Kimberley: 'I am checked.'[95]

Some light skirmishing took place before Methuen was able to reach an armistice with Cronjé on 12 December. Physicians and ambulance units quickly moved on to the battlefield from both sides of the trenches to collect the injured and bury the dead. British casualties approached 1,000, about seven per cent of the entire force.[96] Wauchope, Coode, Goff and Downman were among the many fallen officers. Kelham and Lieutenant-Colonel Codrington were among the many wounded. The Highland Brigade was crippled. More than 75 per cent of the day's casualties came from their ranks. Nearly 40 per cent of the Black Watch, the battalion which led the assault, were dead, wounded or missing. This included 60 per cent of the officers. The Seaforths, who got caught in the Boers' flanking move, also suffered heavily. The casualties to the Guards Brigade were relatively light considering how long they remained on the battlefield. The battalion hardest hit, the 1st Battalion Coldstream, suffered a casualty rate of under eight per cent. Casualties to the other infantry battalions, cavalry regiments and artillery batteries were low. The substantial losses were felt by Scotland and its Highland Brigade. No records were kept which can accurately provide casualty rates for the Boers, but estimates range between 200 and 275, about 25 per cent of the British number.

Under the flag of truce, the Boers directed British ambulances in and around their trenches, helping the British to retrieve their casualties. For this, Methuen was very grateful. As he wrote to his wife, 'Nothing can have been kinder than the Boers letting me bury my dead, and they told my officers they hated fighting us, and were very sorry for us.'[97] Unlike at Belmont, there were no incidents of misbehaviour. Methuen wrote, 'In no case have they fired at my ambulances on which I have had a huge red cross painted, the regulation cross being useless.'[98]

The good feelings between the two opposing forces did not last long, however. At around noon, as the British began to withdraw south towards their camp at the Modder River, the Boer artillery which had remained very quiet during the battle half-heartedly opened fire and shelled the rear guard. The British returned fire and withdrew in 'perfect order'. Methuen's advance to Kimberley had come to an abrupt halt.

THE LESSONS OF MAGERSFONTEIN

In the search for reasons as to why Methuen's attack at Magersfontein failed, it is necessary to analyse several factors of the battle plan and its enactment. We have already seen that Methuen's decision to delay the advance to Kimberley by one week after the Battle of Modder River, as well as his decision to choose the ground in front of Magersfontein Hill as the site for his next encounter, were the correct decisions given the circumstances and limited military information. However, these two decisions did not make the British defeat at Magersfontein inevitable, and in the rest of this chapter I will address the issues which directly concern the events of 10–12 December.

The first issue is that of reconnaissance, and its failure before the Battle of Magersfontein. In general, British reconnaissance, as discussed in the previous chapter, failed throughout South Africa in the early stages of the war because the British had not been properly trained to conduct reconnaissance against a foe armed with modern weapons. Reconnaissance had already failed Methuen at Belmont and at the Modder River. At Magersfontein he had very little information available. He was not aware of the location of his enemy's flanks, he did not know their numbers, nor their exact whereabouts, and he knew little about the ground. All this explains Wauchope's decision to push further ahead towards Magersfontein until his troops, unbeknown to him, had come within 400 yards of the Boer trenches.

The failure of reconnaissance was due to two factors. First, Methuen had few mounted troops, and even fewer mounted troops who were trained scouts. (The cavalry regiments were not trained as professional scouts.) Methuen's only reliable scouts were Rimington's Guides, and there were too few of them to do all that was required. Second, the improved rifle placed in the skilful hands of the mobile Boer made even long-range reconnaissance dangerous. This danger was further aggravated in the area around Magersfontein where there was little cover and several barbed wire obstacles. Indeed, the British were not trained properly to reconnoitre under these conditions, and, if blame must be assigned, it should not to be placed on Methuen or any of his men but on the War Office, which failed to supply and train the necessary troops and provide accurate maps. Caught as he was between the necessity of relieving Kimberley on a timetable caused by political demand from home as well as the real demand of Kimberley's provisions growing sparse, and the inability to gather adequate information about the enemy, Methuen felt that he could not wait. In all likelihood, a further delay would not have brought more information but would simply have given the Boers more time to fortify their left flank and receive reinforcements. Thus he chose correctly to strike when he did.

The second issue which played a role in the failure of the British attack at Magersfontein was Methuen's decision to bombard the Boer position the night before the assault. This issue has been discussed above in detail. It is said the early barrage alerted the Boers to the British plan, eliminating the possibility of surprise. As it was, although the bombardment certainly alerted the Boers to the possibility of an attack at Magersfontein, it did not keep them from being surprised by the night march. Methuen's decision, motivated by his experience at Belmont in which he drove the enemy's artillery from the battlefield, his trust in the uncertain but much-lauded destructiveness of lyddite, his belief in the moral factor of the artillery bombardment, his desire to locate the enemy's artillery, which his reconnaissance had failed to do, and Buller's support, was under these circumstances, the right one.

The third issue to be addressed is Methuen's use of the artillery at Magersfontein. The British artillery was used first to bombard the enemy position before the battle and second to provide cover after the Highlander assault failed. It was rarely used to support an infantry or cavalry offensive, as in the case of the Seaforths' penetration of the Boer line at the Scandinavian post. Even in this case, the artillery had to stop when it exposed its own troops to 'friendly fire'. The British artillery had not yet learned its proper role in modern warfare. Aldershot still taught that the artillery was more important for providing a defensive covering fire than for assisting the offensive bayonet charge.[99] In addition, although the artillery provided necessary cover fire for the British infantry during the day, the actual expenditure of rounds was very low by contemporary continental standards.[100] It was not until 1900 that the British commanders in South Africa were instructed to use the artillery not just to bombard an entrenchment before an infantry attack but also to continue to fire the guns until the moment before the assault began.[101] Thus, although Methuen did not use his artillery well, he used it as any other British commander at the time would have done.[102]

The fourth issue is Methuen's night march and its role in his failure at Magersfontein. Although the night march has been discussed in detail, a few additional comments need to be made in regard to this specific scenario. The night march, as judged by Methuen, was the safest way to get the Highland Brigade within bayonet range of the Boer lines and conduct a frontal assault. Thus, the night march was considered a necessity for achieving a decisive victory. Colvile had issued a memo by Buller to the Guards Brigade which noted that 'Boers will probably retire after a volley or two when charged upon.'[103] Methuen did not want to allow the Boers to retreat, relatively unscathed, just to meet them again at another site of their choosing. And although many critics have questioned his use of this tactic, none has offered an effective alternative. Lacking the necessary mounted troops to conduct a proper flanking move and cognizant of the lack of cover on the battlefield, Methuen's choice was the best one. Considering the conditions, the night march was a remarkable success, taking the Boers almost completely by surprise.[104] After his capture at Paardeberg, Major R. Albrecht, a German volunteer who organized the Orange Free State's artillery and advised Cronjé at Magersfontein, told Major Laurence Drummond, Methuen's ADC, that the British surprised the Boers at Magersfontein and had a very good chance of winning the battle.[105]

Methuen's only error in deploying the night march was in not properly preparing the men for the advance. They did not have sufficient rest and few had the chance to eat before it began. As a result, their fatigue increased dramatically as the day wore on. As the editor of the official German account of the war in South Africa wrote, 'Well-fed troops are far better fitted to undergo the moral and physical exertions incidental to a battle than are those which are placed in a position in which the very greatest demands will be made upon their endurance.'[106] Methuen's haste in getting the men on to the battlefield, a result of a delay in decision-making caused by the bad weather, cost dearly.

A fifth significant factor for the failure at Magersfontein concerns Methuen's deployment and use of his reserves. The reserves were prevented from providing immediate assistance by being placed too far behind the Highlanders. This proved disastrous. When the initial assault failed, the Highlanders fell to the ground in a desperate search for cover. They would not rise without immediate reinforcement. Methuen had no choice but to send in the Guards as support, defying what has since called become a modern military cliché: 'never reinforce failure'.[107] The Guards did not attempt to do anything but prop up the faltering line.[108] As evidenced by their five per cent casualty rate, they made no serious attempt to force the Boer lines.

In fact, the Guards Brigade should not have been used simply as a reserve but should have supported the initial Highlander assault. Frontal attacks could still have succeeded but they required both sufficient numbers and the willingness of the commander to sacrifice a portion of his troops. It was not only the Guards who were unavailable for the initial assault, but also the 9th Brigade, which was used primarily to guard the left flank and the camp. The Gordons too, half of which were used to guard the baggage, were under-utilized. Thus Methuen used barely a third of his men to attempt to dislodge an enemy which numbered roughly twice that of the assaulting force – a serious miscalculation (though he was of course unaware of the precise numbers of the enemy).

Methuen's decision as to the Guards' deployment can only be understood in the context of prevailing military regulation and theory.[109] He was known to carry *The Soldier's Pocketbook*, written by his former commander and the Commander-in-Chief of the British Army, Field Marshal Lord Garnet Wolseley, and certainly knew army regulations. His use of the reserves followed the official British line, which had been successful at Tel-el-Kebir and in other colonial battles. His decision may have also been influenced by Colvile who opposed early reinforcement.[110] Unfortunately, theory regarding the deployment of the reserves had yet to be updated for coping with an enemy armed with modern firepower.

Thus Methuen erroneously decided to hold back a reserve rather than to throw the bulk of his force against the Boer trenches. Like most of his fellow officers, he subscribed to an idea which W. von Scherff called the 'false theory of the necessity of holding back the reserves'.[111] Von Scherff advocated the use of *all* the available troops by the commander to reach his objective. In a period when military strategy was changing as a result of the new technology and many writers had begun to decry the frontal assault, maintaining that the 'spade beats the rifle', others such as von Scherff and Hippolyte Langlois, in anticipation of the tactics of the First World War, still advocated 'the great blow'. The advantage of entrenchment which the Boers possessed had to be countered by the sheer magnitude of firepower directed at their front.

Neither Methuen nor any of the British senior officers in South Africa at the start of the war, however, were ready to make the necessary sacrifices which the 'great blow' required. They had been participants in colonial battles such as Tel-el-Kebir and Omdurman where enemy losses outnumbered their own by 200 to one. To force an enemy armed with modern equipment from a strong position required a great risk and, as Langlois wrote, there existed a utopian belief that the British could succeed without it.[112] Methuen, a highly sensitive commander who took the loss of each man personally, was not ready to commit a large force to a great risk. Except for the Black Watch and the Seaforths, British losses at Magersfontein were comparatively light, bearing in mind the Franco-Prussian War of 1870–71, in which the German infantry suffered 25 per cent losses at Mars la Tour and nearly 30 per cent at St Privat.[113] The Austrian General Staff expected British losses in South Africa to be on the average 26 per cent;[114] at Magersfontein they approached seven per cent.

A sixth factor in the British defeat at Magersfontein can be linked to the War Office's failure to prepare the individual soldier for modern battle. As the size of the battlefield grew larger and the duration of the battle longer, the junior officer increasingly lost control over his men, who were not trained or educated to act independently. Those British soldiers who had battle experience most likely had only seen volley fire. Whereas the individual Boer was a potent force, the individual British soldier still had much to learn about his weapon and his role. This was a defect over which Methuen had no control.

There is one final explanation of the British failure to drive the Boers from Magersfontein, for which Methuen may be fairly indicted. Methuen constructed a suitable plan to break through the enemy's lines. However, once that plan failed, he did little to direct the overall course of the battle. There seems to have been no contingency plan in the event of the Highlanders failing in their attack. Methuen's official orders sent to Buller make no reference to one, and the relative inaction of the British force following the Highlander assault suggests that no such plan existed. It could be argued that Methuen had done his job. As one writer put it: 'When his men had been brought within striking distance of the foe the General's business was done. The rest of the work and of the responsibility devolved upon his subordinates, the brigadiers.'[115] However, Methuen himself never supplied this answer to cover up for what he considered to be his error, and he accepted full responsibility for the battle. For the failure to devise a contingency plan before the battle, or to amend the plan after the initial reverse, there can be no excuse. Whatever blind faith Methuen had in the capability of his men, he still should have prepared for the worst.

The *Sunday Chronicle*, in retrospect, saw Methuen's assault on Magersfontein as a lost cause, fated from the outset:

> The capture of Magersfontein was impossible. So much has been tacitly acknowledged by Lord Roberts, who it is worth noting never even attempted it. Lord Roberts turned Magersfontein – he did not assault it; and he was able to turn it just because he had what Lord Methuen never had – an overwhelming force of cavalry. It needed all French's horses all French's men to scare that rugged old limpet Cronje [*sic*] from the secure shelter of his fastness. Even so, Cronje [*sic*] died hard. The tale of Lord Roberts's losses around that terrible laager at Paardeberg is still to tell. And Lord Roberts,

be it remembered, outnumbered Cronje [*sic*] by ten to one. It is doubtful whether at any time Lord Methuen had before Magersfontein as many soldiers as the Boers had behind it.[116]

In fact, Methuen was not given an impossible task. Indeed, many believed that he had been given an easy task, and he was attacked publicly and privately for his failure to relieve Kimberley. Lansdowne eventually called for his censure, which was unjust. Oddly enough, newspapers such as *The Times* and the *Daily News* remained calm, at least for the time being, blaming no one, praising the brave attempt and respectfully mourning the dead.

To speculate on whether the advance at Magersfontein would have succeeded if the Highlanders had deployed earlier or if the Seaforths had been able to reach the Boer rear offers no reward. Many writers suggest that 'a little confidence would have probably saved the day'.[117] Still, the 1st Division, even with its limited resources, did come close to defeating the Boers at Magersfontein and hence opening the route to Kimberley. Lord Roberts, in time, would relieve Kimberley. With his superior resources he did not have to undertake what Methuen did, that is, to force the Boers from their strong entrenchments. He would be able to use French's cavalry to go around the enemy at Magersfontein – something Methuen could not do. In February at Paardeberg, the British would meet Cronjé's force once again. Lord Kitchener, commanding two infantry divisions, eight battalions of mounted infantry and other troops (a force twice as large as Methuen's) with the additional advantage of nearby reinforcement from Roberts' two other infantry divisions and one cavalry division, would defeat the disheartened Boers with a frontal attack, but only after great loss. Kitchener was to emerge a hero (although Roberts was not too pleased with his command), while Methuen's reputation was tarnished.[118]

The news from South Africa in December 1899 was bad from all fronts. In the west, the advance to Kimberley had failed. Lord Methuen and the 1st Division returned to their base camp at the Modder River and awaited further reinforcements. Several, including Lord Milner[119] and Lord Roberts,[120] questioned Methuen's ability to hold out and urged a withdrawal back to the Orange River. Two days earlier, on 9 December, Gatacre, in the centre, suffered a serious reverse at Stormberg. The British were forced to retreat to Molteno, and Stormberg would not be theirs for another three months. And then, on 15 December, 'Black Week' came to a climax. In the east, General Buller was defeated at Colenso and was forced to retreat to Chieveley. All three British armies serving in South Africa suffered major defeats within one week.[121]

As the year came to a close, the British were forced to make some major changes. Roberts, accompanied by Kitchener, was sent out to South Africa to take over Buller's command. Buller remained, but his status was greatly reduced. Gatacre was sacked and there was debate as to whether Methuen should suffer the same fate. The 6th Division was mobilized and a 7th Division was readied for reserve. Wolseley and the War Office, under intense pressure from the Secretary of War, Lansdowne – and also from the British public – issued orders to call up the Army Reserve, to raise a force of mounted infantry, and to allow for the draft of the volunteer forces.

The one thing Wolseley could not do was to bring the British army into the twentieth century. The Battle of Magersfontein demonstrated that the bravest and the best-drilled troops could not defeat a well-entrenched enemy equipped with modern weaponry. British officers trained in colonial warfare would have to throw out Wolseley's *The Soldier's Pocketbook* and learn new strategies in the field to overcome the challenges posed by modernity. To win the war, the British officer could not wait for slow military reform back in England: he needed an immediate change in military thinking. Lord Esher, who played a major role in the reform of the army after the war, realized this, writing just after Methuen's repulse at Magersfontein: 'This war will do two things – change our whole military system in England, and alter military tactics throughout the world. The old war of "sieges" will begin again. It is clear that a direct attack with modern weapons against good and brave men entrenched is impossible.'[122] The officers remaining in South Africa, including Methuen, simply had to do the best they could, making adjustments as they went along. Methuen himself would have more than two years to redeem his military reputation.

NOTES

1. The 6th Division was commanded by Lieutenant-General Sir T. Kelly-Kenny.
2. Wauchope, who served in the Second Ashanti War, the Egyptian expedition of 1882 (where he had fought alongside Methuen at Tel-el-Kebir), the Nile Expedition of 1884–85 and the Sudan Campaign of 1898, was much beloved in his native Scotland, and came within 690 votes of defeating Gladstone in Midlothian in 1892. See John Morley, *The Life of William Ewart Gladstone* (New York: Macmillan and Co., 1903), III, 492.
3. *The War in South Africa, a German Official Account*, trans. W. H. Walters, (New York: E. P. Dutton, 1904), p. 91.
4. Although in the hospital Methuen did not officially hand over his command to Colvile until 2 Dec. He reclaimed it on 6 Dec. L. S. Amery (ed.), *The Times History of The War in South Africa 1899–1902* (London: Sampson Low, Marston & Co., 1907), II, 389.

5. P. S. Methuen to M. E. Methuen, 8 June 1900, Methuen Papers, Wiltshire Records Office, Trowbridge.
6. See Alfred Kinnear, *To Modder River with Methuen* (Bristol: J. W. Arrowsmith, 1900), p. 132; Amery, *Times History*, II, 391; *The War in South Africa, a German Official Account*, p. 85; and, George Duxbury, *The Battle of Magersfontein*, Battles of the Anglo-Boer War, 1899–1902, no. 9 (Johannesburg: National Museum of Military History, 1979), p. 14.
7. See W. Baring Pemberton, *Battles of the Boer War* (Philadelphia: Dufour Editions, 1964), p. 80.
8. Amery, *Times History*, II, 390.
9. This view is expressed in *The War in South Africa, a German Official Account*, p. 85. And, L. B. Oatts, *Proud Heritage* (London: Thomas Nelson & Sons, 1963), p. 54.
10. Foster H. E. Cunliffe, *History of the Boer War* (London: Methuen, 1901–4), p. 219.
11. 'Report of His Majesty's Commissioners appointed to Inquire into the Military Preparations and Other Matters connected with the War in South Africa', 1904: cd 1790, XL, 16544-26.
12. Kekewich had served in Perak, Sudan and Burma.
13. Methuen Diary, 3 December 1899, Methuen Papers, Wiltshire Records Office.
14. One author went as far as to say that the defeat of Black Week was due 'more to political misdirection and the influence of a supposed political necessity than to blunders in military strategy of tactics'. A belief held by both Methuen and Buller. See Algernon Marshall Methuen, *The Tragedy of South Africa* (London: Methuen, 1905), p. 87.
15. P. S. Methuen to M. E. Methuen, 22 Dec. 1899, Methuen Papers, Wiltshire Records Office. See also, Rayne Kruger, *Good-Bye Dolly Gray* (New York: J. B. Lippincott Co., 1960), p. 124.
16. A. Mahan, *The Story of the War in South Africa* (New York: Collier, 1900), p. 162.
17. Amery, *Times History*, II, 392.
18. Filson Young, *The Relief of Mafeking* (London: Methuen & Co., 1900), p. 86.
19. Duxbury, *The Battle of Magersfontein*, p. 14.
20. Ibid., p. 15.
21. W. Baring Pemberton estimated that the Boer forces at the Battle of Magersfontein numbered 6,000–7,000. Pemberton, *Battles of the Boer War*, p. 81. The *Official History of the War in South Africa* presented three views, the lowest of which was 4,000; the highest, 7,000. Frederick Maurice and M. H. Grant, *(Official) History of the War in South Africa, 1899–1902* (London: Hurst & Blackwood, 1906–10), p. 308. Leo Amery gave no estimate but suggested that only about 4,500 Boers took part in the battle. Amery, *Times History*, II, 395–6. G. R. Duxbury, former Director of the South Africa Museum of National History, put the total number of Cronjé's forces between 8,000 and 8,500. He further added that one-third of these were dismounted due to the fatigue caused by the prior three battles. Therefore, many positioned away from Magersfontein Hill, were not available to take part in the battle. Duxbury, *The Battle of Magersfontein*, p. 15.
22. Young, *Relief of Mafeking*, p. 73.
23. 'Report of His Majesty's Commissioners appointed to Inquire into the Military Preparations and Other Matters connected with the War in South Africa', 1904: cd 1790, XL, 14173.
24. P. S. Methuen to F. Stephenson, 19 Dec. 1899, Methuen Papers, Wiltshire Records Office.
25. As an expert witness, Methuen had supplied information regarding horsemanship, horsemastery, and the quality of horses fit for military service to various War Office Committees including *The Committee on the Number of Horses to be Allowed to Officers Serving in the Field*, 1887.

26. P. S. Methuen to H. E. Wood, 16 May 1914, Methuen Papers, Wiltshire Records Office.

27. 'Report of His Majesty's Commissioners appointed to Inquire into the Military Preparations and Other Matters connected with the War in South Africa', 1904: cd 1790, XL, 15184.

28. P. S. Methuen to M. E. Methuen, 10 Dec. 1899, Methuen Papers, Wiltshire Records Office.

29. The Brigade was accompanied by 'G' Battery RHA, the 18th, 62nd, 65th (Howitzer) and 75th Batteries RFA, as well as a Balloon Section, and some Royal Engineers.

30. The reserve force included the 12th Lancers, some Royal Engineers, and the medical and ammunition units.

31. P. S. Methuen to GOC, 13 Dec. 1899, Methuen Papers, Wiltshire Records Office.

32. Ibid.

33. The British would not learn until the First World War that even the most intense and prolonged bombardment against a fortified enemy would have only a minor effect. See William McElwee, *The Art of War: Waterloo to Mons* (Bloomington, IN: Indiana University Press, 1974), p. 165. C. E. Callwell, writing well after the South African War, rightly concluded that the use of the artillery preparation against an entrenched enemy no longer played a significant role in the outcome of a battle. However, he still believed that the effect on morale was great. Colonel Charles Edward Callwell, *The Tactics of To-day*, 2nd edn (London: W. Blackwood & Sons, 1909), p. 15.

34. P. S. Methuen to GOC, 10–11 Dec. 1899, rewritten 15 Feb. 1900, WO 32/7966, Public Records Office, Kew; and, P. Methuen to F. Stephenson, 19 Dec. 1899, Methuen Papers, Wiltshire Records Office.

35. The function of the artillery was to destroy the enemy's artillery first and then to strike at the enemy's infantry. See Jean De Bloch, *The Future of War in its Technical, Economic and Political Relations* (Boston: Ginn & Co., 1902; repr., New York: Garland, 1972), p. 17; and, Charles Edward Callwell and John Headlam, *The History of the Royal Artillery* (Woolwich: Royal Artillery Institution, 1940), p. 351. Some strategists like C. E. Callwell realized that the days of the classic artillery duel were over. Callwell, *The Tactics of To-day*, p. 12.

36. R. Buller to P. S. Methuen, 6 Dec. 1899, Buller Papers, 7065M/SS4/21, Devonshire Records Office.

37. Duxbury, *The Battle of Magersfontein*, p. 23.

38. The ammunition depot and most of the Boer supply were moved to the Boer laagers after president Steyn's visit. From 3–7 December, President Steyn attempted to heal the growing rift between Transvaalers and Free Staters, created by the retreat at Modder River. See Amery, *Times History*, II, 384.

39. *The War in South Africa, A German Official Account*, p. 87.

40. De la Rey did not actually fight in the Battle of Magersfontein, as he was reconnoitring Kimberley at the time.

41. Duxbury, *The Battle of Magersfontein*, p. 8.

42. Ibid., p. 10.

43. Amery, *Times History*, II, 386, as cited in Johannes Meintjes, *De la Rey* (Johannesburg: Hugh Keartland, 1966), p. 129.

44. See *The War in South Africa, a German Official Account*, pp. 88–9; Amery, *Times History*, II, 386–8; and, Duxbury, *The Battle of Magersfontein*, pp. 11–12.

45. General Charles Warren and his staff did not arrive until 14 December. As a result of the disaster at Colenso, the 5th Division was ordered to Natal.

46. Julian Ralph, *Towards Pretoria* (New York: Frederick A. Stokes, 1900), p. 175.

47. 'Report of His Majesty's Commissioners appointed to Inquire into the Military Preparations and Other Matters connected with the War in South Africa', 1904: cd 1790, XL, 15184.

48. H. Colvile to CSO, 1st Division, 12 Dec. 1899, WO 32/7870, Public Records Office.
49. Colonel C. W. H. Douglas, Methuen's ADC and Chief of Staff, proposed that the Highlanders charge the Boer trenches. Later as Major-General, Douglas commanded the 9th Brigade. P. S. Methuen to M. E. Methuen, 29 Dec. 1899, Wiltshire Records Office.
50. P. S. Methuen to GOC, 10–11 Dec. 1899, rewritten 15 Feb. 1900, WO 32/7966, Public Records Office.
51. See, for example, Thomas Pakenham, *The Boer War* (New York: Random House, 1979), p. 208; and Farwell, *The Great Anglo-Boer War*, p. 103.
52. Maurice and Grant, *(Official) History of the War in South Africa, 1899–1902*, p. 311.
53. Amery, *Times History*, II, 397.
54. 'Battle of Magersfontein, Dec. 1899. A Contemporary Letter', *Journal of the Society for Army Historical Research* 20 (1941): 199.
55. [D'Etechegoyen] Ex-Lieutenant of General de Villebois-Mareuil, *Ten Months in the Field with the Boers* (London: William Heinemann, 1901), p. 21.
56. P. S. Methuen to GOC, 10–11 Dec. 1899, rewritten 15 Feb. 1900, WO 32/7966, Public Records Office.
57. P. S. Methuen to M. E. Methuen, 22 Dec. 1899, Methuen Papers, Wiltshire Records Office.
58. George Douglas, *The Life of Major-General Wauchope* (London: Hodder & Stoughton, 1904), p. 398.
59. As a conciliatory gesture, Major Duff sent a confidential report he wrote on the Battle of Magersfontein to Methuen in September 1903. A. G. Duff, 'Confidential-Magersfontein', 6 March 1900, Methuen Papers, Wiltshire Records Office.
60. Arthur G. Wauchope, *A Short History of the Black Watch, 1725–1907* (London: Blackwood, 1908).
61. Douglas, *The Life of Major-General Wauchope*, p. 402.
62. P. S. Methuen to GOC, 10–11 Dec. 1899, rewritten 15 Feb. 1900, WO 32/7966, Public Records Office.
63. Maurice and Grant, *(Official) History of the War in South Africa, 1899–1902*, p. 317.
64. According to Amery, two rifles were accidentally fired at the start of the advance. The Boers were not alerted. See Amery, *Times History*, II, 397.
65. Amery, *Times History*, II, 399.
66. Lieutenant-Colonel J. W. Hughes-Hallett, commanding officer of the Seaforths, said that the deployment could have come about 200 yards earlier but there was some confusion among the leading battalion. P. S. Methuen to GOC, 10–11 Dec. 1899, rewritten 15 Feb. 1900, WO 32/7966, Public Records Office.
67. R. L. Wallace, *The Australians at the Boer War* (Canberra: Australian Government Public Service, 1976), p. 74.
68. Meintjes, *De la Rey*, p. 130.
69. Duxbury, *The Battle of Magersfontein*, p. 25.
70. P. S. Methuen to GOC, 13 Dec. 1899, Methuen Papers, Wiltshire Records Office.
71. P. S. Methuen to M. E. Methuen, 14 Dec. 1899, Methuen Papers, Wiltshire Records Office.
72. In Methuen's dispatch to Buller after the battle, Methuen rhetorically asked why Wauchope did not deploy sooner when Benson advised and why bayonets were not ready. This question was edited out of the official dispatch. P. S. Methuen to R. Buller, 13 Dec. 1899, WO 32/7870, Public Records Office.
73. Kelham survived the battle.
74. The majority of British soldiers who were killed or were wounded at the Battle of Magersfontein were hit in the first hour of the battle not as they attempted to assault the trenches but as they attempted to fall back. See B. F. S. Baden-Powell, *War in*

      Practice (London: Isbister & Co., 1903), p. 64.

75. P. S. Methuen to GOC, 13 Dec. 1899, Methuen Papers, Wiltshire Records Office.
76. Ibid.
77. Many sources suggest that this advance was stopped by none other than Cronjé, who purportedly got lost during the night and found himself near the rear of Magersfontein Hill with only his staff. Approximately 100 Seaforths led by Lieutenant Wilson were caught between the Boer fire and British artillery fire and were forced to surrender. Both Amery and Duxbury suggest that had these men got through, Magersfontein may have fallen. Since Wilson's movement can not be accurately traced, it is impossible to prove or disprove that theory. See Amery, *Times History*, II, 402–3; and, *The War in South Africa, A German Official Account*, pp. 102–3. For a refutation of this coincidence, see Duxbury, *The Battle of Magersfontein*, p. 27.
78. P. S. Methuen to GOC, 13 Dec. 1899, Methuen Papers, Wiltshire Records Office.
79. Ibid.
80. H. Colvile to CSO, 1st Division, 12 Dec. 1899, WO 32/7870, Public Records Office.
81. Maurice and Grant, *(Official) History of the War in South Africa, 1899–1902*, p. 324.
82. *The War in South Africa, a German Official Account*, p. 105.
83. The Grenadier and the Scots Guards followed the two battalions of the Coldstream Guards.
84. Amery, *Times History*, II, 409.
85. Duxbury, *The Battle of Magersfontein*, p. 30.
86. Lieutenant-Colonel A. D. G. Gardyne, *The Life of a Regiment: The History of the Gordon Highlanders* (London: 1939; Leo Cooper, 1972), III, 100.
87. P. S. Methuen to GOC, 13 Dec. 1899, Methuen Papers, Wiltshire Records Office.
88. Maurice and Grant, *(Official) History of the War in South Africa, 1899–1902*, pp. 326–7.
89. I have found no source which adequately explains the failure of the Guards to notice the threat to the Seaforths' right flank or the failure to relay the information to the Guards.
90. Amery writes that Downman simply thought Hughes-Hallett was ordering a retreat. See Amery, *Times History*, II, 411. In Gardyne's regimental history, he cites Captain Towse, Gordon Highlanders, 'I saw Downman; he came running along the line from the left giving the order to "swing back the right".' See Gardyne, *The Life of a Regiment*, p. 103.
91. T. W. Hughes-Hallett to CSO, 1st Division, 13 Dec. 1899, WO 32/7870, Public Records Office.
92. A. G. Duff to P. S. Methuen, 'Confidential–Magersfontein', 6 March 1900, Methuen Papers, Wiltshire Records Office.
93. Major-General H. Colvile was the only senior officer to object. See H. E. Colvile, *The Works of the Ninth Division in South Africa in 1900* (London: Arnold, 1901), p. 15.
94. P. S. Methuen to GOC, 13 Dec. 1899, Methuen Papers, Wiltshire Records Office.
95. Walter A. J. O'Meara, *Kekewich in Kimberley* (London: Medici Society, 1926), p. 88.
96. GOCC to SSW, 14 Dec. 1899, No. 1816, WO 108, South Africa Telegrams, Public Records Office.

List of Casualties at Magersfontein, 10–12 December 1899

	officers/men killed	officers/men wounded	men missing
RHA 'G' Battery	–	2/4	–
Cavalry Brigade staff	–	1/0	–
9th Lancers	0/1	0/9	–
12th Lancers	0/3	0/17	–
2nd KOYLI, MI	1/0	1/3	–
1st Northumberland Fusiliers, MI	1/0	–	–

1st Bn. Loyal N. Lancashire Regiment, MI	–	0/1	–
Australian Artillery	–	1/0	–
18th Battery RFA	–	0/2	–
62nd Battery RFA	–	0/2	–
75th Battery RFA	–	0/1	–

List of Casualties at Magersfontein, 10–12 December 1899 cont.

3rd Bn. Grenadier Guards	0/1	0/3	–
1st Bn. Coldstream Guards	0/10	5/46	0/7
2nd Bn. Coldstream Guards	1/1	0/23	0/1
1st Bn. Scots Guards	–	0/2	–
Highland Brigade Staff	1/0	2/0	–
2nd Bn. Royal Highlanders	6/62	11/183	0/89
2nd Bn. Seaforth Highlanders	4/34	7/139	1/26
1st Bn. Highland LI	2/10	7/70	0/6
1st Bn. Argyll and Suth. High.	3/20	4/61	0/3
1st Bn. Gordon Highlanders	3/3	2/35	–
1st Bn. York and Lancashire Regt	–	0/8	–
2nd Bn. KOYLI	–	0/8	–
RAMC	–	1/0	1/0
South African Reserve	–	0/2	–

97. P. S. Methuen to M. E. Methuen, 14 Dec. 1899, Methuen Papers, Wiltshire Record Office.

98. P. S. Methuen to GOC, 13 Dec. 1899, Methuen Papers, Wiltshire Records Office.

99. F. N. Maude, 'Military Training and Modern Weapons,' *Contemporary Review* 77 (1900): 319.

100. *The War in South Africa, A German Official Account*, pp. 118–19. 'G' Battery fired 1,179 rounds; 18th Battery, 940; 62nd Battery, 1,000; 75th Battery, 721. Callwell and Headlam, *History of the Royal Artillery*, p. 351.

101. 'Notes for Guidance in South African Warfare', issued 26 Jan. 1900, by Lord Kitchener, Wiltshire Records Office.

102. Long's performance at Colenso, only a few days afterwards, further demonstrated that, tactically, the British artillery had failed to enter the twentieth century.

103. Memorandum on Field Training by R. Buller issued by Major-General Sir H. E. Colvile to the Infantry Brigade, 12 Nov. 1899. *Official Records of the Guards Brigade in South Africa* (London: J. J. Keliher & Co., 1904).

104. The Boers did not see the British advance during the night. In fact, in a gap between the kopjes, British soldiers walked right past Boer guards without seeing them or being seen. G. H. De Villebois-Mareuil, *War Notes* (London: A. & C. Black, 1901), entry of 24 Jan. 1900.

105. Albrecht also told Drummond that the lyddite bombardment did no harm. P. S. Methuen to M. E. Methuen, 3 March 1900, Wiltshire Records Office.

106. *The War in South Africa, A German Official Account*, p. 115.

107. John Keegan, *The Face of Battle* (New York: Vintage, 1976), p. 106.

108. Colvile must share some of the responsibility. Although ordered not to get into a situation from which he could not get out, he did have a great deal of latitude. He made very poor use of the Brigade.

109. *The War in South Africa, a German Official Account*, p. 114.

110. Tactical Directions issued by Major-General Sir H. E. Colvile to the Infantry Brigade, 16 Nov. 1899. *Official Records of the Guards Brigade in South Africa*.

111. W. von Scherff, *The New Tactics of Infantry* (Kansas: Spooner, 1891), p. 26.

112. Hippolyte Langlois, *Lessons from Two Recent Wars* (London: HMSO, 1909), p. 85.

113. Von Heydebreck, 'What Has the Boer War to Teach Us', *Journal of the Royal United Services Institute* 47 (March 1903): 319.
114. Ibid.
115. [Hubert], *Sunday Chronicle* (London), 22 March 1902.
116. Ibid.
117. Young, *Relief of Mafeking*, p. 89.
118. After the war, Piet Cronjé told Methuen that the Boers lost 115 men at Magersfontein and only 70 at Paardeberg. P. S. Methuen to W. Nicholson, 12 Dec. 1908, Methuen Papers, Wiltshire Records Office.
119. A. Milner to R. Buller, 22 Dec. 1899, WO 132/24, Public Records Office.
120. F. S. Roberts to R. Buller, 23 Dec. 1899, WO 105/13/T/8/2, Public Records Office.
121. General Charles Warren and his staff arrived in Cape Town the day before the Battle of Colenso.
122. M. V. Brett (ed.), *Journals and Letters of Reginald Viscount Esher* (London: Nicholson & Watson, 1934), p. 249.

PART THREE

The Restoration of a Career

7

Restoring a Name

On 12 December 1899 Lord Methuen, accompanied by the 1st Division and the Highland Brigade, returned to camp at Modder River having suffered a physical and moral defeat at Magersfontein the day before. The British advance had failed and, as a result, Kimberley remained in a state of siege. Politicians and journalists questioned whether Methuen's force was still strong enough to hold its position since its supply line was vulnerable to a Boer attack. Methuen believed that his position was not in any immediate danger. General Sir Redvers Buller, the Commander-in-Chief of the British forces in South Africa, showing confidence in his subordinate, ordered him to remain at the Modder River, protect his line of communications, i.e. the Western Railway, and do nothing to risk his command. Methuen was told not to make a move until further reinforcement could bolster his inadequate force. Another attempt to break through the Boer lines and free Kimberley was ruled out. Meanwhile, Buller exchanged telegrams with the War Office. At issue was not just the 1st Division's position on the Modder but also Methuen's future in South Africa.

This chapter will continue the narrative of Methuen's command from mid December 1899 through June 1900. It will address several issues, including the reaction in England to the British defeats of 'Black Week', Methuen's new role under Lord Roberts' command, the restoration of confidence in Methuen, and his advance into the Orange Free State. It will demonstrate that Roberts' decision to keep Methuen in South Africa was the correct one.

'BLACK WEEK'

As we have noted in Chapter 6, the war in South Africa was not going well for the British in December 1899. The advances of all three armies had been halted. In the northern Cape Colony, Gatacre and his small force, attempting to seize Stormberg Junction, got lost during their night march on 9 December and stumbled across an undermanned Boer laager. The tired British soldiers, without a battle plan or knowledge of what they were up against, fell back after a feeble attempt to defeat the Boers. Gatacre retreated to Molteno only to learn of the surprising disaster to his force. Although only 29 of his men had been killed, remarkably, over 600 men, 30 per cent of his total force, had been left behind in the confusion. Abandoned by their officers, they had surrendered to the enemy. Neither Gatacre nor any of his junior officers seem to have noticed their disappearance during the retreat.

Methuen's defeat at Magersfontein two days later counted as the second disaster of 'Black Week'. Coming on the heels of Gatacre's reverse, Methuen's defeat increased the urgency for Buller to score a decisive victory over the enemy and thus regain momentum. His soldiers in South Africa and the civilians back at home were in desperate need of some good news to restore their morale. A timely victory would also re-establish the credentials of Buller as well as those of the entire Wolseley Ring in the eyes of Lord Lansdowne and the War Office. Buller, in the east, was thus forced by political exigency to relieve General White's besieged Natal Field Force held up in Ladysmith.[1]

On 15 December Buller attempted to force the passage of the Tugela River near Colenso and thus open up the route to Ladysmith. Colenso, even more than the battles of Magersfontein and Modder River, displayed the disastrous results of employing traditional tactics against an enemy armed with modern weapons. Major-General Arthur Hart's Irish Brigade, misdirected by an African guide, was caught in close order advancing on the enemy. Once the initial advance failed, the Irish were unable to penetrate Boer lines because of the inability of small groups and individuals to function in unison without the direction of a senior officer. Colonel Charles Long, commanding Buller's artillery, was, like Hart, a prisoner of outdated tactics. His faith in the British soldier and, more importantly, his lack of experience in modern warfare, persuaded him to advance the artillery to within a thousand yards of the enemy and into the Boer fire-zone. Once there, enveloped by the fire of Boer rifles and incapable of rescue, the guns were lost.

Another example of British unpreparedness for modern warfare, demonstrated by tactical error, was Buller's decision to leave headquarters and attempt to conduct the course of the battle from the field. A general, personally engaged in a limited action, cannot be cognizant of the details of everything that is going on around him and therefore is likely to make broad decisions based on his own experience, as Buller did in his decision to withdraw at Colenso. A general in such a position is very difficult to communicate with and therefore cannot properly co-ordinate the operations of the battle. This, the third British defeat in one week was devastating. Casualties at Colenso exceeded 1,100 and, even more exhausting to morale back home, ten guns were abandoned by the British.[2] Louis Botha, commanding the Boer forces at Colenso, lost only eight men.

The defeats of 'Black Week' sent shock waves through London. *The Times* declared that this was the worst disaster to hit Britain since the Indian Mutiny.[3] No one in England, even the most alert military critic, could have anticipated the events in South Africa; everyone looked for answers. Challenges to the military system in general appeared in learned journals and daily newspapers alike. Reforms for training, for recruiting and for administering the army were suggested by both experts and novices. Traditional tactics and strategy became suspect, with the suitability of current weapons and the cavalry for use in modern warfare being brought into question. Debates alone, however, would not affect the immediate outcome of the war: decisive action was needed.

The Government did not sit idly by and await the results of these debates. It disassociated itself from the setbacks and took action to restore British authority in South Africa. The War Office, under the leadership of Lansdowne, forced Wolseley's hand. Methuen and Gatacre were to be singled out as scapegoats. On 13 December news of Lansdowne's decision reached South Africa. Sir Charles Warren and the 5th Division were to proceed to the Modder front where Warren would take over Methuen's command. To Warren, Wolseley candidly wrote, 'I look to Sir Redvers Buller and you to put an end to this folly. Our men and Regimental Officers have done splendidly. Our Generals so far have been our weak point.'[4] Buller was informed by Lansdowne that Methuen and Gatacre were to be superseded at once. They were to retreat and avoid further confrontations with the enemy. They were to be assigned responsibilities no greater than that of protecting the lines of communications.[5] On 18 December, three days after Colenso, Lansdowne again telegraphed Buller, this time without Wolseley's knowledge: Buller's name was added to the list of scapegoats and he, too, was to be superseded.

Buller was no fool. His own failure at Colenso had completed the British humiliation of 'Black Week', and he realized that his position in South Africa was precarious at best. Not since the siege of Khartoum and the untimely death of Charles Gordon had the English people been so manipulated by the Government, capitalists and the press in support of a war. This outside interference which had dictated Buller's campaign from the start now threatened his career. Since his appointment six months earlier, he had struggled with both Lansdowne and Wolseley. He was denied the officers he wanted, he failed to receive the numbers he wanted, and he was not allowed to determine overall strategy.[6] He was forced to defer to the plans of Lansdowne and the Cabinet which demanded the division of his forces forthwith.

All this notwithstanding, Buller attempted as best he could to win the war. In mid December 1899 he was losing the war, and the humiliation of 'Black Week' demanded change to restore confidence. British morale both in South Africa and at home was wavering. An immediate decisive victory was now a necessity. The decision to supersede Buller, Lord Esher wrote to Sir William Harcourt, was the culmination of 'the yielding of the Government to the pressure of those who insisted on the holding and the relief of Kimberley'.[7]

If anyone was to be sent out to South Africa to take over his command, Buller expected it to be Wolseley. Field Marshal Lord Garnet Joseph Wolseley, who had turned 66 a few months before the war in South Africa had begun, had held the position of Commander-in-Chief of the British army for five years since the retirement of the Duke of Cambridge. As a young man, he had a host of ideas to reform the British army, some of which were realized, but most of which Cambridge resisted. He had also been a gallant and aggressive soldier who had led his troops to victory in Africa and Asia.

As Commander-in-Chief, however, Wolseley had lost much of his drive. He fought against the continental trend which encouraged the development of a general staff. This would have certainly reduced his personal authority over the army. He also left the fighting to those younger than himself. At the time of the South African War it had been roughly 15 years since he had seen action, and this no doubt affected his ability to perceive the need for reform.

Wolseley was aware, however, of many of the problems facing the British army and in particular of the financial restraints which impeded his ability to address them. Of the many problems in the South African War, Wolseley found greatest fault with the Government's 'refusal to spend money from the very first'.[8] Wolseley had wanted to mobilize an army corps on Salisbury Plain in early June to deter Kruger; he had also wanted to send the Guards Brigade to the Cape in early September. However, with each request came the same answer: no money.[9]

With regard to the direction of the war, Wolseley questioned Buller's decision to divide his forces. Like Buller, he thought White's move across the Tugela River, which had left the Natal field force entrapped in Ladysmith, was a serious mistake.[10] He did not, however, think the best way to break the siege was by sending a force into Natal – an action which resulted in the Battle of Colenso. Wolseley supported a decisive advance on Bloemfontein, such as those that he had commanded to Kumasi and Tel-el-Kebir. He believed that had Buller advanced *en masse* toward Bloemfontein, the troops investing Ladysmith would have been forced to pull back. Wolseley, however, refused to criticize Buller or even to offer him any advice. Trusting his general's judgement, he refused, as he always had, to interfere with 'the man on the spot'.[11]

After the defeat at Colenso, Lansdowne decided that it was necessary to replace Buller. Lord Salisbury and the Cabinet gave the Secretary for War their support. Lansdowne needed a popular figure who could restore the lost morale of the British army and resurrect public confidence. Wolseley was thought to be too old (although age did not prevent the eventual appointment of Roberts). Besides, many of the problems which existed in South Africa were attributed in some circles, especially by those who wanted to eliminate the Commander-in-Chief's office and replace it with a general staff, to poor planning on Wolseley's part. Lansdowne therefore needed someone who could risk incurring the wrath of both Wolseley and Buller and still hope to succeed in the army.

Field Marshal Earl Frederick Sleigh Roberts, 'the greatest soldier of the century',[12] a veteran of the Indian Mutiny and the hero of Kandahar, was the natural choice and he was more than willing to accept the challenge. On 8 December Roberts had written to Lansdowne offering his services. He thought Buller had lost his nerve and that his strategy was destined to lead to more failures. Believing that Wolseley 'would prefer running very great risks [in order to achieve a rapid victory] rather than to see [Roberts] in command', Wolseley was not told of the decision until it was put into effect.[13] To appease Salisbury, who objected that Roberts (aged 67) was, like Wolseley, too old for the South African command, Lord Kitchener, the very popular hero of Omdurman, was appointed his Chief of Staff.[14]

Lansdowne gave Buller no explanation for his supersession. Later, responding to Buller's enquiry, he wrote that the supersession was not a direct result of the defeat at Colenso but that Colenso had shown that the Natal front needed more personal attention, something Buller could not give it if he continued to direct the entire war effort.[15] Ostensibly, Buller was superseded for the failures of 'Black Week'. There were, however, other motives for Lansdowne's decision. Of some importance was the fact that by giving Roberts the South African command, Lansdowne could use the Wolseley–Roberts rivalry to wrestle more power away from the office of Commander-in-Chief. In addition, Wolseley and Buller had both been favourites of the Liberal Party. Roberts' friendship, it was believed, could be a valuable asset for the Conservative Party. Public opinion also played a large role in motivating Lansdowne's decision. Buller's name was now associated with the losses at Magersfontein, Stormberg and Colenso. The popularity of Roberts and Kitchener could reinvigorate both the troops in South Africa and the recruitment drive.

Methuen was disgusted with the Government's decision to supersede Buller. He wrote to his wife, 'My darling, as [Forestier] Walker writes: "I suppose if the House authorities are not satisfied, they will send out the Duke of Cambridge and Lansdowne to succeed Lord Roberts and Kitchener." It seems to me a wretched submission to public opinion, especially Kitchener.'[16] Methuen never criticized Buller's command publicly or privately, supporting his commander and friend throughout the entire controversy.

Lansdowne's successor as Secretary for War, W. St John Brodrick,[17] acknowledged officially that the reason for Buller's supersession was not public pressure, politics, or even the failure at Colenso. Buller was superseded by Roberts because the Government had lost faith in him.[18] This was due to the Cabinet's erroneous belief that Buller was abandoning the Ladysmith and Kimberley garrisons in order to focus on a concentrated thrust to knock the Orange Free State out of the war. This plan, which both Wolseley and Roberts endorsed, had been Buller's original plan, devised in the summer of 1899. He had been forced, however, to discard it because of the political exigency of relieving Ladysmith, Kimberley and Mafeking. After his defeat at Colenso, Buller decided to revert to this earlier strategy: a fateful decision which cost him his command and, in the long run, his career.

On 16 December Buller telegraphed White, still besieged in Ladysmith. Briefly, Buller informed him that he had failed to break through the Boer lines at Colenso, that the Boers were too strong to attempt another direct engagement without reinforcements, and that it would take at least 'one full month' to prepare siege operations. Buller continued: 'Can you last so long? If not, how many days can you give me in which to take up defensive position? After which I suggest you firing away as much ammunition as you can, and making the best terms you can.'[19] Clearly, Buller was not abandoning Ladysmith: he had already diverted Warren's 5th Division to Natal to assist in its relief. He did, however, want to inform White that help was not immediate and that White would have to use his own judgement in determining the fate of Ladysmith.

The *National Review* irresponsibly printed an inaccurate version of Buller's telegram to White which had far-reaching consequences. In it, Buller wired, 'I have been repulsed. You will burn your ciphers. You will destroy all your ammunition. You will then make the best terms you can with the Boers after I have fortified myself on the Tugela.'[20] There was but one way this bogus telegram could be interpreted: Buller had lost his nerve and was abandoning White and Ladysmith. For many in the Government, already tired of Buller after 'Black Week', this was the final straw. What the army needed now, they believed, was a strong commander, not a defeatist. Buller remained in Natal under the supervision of Roberts for another year and then returned to his family's estate in Devon, his military career finished for good.

Although Buller could not prevent his own supersession, he was successful in maintaining Methuen's command on the Modder River. As long as he was still in charge, he would be the one to determine the roles of his subordinates. Some writers, like Kenneth Griffith in *Thank God We Kept the Flag Flying*, have inferred that Buller resisted Lansdowne's attempt to supersede Methuen to justify his own difficulties.[21] Certainly any attempt to defend Methuen's reputation by citing the hardships of the South African terrain, as Buller did, would defend his own reputation and perhaps explain the failure at Colenso. What Griffith fails to consider, however, is that Buller could have used the supersession of Methuen to emphasize the difficulties which the War Office had placed on him from the start, most notably the interference with his command appointments. Although Buller and Methuen were friendly, belonged to the same clubs, and had served together in the Gold Coast, Egypt, and, most recently, the Home District, Buller did not ask for Methuen's service in South Africa. Methuen was Lansdowne's man, not Buller's. Methuen and Lansdowne were amicable Wiltshire neighbours. Both former Whigs, Lansdowne loved Methuen as a son. To command the British forces in Natal, Lansdowne had offered Buller the choice of Methuen or White, but Buller had not wanted either of them. He favoured General Sir Francis Grenfell, a much-decorated veteran of several colonial campaigns. Reluctantly, Buller chose White, although Lansdowne preferred Methuen.[22] Methuen's command of at least a division was thus assured. With White besieged in Ladysmith as a result of his own blunder and Methuen falling back to the Modder River after Magersfontein, Buller could have partially vindicated his current troubles with some finger-pointing.

However, Buller did not let Methuen (or Gatacre) become a scapegoat for the War Office. There were several reasons for this. First, South Africa was Buller's command, and no commanding officer would want to be told how to employ his subordinates.[23] Buller was still in command when he telegraphed Lansdowne objecting to Wolseley's directive on 16 December. Second, Buller apparently sympathized with Methuen's difficulties. He wired, 'I cannot agree with the Commander-in-Chief and allow Methuen, who has done very well, to be superseded by Warren – Commander-in-Chief, comfortable at home, has no idea of the difficulties here. It would, I think, be a fatal policy to supersede every General who failed to succeed in every fight … .'[24] In Methuen's defence, Buller continued:

> The conditions are as follows: the atmosphere is tropical, the sun is vertical, the country is waterless, the watercarts improvised at the Cape are leaky beyond repair, and besides, in Methuen's case, the sandy dust is impregnated with salt. Accordingly you must camp where there is water, and water seldom is to be found at intervals of less than ten miles. Infantry, therefore, cannot move freely more than ten miles from their camp, and the heat dazes them. It is impossible to make accurate reconnaissances, or turning movements on any scale, for Infantry marching in the sun lose fighting power, while the enemy, who are all mounted, are always fresh. … Had it been winter Methuen would, I am sure, have won both his fights at Modder River easily, but in the midsummer the men get so dazed with the hot sun and the scorching that they have no dash left. Willing enough they may be, but they are physically incapacitated. I hope you will approve my orders to leave Methuen in command. The same argument applies to Gatacre.[25]

It is unlikely that this impassioned plea was merely a 'psychological ploy' to defend his own failure at Colenso.

Third, Buller, having just failed at Colenso, was anxious for another opportunity to attempt to break through the Boer line and liberate Lady-smith. As already noted, to do this he would need more men. The only available force was the 5th Division. Therefore, Buller ordered Warren, who had landed at Cape Town on 13 December and was in the process of travelling north to the Modder River, to return to Cape Town and sail to Durban where he could join him. If Methuen was to be superseded, he could not be replaced by Warren. Besides Buller and Warren, Lieutenant-General Sir F. W. E. F. Forestier-Walker was the only officer senior to Methuen in South Africa. Walker, in command of the Cape Colony, already had too many responsibilities. Therefore, even if Buller had wanted to replace Methuen, there was no adequate substitute.

Lastly, there is the explanation which Frederick Maurice offers in *The (Official) History of the War in South Africa*. Based on Walker's advice that any further disturbance would greatly affect the morale of an already weary division, Maurice argues that Buller's decision was simple. To support Methuen and to keep the 1st Division on the Modder River rather than withdraw to the Orange River, an option Roberts, Milner and others supported, was the only means of maintaining morale.[26] Whether Walker was concerned most with the morale of the men, overall strategy, or the reputation of his very close friend, Lord Methuen, is difficult to determine. What is clear is that Buller certainly had several good reasons to justify his objection to Lansdowne's interference.

Lansdowne and Wolseley submitted to Buller's appeal, and did not press him again on the subject.[27] Even Roberts did not interfere, although he was determined to give neither Methuen nor Gatacre an important command again. In time, Methuen would regain Roberts' respect. Gatacre, however, would fail Roberts and be superseded in April.[28] Certainly, the decision not to supersede Methuen or Gatacre in December, at least on Lansdowne's part, was made neither to appease Buller, nor to demonstrate confidence in him. Buller had already been notified of Roberts' appointment when he received word that Methuen could retain his command. Neither was the decision a product of Lansdowne's friendship with Methuen. This could not explain the decision to preserve Gatacre's command. There had to have been some truth in Buller's plea. The failures of 'Black Week' were not the failures of individual generals but rather the failures of the British army to prepare adequately for the war in South Africa. Methuen, Gatacre and Buller could not be held solely responsible.

Ignorant of these larger issues, however, many British soldiers on the Modder River held Methuen solely responsible for their plight. The Highlanders, in particular, blamed Methuen for the destruction of their brigade and the death of their beloved general, Andrew Wauchope. The rumours that Wauchope had resisted Methuen's plan, anticipating his brigade's destruction, and that Methuen had refused to listen, increased their anger. As stories emerged that immediately after the battle, Methuen exonerated himself, placing all blame on the Highlanders, their hatred for him grew. Although these stories are suspect, Brigadier-General Hector MacDonald, who replaced Wauchope in mid January, commented that the entire brigade was relieved when they left Methuen behind at the Modder River in early February to join Roberts' advance on Bloemfontein.[29] Methuen concurred, writing, 'I think the Highland Brigade will never wish to serve under me again.'[30]

The 1st Division, especially the Guards Brigade, continued to demonstrate confidence in Methuen as their commander. One observer wrote, 'Certainly no general was better liked by those around him, and, in spite of all mischievous gossip to the contrary, he was perfectly trusted by his officers and men.'[31] However, the scepticism of the Highlanders and their officers reached Lansdowne, who conveyed his unease to Roberts:

> I am much concerned by the reports which reach me from various sources about Methuen. I am so fond of him that it distresses me to dwell upon this subject, but we must think not of him, but of the troops which he commands. Buller has both blamed and praised him, but the confidence which he [placed] in him at first – a confidence which led to recommend Methuen for second in command – has evidently been shaken. The senior officers under Methuen have certainly formed a very unfavourable opinion of him, and describe him as excitable, wanting in judgement, and neglectful of ordinary precautions.[32]

Roberts responded to Lansdowne that the reports were true and he offered a simple solution to protect the troops: he would 'take care that [Methuen] is not again placed in any responsible position'.[33]

By February, with time and the departure of the Highland Brigade, Methuen regained the confidence of Roberts, Lansdowne, and his men. This change is amply demonstrated by comparing the letters of Colonel H. E. Belfield in January to those written in February. Belfield was assigned to Lieutenant-General Charles Tucker, the commander of the 7th Division, and arrived in Cape Town in mid-January. As a result of a 'series of rows' with Tucker, Belfield was transferred to the 1st Division and replaced Colonel Charles Douglas as Methuen's Chief of Staff.[34] In late January, Belfield wrote to his wife, 'Everyone here [in Capetown] is tremendously down on Methuen. He seems to have made an utter fool of himself and to have forced his troops to destruction against the recommendation of his advisers. Then the story is related that the next day [he] addressed them, completely exonerated himself … .'[35] Such disparaging and indeed damaging, stories continued to circulate in early February in Cape Town. Belfield wrote, 'Wondrous stories are told by Methuen, I fear his troops have lost all confidence in him. Perhaps he is off his head. There is madness in the family.'[36]

However, by the second week of February, Methuen had apparently won back the respect of Belfield and others. Belfield wrote:

A good many reputations have gone during this war: Brabazon and Babington have been degraded. Erroll has disappeared, so has Mainwaring. The English system comes very hard on Generals and their staff on service. In other countries whole divisions, formed as such in peace time, take the field. The General knows his staff and vice versa. ... [In the English System] the staffs are pitch forked together when the show starts and thereby frequently do not work as smoothly as they should.

He [Methuen] was the first to have a fight in which there were many casualties and was accordingly blamed very seriously. He is the kindest hearted, most loyal man in the world, no one more upsets than does he all the loss of life and I know he feels deeply the unkind things that have been said about him.[37]

Methuen's work ethic, his thoughtfulness towards his men, and his burning desire to take Kimberley regained the confidence of those who had lost faith in his ability to lead. If, as Colmar Freiherr von Goltz wrote, 'a General undergoes his hardest trials in the days of disaster', then clearly Methuen was surviving the disaster.[38] The timing of his recovered reputation could not have been more opportune, however, for Roberts needed a strong well-respected Methuen for the February advance on Bloemfontein.

ANXIOUS FOR ACTION

During the hot months of late December and January, Methuen remained on the defensive at his Modder River camp. Roberts, believing that the Boer forces threatened his lines of communications, had wanted Methuen to fall back to the Orange River. He believed Kimberley was safe for the time being.[39] Lord Milner, the Governor of the Cape Colony, also wanted Methuen to fall back to the safety of the Orange River. He was willing to abandon Kimberley indefinitely.[40] As noted above, Buller advised leaving Methuen on the Modder River where he could hold the railway and threaten Cronjé's lines of communication. As long as Methuen remained, he argued, Kimberley was safe.[41] Buller's advice convinced Lansdowne that this was the best strategy and Roberts did not interfere. Buller telegraphed Methuen on New Year's Eve and informed him of the decision. Guns were distributed and the troops entrenched.

Impatiently, Methuen awaited his opportunity to strike at Kimberley again. He was certain that the setback at Magersfontein was only a temporary one. Neither his letters nor his diaries suggest that revenge or the chance to redeem his name were his motivation: he simply wanted to complete the task to which he was assigned. He wrote home optimistically after his Christmas dinner:

> I hope soon to be sharpening my sword again, for I see a good chance, and hope before this note reaches you, to have given Kronje [*sic*] a … licking. I think anxiety does not enter into my mind, and I foresee a [different] campaign under the new regime. If Kelly-Kenny comes here I shall command both divisions, and I hope give Kronje a good licking for he really deserves one.
>
> I have got the reinforcements I asked for. My hope [is] to fight in January with 54 guns, 2 cavalry regiments, 250 mounted infantry, and 11 battalions of infantry; a fine show. If lucky I shall take Jakobsdal [*sic*] and get 12 miles of river bank to Browne's [*sic*] Drift. It will mean constant fighting after, until I relieve Kimberley, which I am quite determined to do. If successful, very likely they will leave me in command of a big force, but I do not want a lot of the rubbish [that] you are now sending out from England, as my casualty bill will be still larger unless they run away.[42]

On 11 January Methuen heard the disconcerting news that he would have to wait for his chance to relieve Kimberley. Roberts, who had arrived a day earlier in Cape Town, ordered Methuen to act 'strictly on the defensive'.[43] The bad news continued:

> It may be even necessary for me to withdraw part of your force, you should consider how your line of entrenchments could be sufficiently reduced to enable you to hold a position with two, instead of three, brigades, and possibly with one or two batteries and one regiment of cavalry less than you have at present. Your request for four of the siege 4.7 inch guns will be complied with and when these reach you, you will doubtless be able to make your position practically impregnable. That the relief of Kimberley cannot be immediately effected I am as sorry for you, as I am sure you must be, but I trust that it will still be possible for you to give the brave garrison at that place a helping hand before they run short of supplies and ammunition.[44]

Methuen had hoped that Lieutenant-General Sir Thomas Kelly-Kenny and the 6th Division, which landed in mid January, would become part of his new command. Now, not only had Methuen lost his chance to relieve Kimberley but Roberts was threatening to reduce, not enlarge, his command.

Life in the Modder River camp during the months of January and early February was monotonous. Methuen wrote home, 'I have had quite a difficult job and it is not right that Pall Mall should condemn us at once. Remaining here inactive is quite enough punishment for want of success … .'[45] Patrols were sent out routinely to reconnoitre the Boers' position at Magersfontein and to check their movement into the surrounding area. Artillery fire was exchanged almost daily with the enemy, but 'the range was too long to be effective, and the result was merely to relieve the monotony of camp life and worry the enemy'.[46] Brief encounters between British reconnaissance parties and the Boers occurred regularly, but no action took place between the two main forces. During this period of waiting, and for the first time, British troops entered the Orange Free State, where they were able to gather information on the area around Ramdam. In addition, the integrity of the railroad, which remained the only lifeline to the Cape, was maintained and protected. Thus Methuen's presence successfully prevented any invasion of the Cape Colony by Cronjé and his forces.

On 8 January, on his own initiative, Methuen sent the 9th Brigade on a raid of the Orange Free State. In what became one of the first of many British raids on civilian property, British soldiers destroyed farm houses and seized sheep and cattle.[47] Reluctantly, Methuen continued this policy with Roberts' approval. Methuen wrote to Roberts, 'To denude this country I must destroy crops of men not on commando for which compensation is given. So far I have done so in order to starve out the Boers. There is [so] much to destroy here that I hesitate [to] incur this great expense. … I think money is well spent as it helps to shorten the war.'[48] Roberts replied, 'It is a sad necessity, but the war must be brought to a close and paying compensation will not cost as much as keeping a large army in the field.'[49] Later this scorched earth policy was incorporated into Roberts' and Kitchener's general plan to weaken the Boer morale and to win the war.

While Methuen and the 1st Division waited on the Modder River, Roberts prepared for the British advance on the Orange Free State. Trying to avoid the same problem which plagued Methuen's advance toward Kimberley, namely the Boers' anticipation of British movements, Roberts decided not to take the most direct route, the Central Railway, which ran from Port Elizabeth in the south, through Bloemfontein, and to Pretoria in the north. Instead, he would rely on the Western Railway for transport and supply. From it, he would conduct a flank march east, between the Riet and Modder Rivers, toward Bloemfontein. Once Bloemfontein fell, Roberts believed, the Orange Free State would surrender, thus forcing the

South African Republic to surrender or to carry on the resistance alone. In addition, an advance on Bloemfontein would ease the pressure on the besieged towns of Kimberley, Ladysmith and Mafeking, by forcing the Boers to divert troops to the Orange Free State. Relief missions would then have an easier task.

In relative secrecy, British forces congregated in and behind Methuen's base camp on the Modder River. In addition to Methuen's 1st Division, Roberts had at his disposal the newly arrived 6th and 7th Divisions, commanded by Kelly-Kenny and Tucker respectively, and the newly created 9th Division, which included the Highland Brigade, commanded by Colvile. The Cavalry Division, commanded by Lieutenant-General John French, and several battalions of mounted infantry comprised the mounted force. In all, Roberts had a marching force of roughly 45,000 men, of whom approximately two-thirds would be used in the invasion.[50] Roberts was not impeded by the manpower shortages which prevented Buller from mounting a similar operation and which likewise crippled Methuen's attempt to relieve Kimberley.

Methuen did not look forward to the introduction of 'the new regime'. Although he liked and respected Roberts, he felt that Buller had done the best job possible under the circumstances. In addition, Methuen did not like Kitchener: he believed him to be undeservedly popular and he feared that he would interfere and restrict his own ability to command. He wrote:

> Lord Roberts … is evidently opting [the plan] which should have been adopted from the beginning, i.e., the one I always named to you, straight to Bloemfontein. From all I gather, I imagine Kitchener is running the show. I question the wisdom of a complete change in the middle of a war, but it must in this case [proceed]. I like Lord Roberts but I have never fancied Kitchener.
>
> … Kitchener is going ahead with a vengeance, and making everyone quite mad except myself. I shall ignore him working with Lord Roberts, but if he requires a [hand] I am always glad to oblige him.[51]

Methuen's frustration grew as his command was reduced. As Roberts had warned, the Highland Brigade departed in mid January to form part of Colvile's 9th Division. In addition, Methuen was stripped of much of his transport and artillery. As he wrote:

> The new regime has begun for I have just got orders to send all my transport to Orange River. I have telegraphed saying I shall be unable to feed my

outposts that my big guns are now fixtures!!! and that I hope I may be left something. … I never complain but I should like to be in Crone's place for a week and I think I should stagger humanity, beginning with the 500 wagon transport, for we know I am useless now.[52]

Methuen directed his anger at Kitchener, for, in his opinion, Kitchener represented the bending of the Government to popular pressure and the subsequent passing of blame, unjustifiably, to Buller and himself. He bemoaned the fact that 'Kitchener consults no one and runs the whole show', and 'will probably take Kimberley for himself and Roberts will let him'. Many comments like these reached Lady Methuen at Corsham Court.[53]

On 8 February Roberts arrived at the Modder River Camp and met with Methuen. The meeting did not go well. Roberts reprimanded Methuen for his treatment of the Highland Brigade after the Battle of Magersfontein and alleged that he had unfairly criticized them, destroying what was left of their shaken morale. Roberts quoted Methuen, from an unknown source, as saying, '[the Highland Brigade] disgraced themselves, and the Brigade, and were a disgrace to the army.' In addition, Roberts accused Methuen of being reckless and incompetent for not reconnoitring the ground around Magersfontein before attacking. Methuen adamantly denied both charges and offered his resignation. Roberts, perhaps unsure of his own accusations, perhaps unsure of the reaction in London, or possibly because he did not want to disturb the planned operations on the eve of the offensive into the Orange Free State, denied the offer 'for the present'.[54]

Roberts' decision to retain Methuen in a position of command was most likely motivated by his inability to substantiate his allegations, which seem to have stemmed from an article printed in the *Morning Post* in late January. Lieutenant-Colonel J. W. Hughes-Hallett, the commander of the Seaforths, responded that he heard Methuen say only positive words to the Highlanders.[55] Methuen's case was further supported by Kelly-Kenny and Major-General Sir G. H. Marshall, the commander of the artillery, who had both recently arrived at the Modder River Camp and had displayed confidence in him. It is unlikely that Roberts' decision to keep Methuen on was made because he feared a negative reaction in London, for although Lansdowne approved of Methuen, he would not have attempted so soon after Roberts' appointment to block his decision. Roberts knew that. He certainly would have replaced Methuen had he believed that there was any wrongdoing. He had already sacked Major-General J. M. Babington,

Methuen's cavalry commander,[56] believing him to have been over-cautious at the engagement at Koedoesberg on 7 February.[57] In the case of Magersfontein, overall responsibility for the failure was diverted away from Methuen and toward Buller, whom Roberts blamed for everything.[58] Later, Roberts publicly acknowledged that 'Lord Methuen could not be blamed for the failure to relieve Kimberley' and therefore he was not relieved of his command. He concluded that the relief of Kimberley, given the size of Methuen's force, was 'almost an impossible task'.[59]

Although Methuen weathered this confrontation, he was less than confident about his future. He had 'lost heart'. His command had been reduced, he had been reprimanded by Roberts and he expected that Lieutenant-General Sir Frederick Carrington,[60] who was sailing to Cape Town, would replace him. Distraught, Methuen wrote home awaiting for what seemed to be the inevitable. 'I am quite out of my element with the India and Egyptian Generals. Therefore you need not pity me if I am ordered home, for Buller and I have happy homes to go to when we are dismissed.'[61]

THE ADVANCE TO BLOEMFONTEIN

On 11 February Roberts' offensive began. With Buller and Warren clamouring for more troops in the east after the defeat at Spion Kop on 24 January, and Gatacre left with a brigade to guard against a possible invasion of the Cape Colony, all available British forces in South Africa were diverted for Roberts' task. The 7th Division and the Cavalry Division advanced from the Modder River camp southeast into the Orange Free State to Ramdam. Kelly-Kenny and the 6th Division followed a day later. The Highland Brigade, which had been protecting the left flank of the force, joined the 9th Division and advanced to Ramdam on 13 February, a day behind the 6th Division. Methuen and the 1st Division remained at the Modder River to protect the lines of communications and form the far left flank of Roberts' advancing force.

Roberts ordered French to advance on Kimberley in a wide flanking move via De Kiel's and Waterval drifts on the Riet River and Klip Drift on the Modder River. The large mounted force allowed Roberts to take Kimberley in a manner in which Methuen could never have accomplished. In December Methuen was without the resources to undertake such a movement. He would have been forced to rely on an infantry advance which could not have been accomplished without enormous amounts of water-bearing transport, which he did not have. In addition, this course

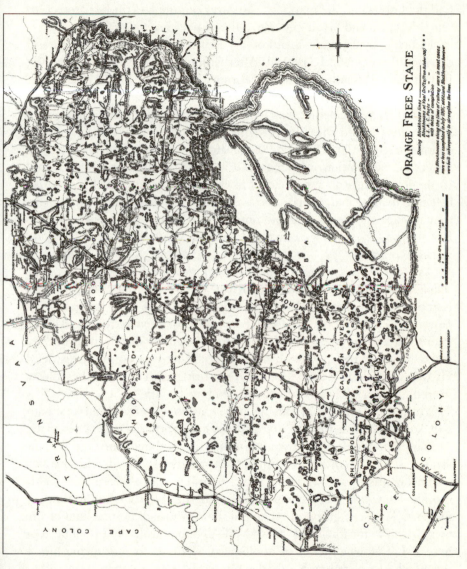

Map 9: The Orange Free State, 1898. Map reproduced from Leo Amery, *The Times History of the War in South Africa*, London, Sampson Low, Marston and Co., 1907.

would have threatened the 1st Division's lines of communication. Aware of this, Methuen did not attempt the march, choosing instead to attack the Boers at Magersfontein. Whereas Methuen had three brigades of infantry, Roberts had five infantry divisions and a cavalry division. Only Roberts had the horses and the manpower to carry out the task and to protect his rear, his flanks and his supply line at the same time.

French's cavalry rode ahead of the British infantry and engaged and defeated the Boers at Klip Drift. After riding 100 miles in four days, the British entered Kimberley on 15 February and ended the 124-day siege. Roberts' move, however successful, was costly. The Cavalry Division was left in tatters by the debilitating heat, the tempo of the march, the lack of horsemanship and the engagements, highlighted by French's cavalry charge at Klip Drift. Of the 5,000 cavalry that set out from the Modder River four days earlier, only 1,200 were ready to continue on 17 February.[62] In the long run, Roberts' decision to divert his force toward Kimberley rather than immediately strike across the Modder and head toward Bloemfontein gave the Boers valuable time to reorganize and prepare for the British invasion. Wolseley estimated that this strategy gave the Boers six weeks to regroup.[63]

As Roberts' force moved into the Orange Free State, Methuen was finally able to depart the Modder River. On 16 February, the day after Kimberley was relieved, his reconnaissance found the Magersfontein entrenchments abandoned and Cronjé and his men retreating toward Paardeberg. Roberts ordered Methuen to march immediately to Kimberley where he was to restore the railway and establish control over the district.[64] He was advised to hold the Modder River bridge and to guard the railway from the Orange River Station to Kimberley.

Much to his dismay, Methuen would have to accomplish this feat with a makeshift division, for the Guards Brigade was ordered to proceed to the Orange Free State where it would participate in the advance on Bloemfontein. Thus, Methuen's command was further reduced.[65] Losing this particular brigade, of which he was a member, was a severe blow to his morale. He wrote, 'My feelings are so awful that I hardly dare to think of the past. The brief glory, and then the shame through no real fault of my own. I believe my force will relieve Mafeking, but probably I shall be kept here.'[66] Lansdowne's letter of apology to Methuen for not giving him a second chance to relieve Kimberley offered little consolation.[67]

Indeed, being denied the honour of relieving Kimberley and having his force further reduced, led the normally sanguine Methuen to become spiteful. When Kitchener made a costly and foolish attack on the Boers at

Paardeberg on 17 February, Methuen expressed only smug satisfaction: 'I have just heard Kitchener has made a frontal attack on the Boers, and has not done even as well as I did on the Modder! Soon people will learn I could not have done much otherwise than I did and my one fault was failing to win.'[68] To some extent he felt vindicated by the Battle of Paardeberg.[69]

The events which led to the Paardeberg attack were as follows. On 17 February Roberts trapped Cronjé and about 4,500 men between French's cavalry and Kitchener's infantry on the banks of the Modder River at Paardeberg, some 30 miles upstream from where Methuen had evicted the Boers nearly three months earlier. Cronjé immediately began to fortify his position. Believing that any British delay could result in either Cronjé's retreat or the arrival of Boer reinforcements, Kitchener, commanding the 6th and 9th Infantry Divisions in Roberts' name, unwisely decided to try to force Cronjé from his strong position.[70] Even though it led to Cronjé's unconditional surrender on 27 February, it proved to be a costly victory.

A comparison of the Battle of Paardeberg and the Battle of Modder River offers much insight as to the difficulties which Methuen faced on 28 November 1899. Like Methuen, Kitchener did not know exactly what he was up against. He estimated Cronjé's force, including possible reinforcements, to be about 15,000 strong. The real number did not exceed 7,500.[71] At the Modder River Methuen seriously underestimated his enemy. Although he suspected Cronjé's force in the area to be about 12,000, he did not think there would be more than 4,000 at the Modder River, assuming the bulk of the force to be further north guarding Kimberley. He was wrong. There were 8,000 Boers at the Modder River that day. Also, the terrain in which the British generals conducted their advances was very similar. Both Kitchener and Methuen had to advance across the Modder where the Boers, able to construct strong breastworks and trenches in the high banks of the river, awaited them on the other side. Methuen also faced the additional difficulty of having to cross the Riet River on his right flank, which proved impossible. Whereas Kitchener had valuable information about the river, which led him to send Major-General Horace Smith-Dorrien's 19th Brigade three miles upstream (where it successfully forded the river), Methuen's maps and reconnaissance had proved faulty, leading him to believe that the Modder was fordable anywhere. As a result only a few British soldiers were able to cross the river, and all on the left flank.

As we have already seen (in Chapter 5) Methuen was heavily criticized for his role at the Battle of Modder River and especially for his use of a frontal attack on the Boer position. His victory at Modder River was considered costly – 60 killed and 300 wounded. At Paardeberg, Kitchener lost more than 1,200 men, yet whereas Methuen's critics were many, his were relatively few. Amery and others wrote off Kitchener's mistakes as errors caused by inexperience,[72] but the truth was far from that. Whereas Methuen was forced to attack the Boers at Modder River (for reasons discussed earlier, see Chapter 5), and was on a timetable to relieve Kimberley, Kitchener had many options open to him. The choices of when, where and how to attack were his. Further, whereas Methuen's use of the frontal attack deserves some criticism it was justified (see Chapter 5). In Kitchener's case there was no justification. By February 1900, unlike November 1899, the frontal attack had been discredited. Against a well-entrenched enemy armed with modern weapons, the tactic could, and did, prove disastrous. Kitchener's inexperience was no excuse. Certainly, he was aware of its earlier difficulties at Modder River, Magersfontein and elsewhere. He had even issued a circular memorandum on 26 January, stating, 'Against such an enemy any attempt to take a position by direct attack will assuredly fail.'[73] He attempted a flank manœuvre, but when this failed, he attempted to do what he had advised all of the other British commanders in South Africa not to do.

Amery also criticizes Methuen's direction of the battle of Modder River. However, so far as Kitchener and his direction of Paardeberg are concerned, the charges of delinquency are more serious. As Methuen knew even before the battle, Kitchener avoided delegating authority, preferring to do everything himself. Although Amery wrote that Kitchener's problems stemmed from the lack of a sufficient staff, it is clear that no staff could have inspired Kitchener's confidence.[74] His failure to delegate left brigades unable to work with each other and, in Smith-Dorrien's case, unable to determine what was going on during the battle.[75] A well-trained staff and improved battlefield communications, which would have made Methuen's job much easier, would probably still have been met with neglect by Kitchener. Thus Methuen's actions both at the Modder River and Magersfontein were vindicated by the Battle of Paardeberg in February 1900, for no longer could the War Office lay blame solely on Methuen, Gatacre and Buller. There had to be underlying causes for the British difficulties in South Africa, and the tactical errors of a few generals could no longer account for all the problems of the British army.

As the British advance continued toward Bloemfontein, Methuen remained behind in Kimberley. There, he had three basic tasks to accomplish.[76] The first was to provision the town and restore communications with the Cape by repairing the railway. Methuen completed this by 20 February, the day he officially took over the Kimberley District as Military

Administrator. He also repaired the railway northward as far as Warrenton. The second and third tasks were to pacify the area north and northeast of Kimberley and to control the northwest section of the Orange Free State. He began these operations in earnest on 21 February. His biggest problem was in containing the guerrillas who were conducting daily raids on the railway; his most annoying problem was Cecil Rhodes.

Although he had been held up in Kimberley for some time, Rhodes had played an important role in the war. It was his presence in South Africa and his influence in London that led to the Government's decision to pressure Buller into sending a force to Kimberley to break the siege – something that Buller had not planned to do. As noted earlier, Rhodes had manipulated the British Government by threatening to surrender the town if help was not dispatched immediately.[77] The Government, of course, did not want to risk losing the town's valuable diamond and gold interests, nor did it want to face the public's wrath if the town's civilian population was turned over to the Boers. This, as noted earlier, was how Methuen came to be assigned to the task of relieving the garrison and evacuating the town. Lieutenant-Colonel R. G. Kekewich and a small garrison defended the town which was subjected to continuous artillery barrages and localized rushes of the Boers. This continued until 15 February, when French's cavalry broke the siege.

Rhodes sent several telegrams to Methuen between December and February offering advice and requesting aid. Rhodes had even written that the Boers would offer no resistance.[78] Methuen refused to reply. Their once amicable relationship had soured since the Jameson Raid, after which Methuen believed that Rhodes was partly responsible for manufacturing the war. He disliked Rhodes for his 'detestable political conduct' which in his view had helped to create the atmosphere in England which forced the Government to replace Buller.[79]

Methuen treated Rhodes as any civilian. When Rhodes wrote him in early December asking if he could raise 2,000 volunteers, Methuen replied to Kekewich, 'I am arranging military defence with you, and Rhodes must understand that he has no voice in the matter.'[80] This policy was supported by Buller, who advised Methuen that 'in dealing with Kimberley, [he] must put De Beers out of the question', and that he should make all decisions 'without favour to any particular capitalist'.[81] Methuen unequivocally addressed the Rhodes problem in a later telegram to Kekewich, writing, 'Rhodes is to leave Kimberley the day after I arrive. Tell him he is not to interfere in military matters.'[82] After Kekewich unwisely showed this telegram to Rhodes, the relationship between Methuen and Rhodes broke down altogether. It should be pointed out though that after Kimberley was relieved, Methuen did meet with Rhodes. At Roberts' insistence, he, Rhodes, Kitchener and Methuen, met on 1 March to discuss the relief of Mafeking, an operation which Methuen desperately wanted to undertake.[83] Rhodes was asked to raise volunteers for a flying column, but failed to do so.[84] Despite these few meetings, Methuen continued to prevent any interference by civilians in the military administration of the Kimberley district.[85]

In March 1900 Methuen concentrated on clearing the area between Boshof and Fourteen Streams, extending British control northeast along the Vaal River toward Hoopstad and Kroonstad, threatening the Boers' flank, and driving towards the besieged town of Mafeking. On 12 March Methuen and a column seized Boshof without firing a shot. A small garrison was left behind and another garrison was established in Warrenton. On 26 March Methuen seized Barkly West, on the Vaal, in the Cape Colony. He returned to Kimberley two days later.

Meanwhile, Roberts' advance was succeeding. Despite French's failure to capture presidents Kruger and Steyn at Poplar Grove, Bloemfontein, the capital of the Orange Free State, fell to the British on 13 March. This was followed two days later by Roberts' offer of amnesty to any Orange Free State Boer who returned home and surrendered his weapon. In the east, on 28 February, Buller successfully relieved Ladysmith after its 120-day siege. He entered the city a few days later. Roberts then ordered Buller to assume a defensive position. The British were also advancing in the centre and on 5 March Gatacre seized Stormberg, driving the Boers north. Ten days later, his force crossed the Orange River into the Orange Free State and seized Bethulie. Rouxville and Smithfield were captured later that week. While the British continued to make small advances, Roberts' main force remained in Bloemfontein, awaiting the surrender of president Steyn and expecting more reinforcements for the march on Pretoria.[86]

THE BATTLE OF BOSHOF

During this time, Methuen was scoring his own successes. On 5 April he learned that a small Boer commando had passed through Tweefontein, five miles south of Boshof. The commando was on its way to the Modder River, where it planned to destroy a section of the railway. It was commanded by Georges Henri Ann-Marie Victor, the 20th Comte de Villebois-Mareuil, 'the Lafayette of South Africa'.[87] Villebois-Mareuil, who had won the cross of the Legion of Honour at Loire in 1870, was the most famous of the many foreign soldiers who fought on the side of the Boers during the war. Cronjé had planned on organizing the German, Dutch, Irish, Scandinavian, French and other foreign volunteers into an international brigade under Villebois-Mareuil's command. Villebois-Mareuil believed Methuen's main force to be still near Barkly West in the Cape Colony.[88] Informed of the commando's movement, Methuen immediately ordered his Imperial Yeomanry, commanded by Brigadier-General Lord Chesham, the Kimberley Mounted Corps, commanded by Lieutenant-Colonel Peakman, and the 4th Field Artillery Battery, commanded by Major Butcher, to 'saddle up at once'.

They arrived before Villebois-Mareuil had a chance to escape. Methuen carried out a successful reconnaissance of the enemy's position before he began the assault, fully utilizing the benefits of his mounted force – a luxury previously denied to him. African guides were also used. Because of the mobility of his troops, Methuen was able to support an attack on one front with two flanking attacks against the enemy entrenched in the kopjes. Fearing that his artillery would hit his own troops, Methuen allowed only three shells from his four field batteries to be fired during the battle.[89] The British pinned down Villebois-Mareuil's commando under a heavy fire from the front and then advanced in small rushes on the flanks. The Imperial Yeomanry took position on the left, Peakman and the Kimberley Mounted Corps took the right, and the centre was able to push slowly forward. Finally, at 25 yards, they charged with bayonets. After Villebois-Mareuil fell, the commando surrendered. Villebois-Mareuil and six others were killed, 11 were wounded and 51 prisoners were taken. In addition, two guns were captured. The British lost only two men, one of whom, Lieutenant A. C. Williams, Imperial Yeomanry, was shot after the white flag had been raised. The assassin was immediately executed under Methuen's order.[90]

Although seemingly a minor incident, the Battle of Boshof was an important one for Methuen and the British. As Filson Young wrote, 'It was as artistic a piece of work as it could be.'[91] First , the resounding success restored Methuen's self-confidence. Second, as Sir Arthur Conan Doyle wrote, 'The affair … came at a time when a success was very welcome.'[92] The fall of Bloemfontein in mid March, followed by Roberts' long delay, had left few successes to report to the demanding crowds back home. And, finally, Methuen's performance helped restore the confidence of others in his ability. For the first time since his arrival in South Africa, Roberts wrote to Lansdowne with something positive to say about Methuen.[93] As a reward, Roberts re-formed the 1st Division into a much stronger fighting unit.[94]

An incident which followed this battle also proved to be an important one for Methuen's future. On the evening of 6 April, in the presence of Kekewich's Loyal North Lancashire Regiment, Methuen gave Villebois-Mareuil a burial with full military honours alongside his own fallen officers in the Boshof cemetery. Methuen allowed Villebois-Mareuil's friend and countryman, the Count Pierre de Bréda, to give a funeral address. During the funeral, Count Bréda turned to Methuen and said, 'We are your prisoners but I thank you in the name of myself and my comrades for your kindness to us, and recognize we are prisoners of a nation whose soldiers are the bravest of the brave.'[95] Methuen's graciousness extended to the cost of Villebois-Mareuil's headstone, which he paid for out of his own pocket.[96] Although not all of the English praised his actions, the French did, and more importantly, the Boers did so as well. This small action greatly added to the reputation for honour and justice which Methuen was building in South Africa. This reputation later played a significant role in restoring post-war Anglo-Afrikaner relations.

Finally, the Battle of Boshof was an important event because it was the first time that the hastily raised Imperial Yeomanry had engaged the enemy. The Imperial Yeomanry, a corps of irregular mounted infantry, had been called up as a result of the failures of 'Black Week'.[97] Within six to seven weeks, with little field training, a very brief musketry drill, and a scarcity of officers, they were sent to South Africa. In their first battle, however, the Imperial Yeomanry 'acted like veteran troops'.[98] Methuen 'was much struck by the intelligent manner in which they carried out the attack and made use of cover'.[99] Both he and Roberts liked what they saw.[100]

PROTECTING ROBERTS' FLANK

After Villebois-Mareuil's funeral, Methuen marched northeast. Preparing for the invasion of the Transvaal and believing that the action might speed up the relief of Mafeking, Roberts ordered Methuen to seize Hoopstad and to threaten Kroonstad. Lieutenant-General Sir Leslie Rundle and the 8th Division would advance to Kimberley to protect Methuen's rear.[101] Methuen's force advanced at once to Zwartkoppiesfontein, which he occupied without resistance.

On 12 April Roberts informed Methuen that his orders had been changed. The 8th Division had been diverted to Thaba 'Nchu in the

Orange Free State and Lieutenant-General Sir Archibald Hunter and the newly formed 10th Division would be sent in their place. Hunter would occupy Kimberley and from there would attempt to force the Vaal River, opening up a path to Mafeking.[102] Methuen, in the meantime, was to halt his advance on Hoopstad, return to Boshof and offer support to Hunter.

Methuen urged Roberts to let him proceed to Hoopstad. He planned to protect his line of communications by setting up a series of small armed posts along the road back to Boshof.[103] This plan partially anticipated the blockhouse system which later was implemented by Kitchener. Roberts, fearing that Methuen would become vulnerable to Boer attack, refused, and on 20 April Methuen began to march back to Boshof.

On 3 May Roberts' advance resumed: however, Methuen was not part of this general attack. With Paget's 20th Brigade assisting Hunter in Christiana and a force of 2,000 Boers north of Boshof, Methuen was ordered to remain behind, where he happily 'chased Boers' and 'gathered supplies'. Roberts underestimated the Boers' ability to resist, assuming that many would lay down their arms and accept his offer of amnesty. He was wrong. Skirmishes with the Boers in and around Boshof continued through early May. Finally, on 14 May, as the situation quieted down, Roberts agreed to allow Methuen and his division to march to Hoopstad.

On 17 May Methuen embarked on a 19-mile night march to Hoopstad and took the Boers completely by surprise.[104] Generals Daniels and du Preez and 40 Boers surrendered with a large stock of rifles and ammunition.[105] In Hoopstad Methuen's orders were to 'encourage the people to give up their arms and ponies and to return to their farms. Make prisoners of all anti-English residents in Hoopstad. Allow no one outside or in the streets after 2000 hours and no one to move in or out of town without a pass.'[106] Hoopstad was but a staging point for an advance on Kroonstad, whose capture was of great importance to Roberts' strategy.[107]

Methuen advanced further into the Orange Free State guarding the extreme left flank of Roberts' march toward Pretoria. After seizing Hoopstad, he continued toward Bothaville, and, after encountering no resistance, he arrived there on 24 May. Next, Roberts ordered Methuen to cross the Vaal and move to either Venterskroon or Parys, depending on the position of the enemy. Before Methuen had a chance to prepare his men and set out from Bothaville, he received disappointing news. Roberts had become unsure of the advance and, fearing that his own rear was becoming endangered, ordered Methuen to move to Kroonstad.[108] Methuen would not protect Roberts' flank as was planned, but would instead guard his rear. On 28 May Methuen and the 1st Division arrived in Kroonstad.

In 15 days Methuen and his men had marched 168 miles through deep sands and over worn roads. Their Boer prisoners could not believe that what had they accomplished could also be done by the British.[109] Only a few months earlier, Methuen's troops had been known for being anything but mobile. By late May, however, they had earned the nickname the Mobile Marvels. Because of Methuen's determination, his knowledge of horsemanship and his use of African guides, his men had become extremely mobile. A popular rhyme, later hummed, went: 'Always somethin' up and doin', Major-General Lord Methuen'.[110] The General always marched alongside his men on foot in the company of his staff officers, and would only call for his horse when trouble started.[111] Methuen's mounted yeomanry also possessed the mobility to fight the Boers on equal terms.

RELIEVING LINDLEY

On the last day of May 1900 Johannesburg fell to the British and the invasion of the Transvaal was well underway. Roberts did not anticipate any continued resistance in the annexed Orange Free State.[112] He erred again. 'Lord Roberts made a miscalculation in thinking that he had left a pacified Free State behind him and when after having reached the Transvaal he learnt that there was some trouble in his rear he refused to believe that it was anything serious until events proved too strong for him.'[113] The Boer siege of Lindley was to take him by surprise.

Confident that the Boers were in retreat, Colvile vacated the town of Lindley, situated on the Valsch River in the Orange Free State, and headed for Heilbron. The next day, he was informed that Lieutenant-Colonel B. E. Spragge and four companies of Imperial Yeomanry, who had marched from Kroonstad to Lindley to join Colvile's division, were stuck in Lindley and surrounded by de Wet's commando with only one day's supplies. Colvile proceeded to Heilbron anyway, advising Spragge to join him or to fall back to Kroonstad. Spragge never received Colvile's message, a fact which Colvile was well aware.[114] Reaching Heilbron on the 29th, Colvile found his own force besieged.

Methuen, who had just reached Kroonstad after a 15-day march, was ordered to proceed immediately to Heilbron, 55 miles northeast, and to relieve Colvile and the Highlanders. Ten miles out of Kroonstad, on 30 May, he learned of Spragge's plight. Spragge wrote that he not could hold out against the Boers' siege beyond 2 June. At once, Methuen changed his course. Leaving Douglas behind to command the division, Methuen, personally accompanying the Imperial Yeomanry, rode 44 miles in 24 hours, over rough terrain with little water, arriving at Lindley early in the morning on the 2nd.[115] After a five-hour fight, he forced his way past 3,000 Boers and their commander, Christiaan de Wet, 'the [Boers] best General and a splendid fellow'.[116] No pursuit of the Boers was attempted, for the horses were too tired.[117] Arriving in Lindley, Methuen found only a few of Spragge's Irish Yeomanry; Spragge and most of his force had already surrendered.[118]

In Lindley, Methuen wrote a letter to Piet de Wet, whose commando was working in co-operation with his brother Christiaan's, asking him to come to Lindley. Methuen hoped to convince de Wet of the futility of continued resistance and to negotiate a surrender. He was also concerned about the numerous times the Boers had fired on his men after a white flag had been raised. De Wet hit back at Methuen, claiming among other things that the British were treating their Boer prisoners badly. Nevertheless, he agreed to come.[119]

Roberts strongly disapproved of this meeting. Apparently, he did not want any negotiations with the enemy to take place unless the Boers initiated the dialogue,[120] in which case he felt that the British would have the upper hand. Methuen strongly disagreed. He approved of any means which would bring the two sides to the table. Thus he met de Wet on 8 June. A six-day cease-fire was negotiated, but de Wet did not surrender.

In the meantime, leaving Paget and the 20th Brigade behind in Lindley, Methuen resumed his march to Heilbron to relieve Colvile. Colvile's condition, which at first had been exaggerated, had deteriorated after a convoy failed to get through to Heilbron on 6 June. Methuen's force, bearing eight days' supplies, arrived there on 7 June after three days of continued fighting. Methuen had now marched 267 miles since leaving Boshof less than a month earlier. His force had earned the nicknames, the 'Salvation Army' and 'Beecham's', because they relieved so many besieged garrisons and isolated outposts! The marches from Kroonstad to Lindley and from Lindley to Heilbron went far in restoring Methuen's reputation.[121] He even enjoyed a brief visit with the Black Watch, who only a few months earlier had treated him with contempt. At last the failure at Magersfontein seemed a distant memory.

On 10 June Methuen, accompanied by the 9th Brigade, his Imperial Yeomanry and some of Colvile's troops, including the 2nd Royal Highlanders (the Black Watch), met Kitchener and Colonel James Spens at the Vredefort Road Station on the Central Railway. They met to discuss the pursuit of Christiaan de Wet, who, with his column, was riding almost at will through the Orange Free State. He had besieged Lindley, attacked Heilbron and most recently captured the Rhenoster River Bridge and Roodewal. The Central Railway, Roberts' main supply line to the Cape Colony, became the primary target for his raids. The Orange Free State had been anything but 'pacified' by the British after its annexation and Roberts' advance into the Transvaal.

The meeting went well. Methuen was put in charge of strengthening all British garrisons along the rail in the Orange Free State. Kitchener praised Methuen for his efficient transport, saying that it was 'the best organized transport in the army, in fact the only division in which the transport was organized'.[122] He also promised not to interfere with Methuen's command – most unusual for an officer whose predilection it was to do everything himself. In conjunction with Colonel Spens, who was ordered west of the railway line, Methuen, on the east of the line, would force de Wet from the Rhenoster River and so reopen the railway. Meanwhile, Roberts ordered Lieutenant-General Ian Hamilton[123] and his two brigades of infantry and large mounted force to Heildelberg, Major-General Ralph Clements and the 12th Brigade to Senekal, and MacDonald and the Highland Brigade to Heilbron.[124] With Rundle south of Senekal and Paget at Lindley, Roberts had hoped that he could tie a rope around de Wet and bring the Orange Free State under order by 23 June.[125]

The following morning, Methuen headed south toward Kroonstad along the railroad line. About 35 minutes later, as expected, he encountered de Wet with 2,000 men and five guns at the Rhenoster River. Methuen directed a heavy artillery barrage against the enemy's position as his infantry closed in. The assault lasted for over four hours. Finally, after a detachment of the Loyal North Lancashires had broken through the Boer lines, the Boers hoisted the white flag. However, by this time, the bulk of the Boer force, including de Wet, had mounted their horses and escaped. Methuen's force was too tired to give chase.[126]

For the next month Methuen protected the lines of communications and pursued de Wet. No longer fighting large enemy forces, he was assigned 'colonel's' work. He wrote home dejectedly, 'Many generals would be very angry, but I am beyond that now.'[127] His work included regularly confiscating cattle and sheep and occasionally burning down a farmhouse. As directed by Roberts' orders, farmers who were suspected of aiding the Boer commandos were subject to penalties or punishment. On 13 June Methuen wrote that he 'had to burn down three farms between [Lindley] and Heilbron because a man in the Highlanders was shot from the house where a flag of truce was flying … and two equally cowardly actions forced the burning of the houses, a proceeding I have hitherto avoided'.[128] Methuen despised this task, avoiding it whenever possible. On 15 June Roberts ordered Methuen to burn down de Wet's farm at Roodepoort,[129] which he duly did the next day. As time went on, however, it became harder for Methuen to carry out Roberts' directives. Later in the war, when he was told to burn down de la Rey's farm near Lichtenberg, he refused. Methuen personally met with Mrs de la Rey. She asked him not to take her cattle and horses, and he did not.[130]

April, May and June were difficult months for Methuen. While Hamilton and Pole-Carew 'got the lion's share' of work (and glory), he remained in the rear, marching back and forth, relieving garrisons and overseeing the lines of communication. During this period, Roberts' attitude toward Methuen is difficult to define, and Methuen constantly received contradictory messages from him. First, in April, he had been ordered to Hoopstad but was then pulled back. He was told that Rundle would be sent to support his movement, then Hunter, but then, as it turned out, Methuen ended up supporting Hunter's move. Also, Methuen became convinced that he was going to be given command of the relief of Mafeking, but on 21 April he learned that this honour was going to Hunter, which led him to write home in disgust, 'He doesn't trust us.'[131] Roberts' explanation, that Methuen was needed to work towards Kroonstad, was far from convincing. For while Roberts was telling Methuen to move on Kroonstad, he was also asking him to send his mounted troops to Hunter to assist in the relief of Mafeking. Methuen could not leave Boshof until this force returned.

A telegram dated 12 April provides a good example of Roberts' conflicting orders and unpredictable attitude. In one sentence, Roberts asks Methuen if he can spare some mounted troops; in the next, he writes, 'I am alarmed at the manner in which you divide your small force.'[132] The biggest surprise came on 25 June, when Roberts decided that 'the fine force' that Methuen had 'looked after so carefully … was unnecessarily large'.[133] Methuen's command, which had been increased only a month earlier, was again decreased. In spite of this harsh treatment, he remained quiescent and loyal to his commander. In H. E. Belfield's words: 'No one has played up more loyally [to Lord Roberts], even to his own detriment, than Methuen.'[134]

Methuen's role in the South African War had changed drastically between December 1899 and June 1900. From commanding the two brigades which were perhaps the most experienced in the army, the Guards and the Highlanders, he was reduced to now commanding an *ad hoc* brigade consisting of raw recruits; only in name did the 1st Division live on. Whereas once he fought set battles with as many as 8,000 opponents, Methuen now sporadically fought and pursued a few thousand Boers at a time in an attempt to stop their guerrilla operations. From spearheading a deliberate drive on Kimberley, he now was forced to relieve beleaguered garrisons. From proceeding along a predictable and reliable line of communication, he now zigzagged across the rugged terrain of the Orange Free State. And, as we have noted, whereas once he did a general's job, he now acted like a colonel.

Despite these frustrations, for Methuen the greatest change from December to June was that confidence in him was restored. It was in a sense a time of reconstruction of his career. After the failure of Magersfontein he had believed his military career to be all but over. Buller had stood by him, but Roberts looked for senior officers, especially those associated with Wolseley's Ring, to blame for the earlier defeats. When Roberts and Kitchener arrived, Methuen's actions were closely watched and judged, and one mistake would have cost him his career. It is to his credit that he was able to function amid this stifling scrutiny and win the respect of both men. Kitchener, later in the war, would even give Methuen free reign to do as he pleased. This change in attitude was largely due to the difficulties at Paardeberg, Poplar Grove and Lindley, where it became evident that the British were not adequately prepared to fight the South African War, and that Methuen and Buller were not responsible for earlier failures.

By June 1900, Methuen's reputation was all but rebuilt. There is no better indication of this than the fact that the Black Watch (whose brigadier, Hector MacDonald, had said after Magersfontein that he would never serve under Methuen again) successfully served under him in June 1900. By that time Methuen's forces had been reduced in size and his role had become a secondary one, protecting Roberts' rear and guarding the lines of communication in the Orange Free State. But to his credit, he succeeded in his role.

By July 1900 Roberts had driven into the Transvaal, capturing both Johannesburg and Pretoria, Buller had secured Natal and was pushing into the Transvaal from the southeast, and most of the towns of the Orange Free State had been captured by the British. Yet, the Boers did not surrender and their resistance in the Orange Free State foreshadowed what was to come in the Transvaal. From then until the close of the war, Methuen would have to fight against guerrilla operations. Never again could he rely on his training and experience since neither prepared him for the task on hand. Instead he was forced to learn in the field. As the drive to Kimberley taught him the lessons of modern firepower, this next phase of the war would teach him how to fight a well-armed, extremely mobile enemy who could strike anywhere and at any time.

NOTES

1. WO 132/24 (p. 29), Public Records Office.
2. F. M. Roberts' son, Freddy, was killed in one of the many futile attempts to rescue the British guns pushed too far forward by the artillery commander Colonel Charles Long.
3. *Times* (London), 16 Dec. 1899: 18.
4. G. Wolseley to C. Warren, 13 Dec. 1899. Cited in Kenneth Griffith, *Thank God We Kept the Flag Flying* (New York: Viking Press, 1974), p. 206.
5. Lord Lansdowne to R. Buller, 14 Dec. 1899, WO 132, p. 31, Public Records Office.
6. C. H. Melville, *Life of General The Right Hon. Sir Redvers Buller* (London: Edward Arnold, 1923), pp. 7–11.
7. Viscount Esher to Sir William Harcourt, 18 Dec. 1899, cited in M. V. Brett (ed.), *Journals and Letters of Reginald Viscount Esher* (London: Nicholson & Watson, 1934), p. 251.
8. 'Report of His Majesty's Commissioners appointed to Inquire into the Military Preparations and Other Matters connected with the War in South Africa', 1904: cd 1790, XL, 8786.
9. Ibid., 8778–93.
10. See Chapter 3. Ibid., 8703.
11. Ibid., 9098.
12. Leo Amery's description, as cited in Byron Farwell, *The Great Anglo-Boer War* (New York: Norton, 1990), p. 151.
13. F. Roberts to Lord Lansdowne, 11 Dec. 1899, as cited in Thomas Pakenham, *The Boer War* (New York: Random House, 1979), p. 253.
14. Philip Magnus, *Kitchener: Portrait of an Imperialist* (New York: E. P. Dutton & Co., 1959), p. 157.
15. Lord Lansdowne to R. Buller, 23 March 1900, WO 32/7902, Public Records Office.
16. P. S. Methuen to M. E. Methuen, 29 Dec. 1899, Wiltshire Records Office.
17. After the autumn election of 1900, Salisbury handed the Foreign Office to Lansdowne. Brodrick, who had been Lansdowne's Under-secretary, replaced him at the War Office.
18. Memorandum by W. St John Brodrick, 4 Nov. 1901, 7101–23–183–10, National Army Museum, London.
19. R. Buller to G. White, 16 Dec. 1899, Telegram No. 88, 7101–23–183–10, National Army Museum.
20. *National Review* (London), as cited in, 7101–23–183–10, National Army Museum.
21. Griffith, *Thank God We Kept the Flag Flying*, p. 206.
22. R. Buller to Lord Lansdowne, 17 April 1900, WO 32/7903, Public Records Office.
23. James Thomas writes that Buller was mostly angry with Lansdowne for not consulting him on the decision. James B. Thomas, 'Sir Redvers Buller in the post-Cardwellian Army: A Study of the Rise and Fall of a Military Reputation' (PhD thesis, Texas A&M University, 1993), p. 142.
24. R. Buller to Lord Lansdowne, 16 Dec. 1899, 7101–23–183–10, No. 9, National Army Museum.

25. Ibid.
26. Frederick Maurice and M. H. Grant, *(Official) History of the War in South Africa, 1899–1902* (London: Hurst & Blackwood, 1906–1910), pp. 378–85.
27. Lord Lansdowne to R. Buller, 23 March 1900, WO 32/7902, Public Records Office.
28. Gatacre was sent home in April 1900 after Roberts questioned his relief operation of Reddersburg. His military career ended shortly afterwards. Major-General Sir H. Chermside took over the command of the 3rd Division.
29. Pakenham, *Boer War*, p. 327.
30. P. S. Methuen to M. E. Methuen, 4 Feb. 1900, Wiltshire Records Office.
31. Filson Young, *The Relief of Mafeking* (London: Methuen & Co., 1900), p. 156.
32. Lord Lansdowne to F. Roberts, 5 Jan. 1900, 7101-23–34, National Army Museum. I have found no evidence to collaborate the statement that any of Methuen's senior officers, other than perhaps Colvile, had formed an unfavourable opinion of him.
33. F. Roberts to Lord Lansdowne, 13 Jan. 1900, WO 105/31, Public Records Office.
34. Douglas had replaced Northcott after the Battle of Modder River. Roberts' appointments of Colvile as the commander of the 9th Division and Pole-Carew as Colvile's replacement as commander of the Guards Brigade left a vacancy in the 9th Brigade. Douglas was given the command.
35. H. E. Belfield to his wife, 25 Jan. 1900, 8111-29, National Army Museum.
36. Ibid., 2 Feb. 1900.
37. Ibid., 8 Feb. 1900.
38. Cited in Sisson C. Pratt, *A Précis of Modern Tactics* (London: HMSO, 1892), p. 10.
39. F. Roberts to R. Buller, 23 Dec. 1899, WO 105/13/T/8/2, Public Record Office.
40. Lord Lansdowne to F. Roberts, 25 Dec. 1899, WO 105/13/T/8/2, Public Record Office.
41. Lord Lansdowne to R. Buller, 24 Dec. 1899, WO 105/13/T/8/2, Public Record Office.
42. P. S. Methuen to M. E. Methuen, 29 Dec. 1899, Wiltshire Records Office.
43. F. Roberts to P. S. Methuen, 11 Jan. 1900, WO 108/328, Public Records Office.
44. Maurice and Grant, *(Official) History of the War*, p. 433.
45. P. S. Methuen to M. E. Methuen, 4 Jan. 1900, Wiltshire Record Office.
46. Herbert M. Guest, *With Lord Methuen from Belmont to Hartebeestfontein* (Klerksdorp, South Africa: H. M. Guest, 1901), p. 45.
47. S. B. Spies (ed.), *A Soldier in South Africa: The Experiences of Eustace Abadie* (Houghton, South Africa: Brenthust Press, 1989), p. 56.
48. WO Confidential telegram, Chapter 6, II, as cited in S. B. Spies, *Methods of Barbarism?* (Cape Town: Human & Rousseau, 1977), p. 121.
49. Ibid.
50. Leo Amery (ed.), *The Times History of the War in South Africa, 1899–1902* (London: Sampson, Low, Marston & Co., 1905), III, 377.
51. P. S. Methuen to M. E. Methuen, 20 Jan. 1900, Wiltshire Records Office.
52. P. S. Methuen to M. E. Methuen, 27 Jan. 1900, Wiltshire Records Office.
53. Ibid.
54. P. S. Methuen to M. E. Methuen, 9 Feb. 1900, Wiltshire Records Office.
55. P. S. Methuen to M. E. Methuen, 17 Feb. 1900, Wiltshire Records Office.
56. Methuen believed that the supercession was unfair. 'The cavalry loved him and he was a good general.' P. S. Methuen to M. E. Methuen, 9 Feb. 1900, Wiltshire Records Office.
57. On 2 February, Roberts ordered Methuen to send the Highland Brigade to Koedoesberg, twenty miles to the west of the Modder River Camp, to seize the drift and to build a small fort. De Wet and roughly 700 men attacked General MacDonald and the Highlanders on 7 February. Methuen dispatched General Babington and a

'scratch' cavalry brigade as per MacDonald's request. Babington showed extreme caution when he arrived at the drift, attempting for over an hour to communicate with MacDonald and gather information on the position of the Boers before he committed his force. Amery, *Times History*, III, 360–4.

58.	P. S. Methuen to M. E. Methuen, 17 Feb. 1900, Wiltshire Records Office. Roberts blamed Wolseley for the failure to protect Ladysmith. F. Roberts to H. Kitchener, 16 March 1900, PRO 30/57/20/o11, Public Records Office.

59.	Copy of an Extract from Parliamentary Debates, CIV (10 March 1902) sent by George Aston to Lady Methuen, 24 Nov. 1932. Lord Roberts' lengthy comment delivered in the House of Lords came on the occasion of Methuen's capture by the Boers at Tweebosch and was made as a statement of support for Methuen. It reads:

> My Lords, as Commander-in-Chief of the Army and one who in South Africa had full opportunities of estimating Lord Methuen's military qualifications as a commander, I feel that it would be unfair to him, and discouraging to the other commanders in the field, were I not to make, on the occasion of this unfortunate occurrence of which we have just heard, some expressions of my appreciation of Lord Methuen's services during the war. When I arrived in South Africa in January, 1900, Lord Methuen was being subjected to very adverse criticism on account of his failure to force the Boer position at Magersfontein. One of the questions I had to decide was whether I should recommend that Lord Methuen should be recalled to England, or whether I should continue to employ him as one of my divisional commanders. I resolved to wait until I could see Lord Methuen myself and the troops under his command, and perhaps have an opportunity of personally inspecting the Boer position. The Boer position occupied a front of some eight miles across the railway. It was very difficult country, and completely blocked the road towards Kimberley. Lord Methuen found himself there with 12,000 men, thirty-five guns, and only 1,000 mounted troops. His orders were to relieve Kimberley; and, influenced by the belief that the garrison and the inhabitants of Kimberley were in far greater straits then eventually turned out to be the case, Lord Methuen decided that he must make an effort to get to them. He saw that to attack by day would involve very heavy loss, and he decided to try a night attack. Night attacks are proverbially risky. But on this occasion the enemy were most certainly surprised, and there seems some reason to believe that, if the Highland alignment had not been broken by the thick bush and the deployment of the men thereby prevented, it is possible he might have succeeded. But I confess that when I had made a careful survey of the Boer position I came to the conclusion that Lord Methuen had been given an almost impossible task. When I arrived at Modder River on February 11th with a view of operating for the relief of Kimberley, I had at my disposal 45,000 men and 136 guns, and of these men 6,000 were mounted. This enabled me to make a wide turning movement, which with Lord Methuen's smaller force was impossible, and the success which was attained on that occasion was due to the greater mobility and strength of the forces which I had under my control. I came to the conclusion, therefore that Lord Methuen could not be blamed for the failure to relieve Kimberley, and I decided, therefore, to keep him in his command ... .

60.	Carrington was an officer with much experience in South Africa. He had recently seen action in Matabeleland and Mashonaland. He did not replace Methuen but was instead given the command of the Rhodesian Field Force.

61.	This is one of the few letters in which Methuen places himself in the Wolseley Ring. In most of his letters after 1885, Methuen attempts to walk a line between the two rings, finding acceptance in both. P. S. Methuen to M. E. Methuen, 17 Feb. 1900,

Wiltshire Records Office. Kitchener had been asking for more 'India men' like Burnett and Bindon Blood. He had also fought against E. Wood, one of Wolseley's men, going to South Africa. F. Roberts to H. Kitchener, 8 Feb. 1900, PRO 30/57/20/o9, Public Records Office.

62. George H. Casser, *The Tragedy of Sir John French* (Newark: University of Delaware Press, 1985), p. 50. Frederick Maurice puts the number slightly higher at 1,500. Maurice and Grant, *(Official) History of the War*, II, 97, as cited in Pakenham, *The Boer War*, p. 346.

63. E. K. G. Sixsmith, *British Generalship in the Twentieth Century* (London: Arms & Armour Press, 1970), p. 24. Wolseley favoured a plan which had the British marching along the railway line across either the Aliwal Bridge or Norval's Point Bridge, rather than the costly flank march from the Kimberley line east to the Bloemfontein line which Roberts chose. Roberts' march resulted in the loss of many transport animals and the bulk of the cavalry. In addition, Wolseley argued, once Bloemfontein fell, there was a long delay in the advance because of the destruction to the transport. 'Report of His Majesty's Commissioners appointed to Inquire into the Military Preparations and Other Matters connected with the War in South Africa', 1904: cd 1790, XL, 9102–9.

64. F. Roberts to Lord Lansdowne, 16 Feb. 1900, WO 32/7964, Public Records Office.

65. Methuen's new command consisted of the 9th Brigade (the 1st Northumberland Fusiliers, the 1st Loyal North Lancashire Regiment, the 2nd Northamptonshire Regiment and the 2nd Yorkshire Light Infantry), 1,000 Imperial Yeomanry, the 20th and 38th Batteries RFA, two Canadian field batteries and the 1st New South Wales Field Battery. An additional brigade consisting of the 1st Highland Light Infantry and three militia battalions were due 10 March. This brigade was formed as the 20th Brigade and was commanded by Colonel Arthur Paget, Methuen's former associate in the Scots Guards.

66. P. S. Methuen to M. E. Methuen, 22 Feb. 1900, Wiltshire Records Office.

67. Lord Lansdowne to P. S. Methuen, 24 Feb. 1900, Wiltshire Records Office.

68. P. S. Methuen to M. E. Methuen, 22 Feb. 1900, Wiltshire Records Office.

69. H. E. Belfield, Methuen's Chief of Staff (who did not witness Magersfontein) wrote in regard to Kitchener's performance at Paardeberg, 'Talk of Methuen! He never committed half such a blunder as that.' H. E. Belfield to his wife, 30 April 1900, 8111–29, National Army Museum.

70. Roberts wrote Kelly-Kenny, '… consider that Lord Kitchener is with you for the purpose of communicating to you my orders … .' Amery, *Times History*, III, 419.

71. Ibid., p. 447.

72. Ibid., p. 449.

73. C. of S. Circular Memorandum No. 5, 'Notes for Guidance in South African Warfare', issued 26 Jan. 1900, by Kitchener, Wiltshire Records Office.

74. Amery, *Times History*, III, 450.

75. Pakenham, *Boer War*, p. 355.

76. Richard Danes (ed.), *Cassell's History of the Boer War* (New York: Cassell & Co., 1903), II, 251–86.

77. Leo Amery, whose praise for Rhodes was much exaggerated in the *Times History*, suggests that Rhodes only threatened to surrender to invoke a quick response from Buller. He goes on to claim, erroneously, that this had no effect on Buller's plan. Amery, *Times History*, IV, 549–51.

78. Brian Gardner, *The Lion's Cage* (London: Arthur Barker Ltd, 1969), p. 61.

79. Methuen believed that attacks by Rhodes and others in the press had forced Lansdowne to supersede Buller. P. S. Methuen to M. E. Methuen, 22 Feb. 1900, Wiltshire Records Office.

80. Maurice and Grant, *(Official) History of the War*, II, 63.
81. R. Buller to P. S. Methuen, 10 Dec. 1899, WO 105/29/150, Public Records Office.
82. Methuen cites this telegram to Kekewich in a letter home. P. S. Methuen to M. E. Methuen, 22 Feb. 1900, Wiltshire Records Office. A slightly different version of the letter is printed in Felix Gross, *Rhodes of Africa* (New York: Frederick Praeger, 1957), p. 383.
83. It is worth noting that Rhodes' relationship with Roberts was very different. Whereas Methuen refused to give Rhodes any role in military matters, Roberts played up to him, often asking for his advice on both military and non-military matters. F. Roberts to C. Rhodes, 27 Feb. 1900, WO 108/238, Public Records Office.
84. Amery, *Times History*, III, 493.
85. Not surprisingly, Milner and Roberts were both against Methuen's policy of 'suppressing' Rhodes. A. Milner to F. Roberts, 23 Jan. 1900, f. 126, Milner Papers, Modern Political Paper Section, Department of Manuscripts, Bodleian Library, Oxford.
86. Pakenham, *Boer War*, pp. 399–400.
87. [D'Etechegoyen] Ex-Lieutenant of General de Villebois-Mareuil, *Ten Months in the Field with the Boers* (London: William Heinemann, 1901), p. 131. For more information on Villebois-Mareuil see Roy Macnab's, *The French Colonel: Villebois-Mareuil and the Boers 1899–1900* (London: Oxford University Press, 1975).
88. For a copy of Villebois-Mareuil's complete plan prepared on the eve of the battle see Louis Creswicke, *South Africa and the Transvaal War* (Edinburgh: T. C. & E. C. Jack, 1901), V, 42–4.
89. 'Report at Tweefontein', 6 April 1900, WO 32/7976, Public Records Office.
90. The 'assassin's' name was Nicolaas de Jung. Macnab, *French Colonel*, p. 208.
91. Young, *Relief of Mafeking*, p. 156.
92. Arthur Conan Doyle, *The Great Boer War* (London: Smith, Elder & Co., 1900), p. 390, as cited in Macnab, *French Colonel*, p. 213.
93. F. Roberts to Lord Lansdowne, 6 April 1900, WO 105/7/126/40, Public Records Office.
94. The composition of the 1st Division in May 1900 was as follows: The 9th Brigade, consisting of 1st Northumberland Fusiliers, 1st Loyal North Lancashire Regiment, 3rd South Wales Borderers, and the 2nd Northamptonshire Regiment, commanded by Major-General Charles Douglas; the 20th Brigade, consisting of 2nd KOYLI, 1st Royal Munster Fusiliers, 4th South Staffordshire Regiment and the 4th Scottish Rifles, commanded by Major-General Arthur Paget; the 3rd, 5th, 10th and 15th Battalions Imperial Yeomanry, 11th Co. Royal Engineers, 4th, 20th and 38th Batteries RFA, and the 37th Howitzer Battery.
95. F. Roberts to Lord Lansdowne, 11 April 1900, WO 105/31, Public Records Office.
96. Methuen sent a letter of sympathy along with the Colonel's ring and a photo of the marble headstone to Villebois-Mareuil's daughter. She wrote back thanking him for his kindness. Simone de Villebois-Mareuil to P. S. Methuen, 6 June 1900, Wiltshire Records Office. The headstone read, 'à la memoire du Comte de Villebois de Mareuil, ancien colonel de la Légion Etrangère du France, Général du Transvaal, mort au champs d'honneur, prés de Boshof, le 5 avril, 1900 dans sa 53 me année. RIP'. Edgar Holt, *The Boer War* (London: Putnam, 1958), p. 218.
97. Sidney C. Peel, *Trooper 8008 Imperial Yeomanry* (London: Edward Arnold, 1901), pp. 1–6.
98. Creswicke, *South Africa and the Transvaal War*, V, 39.
99. 'Report at Tweefontein', 6 April 1900, WO 32/7976, Public Records Office.
100. 'Every man and officer [in the Imperial Yeomanry] trusted [Methuen].' Karl B. Spurgin, *On Active Service with the Northumberland and Durham Yeomanry under Lord Methuen*

(London: Walter Scott Publishing, 1901), pp. 37–42.

101.   F. Roberts to P. S. Methuen, 2 April 1900, WO 108/238, Public Records Office.

102.   F. Roberts to P. S. Methuen, 12 April 1900, WO 108/238, Public Records Office.

103.   P. S. Methuen to M. E. Methuen, 25 April 1900, Wiltshire Records Office.

104.   Mafeking was relieved the same day by Colonel Brian Mahon's flying column.

105.   Guest, *With Lord Methuen*, p. 53.

106.   F. Roberts to P. S. Methuen, 15 May 1900, WO 105/36/s2, Public Records Office.

107.   F. Roberts to P. S. Methuen, 13 May 1900, WO 105/36/s2, Public Records Office.

108.   F. Roberts to P. S. Methuen, 23 May 1900, WO 108/239, Public Records Office.

109.   P. S. Methuen to M. E. Methuen, 29 May 1900, Wiltshire Records Office.

110.   Danes, *Cassell's History*, II, 286. Methuen was, in fact, a lieutenant-general.

111.   Spurgin, *Active Service*, pp. 37–8.

112.   On 24 May 1900, Sir Alfred Milner confirmed Roberts' proclamation of the annexation of the Orange Free State in a telegram to Joseph Chamberlain, the Colonial Secretary. The Orange Free State hence became the Orange River Colony. A. Milner to J. Chamberlain, 24 May 1900, No. 58a, c. d. 261 1900: LVI, 389.

113.   H. E. Belfield to his wife, 7 July 1900, 8111–29, National Army Museum.

114.   F. Roberts to Undersecretary of State for War, 19 July 1900, 'Correspondence relative to the Recall of Major-General Sir H. E. Colvile, k. c. m. g., c. b.', cd 467 1901: XLVII, 557.

115.   Guest, *With Lord Methuen*, p. 54.

116.   P. S. Methuen to M. E. Methuen, 3 June 1900, Wiltshire Records Office. Belfield, writing to his wife, agreed with this assessment of de Wet: 'In addition to proving himself a good general, he has shown himself as [an] honest, chivalrous gentleman, most kind to our wounded.' H. E. Belfield to his wife, 4 June 1900, 8111–29, National Army Museum.

117.   Maurice and Grant, *(Official) History of the War*, III, 125.

118.   Lieutenant-Colonel G. J. Younghusband accompanied by the 5th and 10th Imperial Yeomanry were able to free some more of Spragge's men from the Boers in an encounter on 1 June. Spragge was cleared of any wrongdoing by a Court of Enquiry on 25 Sept. 1900. The court found that 'some irresponsible persons raised white flags'. 'Finding of a Court of Enquiry held at Barberton on 25th September, 1900 to investigate the circumstances under which Lieutenant-Colonel B. E. Spragge, DSO XIIIth Battalion Imperial Yeomanry and others, became prisoners of war', cd 470 1901: XLVII, 557.

119.   P. S. Methuen to M. E. Methuen, 8 June 1900, Wiltshire Records Office; P. de Wet to P. S. Methuen, 6 June 1900, WO 105/8/126/84, Public Records Office.

120.   F. Roberts to P. S. Methuen, 4 June 1900, WO 105/36/s2, Public Records Office.

121.   Danes, *Cassell's History*, II, 287.

122.   This was high praise indeed, for Kitchener introduced a new method of transport when he arrived in South Africa. Only Methuen and Buller could be congratulated for carrying out their transport 'by the book'. P. S. Methuen to M. E. Methuen, 13 June 1900, Wiltshire Records Office.

123.   Roberts had given Hamilton the temporary rank of lieutenant-general.

124.   Roberts sent Colvile home shortly after his inaction which resulted in the capture of Colonel Spragge and for other actions which had shown a want of initiative. Although his role at Magersfontein was not called into question, it should have been. Methuen believed that Colvile had 'lost his nerve'. P. S. Methuen to M. E. Methuen, 18 June 1900, Wiltshire Records Office.

125.   Maurice and Grant, *(Official) History of the War*, III, 135.

126.   On 19 June, near Heilbron, the results were similar when de Wet attacked a convoy guarded by Methuen's force. The British were able to defeat the enemy force but

because of the lack of mounted troops, they failed to capture them. P. S. Methuen to F. Roberts, 20 June 1900, WO 105/8/126/93, Public Records Office.

127. P. S. Methuen to M. E. Methuen, 29 June 1900, Wiltshire Records Office.

128. P. S. Methuen to M. E. Methuen, 13 June 1900, Wiltshire Records Office.

129. The *Times History*, often sympathetic to Roberts, states that this was a mistaken order. Amery, *Times History*, III, 268. Official records suggest otherwise. See F. Roberts 15 June 1900, WO 105/36/s2, Public Records Office; and, F. Roberts to Lord Lansdowne, 15 June 1900, WO 105/13/T/11/8, Public Records Office.

130. J. E. de la Rey, *A Woman's Wanderings and Trials During the Anglo-Boer War* (London: Fisher–Unwin, 1903), p. 23; Johannes Meintjes, *De la Rey* (Johannesburg: Hugh Keartland, 1966), p. 175. Methuen later wrote, ' I am always chaffed for being on such good terms with the Boers, and have always replied that it is because I never burn down a house unless forced to do so.' P. S. Methuen to A. Milner, 23 Feb. 1902, f. 126, Milner Papers, Modern Political Paper Section, Department of Manuscripts, Bodleian Library.

131. P. S. Methuen to M. E. Methuen, 21 April 1900, Wiltshire Records Office.

132. F. Roberts to P. S. Methuen, 12 April 1900, WO 108/238, Public Records Office.

133. F. Roberts to P. S. Methuen, 25 and 28 June 1900, WO 108/238, Public Records Office.

134. H. E. Belfield to his wife, 3 Feb. 1900, 8111–29, National Army Museum.

8

From Notoriety to Obscurity

Historians often separate the South African War into three distinct phases. In the first phase (October–December 1899) the British army, commanded by Sir Redvers Buller, attempted to relieve the besieged towns of Kimberley, Ladysmith and Mafeking. Deliberately advancing toward their targets, the British fought set battles based on the experience of 30 years of colonial campaigns. Against an entrenched adversary, armed with modern weaponry, the British strategy failed and the advances halted. The results surprised the British Government, the British people and the British army itself. The second phase, beginning in the new year, was marked by the arrival of Lord Roberts, the addition of several divisions of infantry, and the mobilization of the volunteers, militia and yeomanry for service in South Africa. With overwhelming numbers, Roberts relieved the besieged towns. Thereafter, with great determination, he drove his force from the Modder River station to Bloemfontein, and then onward to Pretoria. After presiding over the annexation of the Orange River Colony and the Transvaal, Roberts returned to Great Britain. He left Lord Kitchener, his Chief of Staff, behind to consolidate the victory. Roberts' departure at the close of 1900 marks what is commonly viewed as the beginning of the third phase of the South African War: the guerrilla phase. During this phase, Kitchener attempted to strengthen his control over the annexed territories by subjugating the Boer guerrillas through a blockhouse system, a network of concentration camps and a scorched earth policy. Finally, after a year and a half of continued resistance, the Boers surrendered to the British on the last day of May 1902, and the Treaty of Vereeniging was signed.

Lord Methuen was one of only three senior British officers who endured throughout the entire campaign in South Africa.[1] Most of his fellow officers who had arrived with him in late 1899 had either left in ignominy, out of frustration, or because they felt they had served long enough. Several senior officers, such as Andrew Wauchope, did not return alive. Methuen's endurance allows for a study of the entire South African War through his eyes, and his personal experiences give support to the traditional demarcation of the war's three phases. However, the use of Methuen as a model yields a different timetable. The first two phases of the war may still be separated by Roberts' arrival in 1900. However, the third phase, that of the guerrilla warfare, began for Methuen long before Roberts had left South Africa.

As the winter fell on South Africa in July 1900, Roberts continued his drive in the Transvaal. Behind him, in the Orange Free State, he left a few infantry divisions, including Methuen's, to consolidate British authority. The Boers refused to lay down their weapons after the fall of Bloemfontein. Instead, they turned to guerrilla warfare: striking at weak British outposts, destroying communication and transportation networks, and leading British columns on maddening chases. Methuen countered these tactics by confiscating civilian property, burning down farmhouses (though he would not always do this), and preventing the Boer commandos from getting a sound night's rest. Charged with the safety of the garrisons along the railway, and harassed daily by raiding parties, he was more aware than most of his fellow officers that the South Africa War had entered a guerrilla phase. This chapter will demonstrate that the war in South Africa had moved into such a phase prior to Roberts' departure. It will show also how Methuen was able effectively to counter the new Boer tactics, examining his deployment of garrisons, his use of mounted infantry and his unrelenting pursuit of the enemy.

During the final phase of the war, Methuen's greatest adversary was the Free State general, Christiaan de Wet. De Wet took command of all the forces of the Orange Free State in February 1900, when his predecessor, Piet Cronjé, surrendered to Roberts at Paardeberg.[2] To frustrate the British de Wet launched the guerrilla war, which, as Byron Farwell has stated, 'was the start of a whole new war, a war in which … there would be no more set battle pieces; henceforth there would be dozens of small actions, the Boers striking unexpectedly at widely separate locations, snapping up a convoy here, attacking small garrisons there, destroying railroad bridges, blowing up locomotives, sniping'.[3]

De Wet's guerrilla tactics were aimed at interrupting British supply and communication by disrupting the integrity of the Central Railway, the major line of communication. His operations plagued Roberts' campaign and the British effort for the remainder of the conflict. Although Roberts considered this problem to be of secondary importance to his own campaign in the Transvaal, many of the British officers who took part in what became the de Wet chases, including Kitchener, R. G. Broadwood, Robert Baden-Powell, Ian Hamilton, Horace Smith-Dorrien and Methuen, did not. 'Working out a soldier's penance', as Rayne Kruger described, Methuen became the leading figure in the British pursuit of de Wet.[4]

THE GREAT DE WET HUNT

The chase after de Wet, 'one of the most determined and skilful drives of the war',[5] did not officially start until August 1900. By this time Roberts finally had awakened to the fact that de Wet posed a major threat to his rear and that there would be no peace until guerrilla operations had ceased. Only then did Roberts place a high priority on his capture. With Roberts conducting the drive in the eastern Transvaal toward Komati Poort and Portuguese territory, Kitchener was sent to co-ordinate the several British columns involved in the pursuit. The first de Wet hunt began on 6 August and ended with the latter's escape through Olifants Nek on 14 August.

For Methuen, the chase after de Wet had started two months earlier, in June, with the engagements at Lindley and the Rhenoster River. After the engagement at Rhenoster River, Methuen, attempting to capture de Wet, who was wreaking havoc on the Central Railway, followed de Wet as he headed northeast. To prevent him from breaking out westward, Methuen moved to Paardekraal on 20 June. Near Paardekraal, Methuen arrested an important member of the Afrikaner Bond, Andries Wessels, and seized hundreds of cattle and sheep. On 22 June, only a few days after the pursuit began, it was temporarily halted. Methuen was forced to head to Honings Spruit, where an enemy force had been seen threatening the railway. Reluctantly, he gave way to Major-General Ralph Clements and Major-General Arthur Paget, who continued the chase. Until mid July Methuen was occupied with the task of securing the rail line.

On 12 July Methuen was ordered into the Transvaal to relieve the British garrison at Rustenburg and pursue de la Rey's commando. Clements and Paget had successfully trapped de Wet in the northeastern region of the Orange Free State, preventing him from breaking out westward towards the railway. At Kroonstad Station Methuen's small force entrained and departed for Krugersdorp where it arrived on 16 July.[6] Accompanied by Smith-Dorrien's column,[7] Methuen advanced to Hekpoort where he met no resistance. Dividing his force into two columns, one of which was commanded by Charles Douglas, Methuen continued toward Olifants Nek,

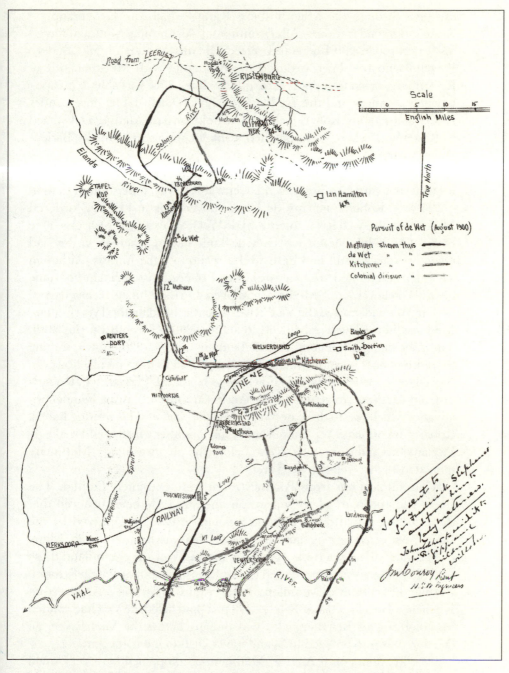

Map 10: Methuen's sketch of the pursuit of de Wet, August 1900. Map reproduced with the permission of the Wiltshire and Swindon Record Office.

the pass through the Magaliesberg Range which the Krugersdorp–Rustenburg road traverses. After continuous skirmishing, Methuen forced his way through 900 Boers and seized Olifants Nek on 21 July. Baden-Powell,[8] who had been ordered to co-operate with Methuen out of Rustenburg, failed to support him and the Boer force was able to escape.[9] Leaving a battery and the 1st Battalion Loyal North Lancashires under Lieutenant-Colonel Robert Kekewich to hold the pass, Methuen advanced to Rustenburg where he dispatched a small contingent to fortify Baden-Powell's garrison.

By this time de Wet had evaded Clements and Paget, and had forced his way westward crossing over the Central Railway at Serfontein Station on 21 July. Roberts, fearing de Wet's movements in his rear, ordered Methuen to the Vaal River to prevent de Wet from exiting the Orange Free State.[10] On 26 July Methuen arrived at Bank Station, where de la Rey had recently attacked and had destroyed a section of the railway. Although Methuen had wanted to engage de la Rey, Roberts insisted that he continue toward Potchefstroom.[11] Methuen complied. On the 29th, he received word that de Wet had crossed the Vaal River and was heading for Tygerfontein. Methuen immediately advanced, reaching Potchefstroom on the 30th. There, he engaged General P. J. Liebenberg outside of the town, forcing his retirement. The information regarding de Wet's movements, however, proved to be incorrect: he was nowhere to be found.[12] Frustrated, Roberts ordered Methuen to remain near Potchefstroom and await Kitchener's advance which was to drive de Wet across the Vaal into his waiting hands. Roberts discouraged Methuen from doing anything which could make de Wet anxious and cause him to flee before the plan was ready. Methuen's men at last got a well-deserved rest.

Communications from Potchefstroom were extremely limited. The Boers had cut many of the telegraph lines, and Methuen believed that those messages that did get through could be easily deciphered by the Boers.[13] Messages sent by hand were just as likely to be intercepted. Many of Methuen's Khoisan runners fell into the hands of the enemy, and those who did not were often too scared to carry messages out of Potchefstroom. Despite these obstacles Methuen did receive his orders on 5 August from Kitchener. He learned that Kitchener's plan had failed: de Wet had evaded his column near Reitzberg and was moving across the Vaal River; he (Methuen) was to proceed to Scandinavia Drift to intercept him.

At 0600 hours on 6 August, Methuen, accompanied by a very small force consisting of the 5th and 10th Regiments Imperial Yeomanry, half of the 1st Battalion Northumberland Fusiliers, two sections of the 4th

Battery, RFA, and two howitzers, set out for Scandinavia Drift to catch de Wet. Near Matgains station, Methuen met with Lieutenant-Colonel G. J. Younghusband, who informed him that de Wet would probably attempt to cross the Vaal near Schoeman's Drift, over ten miles upstream from Scandinavia Drift. Ignoring Kitchener's orders, Methuen headed toward Schoeman's Drift instead, ordering Douglas to advance there as well with his column. He sent detachments downstream to Scandinavia Drift and to Winkel Drift on the Rhenoster River. The disadvantage of this was that Methuen's already small force was becoming dangerously smaller.

On 7 August, after a difficult march of 22 miles, Methuen arrived near Tygerfontein, a position overlooking Schoeman's Drift, only to find de Wet's rearguard. Younghusband's information was accurate: de Wet had headed to Schoeman's Drift instead of Scandinavia Drift. However, because of the delay caused by Kitchener's faulty information, de Wet, president Steyn and 1,500 men had crossed the river earlier that same day by a drift unknown to British maps.[14] To cover his rear, de Wet had left behind another 1,500 men, roughly half of his force. Methuen arrived just in time to strike at this force. The Boers fell back onto the hills between Tygerfontein and Venterskroon under the heavy fire of the British rifles. Methuen's slower force continued to press forward. The Northumberland Fusiliers rushed from kopje to kopje, clearing each hill as they charged, leading Methuen to write to Roberts, 'I have seen nothing finer in this campaign.'[15] The British suffered 17 casualties.[16]

Methuen was determined to capture his prey. He ordered the Imperial Yeomanry under Lord Chesham to ride toward Frederikstad to cut off de Wet.[17] But after their long march the day before, Lord Chesham's men could not keep up with the quick pace set by the Boers.[18] The rest of the force continued to press on after the Boer rearguard. After a 23-mile march the British caught up with and engaged de Wet's rearguard near Leeuw-fontein on 9 August. The British suffered ten casualties but were able to capture five of de Wet's supply wagons. The rest of the Boer force escaped. Meanwhile, Kitchener, alerted to de Wet's movement, ordered Hamilton, Smith-Dorrien, Baden-Powell, Broadwood and Carrington to support Methuen.

The chase after de Wet continued. Methuen ordered Major Alan Gough to move from Potchefstroom and join him in order to reinforce his column. Determined to catch de Wet, Methuen refused to allow his tired force a chance to catch their breath. On the 10th, he headed to Welverdiend Pass after receiving information that de Wet was near Losberg. Methuen's force covered 25 more miles and, near Taaibosch Spruit, they saw Liebenberg's rearguard crossing the Gatsrand. Methuen ordered his artillery to fire, but the Boers, sheltered by the safety of the surrounding kopjes, suffered little. They continued to retreat and managed to elude Smith-Dorrien on Methuen's left flank.

Methuen believed that de Wet would next head toward Olifants Nek and the relative safety of the Magaliesberg Range.[19] Confident that Baden-Powell still held the pass where he had left him, Methuen drove de Wet toward the trap. He informed Kitchener of the plan and Kitchener replied that Hamilton's column would head toward the Pass as well. On 11 August, after another hard march, Methuen reached Frederikstad. The following day, he crossed the Mooi River Bridge and, east of Ventersdorp at Syferbult, his column engaged the Boers for over four hours, capturing a field-gun and seven wagons, and forcing de Wet to abandon 60 British prisoners. De Wet, as expected, continued toward Olifants Nek.

Although it appeared to observers that Methuen and his two columns were pursuing de Wet on their own (since they were the only British forces coming into contact with the Boer leader) this was in fact not the case. Smith-Dorrien was on Methuen's left; Kitchener, Broadwood, Brigadier-General M. O. Little, and Major-General Arthur Hart were on his right; and, Hamilton and Brigadier-General Brian Mahon were further to the east heading toward Olifants Nek. In addition, Baden-Powell was at Rustenburg and Kekewich was at Olifants Nek. Methuen, however, was the driving force in the pursuit, having marched 150 miles in six days, engaging the enemy almost every day. Whereas Broadwood had started his march with fresh cavalry 25 miles ahead of Methuen on 6 August, he had yet to engage the enemy and remained 13 miles behind.[20]

Methuen not only led the chase, he also made most of the decisions for the supporting columns. Although on Roberts' authority Kitchener had command over the many British columns in the pursuit of de Wet, Methuen was Kitchener's senior. Therefore, Kitchener and Methuen had a curious relationship. Kitchener allowed Methuen a great deal of independence, and in this chase, followed his advice to the letter.[21] When Methuen advised Kitchener to close the road to Frederikstad behind de Wet to prevent him from doubling back and turning toward Zeerust, Kitchener complied.[22]

On 14 August Methuen's troops set out at 0100 hours in pursuit of the enemy. They swept toward Magato Nek in a northwesterly movement to prevent the Boers from breaking out toward Zeerust where de Wet could have joined with de la Rey.[23] Methuen was attempting to corral de Wet toward Ian Hamilton's advancing forces and the British garrison which held Olifants Nek. About six miles from the pass, he engaged the Boer rearguard at Buffelshoek. De Wet turned and headed directly for Olifants Nek. At last, Methuen believed, he had captured his prey.

His force pressed on toward Olifants Nek only to see the 'dust' left behind by de Wet's commando still floating in the air.[24] H. E. Belfield wrote:

> We must have encircled De Wet and Steyn with him. We breathed more freely. We were some nine miles from Olifants Nek and feeling pretty confident that we had got him but not a sign of him or his [troops] could we see, but this was not to be wondrous owning to the broken nature of this country. Reports came in that he had crossed the mountains by Olifants Nek, but these were absurd – We [the British] held the Nek. Further reports came in to the same effect and gradually the awful truth dawned on us that this was actually true. Someone had blundered sadly. Poor Methuen was quite overcome, and everyone felt that he had been treated badly. If ever a man had worked hard to obtain an end ... of the war, he has and now owing to some blunder everything has [been] thrown away. It was a sad termination of our labours.[25]

Continued pursuit was useless. The men were exhausted, 16 artillery horses had to be destroyed, and supplies were running low. Again, de Wet had escaped.[26]

Despite Methuen's demands and Kitchener's assurances, the British had failed to hold the pass.[27] Baden-Powell, fearing that the force which garrisoned the pass was too small to stop de Wet, ordered its commander, Kekewich, to abandon his position. Ian Hamilton's force had moved too slowly from Commando Nek to seal off the pass. To make matters worse, Hamilton's column had unwisely marched around the southern side of the range instead of the northern side and thus could not cut off de Wet once he moved north through Olifants Nek.[28] Broadwood, too, failed to make it to the pass in time to stop de Wet. The British recaptured the pass on the 17 August, three days after de Wet rode through.

Methuen concealed the disappointment he surely felt. He wrote to his wife only that 'unfortunately Roberts left open Olifants Nek'.[29] Others demonstrated their feelings more openly. Herbert Guest wrote 'when it became apparent that the pass to which they had hunted their quarry was undefended, the rage and vexation of officers and men was unrestrained, loud and long'.[30] Even Leo Amery sympathized with Methuen when he wrote, 'Of the Generals, Methuen was certainly the soul of the pursuit; often disappointed, he made few mistakes, and never for a moment would he let his quarry go.'[31]

More outrage was expressed by Methuen's men when newspapers such as the *Daily Mail* (London) blamed him for de Wet's escape.[32] It seemed to his Chief of Staff, H. E. Belfield, that the 'papers seemed determined to belittle him in every way, and nothing he can do is right'.[33] However, not a man in his force nor any senior British officer held Methuen responsible for the failure to contain de Wet. When the press attacked his division, Methuen wrote home, '… everyone knows Hamilton is to blame, and my division is furious at the press trying to save him at our expense'.[34]

Blame for the failure to stop de Wet must first be assigned to Roberts himself. As a commander who carefully studied the movements of his subordinates, he was well aware of the overall situation. Kitchener and Methuen kept him abreast of every movement they made. Kekewich, in Baden-Powell's judgement, did not have enough men to stop de Wet at Olifant's Nek, and Roberts should have prepared for this possibility either by sending more troops or ordering Baden-Powell to make a stand and fight despite the risks. Roberts had more than enough men engaged in his own drive toward Pretoria to send reinforcements and should have placed greater importance on de Wet's capture. Some blame must also rest on Hamilton's shoulders for his failure to see the exigency of getting to the Nek quickly.

Clearly, no one should have blamed Methuen for the British failure to stop de Wet. In the pursuit, he proved himself ready to meet the new challenge which the Boers offered.[35] No longer commanding divisions in set battles like those during his attempt to relieve Kimberley, he was forced to be ready to drop everything at a moment's notice and rush off with his small column when a fresh rumour or his reconnaissance presented new information as to the whereabouts of the enemy. Whenever de Wet's force was located, Methuen was single-minded and determined in his pursuit. Few British officers could keep such pressure on the Boers as Methuen did, despite his column's clumsy composition. General A. P. Wavell wrote, 'In sustaining pursuit, mobility is dependent mainly on the personal will and determination of the Commander-in-Chief'[36] – qualities which were clearly demonstrated by Methuen throughout his pursuit of de Wet.

On 15 August, with de Wet now roaming freely north of the Magaliesberg, Roberts gave Methuen new orders. He was to march westwards, relieve Colonel C. O. Hore at Brakfontein on the Elands River and then proceed to Zeerust. There, he would take command of operations in the Marico and Mafeking Districts in the Western Transvaal.

However, like many of Roberts' plans for Methuen, this one was also to change. Methuen did not go to Brakfontein to relieve Hore. Instead,

Kitchener was ordered to rescue Hore, and Methuen proceeded directly for the western districts. After skirmishing with Liebenberg at Magato Pass, he changed direction and, via Zeerust and Ottoshoop, marched toward Mafeking, where his force arrived on the 28th. The force remained there through the first week of September, enjoying a well-deserved rest.[37] Methuen was to remain in the Western Transvaal for the rest of the war.

In the first week of September 1900 Roberts annexed the Transvaal, Buller seized Lydenburg, French captured Carolina, and the president of the former South African Republic, Paul Kruger, fled to Lorenço Marques in the Portuguese colony at Delagoa Bay. The British continued their drive into the Eastern Transvaal and the Orange Free State and restored their control over northern Natal. Methuen, far off from the main sectors of the war, took up the administration of the sparsely populated Western Transvaal – an area deemed strategically unimportant by both Roberts and Kitchener. However, Methuen never felt that his command was any less important than any other British command. He was determined to do whatever he could to defeat the Boers, and he would rather hold a less exciting post than idly await the day when he could sail home.

Methuen's men were highly motivated by their commander's determination to stay and fight the enemy, and they greatly respected his strong will and diligence. Karl Spurgin, in a book about his experiences while serving in the Northumberland and Durham Yeomanry, described an incident which demonstrated Methuen's courage and quick-thinking. As his men rested in Mafeking in early September, Methuen personally led a small patrol to reconnoitre the area on 3 September. When he came across a river,[38] Methuen sent an empty wagon into the water drawn by 16 oxen with two African drivers to determine if it was fordable. The wagon made it across successfully, but on its return trip a pair of the oxen went under, got confused and began to head upstream. A conductor, astride his horse, jumped into the water to grab the team but fell, losing control of the oxen. Without thinking of the risk, Methuen jumped into the river and grabbed the oxen himself. His action was best summed up by Spurgin: 'No wonder the men under his command look up to him and admire his grit.'[39]

Another example of Methuen's relationship with his men is described by Herbert Guest in an incident outside of Bloedzuikerspan. In this account, Methuen displayed the paternal instincts he had for his men. 'At this place there was a well, the convenience for drawing the water being a Bakkies [*sic*] pump, usually worked by an ox or a horse. Lord Methuen, with Lord Loch, rode on in front, and when the infantry arrived they found their General and Lord Loch at the pump, forcing up a supply of water for the parched and travel-worn soldiers.'[40] Methuen was loved by his men because he was willing to do anything for them. He never asked anything of them which he did not ask of himself. If there remained some doubts among others about his ability to command, none existed among his men. His concern for his men never flagged and because of the faith they had in him, they would have followed him anywhere. After meeting Methuen for only 30 minutes, one colonial officer said to Methuen's adjutant, 'You know, I would kill myself for your Chief.'[41]

LORD ROBERTS AND THE CAPTURE OF ZEERUST

By 7 September Methuen felt that his men were ready to leave Mafeking and to get back to work. He urged Roberts to allow him to take the town of Zeerust, believing it to be the key to the entire Marico District. Convinced that the Boers were weakening, Methuen believed that if Zeerust fell, they would probably surrender. In addition, a strong demonstration against Zeerust would also be seen as a sign of support for the loyalists in the area, who Methuen feared were becoming increasingly apprehensive about the British army's ability to protect them.[42] Roberts, however, frustrated Methuen's plan. He was concerned not as to whether Methuen could take Zeerust, but whether he could hold it. Dividing his force to provide adequate garrisons for numerous points, Roberts believed, would make Methuen too weak to face any sizeable Boer force.[43] As he was endeavouring to establish martial law in the recently annexed Transvaal, Roberts felt that he could not spare any reinforcements: thus Methuen was persuaded temporarily to put aside thoughts of capturing Zeerust.[44]

After garrisoning Mafeking with over 1,000 troops, and dispatching a secondary column under Major-General Douglas to Lichtenburg, Methuen proceeded to clear the country around Ottoshoop and Zeerust.[45] If he could not seize Zeerust, at least he could cut it off from reinforcement. As usual, the Boers resisted. On 8 September a small skirmish took place at Grootfontein. The following day Methuen met Vermaas's commando at Melopo Oog, just southeast of Ottoshoop, and took 30 prisoners, along with over 40,000 rounds of ammunition.[46] The Boers fled after each encounter.

Although they no longer came forward to meet the British in pitched battles, the Boers made their presence felt by striking at weak British garrisons and their supply lines. Belfield described this situation as 'the utter collapse of any true resistance among the Boers and the adoption by them of purely guerrilla warfare, secreting themselves in almost

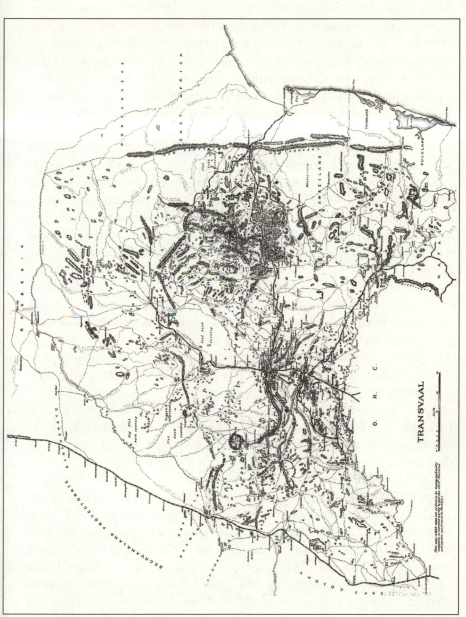

Map 11: The Transvaal, 1899. Map reproduced from Leo Amery, *The Times History of the War in South Africa*, London, Sampson Low, Marston and Co., 1907.

inaccessible hills and sallying forth merely to snipe at convoys or cut off any opposition'. Though the enemy was there, 'in fact nothing could be seen of the[m]'.[47] Belfield was correct in suggesting that any unified resistance had collapsed. As Byron Farwell has demonstrated, after June 1900 there was no longer any real Boer strategy or policy for continuing the war. But Belfield was wrong in suggesting that the adoption of guerrilla warfare was the result of the collapse of Boer resistance. Indeed, resistance had not collapsed, it had just changed form. Boer resistance was no longer unified behind the Boer presidents, but had broken down into the individual efforts of localized commando leaders.[48]

Fighting the Boer guerrillas was infuriating for British officers trained to meet the enemy's army head-on in one decisive battle. Whether at Amoaful, Tel-el-Kebir or Omdurman, the British knew that the entire war would end as soon as the decisive battle was over. In South Africa, departure dates were continually pushed back by those British officers foolish enough to choose them. Although Methuen did not let on until much later in the war that this type of guerrilla fighting exacerbated him, Belfield spoke very clearly:

> Ours [the task in hand] is not a noble one. We are to travel about our district and by living on the country exhaust it of supplies so that it will be impossible for any commando to live there. I doubt its success. The next step will be that we shall [not] feed the inhabitants. It's dirty work and I hate it. Who on earth draws up Lord Roberts' proclamation should be fitted with more brains then he apparently has.[49]

Engaging in this kind of warfare would seriously test the morale of the British soldiers, many of whom were seeing combat for the first time in their lives.

On 12 September Methuen received orders to march to Schweizer Reneke where 2,400 Boers were reported to have surrounded the British garrison there. Major-General Settle would join him from Vryburg. Methuen moved at once. Far from the rugged hills surrounding the Witwatersrand, the 1st Division moved on to the flatlands near the southwest corner of the Transvaal. Methuen reported that the farms along the way were deserted of humans, but that there were plenty of sheep, cattle, oxen, donkeys and horses to be found. All of these, as well as the occasional prisoner, became property of the British army. However, by the time the force reached Polfontein on the 14 September, as the terrain hardened and water became more difficult to find, the animals disappeared.

On 19 September Methuen encountered Tollie de Beer and 400 Boers outside of Jaksraal. Once again his force scattered the enemy, and 28 Boers, several wagons and several thousand cattle and sheep were captured. Most satisfying was the retrieval of a 15-pr gun which had been lost by Buller at Colenso. With Methuen's defeat of this force and Settle's successful advance to Schweizer Reneke, the garrison was relieved. Methuen headed at once northeast toward Rustenburg.

By late September 1900 Methuen had received word that Roberts planned to leave South Africa. With the capture of Johannesburg and Pretoria and the annexation of the Transvaal, Roberts believed that his work was done. There was much speculation among Methuen's staff about their commander's fate as well as their own. Methuen, for one, was initially delighted with the news. With Roberts' departure, he assumed that Buller would once again be his 'master' which would mean 'a free hand, definite orders and no more rushing about from pillar to post'.[50] Methuen wrote to Edward Cecil, who was acting as an emissary for Alfred Milner, gathering information regarding Roberts' direction of the war, that Lord Roberts was largely to blame for the slow pace of the war and the failure of the British to defeat the Boers.[51]

By late October new information had altered Methuen's expectations. On 24 September Buller set sail from Cape Town for England, never to return. Although Methuen made no comment on this in his letters home, H. E. Belfield wrote what Methuen himself must have been thinking: 'I hear that Buller has gone home, this means Methuen is the next senior to Roberts in South Africa. ... As they certainly won't leave him in command he will probably go home before or at the same time as Roberts. This may mean that I shall go too – I hope so, I've had quite enough by this.'[52] As senior officer in the field, any option other than returning home would have been humiliating, for it would have meant his supersession by a subordinate. He wrote to his wife in mid November that he would be leaving South Africa shortly after Roberts.[53]

Believing that he would set sail for home any day, Methuen set off in late September for what he expected would be his last trek during the South African War. He returned to Rustenburg to clear the district and to try to intercept President Steyn, who was rumoured to be in the vicinity. On 28 September Methuen engaged Lemmer's commando twice near Brockhorst-fontein. He continued to act in and around Rustenburg until 9 October, when he moved north to pursue de la Rey. Douglas manœuvred de la Rey toward Boschoek Nek and toward Methuen's column. De la Rey, however, had no desire to fight the strong British force. He fled westward and, as a result of his mobility, escaped. Methuen had asked for more horses to reduce de la Rey's chance of evading him again, but Roberts sent him none.

Methuen headed west toward Zeerust, careful not to get trapped between Lemmer and de la Rey. The enemy continued to harass his flanks but refused to engage him in any battle. On the 16th, Methuen caught Lemmer and successfully forced his retreat. The following day he turned on de la Rey and again had some minor success. On 18 October the British marched into Zeerust.

Despite Roberts' objections Methuen at last got the position he wanted by occupying Zeerust. He had believed, as explained above, that this was the key position for holding the Western Transvaal and forcing the Boers' surrender. Roberts telegraphed sarcastically, 'I believe Zeerust is not an easy place to defend but you have of course satisfied yourself.'[54] Roberts' position on Methuen's action was clear:

> Large as the force appears to be in South Africa, it has proved all too small for the duties it has been required to perform, and I have found it impracticable to occupy in sufficient strength the many places it would have been advantageous to have held. Every garrison thus isolated not only reduces the power and mobility of the several columns in the field, but necessitates the withdrawal of these columns from other important duties to periodically escort convoys of supplies for its use.[55]

Methuen was also well aware of the problems of stretching his forces and leaving behind isolated garrisons in hostile territory, but he saw no other means to protect sympathetic settlers and to prevent the Boer commandos from resupplying themselves. Roberts did not suggest any alternatives.[56]

The capture of Zeerust did not force the Boers to surrender as Methuen had hoped. He believed that there were three reasons for this. First, the Boer leaders believed that they would be exiled for life to remote colonies and therefore they saw no other option but to continue to fight. To scotch this belief Methuen sent a letter to de la Rey encouraging him to surrender and giving him his word that he would be 'sent to St Helena only until the colony was quiet'.[57] Second, Methuen had heard rumours that many Boers who had previously surrendered and who did not want to fight any more were forced back into service. Third, he thought that many held strong beliefs that God was going to intervene on their behalf: 'The commandants have told the Boers that the English mean to leave the Transvaal October 15; that a plague has killed 1,000s in our army, and that God has rained stones in England which have killed 1,000s, and sunk thirteen of our finest ships.'[58] Despite the Boers' reasons for continuing the war, Methuen desperately wanted to put an end to it: 'My [sole] object is to save further loss of life.'[59]

Throughout the rest of October and November, as the Boers struggled to retake the offensive with an invasion of the Cape Colony and attacks on Balmoral and Dewetsdorp, the British continued to be frustrated in their attempt to bring order to the Western Transvaal. After leaving behind a garrison at Zeerust, Methuen headed toward Ottoshoop to prevent Louis Botha and his 3,000 men from moving west toward Mafeking and joining de la Rey. Douglas, working in conjunction with Methuen, drove Lemmer and Botha towards his awaiting force near Kaffir Kraal. After a heavy skirmish on the 24th, the Boers escaped when Lord Erroll's yeomanry failed to move decisively.[60] In such encounters the British often captured a number of the enemy and a great deal of supplies, yet they failed to prevent the majority of the commando from getting away.[61]

Methuen next moved to the Lichtenburg district to carry out Roberts' scorched-earth policy. This policy was initiated in the field by Kitchener. To clear the district of resistance, Methuen was ordered to destroy all crops which potentially could be used to feed the enemy forces, and to send anyone caught assisting the commandos to concentration camps. Roberts had referred to this policy as 'a sad necessity' to bring the war to a close,[62] and Methuen too was unenthusiastic.[63] As we have already noted (Chapter 9), after the war Methuen was proud of the fact that he 'never burnt down a farm that he didn't have to'. But his disgust for the scorched-earth policy and his concern for the innocent Boer farmers went further than postwar boasts. He often gave several warnings to the wives of the burghers on commando who remained on their farms during the war before taking action. At other times he simply ignored the directives. In addition, he pitied the destitute left behind by the scorched-earth policy, delivering many to concentration camps. Although this might seem a dubious act of kindness, the camps being a form of detention or imprisonment, Methuen took this action for the simple reason that he felt many of these people would die without British assistance. This action eventually forced Roberts to complain: 'Is there an advantage in sending old men and women? I have steadily refused to sanction this procedure ... and H. C. [High Commissioner] begs that no more may be similarly treated.'[64] It was becoming too expensive and too much work to care for the poor in the already overcrowded camps.

From November through to December, Methuen's forces tried to keep all of the garrisons in the area supplied and the district quiescent.

Accompanied by only 1,500 troops, most of which were yeomanry, this task was becoming more difficult. Douglas, who, after serving as Methuen's Chief of Staff commanded the 9th Brigade under him, left with his column in early November to join French at Klerksdorp. Methuen lost a valuable officer and roughly 2,300 men, including 800 mounted troops. His force was reduced and, from this point on, operations in the Western districts were greatly hindered. While Methuen's force diminished, the size of the Boer force grew apace, and resistance in the west grew along with it. Caught as he was between de la Rey and de Wet, Methuen's position grew more precarious.

On 28 November, while near Lichtenburg, Methuen heard from Roberts for the last time. Roberts was leaving South Africa and command of the British forces in South Africa was being passed to Kitchener (who was given a corresponding senior local rank). Methuen, on the other hand, surprisingly was going nowhere. The departing Commander-in-Chief of the South African forces wrote: 'Sorry not to say goodbye in person, but you are too far off. ... I have watched with great interest the many difficult marches you have had to make, and the great number of times while your columns have been engaged with the enemy. On every occasion you have been successful. ... I congratulate you.'[65] In response to the letter Methuen wrote to his wife:

> Lord Roberts ... made out peace when there was no peace, and going home himself [and] sending home our troops has made the Boer think we do not intend to hold the country permanently, and all they have to do is to hold on. Losing our chance of catching De Wet saved closing the war in August. ... I expect [Pole] Carew will become Military Secretary, and should do well. I only hope Lord Roberts may come up to public expectation as Commander in Chief. Kitchener will be hated out here, and has not done anything that makes one to have the slightest confidence in him.[66]

Clearly, Methuen was not happy with the situation which Roberts was leaving behind and held him largely responsible for it. What changes would follow under Kitchener's command, he could not anticipate.[67]

SERVING UNDER KITCHENER

If Methuen could not anticipate what would follow, his chief of staff could. He knew exactly what effect Kitchener's new position would have on Methuen: he would continue to do whatever he was ordered to do and would do it well. Belfield wrote: '[Methuen] is the most loyal man in the world and will play up to Kitchener, just as heartily as he did to Roberts. He might have done better had he been a little less loyal and more selfish.'[68]

Many historians view Roberts' departure from South Africa and Kitchener's ascendancy to command as the beginning of a new phase in the South African War. This phase comprised the transition from a major offensive aimed at key strategic centres to a 'mop up' operation. The British would now have to concentrate on eliminating individual Boer commandos still operating in the areas free from their overall control. In the case of Methuen and the Western districts of the Transvaal, Roberts' departure changed little. The guerrilla phase of the war continued. The only essential change for Methuen was the increased independence he was given. Whereas Roberts consistently harassed Methuen with a barrage of orders and demanded constant updates, Kitchener, very surprisingly, left Methuen to his own devices. Although Kitchener still kept a watchful eye on his other subordinates, Methuen, along with French, was given an amazing amount of independence.

For the remainder of 1900, Methuen continued to patrol the Lichtenburg district. Meanwhile, the area of his command was extended as far south as the Orange River.[69] The increased size of his command seems to have had little to do with the demand of the actual state of affairs. The Western districts were still far from 'pacified'. Indeed, a serious action on 14 December outside of Ottoshoop had resulted in the death of the Boer general, H. L. Lemmer, and the capture of five prisoners and the entire Boer laager including 15,000 rounds of ammunition, 1,500 cattle and 2,000 sheep.[70] However, de la Rey, Smuts and Vermaas remained in the area; de Wet was just to the east; and, du Toit, de Villiers, Celliers and Liebenberg remained in striking distance to the southeast. The area of Methuen's command was growing, his forces were shrinking and Boer resistance continued. Of Methuen's lines of communications which now stretched over 2,000 miles, Belfield wrote, 'I do not think an attempt has ever previously been made to guard such a length of line.'[71] As far as the Western districts were concerned, Kitchener had inherited no easy task from Roberts.

After the key garrisons of Zeerust and Lichtenburg were provisioned for the next six months and the Ottoshoop garrison was withdrawn, Methuen and his small force headed for Griqualand West. The area around Griqualand West had grown restive and the security of Bechuanaland was threatened. A week of Methuen's men marching back and forth and demonstrating in the area seemed to have scared off the Boers. The Boers

fled for safer areas in the east and the area was pacified. On New Year's
Eve 1901, Methuen boarded a train in Vryburg and headed for Taungs
via Schweizer Reneke to denude the Boer farms of their capabilities to
support the guerrillas still operating in the southwest of the Transvaal.

The relative quiet of the early summer months did not afford Methuen
and his men much rest, since they were still needed to patrol the Western
Districts. By February, when Kitchener ordered them east toward Klerksdorp, the toll of a year's incessant marching had begun to wear them down.
As Belfield wrote to his wife:

> The constant movement is telling even on Methuen I think, and he is at last
> beginning to understand that everyone is not so strong as himself. His energy
> is as boundless as ever. It was the knowledge of his appalling energy that
> proved one of the strongest obstacles against his getting the Aldershot
> command. It was argued that if he were sent there he would so tire out the
> men … that recruiting would be seriously affected.[72]

The British war effort was dragging in all sectors of South Africa as
Kitchener awaited the arrival of 30,000 additional mounted troops. In the
Western Transvaal, Methuen marched east toward Klerksdorp after
receiving reports which suggested that several commandos led by S. P. du
Toit, Jan Celliers and P. J. Liebenberg were gathering there. With co-
operation from Brigadier-General Cunningham and 2,300 men to the east
near Roodepoort, and from Major-General J. M. Babington[73] and 2,000
more men to the northeast near Naauwpoort, Methuen left Taungs on the
2nd. After an 11-day march, constantly harassed by General de Villiers'
Bloemhof commando, Methuen's force finally reached Wolmaransstad on
14 February. They continued to press on toward Klerksdorp. While encamped at Paardeplaats, a day's trek away from their destination, Methuen
located a large Boer force which held several British prisoners just to his
southeast. On 17 February he ordered his men to attack the next day at
0500 hours.

About 1,500 Boers were situated high in the hills at Hartebeestfontein.
They occupied fortified positions on both flanks of the Klerksdorp road
that descended down into the valley as well as at the *nek* where the road
passed through the kopjes. Methuen, with his much smaller force, was
determined to break through the Boer defences. Failure to do so could have
allowed de Villiers to advance from the rear, cut off any possible retreat
and surround the British in this most dangerous position. This would be,
as Methuen put it, 'the hardest nut he had to crack since Magersfontein'.[74]

M. H. Grant, in the *(Official) History of the War in South Africa*, described Methuen's attack as 'brilliant'.[75] Methuen struck simultaneously at both sides of the road with his yeomanry, while holding back his few companies of regulars to escort the supplies and non-combatants through the pass. On the right, the 5th Yeomanry rushed the west flank, and, in a mad dash, drove the Boers from their position. On the left, the 10th Imperial Yeomanry had a much more difficult struggle, since the Boer position was held in a series of ridges. The initial assault was repelled. Methuen, believing that it was still too dangerous to try to force the *nek* even after the capture of the right flank, ordered more of the 10th into the fray. They forced their way up the steep embankment under the heavy fire of the Boer rifles. The poorly trained British irregulars continued to advance and forced back the Boers. Although the Boers were able to locate new positions and continue to offer strong resistance, they had been pushed too far back to assist the forces holding the *nek*. Methuen then ordered the Loyal North Lancashire to advance along the open road toward the *nek*. With the aid of the artillery, they forced their way through the Boer lines, and, under a deliberate fire, seized the *nek* as well as the Boer laager. The 5th and 10th Yeomanry then methodically pulled back and retreated through the pass behind the Loyal North Lancashires Regiment.[76] The British supply wagons and non-combatants were given ample time to escape through the pass as well. Methuen walked through the lines to congratulate the soldiers, shaking their hands and chatting with them. Two days later, the force entered Klerksdorp.

Methuen's march to Klerksdorp was a superb feat. While constantly being harassed by enemy skirmishing parties and snipers, his force had covered over 150 miles in seven days. At Hartebeestfontein, Methuen gave further justification for his presence in South Africa. He had gathered over a year's experience since Magersfontein. He understood his enemy's tactics and no longer put his faith in the unlimited capabilities of his artillery. He had also gained an understanding about the limits of his own men, who could not be compared to the crack regiments of the Guards and Highlander Brigades. Dargai tactics, where the Gordons defiantly charged a virtually impenetrable position under heavy fire, were now the farthest thing from Methuen's mind.[77] The bulk of his force was comprised of hastily raised yeomen and he now had a much better awareness of what they could be expected to do and to endure.

Throughout the autumn Methuen continued his operations in the Western Transvaal. After excursions to Hoopstad[78] and Ventersdorp, his force returned to the Western Railway which ran parallel to the Transvaal–

Cape Colony border. In mid March 1901 they crossed the Vaal River and entered Warrenton. Methuen, feeling unwell, placed himself on the sick list and handed his command over to the Earl of Erroll. Without him, his men headed north to Mafeking to chase after de la Rey. Methuen remained in Warrenton and did not retake the field until the first of May. He finally got a much-deserved rest.

THE LAST YEAR OF THE WAR

In early May 1901 Kitchener's operations entered their final phase. The Blockhouse system, designed to protect the railroads from guerrilla activity, and the concentration camps, constructed to break morale and prevent sympathizers from feeding the guerrillas, were established through South Africa. The enforcement of Martial Law was also spreading over the annexed colonies. With reinforcements of cavalry, mounted infantry, yeomanry and South African irregulars strengthening his mounted force to over 50,000, the effective fighting force of Kitchener's army in South Africa numbered over 160,000 – a far cry from Buller's small force which took the field at the close of 1899.[79] With this large force, Kitchener could now overwhelm the Boers by taking control of both the countryside and the important urban centres.

Although the size of the British army was growing in South Africa, Kitchener believed that securing the Western Transvaal was of little importance. Like Roberts, he underestimated the Boers' capability to resist. Methuen's division received no reinforcements. With so few men, and the other British columns operating in the Western Transvaal unable to lend support due to poor communication or other responsibilities, Methuen could do little more than chase after shadows.[80] Thus the enemy continued to evade his grasp.

On 1 May Methuen retook the field with 150 infantry, 1,163 mounted infantry, ten guns, and two machine guns near Lichtenburg.[81] His job was to strengthen the garrisons, to pacify the Lichtenburg district and to capture de la Rey and Kemp who were harassing the weak outposts. Through August, Methuen's force marched back and forth from Lichtenburg to Zeerust to Mafeking to Klerksdorp; ground which became so familiar to all of the soldiers that maps were rarely needed. Still, the Boer commandos managed to elude Methuen and the other British columns. Garrisons and outposts continued to be raided, rails destroyed and ambushes attempted, but the Boers refused to end their resistance. With Kitchener's eyes on the

Eastern Transvaal where similar events were taking place, the numbers of British soldiers in the Western Transvaal continued to decrease despite Methuen's inability to pacify the area.

By mid August 1901 Methuen had been working in the Western Transvaal for a year. The routine of strengthening outposts, repairing rail and telegraph lines, and chasing after the Boers, as described above, had not changed. There were, however, some differences in Methuen's force and in his attitude one year later. The composition of his force had changed radically. When his Northumberland and Durham Yeomanry entrained on 14 May for Cape Town, on their journey to England, Methuen's 'heart was too full to allow him to attempt a speech'.[82] He had a word with each man and shook their hands and wished them luck. The Shropshire Yeomanry, which had also served him well since the winter of 1900, had also departed. Increasingly, Methuen was getting raw troops which were of very little value on the battlefield. He complained often, but there was nothing Kitchener could do except to offer his sympathy. He telegraphed in June, 'Very sorry to hear that your new yeomanry are so unreliable. Hope by steady training they will improve.'[83] Kitchener was counting on one of two things: either the war would last long enough for these raw recruits to get seasoned or these troops would not be needed for heavy combat. Methuen could not be expected to do much with these troops; certainly Kitchener could not have expected much. Besides, Kitchener was more concerned with other areas of the war.

Methuen's attitude to the Boers was also changing: he was becoming increasingly sympathetic towards them and had developed amicable relations with several Boer officers. In a letter to Alfred Milner he displayed the mutual respect he and the Lichtenburg commando general, J. G. Celliers, had for each other: 'Directly [after] the fighting is over he sends a man to show me where any wounded man may be. As far as escort to an ambulance I never think of such a thing, for the Boers trust me, and I trust them.'[84]

Methuen had always displayed respect and kindness toward his enemy as well as sympathy toward the non-combatants, and his belief that his government was pursuing a ruthless policy against civilians only strengthened his convictions. In the field, he continued to abhor the orders to burn the homes of those out on commando and force their families into concentration camps. At the refugee camps, he witnessed several abuses by the civilian administrators: inmates being worked excessively hard, women and children inadequately clothed, a lack of supplies such as fuel, food and medicines. He also received reports of overcrowding and poor climate at other camps.[85] He believed that the general treatment of the Boers would only stiffen their resolve to continue the fight and thus delay the end of the war. In addition, he believed that it would make reconciliation afterwards even more difficult.

Methuen conveyed his views to Henry Campbell-Bannerman, former Secretary of War and a current leader of the Liberal Party. This had a great impact on the Liberal Party's position on Kitchener's blockhouse system and the scorched-earth policy.

> The Boers were less accessible to compromise in August 1901 than formerly because their hearts had been hardened by the methods of warfare, which would alienate them the more the longer we pursued them. … It should be repeated as often as possible that such a victory [attained by such methods] will be only the beginning of a long agony of constitutional strife culminating in a final and probably successful revolution.[86]

Even before the war ended, Methuen anticipating future difficulties, favoured a 'humane policy' which would foster goodwill between the two peoples. He saw no other way out of the conflict.

In late August, Boer operations on all fronts heated up after President Steyn, de Wet, Botha and others in a Council of War rejected a British plea for a Boer surrender. They took the offensive, an action highlighted by Smuts' invasion of the Cape Colony and Botha's march on Natal. In the Western Transvaal, the forces of de la Rey and General Christoffel Kemp once again renewed activity directed at interrupting British communication and supply and driving the British to their physical breaking point.

Kitchener quickly responded to the Boer threats on the Cape Colony and Natal by sending several columns to reinforce the British troops already there. However, once again he neglected the Transvaal. He scraped up only a few columns (those commanded by Allenby, Kekewich, Colonel William Hickie, Lieutenant-Colonel Ingouville-Williams and Brigadier-General Gilbert Hamilton) to aid Methuen, and on 1 September this force rode to intercept Kemp at Roodewal. The inadequate British force was not large enough to contain the enemy, Methuen having fewer than 500 men to guard the west flank, and Kemp – with a force twice as large – easily drove through his thin lines.

On 4 September Methuen headed for Zeerust.[87] After a brief skirmish on the 4th, he was attacked on the 5th by Kemp and de la Rey near Wonderfontein in the Marico River Valley. Greatly outnumbered, he nonetheless was able to temporarily hold back the enemy forces. He then continued toward Zeerust. Throughout the month, Methuen continued to skirmish with the Boers as he marched from Zeerust, to Lichtenburg and to Mafeking, refitting and dropping off supplies where needed. As the British failed to stop de la Rey and Kemp, so too did the Boers fail to stop Methuen. Methuen's success brought more enemies upon him as Commandants F. C. van Tonder, Daniel Botha, Liebenberg and Lemmer joined de la Rey and Kemp in their pursuit.[88] The British response was just the opposite. In early October, when Methuen required more troops to stop the Boers, Kitchener unwisely diverted most of the British columns from the Western Transvaal to Natal – an area deemed vital to British interest and more at risk. This left only Methuen, Kekewich and Hickie to guard the outposts and garrisons and to break Boer resistance.[89]

British operations in the Western Transvaal were floundering. With few troops, there was little Methuen could do to stop the Boer guerrillas. He was able to maintain authority over the towns and outposts which his forces occupied but could make little headway in expanding his zone of control northeast into the Witwatersrand or southeast toward the Vaal River. Kitchener seemed satisfied with this temporary stalemate. He believed that with time, resistance would decline. He also believed, with little evidence, that de la Rey could not hold out much longer. In mid September, Kitchener telegraphed Methuen: 'De la Rey is very nearly done. He has been much hustled lately and a little more would result in collapse in the whole Western Transvaal. I hope you will be able to give him the little more necessary and give him no rest.'[90] Perhaps Kitchener's claim was a justification for not sending Methuen any reinforcements. Nevertheless, Methuen's sole objective, at least in theory, became the capture of de la Rey.[91]

Had the capture of de la Rey been Methuen's only responsibility, events might have unfolded differently, but as it was he had much else to worry about. With roughly 3,000 men under his command, and another 2,000 under Kekewich and Hickie, he had to administer the Western Transvaal from its western frontier to the Zeerust–Lichtenburg–Wolmaransstad line in the east and the northern Cape Colony from Mafeking to Fourteen Streams.[92] He could not devote himself to the single purpose of capturing de la Rey, since he was needed to garrison towns and outposts, provide supplies where necessary, ensure the safety of the loyalists and make repairs on bridges and rails, among other tasks. In addition, the size of the force he actually had at his disposal for offensive operations never exceeded 2,000 – much too small to seriously attempt to stop de la Rey.[93]

Methuen utilized his few troops the best he could, employing them to destroy crops, seize stock and skirmish with the enemy. In October he cooperated with Kekewich around Zeerust; in November, he pursued the Boers near Klerksdorp; whilst December saw him moving west toward Wolmaransstad. There, he twice took Commandant Potgieter by surprise, enabling the British to seize prisoners, wagons, grain and thousands of sheep.[94] Through the New Year and into January, fighting off heavy rains and *rinderpest* (a cattle disease), Methuen marched northwest to Vryburg and then on to Lichtenburg. In February, he returned by rail to Klerksdorp, and caught Potgieter once again outside of Wolmaransstad and captured 36 more burghers. He then returned to Vryburg for a rest and to take care of some long overdue administrative work. Colonel Stanley von Donop took command of his column in the meantime.[95]

As the war went into its third year, the Boers had begun to lose their drive. For the moment, it seemed Kitchener was right in his assessment of the Western Transvaal. A stalemate had been reached and Methuen's administered districts were quieting down. The blockhouses and the often ruthless policies carried out against the civilian populations were taking their toll on the Boers. Fewer mounts were to be found and the Boers were running low on ammunition. De la Rey remained elusive, but the British, with fewer and fewer men, were able to maintain relative order in the Western Transvaal and continue to make gains in the other theatres of the war.

Despite having met little serious opposition during his marches across the Western Transvaal in the last five months, Methuen was far from confident. He worried that he did not have enough men in his district to contain any strong Boer offensive or to conduct a British offensive. The few men he had were raw recruits, growing increasingly tired due to the demands put on each man for the work of many.[96] His fear became reality on 24 February when von Donop and a force of nearly 700, escorting 150 empty wagons to Klerksdorp, were ambushed at Yzer Spruit by de la Rey and 1,300 Boers. The British force was captured after a brief struggle which left over 50 of them dead and 130 wounded. Methuen, fearing that this disaster could give the Boers a morale boost and lead to further activity, immediately requested more experienced infantry. His request was turned down by Ian Hamilton, Kitchener's Chief of Staff.[97] Kitchener would recognize too late that this incident and the failure to send more troops to support Methuen began a chain of events which seriously set back the British war effort in South Africa.[98]

Methuen took von Donop's defeat personally. After all, he had been in the field with these same men for months and had watched over and cared for them like a father. Paper-work had only recently forced him from their company. Furious over the convoy disaster, he wrote to his wife, 'Directly [after] I left the column the Boers captured my convoy, 100 wagons, and all the laager escorts surrendered. It is maddening and really I can blame no one. The fact is they won't fight me, but the moment my back is turned, go for my successor.'[99]

Methuen sought revenge against the Boers. No doubt, chasing de la Rey for most of the past two and a half years had worn down his patience. Although he had recently received orders to return home to England, he gathered together all the forces that he could spare in the Western Transvaal into what Leo Amery called 'one of the most extraordinary columns which ever took the field in South Africa' to make one last attempt to catch de la Rey.[100] Methuen believed that it was necessary 'to stop the captured convoy and guns from being taken to the Marico' which would be used in strengthening Boer resistance north of Zeerust.[101] His 1,300 men which made up the 'Kimberley Column' came from 14 different units, the majority of which were irregulars, many of which had never seen action.[102]

DEFEAT AT TWEEBOSCH

On 2 March Methuen left Vryburg with his column and headed toward Rooirantjestfontein, an important crossroads, 20 miles south of Lichtenburg. At Rooirantjestfontein, Methuen's column was to be strengthened by the addition of Lieutenant-Colonel H. M. Grenfell's 1,600 mounted troops. Colonel A. N. Rochfort and a force of 1,000 was also marching north to join Methuen. Thus reinforced, Methuen would then march northeast and intercept de la Rey and the captured convoy as they attempted to escape into the Marico Valley.

At nightfall, Methuen reached O'Reill's Pan and encamped. On the 3rd, the force reached Bester's Farm; the 4th, Mooiplaats; and, on the evening of the 5th, it reached Barber's Pan with a welcome of sniper fire from the Boers. On the 6th, Methuen's force skirmished with Commandant Louis Jacobus van Zyl. The Boers broke off the unsuccessful attack but not before 'it became evident … that the [British] troops were not efficient, the officers los[t] their head and the men lack[ed] coolness and fire discipline'.[103] Methuen had no choice but to rely upon his raw yeomanry. As Kitchener had directed, they would have to gain their experience in the field.

Methuen crossed Great Hart's River and moved to Leeuwspruit. After finding no water there, he was forced to abandon his position and move to Tweebosch. Methuen had wished to avoid Tweebosch and to give Klip

Drift, a position which he had not yet reconnoitred, a 'wide berth'. However, 'want of water' forced him to go there.[104] Twenty-five miles from Rooirant-jestfontein, Methuen had yet to hear anything from Grenfell or Rochfort about his expected reinforcements. However, he was not overly concerned. Although he now knew van Zyl was near, his information led him to believe that the main Boer force under de la Rey was still to the south.[105] Unbe-known to Methuen, de la Rey, notified by van Zyl of the British movement, had arrived during the night bringing the strength of the Boer force up to 1,500.[106]

On 7 March, at 0300 hours, Methuen and an oxen convoy accompanied by the 86th Co. Imperial Yeomanry, the 300 regular infantry, a section of the 4th Battery, RFA, and some of the Cape Police, moved out toward Leeuwkuil. An hour later, the more mobile second column, commanded by Major Paris, followed. At 0500 hours, just as day broke, the front column reached Klip Drift. At the same time, the rear of the second column was hit by a heavy fire. Although a mile ahead of the engagement, at the first shots, Methuen's Khoisan drivers panicked and hid for cover under their oxen. Methuen could neither move his column to safety nor support Paris' column. At 0530 hours, Methuen ordered his column to halt and to prepare for a Boer attack. Immediately, he reinforced the rearguard.

At around 0600 hours, de la Rey ordered his troops to spread out and strike at both the right flank and the right rear of the second column. Major Paris ordered Ashburner's Light Horse and Cullinan's Horse, who had formed the advanced guard, to strengthen the rearguard, and some of the Cape Police to strengthen the failing right flank. At about 0630 hours, just as Paris was moving more of his men to the right flank, de la Rey boldly ordered his force to charge. This was an extremely unconventional tactic for the mounted Boer burghers.[107] The British irregular troops, many of whom had not seen fire before, broke ranks. As the fleeing forces merged with the reinforcing yeomanry, the latter joined the rout. The confusion spread as the collapsing right flank stampeded over the left flank. Amery wrote, 'The horde of fugitives swept along the left flank of both convoys, crossed the river, sucked into the current of flight the 86th Yeomanry and Cape Specials, who had not fired a shot, and never drew rein till they reached the top of a rise some three miles away.'[108] Only a few brave men who had managed to hold their position remained to guard the section of the 38th Battery, RFA, and the Diamond Fields pom pom; all that was left of Paris's column. Every man of the 38th Battery was shot down and when their commander, Lieutenant Cuthbert Nesham, refused to surrender, he too was killed.[109]

As Major Paris attempted, in vain, to rally the routed troops,[110] Methuen, with most of his left flank gone, directed his infantry to hold and stand against the anticipated Boer charge. The 300 Northumberland Fusiliers and Loyal North Lancashires held their ground as the superior Boer force now overwhelmed the lead column. For over two hours Methuen's men held out. The fate of the gunners of the 4th Battery was similar to that of the 38th Battery. Methuen, who had stayed with his guns, was shot twice, the second bullet severely wounding his thigh. His horse was shot from beneath him and collapsed on him, breaking his leg. The doctor sent to Methuen's aid was killed before reaching him. At 0935 hours, the white flag was raised and the British surrendered.

The defeat at Tweebosch was the most serious British disaster since the first stage of the conflict. British casualties were substantial: 68 killed, 121 wounded, and 205 – including Methuen – taken prisoner.[111] In addition, the Boers captured six guns and supplies, and eliminated the main British force in the Western Transvaal. Kitchener, who fell ill when he heard the news, was forced to divert three columns to the west.[112] This was also the first time during the war that a British general had been captured by the Boers and, as Roberts wrote to Kitchener, 'it naturally caused a certain amount of excitement in [England]'.[113]

The effects of the disaster were far-reaching. Roberts, the new Commander-in-Chief of the British army, was forced to defend Methuen before those in parliament who wondered why he had not been recalled after the defeat at Magersfontein. Of course, Roberts was defending his own decision as well as Kitchener's decision to let Methuen remain in the field with so few trained men. William St John Brodrick, the War Secretary, claimed that Methuen's capture was the worst disaster since Colenso and that it meant a great loss of prestige and weakened the war effort.[114] As a result of such a large number of soldiers refusing to obey orders and fleeing from the battlefield, the War Office was forced to rethink its policy regarding insubordination and desertion. In South Africa, Kitchener immediately punished the soldiers who fled to discourage a similar rout from occurring. J. L. Garvin and others have suggested that the greatest result of the Boer victory at Tweebosch was that the Boers now felt that they could indeed gain an honourable peace from the British.[115]

Interestingly, this military defeat did not harm Methuen's career, in fact to some extent it enhanced his reputation. While some questioned why he took to the field with his ragged force, none challenged his decisions or his behaviour during the battle. Instead, the War Office was criticized for providing such inferior troops. Some blamed Kitchener for sending so few men to the Western Transvaal; while others blamed those who had failed to make peace with the Boers. But almost no one blamed Methuen. They thought his tactics were sound and his personal action was heroic. Of course, his reconnaissance had failed and, as a result, he was taken by surprise. Thus, he shared a certain responsibility for the defeat. However, the main cause for his defeat was clearly the inefficiency of his troops. Besides, Methuen's personal actions were indeed unquestionably heroic. In fact, his capture served to remind many of his successes throughout the course of the war. In addition, the press re-investigated his role in the defeat at Magersfontein and the drive after de Wet, and, at last, he was given the recognition that was long overdue.

Methuen received public and private tributes from many sources. The new king, Edward VII, Lord Minto and others praised him for the good work he had done and offered their support. His captor, de la Rey, wrote to his comrade Christiaan de Wet that Methuen's fighting 'was beyond praise'.[116] Kitchener wrote in an official dispatch that Methuen had 'done more than most officers towards maintaining throughout this campaign the high standard for personal courage, modesty and humility, which characterizes the British Army'.[117] In *After Pretoria: The Guerrilla War*, Herbert Wilson observed:

> No officer had more endeared himself to the British nation, and there was none whose efforts it would have preferred to see crowned with victory; for, of all those who went out in high command, he alone remained to the last, refusing to come home before the war was over, and striving manfully to retrieve the discredit which he thought that the sad reverse of Magersfontein had brought upon his name. Younger men were placed above him; his command was reduced at times to a single weak column; yet he continued to serve his country with unabated constancy and zeal. His chivalrous spirit was proof against all slights and discouragements.[118]

After the white flag was raised, de la Rey took Methuen as his personal prisoner, treating him with great respect. Although his wounds were not life-threatening, his life was still at risk. There were many in the commando who, having grown tired from years of fighting, favoured his execution. Methuen had often been their adversary and they blamed him for their own hardships in the field and for those of their families. (Indeed, it is quite likely that Methuen was directly responsible for destroying many of their farms.) However, de la Rey spared Methuen's life and, although he would have been a valuable hostage, released him. Paul Kruger, in exile in Europe, applauded these actions.[119] On meeting de la Rey, Methuen asserted, 'You are the better man. We've been fighting for nearly three years and now you have got me down. Incidentally, that was a magnificent charge. If those are going to be your tactics in [the] future, you still have a chance to win the war!'[120]

The story of Methuen's capture and his treatment by de la Rey became legendary in England and in South Africa. Methuen, who refused to see visitors, agreed to see de la Rey's wife. He was brought face to face with the woman whom he had forced from her home earlier in the war. While at Lichtenburg, he was ordered to burn her house, because, it was suspected, that she was supplying her husband with food and giving him shelter. Methuen had personally met with Mrs de la Rey and after she pleaded with him not to destroy her house and to take her cattle and horses, he left them unharmed. She later wrote, 'He gave me his hand and he said, "it shall not be taken away from you".'[121] In a twist of irony, the two now met again and Mrs de la Rey had the opportunity to return the earlier favour by showing sympathy to him. For the anguish the war had caused her, Methuen begged for her forgiveness, and she gave it to him. She even sacrificed her last chickens to prepare him a meal. She sent a telegram to Lady Methuen informing her that her husband was in no danger, and he, on his release, as promised, sent a telegram to the de la Rey children in Pretoria on the health of their parents.[122]

Many years later (in 1929), in a speech at a dinner for the veterans of the South African War, Ian Hamilton added another episode to the Tweebosch legend which further serves to demonstrate the affability of the Methuen–de la Rey relationship:

> I defy anyone to produce, out of all the hundreds of books being written about the Great War, one single incident to hold a candle to that of Field Marshal Lord Methuen and General De la Rey after the battle of De Klip Drift on 7 of March 1902. The British Commander lying badly wounded in a tent; the Boer Commander attending to him with something uncommonly like affection. Next, the entry of a rough back veldt Boer who, from sheer force of habit, begins to unbutton the gaiter of Lord Methuen's unwounded leg [to claim as a souvenir] and then – the great De la Rey, literally, very literally, kicking the intruder clean out of the tent. Afterwards, as we all know, although Lord Methuen would have been of priceless value to the Boers as a hostage, he is handed over to the British in their lines at Kraai Pan.[123]

Methuen was brought to Klerksdorp on 13 March and afterwards was sent to Cape Town where he was reunited with his wife. For him, the war was finally over. Roberts insisted that he return to England as soon as he was well enough to travel.[124] He left aboard the *Assaye* on 21 June, only two days before Kitchener, French and Hamilton sailed for home. The war had ended on the last day of May, when the terms of surrender were signed in Pretoria by a Boer delegation which included President Steyn, Christiaan de Wet and J. H. de la Rey. The Boers had reached their physical breaking point. Faced with continuing a war against an enemy with seemingly inexhaustible reserves and supplies, they had at last given up. The victory at Tweebosch had been their last great moment of military glory.

NOTES

1. The others were John French and Neville Lyttelton.
2. Byron Farwell, *The Great Anglo-Boer War* (New York: W. W. Norton & Co., 1976), p. 257.
3. Ibid., p. 324.
4. Rayne Kruger suggests that Methuen's perseverance in the de Wet chases was a result of his need to right an earlier wrong, i. e. the failure at Magersfontein. Although 'penance' is perhaps too strong a word, Methuen desperately wanted to restore his reputation. Rayne Kruger, *Good-Bye Dolly Gray* (New York: J. B. Lippincott Co., 1960), p. 334.
5. H. S. Gaskell, *With Lord Methuen in South Africa* (London: Henry J. Drane, 1906), p. 175.
6. Methuen's force consisted of the 1st Loyal North Lancashire Regiment, 2nd Northamptonshire Regiment, 1st Northumberland Fusiliers, and the 5th, 10th and 15th Battalions Imperial Yeomanry – in all, roughly 1,200 Mounted Infantry and 2,400 Infantry. In addition, the force was armed with 12 field guns, two howitzers, two pom-poms, and seven machine guns. See Herbert M. Guest, *With Lord Methuen from Belmont to Hartebeestfontein* (Klerksdorp, South Africa: H. M. Guest, 1901), p. 56; and, F. Roberts to Lord Lansdowne, 10 Oct. 1900, report of 14 August 1900, WO 32/8000, Public Records Office, Kew.
7. Major-General Horace Smith-Dorrien, a graduate of Sandhurst, served in the Zulu War, in Egypt in 1881 and in the Sudan Campaigns of 1884–45 and 1898. He also participated in the Tirah Expedition of 1897–98 with Methuen. He commanded the 19th Brigade in the South African War.
8. Major-General R. S. S. Baden-Powell served in the Ashanti campaign of 1895 and the Matabele campaign of 1896. Baden-Powell, who later earned much fame for establishing the Boy Scouts, commanded the garrison of Mafeking which was besieged by the Boers for nearly seven months. Methuen thought that both Smith-Dorrien and Baden-Powell were 'good men'. P. S. Methuen to M. E. Methuen, 16 July 1900, Wiltshire Records Office, Trowbridge. Methuen continued to enjoy a friendly relationship with Baden-Powell after the war.
9. George Aston, Diary entry, 27 July 1910, 1/3, Aston Collection, Liddell Hart Centre for Military Studies, King's College, London University, London. Tim Jeal writes that Baden-Powell could do nothing to aid Methuen because his own command was

dangerously small. Tim Jeal, *The Boy-Man: The Life of Lord Baden-Powell* (New York: Wm Morrow & Co., 1990), pp. 320–1.

10. F. Roberts to P. S. Methuen, 27 July 1900, WO 105/36/s2, Public Records Office.
11. Jeal, *The Boy-Man*, p. 320.
12. P. S. Methuen to F. Roberts, 3 Aug. 1900, WO 105/10/126/147, Public Records Office.
13. F. Roberts to Lord Lansdowne, 1 Aug. 1900, WO 105/13/T/11/17, Public Records Office.
14. H. Belfield to his wife, 7 Aug. 1900, 8111–29, National Army Museum, London. Leo Amery claims that the Boers were able to cross the Vaal because Methuen's force was too small. This was not the case. Leo S. Amery (ed.), *The Times History of The War in South Africa 1899–1902* (London: Sampson Low, Marston & Co., 1907), IV, 422.
15. P. S. Methuen to F. Roberts, 25 Aug. 1900, WO 105/10/126/161, Public Records Office.
16. Karl B. Spurgin, *On Active Service with the Northumberland and Durham Yeomanry under Lord Methuen* (London: Walter Scott Publishing, 1901), pp. 113–16.
17. Lord Chesham was a member of the Imperial Yeomanry Committee which raised and helped to outfit the Imperial Yeomanry.
18. E. W. Gladstone, *The Shropshire Yeomanry* (London: Whitethorn Press, 1953).
19. P. S. Methuen to F. Roberts, 25 Aug. 1900, WO 105/10/126/161, Public Records Office.
20. Spurgin, *On Active Service*, p. 113.
21. After the first de Wet hunt, Kitchener took a great deal of credit for the pursuit in the press. In disgust, Belfield wrote to his wife, 'I see by the papers that Kitchener has been making such a good story for himself regarding the chase of De Wet. His telegrams read as if he had directed operations entirely whereas it was Methuen, who is far senior to him, who did that. He worked in his own lines and *requested* Kitchener to fall in with his wishes, which in the main, he did.' H. Belfield to his wife, 28 Aug. 1900, 8111–29, National Army Museum.
22. P. S. Methuen to F. Roberts, 25 Aug. 1900, WO 105/10/126/161, Public Records Office.
23. Fransjohan Pretorius, 'Die Eerste Dryfjag op Hoofkmdt. C. R. de Wet', (MA thesis, University of Pretoria, 1975), pp. 172–3.
24. P. S. Methuen to F. Roberts, 25 Aug. 1900, WO 105/10/126/161, Public Records Office.
25. H. Belfield to his wife, 16 Aug. 1900, 8111–29, National Army Museum.
26. On the evening of 13 August, De Wet had sent a scouting party to reconnoitre the nek. They learned that Kekewich's force had abandoned it and that Commandant K. Boshoff's Pretoria Commando were occupying it. Pretorius, 'Die Eerste Dryfjag op Hoofkmdt. C. R. de Wet', p. 169.
27. Roberts blamed Hamilton for the failure to hold Olifants Nek. In a telegraph to Kitchener, he wrote, 'I told Ian Hamilton to send troops there but he seemed to think it unnecessary.' F. Roberts to H. Kitchener, 16 Aug. 1900, WO 108/241, Public Records Office. This is a most surprising statement coming from an officer who refused to allow Methuen to do anything without his approval and insisted on 'fuller and more frequent accounts of [his] proceedings'. Roberts later telegraphed Methuen thanking him for his unrelenting pursuit of de Wet. F. Roberts to P. S. Methuen, 24 Aug. 1900, WO 108/241, Public Records Office.
28. George Aston, Diary entry, 27 July 1910, 1/3, Aston Collection, Liddell Hart Centre for Military Studies, King's College, London University.
29. P. S. Methuen to M. E. Methuen, 23 Aug. 1900, Wiltshire Records Office.

30. Guest, *With Lord Methuen*, p. 58.
31. Amery, *Times History*, IV, 432.
32. The *Diamond Fields Advertiser* printed a strong denouncement of the *Daily Mail*'s 11 August report which blamed Methuen for taking a wrong turn and losing de Wet. It stated that in conclusion

> Had the Magato Pass and Olifants Nek been occupied, De Wet would have been flung back into the arms of his pursuers, and nothing could have averted his capitulation. These are the plain facts, and we do not think they can be controverted. It is certainly only fair therefore that an explanation should be forthcoming as to why there were no troops in position at Magato Pass and Olifants Nek before placing blame on Methuen's Division, and withholding the praise due to them for such splendid marches ... accomplished by men who have been constantly on the march since early May, and started out on tired horses, but who nevertheless chased De Wet with a doggedness and determination which, though not commanding success, deserved it in the fullest degree (*Diamond Fields Advertiser* (Kimberley), 4 Sept. 1900).

33. H. Belfield to his wife, 6 Sept. 1900, 8111–29, National Army Museum.
34. P. S. Methuen to M. E. Methuen, 5 Oct. 1900, Wiltshire Records Office.
35. Methuen's experience in Bechuanaland from 1884 to 1885 aided him in the transition.
36. John Keegan, *Mask of Command* (New York: Penguin Books, 1988), p. 65.
37. Methuen's force in September 1900 consisted of two columns. He personally led a column consisting of the 1st Brigade Imperial Yeomanry, commanded by Lord Chesham, 4th Battery RFA, one section of the 11th Field Co. Royal Engineers, 1st Loyal North Lancashire Regiment, 1/2 of 2nd Northamptonshire Regiment, the 1st Royal Munster Mounted Infantry, one section 2nd Battery Rhodesian Field Force and two pom-poms. Major-General Douglas commanded the second column consisting of half of the 1st Northumberland Fusiliers, 2nd Brigade Rhodesian Field Force, two sections of the 88th Battery RFA, two sections of the 2nd Battery Rhodesian Field Force, one section of the 27th Battery RFA, two pom-poms and a howitzer.
38. Spurgin misidentified the river as the Vaal. In all likelihood it was the Molopo or one of its tributaries.
39. Spurgin, *On Active Service*, pp. 274–5.
40. Guest, *With Lord Methuen*, p. 69.
41. L. E. Belcher to G. Aston, Aston Papers, 6/11, Liddell Hart Centre for Military Archives, Kings College, London University, London.
42. P. S. Methuen to F. Roberts, 24 Aug. 1900, WO 105/13/T/11/17, Public Records Office.
43. F. Roberts to P. S. Methuen, 27 Aug. 1900, WO 105/37/s2, Public Records Office.
44. The British Government had given Roberts authority to annex the South African Republic in early July, 1900. 'Further Correspondence relating to the Affairs of the South African Republic', J. Chamberlain to A. Milner, 4 July 1900, No. 2, p. 9; cd 420, 1900: lvi, 595. The actual date of the annexation was 1 September. Milner was given the authority to administer the Transvaal as well as the Orange River Colony on Roberts' departure (Ibid., 7 Dec. 1900, No. 5, p. 10; cd 547, 1901: xlvii, 1).
45. In addition to Douglas's force, Methuen acted in co-operation with Brigadier-General Lord Erroll's force of yeomanry, Bushmen and Australian Imperial Rifles at Ottoshoop and Major-General Settle's flying column at Vryburg.
46. Guest, *With Lord Methuen*, p. 59.
47. H. Belfield to his wife, 19 Oct. 1900, 8111–29, National Army Museum.
48. Farwell, *The Great Anglo-Boer War*, p. 324.
49. H. Belfield to his wife, 8 Sept. 1900, 8111–29, National Army Museum.

50. P. S. Methuen to M. E. Methuen, 21 Sept. 1900, Wiltshire Records Office.

51. Ibid.

52. H. Belfield to his wife, 31 Oct. 1900, 8111–29, National Army Museum.

53. P. S. Methuen to M. E. Methuen, 11 Nov. 1900, Wiltshire Records Office.

54. F. Roberts to P. S. Methuen, 27 Oct. 1900, WO 105/38/s2, Public Records Office.

55. F. Roberts to Lord Lansdowne, 10 Oct. 1900, as cited in Guest, *With Lord Methuen*, p. 60.

56. Roberts wrote in his official report: 'I arranged for the permanent occupation of Zeerust.' Ibid.

57. P. S. Methuen to F. Roberts, 4 Oct. 1900, W.O. 105/11/126/195, Public Records Office.

58. P. S. Methuen to M. E. Methuen, 5 Oct. 1900, Wiltshire Records Office.

59. P. S. Methuen to F. Roberts, 5 Oct. 1900, WO 105/13/T/11/25, Public Records Office.

60. Of Lord Erroll, Captain R. S. Britten, Bucks Company, IY, wrote 'Erroll is … an old woman. If it was not for Lord Methuen and his staff being with us we wouldn't go one yard under him.' Undated diary entry, 7812–34, National Army Museum.

61. Six Boers were killed, four were wounded and 25 were taken prisoner. In addition, cattle, sheep, wagons and ammunition were captured. The British suffered nine casualties. The Boer force was estimated to be between 500 and 700. This was roughly 16 per cent of the entire Boer force in the Marico District. P. S. Methuen to F. Roberts, 24 Oct. 1900, WO 105/11/126/214, Public Records Office; and, Maurice, Frederick and M. H. Grant, *(Official) History of the War in South Africa, 1899–1902* (London: Hurst & Blackwood, 1906–10), III, 510–14.

62. F. Roberts to P. S. Methuen, 1 Nov. 1900, WO 108/243, Public Records Office.

63. Johannes Meintjes tells a story of two Boers reminiscing about Methuen after the war. The first one said 'Methuen was a perfect Christian knight – there could not be a nobler gentlemen.' The second man replied, 'But he destroyed your farm.' The first man answered, 'Agh. That was war; just war.' Johannes Meintjes, *De la Rey* (Johannesburg: Hugh Keartland, 1966), p. 297.

64. F. Roberts to P. S. Methuen, 22 Nov. 1900, WO 108/243, Public Records Office.

65. F. Roberts to P. S. Methuen, 28 Nov. 1900, WO 108/243, Public Records Office.

66. P. S. Methuen to M. E. Methuen, 27 Nov. 1900, Wiltshire Records Office.

67. H. Streatfield accompanied Roberts home as his private secretary. Streatfield was the last remaining officer of Methuen's original divisional staff. J. A. Bell-Smyth, R. B. Mainwaring, and R. H. L. Warner had already returned home. H. P. Northcott had been killed at the Battle of Modder River and E. D. Loch had been invalided home in September after being wounded in action at Bronhorstfontein.

68. H. Belfield to his wife, 11 Dec. 1900, 8111–29, National Army Museum.

69. Belfield wrote: 'Methuen's command is now huge, extending from Mafeking in the north to the Orange River in the south, bordered in the east by a line through Zeerust, Lichtenburg, Boshof, Hoopstad, and Fairesmith and in the west by German territory and the Atlantic.' H. Belfield to his wife, 2 Jan. 1901, 8111–29, National Army Museum.

70. Guest, *With Lord Methuen*, p. 61.

71. H. Belfield to his wife, 7 Feb. 1901, 8111–29, National Army Museum.

72. H. Belfield to his wife, 13 Feb. 1901, 8111–29, National Army Museum.

73. Babington had commanded Methuen's cavalry in the advance toward Kimberley.

74. 'The Yorkshire Yeomanry with Lord Methuen', *Yorkshire Post*, 19 March 1901.

75. Maurice and Grant, *(Official) History of the War*, IV, 132.

76. British casualties were surprisingly low. Sixteen were killed and 32 were wounded. Maurice and Grant, *(Official) History of the War*, IV, 133. On their way through the pass, the British counted 18 dead Boers. Guest, *With Lord Methuen*, p. 66.

77. See Chapter 3.
78. At Commando Drift, the Vaal River had risen too high, and had prevented Methuen from crossing and relieving Hoopstad. He was forced to return to the railway and cross the river at Fourteen Streams. Erroll led the relief mission after the force reached Fourteen Streams. Maurice and Grant, *(Official) History of the War*, IV, 134–7.
79. Effective Fighting Strength of 19 June 1901

Cavalry	10,430
MI	12,677
IY	13,970
Overseas Colonials	5,561
SA Irregulars	16,712
Colonial Defence Force	3,577
RA	11,911
Engineers	3,822
Infantry, Regular	62,000
Infantry, Militia	16,000
Infantry, Volunteer	3,742
Non-combatants	3,577
Total	163,979

Cited in Amery (ed.), *The Times History*, V, 249.
80. The Boer commandos were being chased throughout South Africa by British troops. Lieutenant-General Sir Bindon Blood and Brigadier-General H. C. O. Plumer were high up in the hills of the Northeast Transvaal while French, with Major-General Horace Smith-Dorrien, Brigadier-General E. A. H. Alderson, Brigadier-General Dartnell, and Colonel E. H. H. Allenby, were driving the Boers in the Eastern Transvaal. In the Orange Free State, General Neville Lyttelton, Major-General Bruce Hamilton, and Major-General Douglas Haig acted in the south; Major-General Charles Knox worked in the central district; Major-General E. Locke Elliott and Brigadier-General R. G. Broadwood patrolled the north; and, Lieutenant-General Leslie Rundle occupied the northeast. In the Western Transvaal, Babington and Colonel Shekleton were in the north near Ventersdorp, Colonel Henry Rawlinson was in the east, Lieutenant-Colonel G. E. Benson (who had led Methuen's night march at Magersfontein) was outside of Gatsrand, and Brigadier-General H. G. Dixon was in the Krugersdorp District.
81. Maurice and Grant, *(Official) History of the War*, IV, 197.
82. Spurgin, *On Active Service*, p. 297.
83. H. Kitchener to P. S. Methuen, 24 June 1901, WO 108/96, Public Records Office.
84. P. S. Methuen to A. Milner, 5 June 1901, f. 126, Milner Papers, Modern Political Papers, Department of Manuscripts, Bodleian Library, Oxford.
85. P. S. Methuen to (unnamed) Adjutant General, 25 July 1901, Wiltshire Records Office. See also, P. S. Methuen to M. E. Methuen, 30 Sept. 1901, Wiltshire Records Office.
86. P. Methuen to H. Campbell-Bannerman in G. B. Pyrah's *Imperial Policy and South Africa 1902–1910* (Oxford: Clarendon Press, 1955), pp. 62–3.
87. By this time Methuen's appearance, accented by a slouch hat, was indistinguishable from that of the rest of the troops. Belfield wrote, 'He's hanged if he's going to be shot by wearing a distincting [*sic*] helmet so has invested in a terrible looking wide-awake.' H. Belfield to his wife, 1 May 1901, 8111–29, National Army Museum.
88. Herbert Wrigley Wilson, *After Pretoria: The Guerrilla War* (London: Amalgamated Press, 1902).
89. Periodically, both Hickie and Kekewich were assigned the duty of guarding the

construction of the blockhouses in the Western Transvaal and were not available for active field service.

90. H. Kitchener to P. S. Methuen, 17 Sept. 1901, WO 108/96, Public Records Office.

91. H. Kitchener to P. S. Methuen, 26 Nov. 1901, WO 108/96, Public Records Office.

92. Amery, *Times History*, V, 496.

93. Maurice and Grant, *(Official) History of the War*, IV, 303, 406.

94. From 16–23 December, Methuen's small force captured 250 prisoners, 11,280 rounds of ammunition, 163 wagons, 1,200 horses, 8,600 cattle and several thousand sheep. H. Kitchener to William St. John Brodrick, 23 Dec. 1901, WO 108/235, *South Africa Telegrams*, XIV, Public Records Office.

95. In mid December 1901, Belfield left Methuen as his chief of staff to become the AAG of the 7th Division.

96. P. S. Methuen to I. Hamilton, 27 Feb. 1902, Wiltshire Records Office.

97. I. Hamilton to P. S. Methuen, 28 Feb. 1902, WO 108/99, Public Records Office.

98. H. Kitchener to W. St. John Brodrick, 9 March 1902, 30/57/22/Y131a, Public Records Office.

99. P. S. Methuen to M. E. Methuen, 26 Feb. 1902, Wiltshire Records Office.

100. Amery, *Times History*, V, 501.

101. P. S. Methuen to A. Milner, 3 Jan. 1903, f. 126, Milner Papers, Modern Political Papers, Department of Manuscripts, Bodleian Library.

102. The Kimberley Column included men from the 1st Northumberland Fusiliers, 1st Loyal North Lancashire Regiment, 4th and 38th Batteries, RFA, Diamond Field Horse, Cullinan's Horse, 43rd and 86th Columns Imperial Yeomanry, Cape Police, BSA Police, Dennison's Scouts, Ashburner's Light Horse, Cape Special Police and details from the 5th Battalion Imperial Yeomanry. Besides British regulars and irregulars, the force consisted of both South African English speakers and Dutch speakers, as well as Khoi-San and other indigenous people. Amery, *Times History*, V, 501–2.

103. Amery, *Times History*, V, 503.

104. P. S. Methuen to I. Hamilton, n.d. 1902, Methuen Papers, Wiltshire Records Office.

105. Maurice and Grant, *(Official) History of the War*, IV, 417. Leo Amery's claim that Methuen was aware that de la Rey, with a large force, had joined van Zyl cannot be substantiated. See Amery, *Times History*, V, 503.

106. *Report from Lt. Gen. Lord Methuen on the Action that took place near Tweebosch on the 7th March 1902*, 1902, cd 967, lxix, 287.

107. J. H. de la Rey to C. de Wet, 13 March 1902, Methuen Papers, Wiltshire Records Office.

108. Amery, *Times History*, V, 506.

109. *South Africa Dispatches*, 7 March 1902, cd 984, lxix, 153.

110. At a cattle-kraal, some 800 yards away, Major Paris was able to rally about 40 men. After holding out for two hours, they surrendered to Celliers. See *South Africa Dispatches*, 7 March 1902, cd 984, lxix, 153.

111. *South Africa Dispatches*, 7 March 1902, cd 984, lxix, 153; and, Maurice and Grant, *(Official) History of the War*, IV, 420.

112. Thomas Pakenham, *The Boer War* (New York: Random House, 1979), p. 583.

113. F. Roberts to H. Kitchener, 14 March 1902, Kitchener Papers, 30/57/20/o64, Public Records Office.

114. W. St John Brodrick to H. Kitchener, 15 March 1902, 30/57/22/Y132, Public Records Office.

115. J. L. Garvin, *The Life of Joseph Chamberlain* (London: Macmillan & Co., 1934).

116. J. H. de la Rey to C. de Wet, 13 March 1902, Methuen Papers, Wiltshire Records Office.

117. *South Africa Dispatches*, 1920, cd 988, lxix, 193.
118. Wilson, *After Pretoria*, p. 956.
119. Meintjes, *De la Rey*, p. 242.
120. Ibid., p. 236. When Methuen met de la Rey for the first time after the war, 'there was [*sic*] no histrionics; it was a cordial affair, as between two old comrades-in-arms. These men had nothing that was petty in them.' See F. V. Engelenburg, *General Louis Botha* (London: George Harrap & Co., 1929), p. 67.
121. J. E. de la Rey, *A Woman's Wanderings and Trials During the Anglo-Boer War* (London: Fisher Unwin, 1903), p. 23.
122. Ibid., p. 70.
123. Text of a speech given in honour of Lord Methuen at Windsor Castle at the 1st Dinner of South African War Veterans, 1929, Ian Hamilton papers, 39/12/298, King's College, London University.
124. F. Roberts to H. Kitchener, 18 April 1902, Kitchener Papers, 30/57/20/o69, Public Records Office.

9

Continuing to Serve

The British army emerged from the South African War with grave problems. Entire departments ranging from the Commander-in-Chief's office to Military Intelligence and institutions from the Yeomanry and Volunteers to the Staff College had failed during the war. Strategy and tactics were antiquated, training procedures were inadequate, and leadership was old and uninspired. The problems could not be kept hidden from the watchful public. Many questioned whether there was still a place in the Edwardian army for Lord Methuen and the other great Victorian generals. The pressure generated by the penny press, popular war literature and military reformers made sure that, unlike after the Crimean War, the War Office would enact sweeping changes to force the British army into the twentieth century. The safety of Great Britain and the interests of the empire had to be maintained.

Without the latitude which universal conscription could offer, British resources were stretched to their limits in order to field an army large enough to sustain the war effort. There was no plan to call up men to serve overseas in an emergency. The reserve force was needed almost as soon as the war started not only to fill holes in regimental lines, as intended, but also to form new battalions as well as to overcome the problems of desertion, discharge, and the poor health of many regulars. As new divisions were formed, it became impossible to field an army consisting solely of regulars and reserves. In time, the militia, yeomanry and volunteers would be mobilized to fill the need, but often they arrived in South Africa with little training or experience. In 1902 the effective size of the British army, including its Indian contingent, numbered 808,758.[1] Over half of this force was used in South Africa, leaving behind a bare skeleton to guard Britain and its empire. One in every seven of the United Kingdom's men between the ages of 18 and 40 wore some sort of military uniform during the South African War and this still was not enough.[2]

There were few areas of the British Empire untouched by the war. Casualty rates were high, affecting Regulars, Volunteers and Colonial soldiers alike. Of the nearly 450,000 men who sailed to South Africa to fight under the flag, roughly 100,000 received some sort of wound, contracted an illness or were captured by the Boers.[3] Twenty thousand of these soldiers did not return.[4]

In economic terms the war was costly. The price for paying, feeding and clothing an army in the field rose dramatically every year from £20,096,373 in 1900, to £43,065,398 by 1901, to an incredible £91,343,544 by 1902.[5] Due to time restraints and transportation costs, the War Office attempted to buy most of the supplies it needed in South Africa. Ordnance and supply departments were frustrated at every step by greedy merchants and untrustworthy entrepreneurs. Goods were scarce, prices were enormously high, and quality was lacking. Regardless, the purchases were made. Had the Government provided the Militia, Yeomanry and Volunteers with the supplies they needed, the price tag would have been even higher.[6] Adding to the total cost of the war were the maintenance of the concentration camps and retribution for the destruction of Boer lands and livestock. Not surprisingly, the South African War became the most expensive 'expedition' the British ever launched. The British people deserved a thorough investigation of the war to explain its costly nature.

Obviously, the Government was interested in studying the course of the war to determine the strengths and the weaknesses of the British army. It was clear that unless the War Office initiated and carried out serious reforms, the British army could not satisfactorily protect strategic and economic interests. The Elgin Commission, or the Royal Commission appointed to inquire into the military preparations and other military matters connected with the war in South Africa, was established to undertake this investigation. It met between October 1902 and February 1903. Its findings demonstrated to the British Government that there were serious structural problems within the army.

THE ROYAL COMMISSION ON THE WAR IN SOUTH AFRICA

The Government never considered the investigation to be a witch-hunt. It already had a long list of scapegoats including William Gatacre, Henry Colvile and, of course, Redvers Buller. In fact, neither the field officers who served in South Africa nor the staff officers who remained at home during the war, working in various administrative departments such as ordnance or military intelligence, were allowed to question the decisions made by their superiors. The commissioners made it quite clear from the onset of the proceedings that they were not interested in recording a military history of the war. Any discussion on the strategy and tactics used by British officers during the war by the witnesses was to be limited. With this in mind, the witnesses were to provide 'evidence regarding the efficiency of the organization of the Army, and the use of the different arms under the conditions of modern warfare … .'[7] Certainly, one question puzzled Methuen and others: How could they discuss the efficiency of the army and conditions of modern warfare while avoiding the subject of strategy and tactics? Nonetheless, the witnesses did their best to answer the commissioners' questions within the proper framework.

On 13 February 1903 Lieutenant-General Lord Methuen was called before the Earl of Elgin's Royal Commission to investigate the South African War. It was the 34th day of the proceedings. The Commission would meet for 55 days, during in which time it examined 114 witnesses ranging from the former Commander-in-Chief, Field Marshal Viscount Wolseley, to the Undersecretary of State at the War Office, Sir Ralph Henry Knox, to the Deputy Assistant Adjutant-General for Supplies and Transport, Colonel Sir W. D. Richardson. Methuen was but one of the many senior line officers questioned.

The problems which plagued the British army in the South African War are too numerous to list in this short study. However, some of the greater difficulties which field officers faced can be addressed. Methuen's 334 answers to the Royal Commission's questions and his brief précis submitted to that same commission provide valuable information about his character and assist in a summation of the overall defects which troubled the British army.

Transport problems

The Royal Commission's examination of Methuen was rigorous, yet respectful. Not once did the commissioners forget that they were addressing a peer and one of Britain's senior generals. Methuen was granted the deference which he deserved, but the commissioners did not avoid sensitive issues such as his decision to fight the Boers at Magersfontein. Nor did they avoid debating the witness on his views on the militia and volunteers. Questions were reiterated if Methuen attempted to avoid the subject or hedged his answer. However, his actions and leadership in South Africa were never seriously challenged or criticized.

The first important issue which Methuen addressed in his evidence was transport. He was steered to this subject by Lord Elgin's questions about his decision to adhere to the course of the railway during the attempt to relieve Kimberley.[8] Methuen explained that problems of transport were abundant during the war due to the failure of the War Office to provide the necessary numbers of mules, oxen and wagons. Roberts and Kitchener were stunned to find transport in a state of almost total disorganization when they arrived in South Africa in 1900. Kitchener blamed Buller's creation, the Army Service Corps, for failing to establish an effective transport service and encouraged the establishment of a new transport department.[9] As already noted, Kitchener felt that prior to Roberts' command, no British officer, with the exception of Methuen and Buller, knew the first thing about transport. The Staff College had failed to provide its students with an understanding of the workings of an efficient transport system.

Horses and the role of the cavalry in future wars

Since Methuen knew how to employ his transport according to the guidelines established by the Army Service Corps, his problem was not with its implementation but with available resources. Leaving Orange River Station, Methuen had only mule transport to carry his supplies. The mule transport only met the requirements of the regiments and his staff.[10] Divisional requirements, such as food and water, had to be supplied by rail. Despite his requests for oxen, which would have provided more flexibility in selecting his route to Kimberley, that form of transport did not become available until after he had already reached the Modder River. At that point, Methuen rejected the offer of oxen transport for he had already made up his mind to strike at Magersfontein and the oxen would have only slowed up his division.[11]

From mules and oxen, Methuen moved on to testify about horses, horsemanship and what he called horsemastership, or the care of horses. At the Battle of Belmont, Methuen noticed that his horse artillery were unable to drag their heavy guns on to the heights of Table Mountain because the horses were still tired from their trip to South Africa. The failure of the British to adequately acclimatize the horses after their arrival was an issue about which many officers had already presented evidence. Methuen testified that upon his arrival at Orange River Station, the health of the horses which had acclimatized was only marginally better than those that had not. This was a result of both poor supply and intelligence. Buller had informed Methuen, based on the findings of military intelligence, that horses would have no trouble grazing between the Orange River and Kimberley.[12] This turned out to be only partially true. Because of the time spent at Orange River Station awaiting reinforcement, the land had been exhausted for foraging. The limited supply of hay and oats failed to ameliorate the situation. As a result the horses were weakened and many ridden by poor horsemen had to be destroyed.

The destruction of overworked or ill-used horses was fairly common during the war. Methuen testified that 'the Yeomanry and the Colonials seemed at first to have an idea that I had an unlimited supply of horses always ready for them at a moment's notice'.[13] As a result, they paid little attention to the care of their mounts. Because it was so hard to acquire more horses, and the quality of reinforcement from Great Britain, Argentina or the Cape was often poor, Methuen made an effort to teach each and every horseman the correct way of handling his mount in the South African climate. Those that did not take good care of their horses would be forced to walk alongside them. Often, new arrivals to Methuen's division were attached to regiments that were well-versed in horsemastery.

Methuen's views on horsemanship can be discussed in the larger context of the cavalry and mounted infantry. There was a dearth of British mounted troops at the beginning of the war. Earlier chapters have dwelt at length on the consequences of the lack of mounted troops for Methuen's advance. Horsemanship became a problem for the British when irregular mounted troops were hastily raised for Roberts' drive. Many of these men, who filled the numerous battalions of the Imperial Yeomanry, knew very little about horses at all. However, those that could ride and shoot proved superior to the regular cavalry. The mounted infantry fitted the needs of the South African War far better than the cavalry.

A debate raged for the next decade about what role, if any, the cavalry should have in future wars. Many, including Methuen, believed that the cavalry was an obsolete force. They argued that cavalrymen could not act individually, that they could not fight dismounted on the battlefield, and that they could not conduct proper reconnaissance. Methuen was one of those who argued that the answer to the dilemma posed by modern weapons was to dismantle the cavalry and create an efficient mounted infantry, a force which consisted of 'men as good on foot as they are on horseback'.[14] When Lord Strathcona asked Methuen what he thought about the mounted infantry, Methuen unequivocally replied, 'I consider them a most useful body.'[15] The mounted infantry, unlike the cavalry, could provide the army with mobility without sacrificing the benefits which came from utilizing modern weaponry.

Training

In order to meet the requirements of modern warfare, according to Methuen, the British army needed a better type of recruit: one more intelligent, who could act on his own; and, one with a stronger physique, who could endure the hardships of war. In an age when the firepower of the rifle was improved in range, accuracy, destructiveness and speed, the use of cover became more important than ever. The average British soldier, however, had little experience building trenches or seeking the safest ground. Unlike his Boer counterpart, who had hunted in the veldt and knew how 'to stalk game', the British soldier, according to Methuen, could not be expected to have the 'cunning and shrewdness' to make the best use of cover.[16] Therefore, the British soldier would have to rely on intelligence. As things stood, a career in the army was not all that attractive, and recruits seldom had a substantial general or military education. Methuen believed that this had to be corrected.

Besides intelligence, the British soldier was lacking in physique. Methuen described the physical condition of his men as poor at best. In his opinion, 'if you get a wretched set of men like that, you may be perfectly certain that if they get into a tight corner they will not face it'.[17] Again, the solution was to get a better recruit by offering a more substantial life in the military and to improve the drill and training of all recruits. Both of these methods would require the Government to spend more money on the army.

In his analysis of the organization and the training of the British army, Methuen harked back to an issue which had been so dear to him in the early 1880s when he served as Assistant Adjutant-General of the Home District: the role of the junior officer. Methuen felt that the junior officer was underutilized off the battlefield, and when it came to taking action on the battlefield, he often failed to take responsibility and did not have the necessary skills to command. With men fighting on widened fronts and in extended marching orders, a lone senior officer could no longer direct all battlefield movements. The battles at Modder River and Magersfontein demonstrated the poor battlefield communications of the British army. In the age of modern firepower, it was necessary for junior officers to take on much greater roles. However, they were not properly trained for this task. Methuen argued that the junior officer had to be required to drill with his men, to take on more responsibility for their care, and to be given a greater role in the regimental company by his senior officer. If the rank and file required additional individual training to fight on the modern battlefield, the junior officer would have to provide it.

Failure of the staff

Methuen's most lengthy comments before the Elgin Commission addressed the role of the Staff College and the failure of staff officers in the South African War. Few witnesses who testified before the Royal Commission spoke approvingly about the performance of staff officers in the war. As Brian Bond wrote in his study of the Staff College, 'there is abundant evidence that the lack of a properly organized staff system was a serious handicap, and that incompetent staff work played a conspicuous part in many of the muddles and disasters [of the war]'.[18] A general's staff was to provide him with all the necessary information regarding supply, transport, intelligence, weapons' capabilities, and so on. As Methuen stated: 'It is essential if a General is to be well served, and to have his brain free to think out the general scheme, that he should be able with confidence to leave all details in the hands of his staff.'[19] Needless to say, few senior officers could rely on the competency of their staff because so few officers were trained for this duty. As explained in an earlier chapter, there was still a stigma attached to attending the Staff College. The most successful staff officers in the South African War were often not Staff College graduates, but regimental officers who had previously performed the duties of staff officers in other campaigns.[20]

In presenting his evidence about staff officers, Methuen stressed the need to elevate the status of the Staff College in the eyes of regimental officers. The problem, as he saw it, was that there was no incentive for a young officer to sacrifice two years of his life away from his regiment for school. Many young officers feared, as he did when he made his decision not to attend, that they faced a very uncertain future once they left their regiment for any period of time. There was a chance that on their return they would be passed over for assignments in favour of men with practical experience rather than theoretical knowledge. Methuen explained that some potential Staff College candidates believed that they would never be employed again if they left their regiments.[21] For that reason the college did not always attract the best candidates for staff work.

Methuen argued that the British Staff College had to take on a role similar to its German counterpart. It had to raise its qualification standards and only accept the best candidates. A message had to be sent through the army that the responsibilities of staff officers were important. Men who took time off from their regiments to attend had to be rewarded rather than punished. Only after these changes could a suitable pool of staff officers be created to serve the needs demanded by modern warfare. Until then Methuen and other senior officers would be forced to rely on untrained regimental officers for their staff work, and that, as demonstrated by the South African War, could prove dangerous.

Problems of intelligence

Another problem which field officers faced in the South African War was acquiring information about the enemy and the ground which it held. As previously demonstrated, the difficulties of reconnaissance grew considerably with the introduction of the long-range rifle – an outcome which the War Office had failed to predict. Except for discussing the unsuitability of the cavalry to reconnoitre, Methuen made no reference to this subject. Tactical issues were to be avoided unless raised by the commissioners. The Royal Commission did, however, ask Methuen about his maps.

Military intelligence in the South African War failed. The War Office did little preparation prior to the war to acquire necessary information about the enemy and the South African terrain. Lieutenant-Colonels E. A. Altham and W. R. Richardson were two of the several intelligence officers which the Royal Commission questioned. Lack of money and the political situation prior to the war were used by these officers as excuses for the failure. What the commissioners, Sir George Taubman-Goldie and Sir Frederick Darley, wanted from Methuen was an account of how the weakness of the Military Intelligence Department affected him during the course of the war.

Methuen's answers to the commissioners on this subject were concise. They do not suggest that he wanted to pass the responsibility for his difficulties at Modder River and Magersfontein on to someone else, but they do reveal his desire to set the record straight. He explained that his tactics at the Battle of Modder River were chosen in part because of the information supplied to him by maps and intelligence. That the Riet River was not fordable, he learned only after the battle began. That the Modder River could be crossed at only one point on the battlefield, he learned by chance.[22] Methuen had no maps of the Transvaal, Orange Free State or even the Cape Colony sufficient for tactical movements. It was not until he got hold of a copy of Jeppe's map, a Boer land survey, that he could devise tactics safely according to terrain.[23]

The Volunteers

Finally, one last issue which Methuen commented on was the nature of his reinforcements – the Militia, Yeomanry and Volunteers. Since this was an issue which interested many of the commissioners, they kept steering Methuen to it throughout his testimony. Methuen was in fact something of an expert on this matter. He had worked with the Volunteers when he commanded the Home District and always had an interest in it since his father had been the Queen's chief adviser on the subject. (Other Royal Commissions would address this subject in years to come, and they too would summon Methuen to sound out his views.) It was clear to all present, that without universal conscription, Britain would have to rely increasingly on these forces for its home defence and for the defence of the empire. Could His Majesty's subjects sleep easy knowing this?

Naturally, Methuen had some animosity towards these voluntary recruits who reinforced his division late in the war. His defeat and capture at Tweebosch was caused largely by their failure to stand and fight. However, Methuen's testimony displays no ill-feeling and seems quite objective. As noted above, the intelligence and physique of many of the volunteers was very unsatisfactory, as was the horsemanship of many of the yeomanry. Methuen claimed that on the whole, with some experience, the Militia and Volunteers became efficient at marching and performing most tasks that were not battle-related. Marksmanship, however, was much in need of improvement. This was not the fault of the men, but the failure of the Government to provide them with adequate training facilities, drill instructors and the time they required to practice.[24] This, of course, was determined not by the needs of the War Office but by the Treasury.

As to the question of whether the volunteer forces could substitute for regular troops in battle, Methuen made his opinion quite clear. The volunteer forces of Britain were far from a competent fighting force. It would be possible, with much time and money, to bring them to a higher state of efficiency. However, they should never be expected to take the place of regular troops or to act as anything more than a supplement to them. When Sir John Edge asked Methuen, 'Are you speaking of efficiency from the point of view of having a [volunteer] force that is capable of manœuvring in the field?', Methuen replied, 'I do not speak of brigade work; I only speak of work which I think Volunteers ought to be able to do.'[25] In Methuen's opinion, what Britain should expect from its Volunteers was that they all could shoot, some ride, and in an emergency provide support to the regular troops. Over the next decade, he would dedicate much of his time and energy to increasing the efficiency of the volunteer forces.

PUTTING THE WAR BEHIND HIM

After testifying before the Royal Commission, Methuen took a brief vacation and then returned to business. His military career did not end with the close of the war in South Africa. After receiving several decorations for his service,[26] and replacing HRH Arthur, the Duke of Connaught and Strathearn as the Colonel of the Scots Guards, he became the Chairman of Army Temperance in 1903. He presented evidence to the Elgin Commission and the Duke of Norfolk's Royal Commission on the Militia and Volunteers, and sat on Esher's committee on the expeditionary forces and auxiliary forces. And, after being promoted to a full General, he was given the command of the 4th Army Corps.

The command of the 4th Army Corps, which became known as the Eastern Command in June 1905, came as an unwelcome surprise to Methuen. He had hoped that the War Office would employ him, but the newly created Army Council and General Staff, which had replaced the Commander-in-Chief's role in army administration after Roberts' resignation, opted for younger men whose records were not tarnished by the South African War. When Methuen received the news of his employment, he wrote to his wife, 'The command is not one I like, but I cannot refuse it ... .'[27]

The Home defences of Great Britain were divided into five commands under five Generals. Methuen's command included London, Canterbury, Windsor and Oxford. His responsibilities included the training of all local troops, the administration of the several districts in the area, the preparation and maintenance of all local defence schemes, and the overseeing of all auxiliary forces under his command. He held this position until 1908, and during this time advised Hugh Arnold-Forster (Secretary of State for War) and worked closely with Arnold-Forster's Liberal successor, R. B. Haldane, on reforming Britain's defences.

As early as January 1907 Haldane had talked to Methuen about returning to South Africa once General Henry Hildyard's term as General Officer Commanding-in-Chief of the British forces in South Africa ended. Although Methuen had no desire to leave Britain, he made it clear that he would 'look on the King's wish as a command'.[28] Ironically, it was Methuen who had suggested that Hildyard would be best suited to reorganize the

British infantry for it opened up the job in South Africa.[29] In late March 1908 Methuen sailed to Cape Town where he took up his new command on 4 April. During a speech in 1910 in the Orange Free State, he declared, 'I had hoped to retire to my property and my family when my last command in England was drawing close, but Mr Haldane, the Secretary of State for War, asked me to come out to South Africa ... .'[30] Again, he put national service above his own self interest.

Until 1910 and the formation of the Union of South Africa, Methuen served as Great Britain's last GOC in South Africa.[31] In addition to this position, he held the offices of Governor and High Commissioner of the Natal and Deputy Governor of the Transvaal, the responsibilities of which were mainly administrative and functionary. He advised Lord Selbourne, the Governor of the Transvaal, and Lord Gladstone, Britain's first Governor-General of South Africa, on military matters. He established the cadet corps in South Africa to promote interest in the army and to aid in the training of recruits. Assisted by his adjutant, Major-General Sir George Aston, he incorporated the defence of South Africa into the scheme of Imperial Defence. He also did much to promote the use of modern technology in agriculture and the fair treatment of Indians and Zulus in the Natal.

Above all, Methuen helped heal many of the wounds of the South African War by re-establishing contacts between the British and the Afrikaners. This was not an easy task to accomplish. Many participants of the war still harboured bitter animosities. Methuen wrote to his friend Lord Grenfell:

> I defy the ablest man to know the feeling of the Dutch, unless he has been in the country for far longer than I have been, and travelling amongst them in the Veldt, speaking [to them] in Afrikaans – tour a little, stay in their houses ... .
>
> There are men like Botha, De la Rey and others who never wished for a war. ... There are other men like Smuts of whom I am not sure, but who are sure that it is in their interest and that of their country to be united. There are men like Merriman, Fischer ... devoid of principle. There are men in the Natal, who are too stupid for words. There are fanatics like Hertzog and Hofmeyer who believe 'union' may strengthen the Dutch case. Those are the leaders. Behind these men in the Veldt are the Boers who only wish to be left alone. So much for the Dutch party. –The English – They are much more outspoken, and give one the idea of being far more bitter than the Dutch. I am not thinking of the idiots, who wave the flag in one's face.

> I am thinking of sensible people, and they assure me in the schools and in
> their society they do all they can to be nasty, to let them understand they
> have now got, or will get all into their own hands, and lord it over them.[32]

Nevertheless, Methuen tried his best to bring the sides together. Aston called
Methuen 'the prime conciliator between Briton and Boer',[33] and there were
few who disagreed. As Lord Gladstone wrote to Methuen: 'Few people
know the vast extent and value of your untiring activities in the public
interest. You have contributed much more then anyone else … to establish
and strengthen good relations between British and Dutch.'[34]

Methuen's greatest contribution to the Union of South Africa was his
participation in the South Africa Defence Act. Although he had intended
to return home in 1910, he felt that he could not refuse the personal request
of two of South Africa's most honoured soldiers and statesmen, Jan Smuts
and Louis Botha, to remain until the Act was passed.[35] Methuen and Aston
worked side by side with Botha and Smuts to prepare South African
defences for the removal of its British garrisons. Time was of the essence
and the safety of South Africa from a German attack, launched from its
colony in southwest Africa, had to be ensured.[36] Almost all of Methuen's
final revisions were accepted by Smuts and the Bill was passed in April
1912.[37] Prime Minister Botha personally thanked Methuen for all the help
he had given South Africa and especially for the two years of his life he
had sacrificed in completing the Defence Bill.[38] Upon leaving South Africa
Methuen wrote a few poignant words to his friend Lord Gladstone: 'I
remember Cromer saying of Gordon that he died at the right time. In my
small way, I feel this is the moment I should depart not only from South
Africa, but from a world which has been kind to me.'[39]

In 1912 Methuen returned to Britain as a Field Marshal, and retired
from active duty. Subsequently he dedicated much of his time and energy
to strengthening British home defences without resorting to national
service. He became a champion of Haldane's Territorial Army, and, as
sometime President of the National Defence Association, worked hard for
the establishment of a cadet corps system in Great Britain. In his spare
time, when not fishing, walking or attending meetings at the local Masonic
lodge, where he held one of the highest honours of Senior Grand Warden,
he did much philanthropic work for Wiltshire charities and ex-servicemen.
Despite all of these commitments, in 1912, the 66-year-old Methuen found
the time to travel to Japan to represent the British throne at the Japanese
Emperor's funeral.

When the First World War erupted in August 1914, Methuen expected to do nothing more than follow the events from his home in Corsham. However, the following February, he was asked to serve and he agreed. Sir Edmund Franklyn, who was to have succeeded General Henry Leslie Rundle as Malta's Governor and Commander-in-Chief, died suddenly in early 1915. Methuen was asked to fill the vacant position. He wrote H. Spenser Wilkinson, 'My German friends in olden days used to say that a man should not say where he wished to go, but go where he is told.'[40] Although this was not a battlefield command, Methuen was proud to perform the task of turning Malta into the 'nurse of the Mediterranean'.[41] When the first patient arrived in May 1915, there were only enough hospital facilities to care for 3,000 soldiers. By the war's end, Methuen had completely transformed the island: it was now staffed and equipped to care for up to 25,000 patients.[42] He established many relief organizations, helped integrate Protestant and Catholic organizations, and set up the Boy Scouts, with the help of the organization's founder and his friend, Robert Baden-Powell.

In March 1919 Methuen returned to Britain. He was presented with the Grand Cross Legion of Honour by the French Government and a GCMG (Grand Cross of St Michael and St George) by George V. He was also given the honorary title of Constable of the Tower of London.

For the rest of his life Methuen continued to be active in military and social affairs. As late as 1931, at the age of 85, he rose in the House of Lords to give a stirring speech in support of the cadet corps. He died at his home at Corsham Court on 30 October 1932, 'a perfect knight who never swerved a hair's breadth from the path of truth and honour, and would never believe evil of another man'.[43]

NOTES

1. The normal establishment of the army was 934,050. Army Estimates. 1902: lvi, 1.
2. M. D. Blanch, 'British Society and the War', in Peter Warwick (ed.), *The South African War* (Harlow: Longman, 1980), as cited in Ian F. W. Beckett, *The Amateur Military Tradition, 1558–1945* (Manchester: Manchester University Press, 1991), p. 205.
3. Thomas Pakenham, *The Boer War* (New York: Random House, 1979), p. 607.
4. Return of Military Forces. 1903: cd 990 lviii, 21.
5. Army Estimates. 1900: xlviii, 1; 1901: xxxviii, 1; 1902: lvi, 1.
6. John K. Dunlop, *The Development of the British Army 1899–1914* (London: Methuen, 1938), pp. 90–5.
7. 'Report of His Majesty's Commissioners appointed to Inquire into the Military Preparations and Other Military Matters connected with the War in South Africa', 1904: cd 1790, XL, 4.
8. Ibid., cd 1790, XL, 14147–56.

9. Ibid., cd 1789, XL, 186–220.
10. Ibid., cd 1790, XL, 14149.
11. Ibid., 14158.
12. Ibid., 14164.
13. Ibid., 14219.
14. Ibid., 14350.
15. Ibid., 14349.
16. Ibid., 14223–6.
17. Ibid., 14230.
18. Brian Bond, *The Victorian Army and the Staff College 1854–1914* (London: Methuen, 1972), p. 187.
19. 'Report of His Majesty's Commissioners appointed to Inquire into the Military Preparations and Other Matters connected with the War in South Africa', 1904: cd 1790, XL, 14290.
20. Viscount Esher to M. V. Brett, 25 Sept. 1902, in M. V. Brett (ed.), *Journals and Letters of Reginald Viscount Esher* (London: Nicholson & Watson, 1934), p. 353.
21. 'Report of His Majesty's Commissioners appointed to Inquire into the Military Preparations and Other Matters connected with the War in South Africa', 1904: cd 1790, XL, 14292.
22. Ibid., 14376.
23. Ibid., 14453.
24. Ibid., 14203–4.
25. Ibid., 14394.
26. These included the Queen's medal with four clasps, the King's medal with two clasps, the KCB (Knight Commander of the Order of the Bath), the GCB (Knight Grand Cross of the Order of the Bath) and the Grand Cross of the Leopold Order from Emperor of Austria–Hungary, Franz Joseph II.
27. P. S. Methuen to M. E. Methuen, 24 Feb. 1904, Methuen Papers, Wiltshire Records Office.
28. P. S. Methuen to R. B. Haldane, 30 Jan. 1907, Methuen Papers, Wiltshire Records Office.
29. P. S. Methuen to H. O. Arnold-Forster, 16 Feb. 1905, Methuen Papers, Wiltshire Records Office.
30. Gladstone Papers, 46009, British Library.
31. He received a GCVO (Knight Grand Cross of the Victorian Order) in Nov. 1910.
32. P. S. Methuen to F. Grenfell, 11 July 1909, Methuen Papers, Wiltshire Records Office.
33. Major-General Sir George A. Aston, 'Methuen Obituary', *Household Brigade Magazine* (1932): 257.
34. H. Gladstone to P. S. Methuen, 24 April 1912, Gladstone Papers, 46009, British Library.
35. WO 32/7111, Public Records Office, Kew.
36. John Adye to DMO, 11 Feb. 1910, WO 32/7111, Public Records Office.
37. J. Smuts to P. S. Methuen, 20 Nov. 1911, Methuen Papers, Wiltshire Records Office.
38. L. Botha to P. S. Methuen, 22 April 1912, Methuen Papers, Wiltshire Records Office.
39. P. S. Methuen to H. Gladstone, 24 April 1912, Gladstone Papers, 46009, British Library.
40. P. S. Methuen to H. S. Wilkinson, 15 Feb. 1915, National Army Museum, OTP 13/27, London.
41. Edith Dobie, *Malta's Road to Independence* (Norman, OK: University of Oklahoma Press, 1967), p. 73.
42. Albert Victor Laferla, *British Malta* (Malta: A. C. Aquilina and Co., 1947), p. 200.
43. Aston, 'Methuen Obituary', *Household Brigade Magazine* (1932): 259.

10

Conclusion

For Methuen and the British army the South African War was in fact a struggle against two different enemies: the Boers and the changing nature of warfare. In this study we have tried to examine the problems posed by both these agents, and Methuen's career in particular provides an excellent case study of an individual officer's capacity for adaptation.

Howard Bailes's assertion that the Victorian Army 'could be an effective instrument of imperialism' is indeed correct.[1] Most of Britain's small wars were carried out smoothly and successfully with little loss of British life and little cost to the Treasury. However, the Victorian army was riddled with severe problems. Its officers were not required to attend military schools and the schools that existed were poor. The drill, or set of training exercises, of the rank and file was obsolete and the average soldier had yet to learn how to act on the battlefield as an individual. The cavalry, as an arm of the military, was anachronistic and the artillery had yet to learn the limits and effects of their new equipment. Strategy and tactics had yet to catch up with modern technology. Britain still lacked a general staff to bring the armed forces together for the co-ordination of a military effort, to prepare offensive and defensive plans, and to oversee military relations with the colonies. The list of problems goes on and on, but perhaps the army's greatest problem was psychological, resting in the belief of the vast superiority of the British soldier to any foe. This belief, strengthened by 30 years of victories in Africa and Asia, made reform seem unnecessary and encouraged officers to put their faith in their men rather than in their own ability to command.

Another problem the Victorian army faced was that although it may have been ready for a small war, it was not ready to meet a strong entrenched enemy armed with modern weapons. The indecisiveness of Lansdowne in the months before the South African War, and the War Office's failure to estimate the enemy's resolve, proved costly. The department of Military

Intelligence, understaffed and underfunded, failed to supply British staff officers with accurate knowledge of the enemy's terrain. Structural problems were demonstrated almost at once in the field as officers and men alike failed to understand the capabilities of either their own or enemy weapons.

The inadequacies of the British army were demonstrated by its failure to overcome the Boer defences in the opening phase of the South African War. At Belmont, Graspan and Modder River, Methuen engaged his adversaries and left each battlefield unsatisfied with the results. At Magersfontein he was forced to retire. In his first divisional command, he failed. Other senior British officers failed as well and the result was the ignominious 'Black Week'. The British reversal was due to a lack of cavalry, poor intelligence, a restrictive strategy, and, most significantly, to the failure to understand the changing nature of war. Like so many of his fellow officers trained in the tactics of colonial warfare, Methuen was unable to improvise to meet the new challenges which the opening phase of the South African War offered, relying instead on the tried and tested methods of the past.[2]

Not only did the British army suffer defeat in the opening phase of the South African War, it failed to adjust during the guerrilla phase of the war. After June 1900 Roberts and Kitchener, concentrating on strategic targets, ignored the Boer guerrillas beyond the periphery of the central theatre of operations. Education and experience had led Roberts and Kitchener to believe that an enemy would capitulate once its capital fell. British attempts to bring the war to its end after the fall of Bloemfontein were hasty and indecisive. The front remained strong but the flanks of the British advance, often spread out over vast areas of hills and rugged veldt, were weak. Officers like Methuen were forced to make the best of bad situations as the only reinforcements they received were inexperienced yeomen and volunteers. Disaster in these sectors was more common than not.

Methuen was one of only a few senior officers who eventually was able to make the transformation which the new type of warfare demanded. Although at the start of the war he had marched toward Kimberley with Wolseley's *Soldier's Pocketbook* in his breast pocket, by mid 1900 he had left this obsolete manual behind.[3] Since the Boers were not playing by the same rules and the author of the *Pocketbook* had not taken into consideration the affects of modern technology on warfare, the rule book had to be thrown out. The set battle, along with the cold steel charge, were things of the past. Methuen was forced to rely on his common sense, rather than on his colonial experience.

His ability to make the transition required to defeat the enemy despite the British army's tactical and strategical tradition bore the mark of a true commander. J. F. C. Fuller, one of Britain's foremost military analysts of the twentieth century, wrote that the ability to set aside conventions and established military practices, and rely instead on common sense and immediate conditions is a talent that only great leaders possess.[4] To ignore a decade of peacetime manœuvres, 30 years of colonial expeditions, and a lifetime of studying military manuals and histories, was by no means an easy task. General Ulysses S. Grant's experience in the American Civil War, half a century earlier, is telling and can be applied to the British officers in the South African War. He wrote: 'Some of our generals failed because they worked out everything by rule. They knew what Frederick did at one place, and Napoleon at another. They were always thinking about what Napoleon would do. Unfortunately for their plans, the rebels would be thinking about something else. ... If men make war in slavish observances of the rule, they will fail.'[5] Methuen was able to succeed because he was able to free himself from tradition and learn quickly on the battlefield.

Nineteenth-century conventional tactics and strategy had to abandoned. Technological innovations and inventions had forever changed the nature of warfare. In the years which followed the South African War, veterans like Ian Hamilton, Douglas Haig, and B. F. S. Baden-Powell, would argue that new tactics could overcome modern technology. These ranged from the use of defensive tactics like the night march, to improving the condition of the individual soldier, to undermining the enemy by the increasing use of shock tactics.[6] Jean de Bloch, the Polish expert on military theory, concluded that the only way to overcome the effects of modern firepower, as displayed in the South African War, would be to raise armies numbering in the millions and engage in siege-type wars. But in doing so, he argued, the social order of the state would be convulsed by economic and psychical strains.[7] Others agreed with Bloch's gloomy prognostication of the future of warfare.

Methuen was well aware of the revolution that was going on around him. He had witnessed the failures of the current system at Modder River and Magersfontein. Once he had recognized the changes, he was able to implement new measures and adapt to fight his adversary. By 1900 only Roberts and lack of manpower prevented him from demonstrating his full potential as an officer. Regardless, he trudged on through the war until its bitter end came for him at Tweebosch. When he returned to Britain in 1902, he was recognized as a hero by the public, and more importantly for him, appreciated by his fellow officers as an excellent general.

As Rayne Kruger wrote in *Good-bye Dolly Gray*, 'Methuen occupied that special place in English minds reserved for men who did not give way to adversity.'[8] After failing in the first phase of the South African War, he toiled in obscurity for its remainder, proficiently adapting to the changing nature of warfare, and, ultimately, playing a key role in the war's end.

NOTES

1. Howard Bailes, 'Technology and Imperialism: A Case Study of the Victorian Army in Africa', *Victorian Studies* 24 (1980): 85.
2. Edward M. Spiers, *The Late Victorian Army 1868–1902* (London: St Martin, 1992), p. 156.
3. John F. C. Fuller, *The Last of the Gentlemen's Wars* (London: Faber & Faber, 1937), p. 20.
4. J. F. C. Fuller, *The Generalship of Ulysses S. Grant* (London: J. Murray, 1929; repr., New York: Da Capo Press, 1958), pp. 185–6.
5. William Conant Church, *Ulysses S. Grant* (New York: 1906), pp. 188–9; cited in Fuller, *The Generalship of Ulysses S. Grant*, pp. 186–7.
6. See T. H. E. Travers, 'Technology, Tactics, and Morale: Jean de Bloch, the Boer War, and British Military Theory, 1900–1914', *Journal of Modern History* 51 (1979): 264–86.
7. Ibid., pp. 266–7.
8. Rayne Kruger, *Good-Bye Dolly Gray* (New York: J. B. Lippincott Co., 1960), p. 454.

10

Bibliography

I ARCHIVES AND MANUSCRIPT COLLECTIONS

Note that unless otherwise indicated archives and manuscripts are located in London.

Trowbridge. County Hall, Wiltshire Records Office. Paul Sanford, 3rd Baron Methuen, Corsham. Miscellaneous correspondence and papers 1881–1932 (NRA list 812) WRO 1742.

Exeter. Devonshire Records Office. Sir Redvers Buller Papers. 7065M/SS4.

Hove. Central Library. Sir Garnet Wolseley Papers.

London. British Library. Gladstone Papers. 46003–9.

British Library. Miscellaneous Methuen Letters. 46056, ff. 9, 51; 46072 ff. 77–9; 46299, f. 313.

Liddell Hart Centre for Military Archives, Kings College, London University. General George Aston Papers. 1/2, 1/3, 1/4, 1/5, 6/11.

Liddell Hart Centre for Military Archives, Kings College, London University. Sir Ian Hamilton Papers. 3/25, 7/1/8, 13/1/14, 29/12/298, 39/12/154, 39/12/154.

National Army Museum. Colonel H. Belfield Papers. 8111–29.

National Army Museum. Captain R. Britten Papers. 7812–34.

National Army Museum. Lord Roberts Papers. 7101/23.

Public Records Office. Sir Redvers Buller Papers. WO 132.

Public Records Office. Cabinet Reports. CAB 8/5/41, CAB 11/32–6, CAB 37/27, CAB 41.

Public Records Office. Imperial Defence. CO 537/358.

Public Records Office. Lord Kitchener Papers. PRO 30/57.

Public Records Office. Miscellaneous Reports. WO 33/32, 34, 48, 52, 57, 69, 218, 221, 249, 256, 439, 468.

Public Records Office. Natal. CO 180/12.

Public Records Office. Regimental Records. WO 27/489, 25/843.

Public Records Office. Registered Papers. WO 32/6051, 6083, 6360, 6734, 6917,

6928, 7111, 7116–18, 7870, 7890–3, 7903, 7962, 7964, 7966, 7969, 7971, 7976, 7982, 7996, 8000–1.

Public Records Office. Lord Roberts Papers. WO 105.

Public Records Office. South Africa. CO 879/56, 59, 62, 103, 106.

Public Records Office. South Africa Defence. CO 632/2.

Public Records Office. South African War. WO 108/96–9, 229 243.

Oxford. Bodleian Library, Department of Western Manuscripts, Oxford University. Lord Milner Papers. f. 126.

II PARLIAMENTARY PAPERS

Further Correspondence Respecting the Ashantee Invasion, 1874: xlvi 1, 245, 483, 755, 819, 831, 890–4, 921–2, 943, 1006, 1045.

Despatches from Sir Garnet Wolseley, 1874: xlvi, 905.

Education of Officers, 1883: xv, 485.
    1889: xvii, 73.
    1893–94: xvii.

Committee on Military Educational Establishments A117, 1888.

Report of the Royal Committee Appointed to Enquire into the Civil and Professional Administration of the Naval and Military Departments, 1890.

Infantry Drill. London: HMSO, 1890.

Record of the Proceedings During a Staff Ride Between Brighton and Red Hill, 1895.

Further Correspondence relating to the Affairs of the South African Republic.
    1899: c 9530 lxix, 751.
    1900: cd 43 lvi, 121; cd 261 lvi, 389; cd 420 lvi, 595.
    1901: cd 547 xlvii, 1.
    1902: cd 903 lxvii, 1; cd 1163 lxvii, 213.
    1903: cd 1463 xlv, 1.

Army Estimates.
    1900: xlviii, 1.
    1901: xxxviii, 1.
    1902: lvi, 1.

Return of Military Forces.
    1900: cd 421 xlix, 277.
    1902: cd 462 xxxix, 639; cd 578 xxxix, 643.
    1903: cd 892 lviii, 17; cd 990 lviii, 21.

South African Despatches, 1901: cd 457 xlvii, 87; cd 458; cd 463 xlvii, 365.

Correspondence relative to the Recall of Major-General Sir H. E. Colvile, k.c.m.g., c.b., 1901: cd 467 xlvii, 557.

Finding of a Court of Enquiry held at Barberton on 25th September, 1900 to investigate the circumstances under which Lieutenant-Colonel B. E. Spragge,

DSO XIIIth Battalion Imperial Yeomanry and others, became prisoners of war, 1901: cd 470 xlvii, 557.

Kitchener Despatches.

1901: cd 522 xlvii, 391; cd 605 xlvii, 433; cd 695 xlvii, 469.

1902: cd 920 lxix, 1; cd 823 lxix, 69; cd 824 lxix, 81; cd 890 lxix,104; cd 965 lxix, 118; cd 970 lxix, 129; cd 984 lxix, 154; cd 986 lxix, 169; cd 988 lxix, 193.

Report from Lt.-Gen. Lord Methuen on the Action that took place near Tweebosch on 7th March, 1902. 1902: cd 967 lxix, 287.

Report of the Committee appointed to Consider the Education and Training of Officers in the Army, 1902: cd 982 x,193.

Report of His Majesty's Commissioners appointed to Inquire into the Military Preparations and Other military Matters connected with the War in South Africa, 1904: cd 1789 xl, 1; cd 1790 xl, 325; cd 1791 xli, 1; cd 1792 xlii, 1.

Militia and Volunteers.

1904: cd 2062, 2063 xxx, 259.

1904: cd 2061 xxx, 175.

1904: cd 2064 xxxi, 287.

Report of the War Office (Reconstitution) Committee, 1904: cd 1932 viii, 101; cd 1968 viii, 121; cd 2002 viii, 157.

III CONTEMPORARY BOOKS

Amery, L. S. *The Problems of the Army*. London: Edward Arnold, 1903.

Amery, L. S. (ed.). *The Times History of the War in South Africa 1899–1902*. London: Sampson Low, Marston & Co., 1907.

Arnold-Forster, Hugh Oakley. *The War Office, the Army and the Empire*. 2nd edn New York: Cassell & Co., 1900.

Arnold-Forster, Hugh Oakley. *The Army in 1906*. New York: E. P. Dutton, 1906.

Arnold-Forster, Hugh Oakley. *Military Needs and Military Policy*. London: Smith, Elder, 1909.

Aston, George G. *The Defence of United South Africa as Part of the British Empire*. Cape Town: Cape Times Ltd, 1910.

Aston, George G. *Staff Duties and Other Subjects*. London: Hugh Rees, 1913.

Atkinson, John Clayton. *A B C of the Army*. London: Gale & Polden, 1910.

Baden-Powell, B. F. S. *War in Practice*. London: Isbister & Co., 1903.

Balck, William. *Tactics*. Ft Leavenworth, Kansas: US Cavalry Assn., 1915.

Bethell, H. A. *Modern Artillery in the Field*. London: Macmillan, 1911.

Biddulph, Robert. *Lord Cardwell at the War Office*. London: Murray, 1904.

Blunt, Wilfrid S. *Secret History of the English Occupation of Egypt*. London: T. Fisher Unwin, 1907.

Boyle, Frederick. *Through Fanteeland to Coomassie*. London: Chapman & Hall, 1874.

Brackenbury, Henry. *The Ashantee War of 1873–74*. London and Edinburgh: William Blackwood & Sons, 1874.

The British Army by a Lieutenant-Colonel in the British Army. London: Sampson Low, Marston & Co., 1899.

Butler, William Francis. *Akim-Foo*. London: Sampson Low, Marston, Low & Searle, 1875.

Cairns, W. E. *The Absent Minded War*. London: John Milne, 1900.

Cairns, W. E. *Social Life in the British Army*. London: Long, 1900.

Callwell, Charles Edward. *Lessons to be Learnt from Small Wars Since 1870*. London: Aldershot, Gale & Pulden, 1895.

Callwell, Charles Edward. *Small Wars: Their Principles and Practice*. rev. edn London: HMSO, 1899.

Callwell, Charles Edward. *Tactics of Home Defence*. London: Aldershot, Gale & Pulden, 1908.

Callwell, Charles Edward. *The Tactics of To-day*. 2nd edn London: William Blackwood & Sons, 1909.

Callwell, Charles Edward. *Tirah, 1897*. London: Constable & Co., 1911.

Callwell, Charles Edward and John Headlam. *The History of the Royal Artillery*. Woolwich: Royal Artillery Institution, 1940.

Clery, C. Francis. *Minor Tactics*. London: Kegan Paul, 1893.

Creswicke, Louis. *South Africa and the Transvaal War*. Edinburgh: T. C. & E. C. Jack, 1901.

Crombe, J. *The Highland Brigade*. London: Stirling, 1902.

Cromer, Earl of. *Modern Egypt*. London: Macmillan, 1911.

Cunliffe, Foster H. E. *History of the Boer War*. London: Methuen, 1901–4.

Cust, Lionel H. *History of Eton College*. New York: Scribner's, 1899.

Danes, Richard (ed.). *Cassell's History of the Boer War*. New York: Cassell & Co., 1903.

Davies, C. Collin. *The Problem of the North-West Frontier 1890–1908*. Cambridge, 1932; repr., New York: Barnes & Noble, 1974.

Davitt, Michael. *The Boer Fight for Freedom*. New York: Funk & Wagnals, 1902.

De Bloch, Jean. *The Future of War in its Technical, Economic and Political Relations*. Boston: Ginn & Co., 1902; repr., New York: Garland, 1972.

Dilke, Charles W. and Spencer Wilkinson. *Imperial Defence*. New York: Macmillan, 1892.

Doyle, Arthur Conan. *The Great Boer War*. London: Smith, Elder & Co., 1900.

Dressler, Friedrich August *Moltke in His Home*. London: John Murray, 1907.

Dunlop, John K. *The Development of the British Army 1899–1914*. London: Methuen, 1938.

Edwards, FitzJames. *The Defence and Defensive Positions*. London: William Clowes, 1902.

Forbes, Archibald, *et al. Battles of the Nineteenth Century*. London: Cassell & Co., 1901.

Fortescue, John W. *A History of the British Army*. London: Macmillan, 1899–1912.

Fortescue, John W. *Military History*. Cambridge: Cambridge University Press, 1914.

Fuller, John F. C. *Imperial Defence*. London: Siffon, Praed, 1926.

Fuller, John F. C. *The Last of the Gentlemen's Wars*. London: Faber & Faber, 1937.

Fuller, John F. C. *The Conduct of War*. New Brunswick, NJ: Rutgers University, 1961.

Furse, George A. *The Organization and Administration of the Lines of Communication in War*. London: William Clowes, 1894.

Furse, George A. *Information in War*. London: William Clowes, 1895.

Furse, George A. *Provisioning Armies in the Field*. London: William Clowes, 1899.

Gall, Herbert R. *Modern Tactics*. London: W. H. Allen, 1899.

Gardyne, A. D. G. *The Life of a Regiment: The History of the Gordon Highlanders*. London: 1939; repr., London: Leo Cooper, 1972.

Godwin-Austen, A. R. *The Staff and the Staff College*. London: Constable, 1927.

Goodenough, W. H. and J. C. Dalton. *The Army Book for the British Empire*. London: HMSO, 1893.

Goodrich, Caspar Frederik. *Report of the British Naval and Military Operation in Egypt*. Washington: Government Printing Office, 1883.

Gordon, Hampden. *The War Office*. London: Putnam, 1935.

Grierson, James Moncrieff. *Scarlet into Khaki: The British Army on the Eve of the Boer War*. London: Sampson Low, Marston & Co., 1899; repr., London: Greenhill Books, 1988.

Gwynne, H. A. *The Views of the Army on Itself*. London: Frederick Warne & Co., 1904.

Haliburton, Arthur. *Army Organization: The Arnold-Forster Scheme*. London: E. Stanford, 1905.

Hall, John. *The Coldstream Guards 1885–1914*. Oxford: Clarendon Press, 1929.

Hamilton, Ian. *Soul and Body of an Army*. London: Edward Arnold, 1921.

Hamilton, Ian. *Listening for the Drums*. London: Faber & Faber, 1944.

Hamilton, Ian. *The Commander*. London: Hollis & Carter, 1957.

Hamley, Edward Bruce. *The Operations in War*. London: William Blackwood & Sons, 1866.

Henderson, George Francis Robert. *The Science of War*. London: Longman, Green & Co., 1912.

Henty, George A. *The March to Coomassie*. 2nd edn London: Tisley Bros, 1874.

Hillegas, Howard C. *The Boers in War*. New York: Appleton & Co., 1900.

Hohenlohe-Ingelfingen, Kraft zu. *Letters on Strategy*. London: Kegan Paul, Trench, Trüber & Co., 1898.

Home, Robert and Sisson C. Pratt. *A Précis of Modern Tactics*. 2nd edn London: HMSO, 1896.

Howland, Frederick Hoppin. *The Chase of De Wet*. Providence: Preston & Rounds, 1901.

James, Lionel. *The Indian Frontier War*. New York: Charles Scribner's, 1898.

Jeans, T. T. (ed.). *Naval Brigades in the South African War, 1899–1900*. London: Sampson, Low, Marston & Co., 1901.

Kearsey, A. H. C. *War Record of the York and Lancaster Regiment 1900–1902*. London: G. Bell & Sons, 1903.

Langlois, Hippolyte. *Lessons from Two Recent Wars*. London: HMSO, 1909.

Low, Charles Rathbone. *Battles of the British Army*. London: Routledge & Sons, 1908.

MacDougall, P. L. *Theory of War*. 2nd edn London: Longman, 1858.

Mahan, Alfred T. *The Story of the War in South Africa*. New York: Collier, 1900.

Malet, Edward. *Egypt, 1879–1883*. London: John Murray, 1909.

Maurice, Frederick Barton. *The History of the Scots Guards*. London: Chatto & Windus, 1934.

Maurice, Frederick and M. H. Grant. *(Official) History of the War in South Africa, 1899–1902*. London: Hurst & Blackwood, 1906–10.

Maurice, John Frederick. *The Ashantee War*. London: H. S. King, 1874.

Maurice, John Frederick. *The Military History of the Campaign of 1882 in Egypt*. London: HMSO, 1887.

Mayne, C. B. *The Infantry Weapon and Its Use in War*. London: Smith, Elder & Co., 1903.

Methuen, Algernon Marshall. *The Tragedy of South Africa*. London: Methuen, 1905.

Mills, H. Woosnam. *The Tirah Campaign*. Lahore: C. & M. Gazette Press, 1898.

Murray, Stewart. *Discipline: Its Reason and Battle-Value*. London: Gale & Polden, 1894.

Official Records of the Guards Brigade in South Africa. London: J. J. Keliher & Co., 1904.

O'Meara, Walter A. J. *Kekewich in Kimberley*. London: Medici Society, 1926.

Ralph, Julian. *Towards Pretoria*. New York: Frederick A. Stokes, 1900.

Reade, Winwood W. *The Story of the Ashantee Campaign*. London: Elder & Co., 1874.

Rompel, Frederick. *Heroes of the Boer War*. London: Review of Reviews Office, 1903.

Royle, Charles. *The Egyptian Campaigns 1882 to 1885*. rev. edn London: Hurst & Blackett, 1900.

Shadwell, L. J. *Lockhart's Advance Through Tirah*. London: W. Thacker & Co., 1898.

Shaw, Wilkinson J. *Elements of Modern Tactics*. London: Kegan Paul, 1894.

Stanley, Henry M. *Coomassie: The Story of the Campaign in Africa 1873–4*. London: Sampson, Low, Marston & Co., 1896.

Swinton, Ernest Dunlop. *The Defence of Duffer's Drift*. London: *United Services Magazine*, 1907; repr., Wayne, New Jersey: Avery Publishing Group, 1986.

Theal, George McCall. *History of South Africa from 1873 to 1884. Twelve Eventful Years*. Vol. 11. *History of South Africa*. London: George Allen & Unwin, 1919.

Vogt, Hermann. *The Egyptian War of 1882*. London: Kegan Paul, 1883.

Walker, H. M. *History of the Northumberland Fusiliers*. London: John Murray, 1919.

The War in South Africa, a German Official Account. Translated by W. H. Walters. New York: E. P. Dutton, 1904.

Wauchope, Arthur G. *A Short History of the Black Watch, 1725–1907*. London: Blackwood, 1908.

Wheeler, Owen. *The War Office: Past and Present.* London: Methuen, 1914.

Wilkinson, H. Spenser. *Lessons of the War.* Philadelphia: J. B. Lippincott Co., 1900.

Wilmot, Alexander. *The History of Our Own Times in South Africa.* London: J. C. Juta, 1898.

Wilson, Herbert Wrigley. *With the Flag to Pretoria.* London: Harmsworth Bros., 1901.

Wilson, Herbert Wrigley. *After Pretoria: The Guerrilla War.* London: Amalgamated Press, 1902.

Wolseley, Viscount. *The Soldier's Pocket Book.* 4th edn London: Macmillan, 1882.

Wood, Henry Evelyn. *Battles on Land and Sea.* London: Cassell & Sons, 1915.

Wood, Henry Evelyn. *Our Fighting Services.* New York: Cassell & Cassell, 1916.

Wood, Walter. *The Northumberland Fusiliers.* London: G. Richards, 1901.

Wylly, H. C. *History of the King's Own Yorkshire Light Infantry.* London: Humphries, 1926.

Wylly, H. C. *The Loyal North Lancashire Regiment.* London: RUSI, 1933.

Young, Filson. *The Relief of Mafeking.* London: Methuen & Co., 1900.

IV CONTEMPORARY MEMOIRS, DIARIES AND AUTOBIOGRAPHIES

Adye, John. *Recollections of a Military Life.* London: Smith & Elder, 1895.

Adye, John. *Soldiers and Others I Have Known.* London: H. Jenkins, 1925.

Aston, George G. *Memories of a Marine.* London: John Murray, 1919.

Bennett, Ernest C. *With Methuen's Column on an Ambulance Train.* London: Sonnenschein, 1900.

Brackenbury, Henry. *Some Memories in My Spare Time.* London and Edinburgh: Blackwood & Sons, 1909.

Brett, M. V. (ed.). *Journals and Letters of Reginald Viscount Esher.* London: Nicholson & Watson, 1934.

Butler, William F. *An Autobiography.* London: Constable & Co., 1911.

Cecil, Lady Gwendolin. *The Life of Robert Marquis of Salisbury.* London: Hodder & Stoughton, 1921.

Colvile, H. E. *The Works of the Ninth Division in South Africa in 1900.* London: Arnold, 1901.

de la Rey, J. E. *A Woman's Wanderings and Trials During the Anglo-Boer War.* London: Fisher Unwin, 1903.

de Villebois-Mareuil, G. H. *War Notes.* London: A. & C. Black, 1901.

de Wet, Christiaan Rudolf. *Three Years' War.* Westminster: Archibald Constable & Co., 1903.

[d'Etechegoyen] Ex-Lieutenant of General de Villebois-Mareuil. *Ten Months in the Field with the Boers.* London: William Heinemann, 1901.

Gaskell, H. S. *With Lord Methuen in South Africa.* London: Henry J. Drane, 1906.

Gatacre, Beatrice. *General Gatacre.* London: John Murray, 1910.

Goldmann, Charles Sydney. *With General French and the Cavalry in South Africa.* London: Macmillan, 1902.

Grenfell, F. W. *Memoirs of Field Marshal Lord Grenfell*. London: Hodder & Stoughton, 1925.

Guest, Herbert M. *With Lord Methuen from Belmont to Hartebeestfontein*. Klerksdorp, South Africa: H. M. Guest, 1901.

Haldane, R. B. *An Autobiography*. London: Hodder & Stoughton, 1929.

Kinnear, Alfred. *To Modder River with Methuen*. Bristol: J. W. Arrowsmith, 1900.

Mackenzie, John. *Austral Africa. Losing It or Ruling It*. London: Sampson, Low, Marston, Searle & Rivington, 1887.

Melville, C. H. *Life of General The Right Hon. Sir Redvers Buller*. London: Edward Arnold, 1923.

Morley, John. *The Life of William Ewart Gladstone*. New York: Macmillan & Co., 1903.

Peel, Sidney C. *Trooper 8008 Imperial Yeomanry*. London: Edward Arnold, 1901.

Phillipps, L. March. *With Rimington*. London: Edward Arnold, 1901.

Piennar, Philip. *With Steyn and De Wet*. London: Methuen, 1902.

Pollock, Arthur William. *With Seven Generals in the Boer War*. London: Skeffington, 1900.

Prior, Melton. *Campaigns of a War Correspondent*. London: Edward Arnold, 1912.

Pullin, Dudley. *A Devonshire Volunteer With Methuen's Horse in Bechuanaland under Sir Charles Warren*. Sidmouth: Frank Carter, 1886.

Robertson, William. *From Private to Field Marshal*. London: Constable, 1921.

Robinson, Phil. *How I Found Methuen*. London: 1882.

Schowalter, A. *Amtliche Berichte des Generals J. H. de la Rey, des Generals J. C. Smuts unde des Generals P. J. Liebenberg sowie andere Urkunden über den Südafrikanischen Krieg*. Munich: J. F. Lehmanns Verlag, 1902.

Smith-Dorrien, Horace. *Memories of Forty-Eight Years' Service*. London: John Murray, 1925.

Spurgin, Karl B. *On Active Service with the Northumberland and Durham Yeomanry under Lord Methuen*. London: Walter Scott Publishing, 1901.

Stephenson, Frederick Charles Arthur. *At Home and on the Battlefield*. Collected by Mrs Frank Pownall. London: Murray, 1915.

Wilkinson, H. Spenser. *Thirty-Five Years*. London: Constable, 1933.

Wolseley, Garnet. *The Story of a Soldier's Life*. New York: Scribner's, 1903.

Wood, Henry Evelyn. *From Midshipman to Field Marshal*. London: Methuen, 1906.

Wood, Henry Evelyn. *Winnowed Memories*. New York: Cassell & Co., 1917.

V CONTEMPORARY JOURNALS AND MAGAZINES

Adye, John. 'The British Army'. *Nineteenth Century* 6 (1879): 344–60.

Adye, John. 'Has Our Army Grown with Our Empire?' *Nineteenth Century* 39 (1896): 1012–36.

[Army Instructor]. 'The Case of the British Army Officer'. *Contemporary Review* 79 (1901): 406–12.

Atkinson, B. 'Army Reform'. *Quarterly Review* 193 (Jan. 1901): 171–201.

Atkinson, B. 'Administrative Reform in the Army'. *Edinburgh Review* 200 (Oct. 1904): 477–501.

Atkinson, B. 'The Truth About the Army'. *Edinburgh Review* 198 (Oct. 1903): 438–62.

Atkinson, B. 'German General Staff on Lord Roberts' Campaign'. *Blackwood's Magazine* (April 1905): 482–97.

Balck, Major. 'The Lessons of the Boer War and the Battle-Working of the Three Arms'. *Journal of the United States Cavalry Association* 15 (Jan. 1905): 698–722.

'Battle of Magersfontein, December 1899. A Contemporary Letter'. *Journal of the Society for Army Historical Research* 20 (1941): 198–200.

Biddulph, H. 'The Era of Army Purchase'. *Journal of the Society for Army Historical Research* 12 (1933): 221–3.

Brabant, E. H. 'Lessons of the Transvaal War'. *Quarterly Review* 195 (Jan. 1902): 295–326.

Brackenbury, Henry. 'Military Reform'. *Fraser's Magazine* Dec. 1866; Aug. 1867.

[British Officer]. 'The Literature of the South African War'. *American Historical Review* 11 (1907): 299–321.

Bürde, J. 'The War and Modern Tactics'. *Contemporary Review* 78 (1900): 142–52.

Court, Charles À. 'Lessons of the War: Suggestions From the Front'. *Nineteenth Century* 47 (1900): 702–16.

de Bloch, Jean. 'Some Lessons of the Transvaal War'. *Contemporary Review* 77 (1900): 457–71.

Dicey, Edward. 'After the Present War'. *Nineteenth Century* 46 (1899): 693–707.

Ducrot, L. H. 'Guns in South Africa'. *Journal of the Proceedings of the Royal Artillery Institution* 28 (1901): 203–8.

Ellison, G. F. 'Our Army System in Theory and Practice'. *Army Review* 3 (1912): 382–96.

Forbes, Archibald. 'War Correspondents and the Authorities'. *Nineteenth Century* 7 (1880): 185–95.

Hale, Lonsdale. 'An Army Without Leaders'. *Nineteenth Century* 39 (1896): 357–65.

Hale, Lonsdale. 'Our Peace Training For War. Guilty or Not Guilty?' *Nineteenth Century* 47 (1900): 227–43.

Hamilton-Gordon, A. 'Fourteen Days Howitzer work on Service'. *Journal of the Proceedings of the Royal Artillery Institution* 27 (1900): 347–64.

Henderson, G. F. R. 'The Training of Infantry for Attack'. *United Service Magazine* (Aug. 1899): 491–512.

'Lessons of the South African War'. *Contemporary Review* 82 (1902): 305–40.

Low, Sydney and Sydney Shippard. 'South African Problems and Lessons'. *Nineteenth Century* 46 (1899): 865–90.

MacDougall, Patrick. 'Have We an Army?' *Nineteenth Century* 15 (1883): 501–16.

MacDougall, Patrick. 'Our System of Infantry Tactics: What is it?' *Nineteenth Century* 17 (1885): 833–46.

MacMunn, G. F. 'The Boer Position at Magersfontein'. *Journal of the Proceedings of the Royal Artillery Institution* 27 (1900): 97–102.

Maude, F. N. 'Military Training and Modern Weapons'. *Contemporary Review* 77 (1900): 305–22.

Mayne, C. B. 'The Training of Infantry for the Attack'. *United Services Magazine* Dec. (1899): 289–95.

Mead, A. R. 'Night Attacks in the Transvaal War'. *United Services Magazine* (May 1904): 200–10.

[Miles]. 'Lessons of the War'. *Contemporary Review* 77 (1900): 153–73.

[Officer]. 'The Government and the War'. *Contemporary Review* 76 (1899): 761–3.

[Officer]. 'The War in South Africa'. *Contemporary Review* 77 (1900): 143–52.

Robinson, Phil. 'The Army, the Volunteers, and the Press'. *Contemporary Review* 42 (1882): 973–8.

Simmons, J. L. A. 'The Weakness of the Army'. *Nineteenth Century* 13 (1883): 529–44.

Simmons, J. L. A. 'The Critical Condition of the Army'. *Nineteenth Century* 14 (1883): 165–88.

[Staff Officer]. 'The War and the Drill Book'. *Contemporary Review* 78 (1900): 203–12.

Stopford, J. G. B. 'The Volunteers'. *Nineteenth Century* 47 (1900): 29–35.

Thring, Lord, Charles À Court, and A. Hurd. 'Lessons of the War'. *Nineteenth Century* 47 (1900): 695–729.

Vincent, Howard. 'Lessons of the War'. *Journal of the Royal United Services Institute* 44 (June 1900): 605–62.

Von der Goltz, Colmar. 'What Can We Learn from the Boer War?' *Journal of the Royal United Services Institute* 46 (Dec. 1902): 1533–9.

Von Heydebreck. 'What has the Boer War to Teach Us?' *Journal of the Royal United Services Institute* 47 (Jan. 1903): 48–56; (Feb. 1903): 186–95; (March 1903): 314–25.

Wilkinson, Spenser. 'The War in South Africa and the American Civil War'. *Contemporary Review* 77 (1900): 793–804.

Wolseley, Garnet. 'England as a Military Power in 1854 and in 1878'. *Nineteenth Century* 3 (1878): 433–56.

Wolseley, Garnet. 'Long and Short Service'. *Nineteenth Century* 9 (1881): 558–70.

VI MODERN BOOKS

Adjaye, Joseph K. *Diplomacy and Diplomats in Nineteenth-Century Asante*. New York: University Press of America, 1984.

Agbodeka, F. *African Politics and British Policy in the Gold Coast 1869–1900*. Evanston, IL: Northwestern University Press, 1971.

Andrzejewski, Stanislaw. *Military Organization and Society*. London: Routledge & Kegan Paul, 1957.

Anglesey, George Charles Henry Victor Paget, Marquis of. *A History of the British Cavalry*. London: Leo Cooper, 1982.

Atkinson, C. T. *The South West Borderers 24th Foot.* Cambridge: Cambridge University Press, 1937.

Avant, Deborah D. *Poltical Institutions and Military Changes.* Ithaca: Cornell University Press, 1994.

Barnett, Corelli. *Britain and her Army.* New York: William Morrow & Co., 1970.

Beet, Arthur J. *Kimberley Under Siege.* Kimberley: Kimberley Siege Veteran's Reunion Committee, 1950.

Belfield, Eversley. *The Boer War.* Hamden, CT: Anchon Books, 1975.

Bond, Brian (ed.). *Victorian Military Campaigns.* New York: F. A. Praeger, 1967.

Bond, Brian (ed.). *The Victorian Army and the Staff College 1854–1914.* London: Methuen, 1972.

Bowie, John. *Empire at War.* London: Batsford, 1988.

Cannadine, David. *The Decline and Fall of the British Aristocracy.* New York: Anchor Books, 1990.

Carver, Lord. *The Seven Ages of the British Army.* New York: Beaufort Books, 1984.

Charters, David A., M. Milner, J. Brent Wilson. *Military History and the Military Profession.* Westport, CT: Praeger, 1992.

Cole, Juan Ricardo. *Colonialism and Revolution in the Middle East.* Princeton, NJ: University Press, 1993.

Cunningham, Hugh. *The Volunteer Force.* Hamden CT: Archon, 1975.

D'Ombrain, Nicholas. *War Machinery and High Policy.* Oxford: University Press, 1973.

Duxbury, George R. *The Battle of Magersfontein.* Battles of the Anglo-Boer War, 1899–1902, No. 9. Johannesburg: National Museum of Military History, 1979.

Farnie, D. A. *East and West of Suez. The Suez Canal in History 1854–1956.* Oxford: Clarendon Press, 1969.

Farwell, Byron. *Queen Victoria's Little Wars.* New York: Harper & Row, 1972.

Farwell, Byron. *The Great Anglo-Boer War.* New York: W. W. Norton & Co., 1976.

Farwell, Byron. *Mr Kipling's Army.* New York: W. W. Norton & Co., 1981.

Farwell, Byron. *Eminent Victorian Soldiers.* New York: W. W. Norton & Co., 1985.

Fergusson, Thomas G. *British Military Intelligence 1870–1914.* Frederick, MD: University Publications of America, 1984.

Gardner, Brian. *The Lion's Cage.* London: Arthur Barker Ltd, 1969.

Gibbs, Norman H. *The Origins of Imperial Defence.* Oxford: Clarendon Press, 1955.

Gladstone, E. W. *The Shropshire Yeomanry.* London: Whitethorn Press, 1953.

Gooch, John. *The Plans of War: The Central Staff and British Military Strategy.* New York: John Wiley & Sons, 1974.

Griffith, Kenneth. *Thank God We Kept the Flag Flying.* New York: Viking Press, 1974.

Gross, Felix. *Rhodes of Africa.* New York: Frederick Praeger, 1957.

Hamer, W. S. *The British Army: Civil–Military Relations, 1885–1905.* Oxford: Clarendon Press, 1970.

Harries-Jenkins, Gwyn. *The Army in Victorian Society.* Toronto: University of Toronto Press, 1977.

Harrison, Robert T. *Gladstone's Imperialism in Egypt.* Westport, CT: Greenwood Press, 1995.

Holt, Edgar. *The Boer War*. London: Putnam, 1958.

Howard, Michael. *Studies in War and Peace*. London: Temple Smith, 1970.

Howard, Michael. *The Continental Commitment*. London: Temple Smith, 1972.

Howard, Michael (ed.). *Soldiers and Governments: Nine Studies in Civil–Military Relations*. Bloomington: Indiana University Press, 1959.

Hull, Richard W. *Southern Africa: Civilization in Turmoil*. New York: New York University Press, 1981.

Jeal, Tim. *The Boy-Man: The Life of Lord Baden-Powell*. New York: William Morrow & Co., 1990.

Johnson, Franklyn A. *Defence by Committee*. New York: Oxford University Press, 1960.

Keegan, John. *The Face of Battle*. New York: Vintage, 1976.

Keegan, John. *Mask of Command*. New York: Penguin Books, 1988.

Keppel-Jones, Arthur. *Rhodes and Rhodesia: The White Conquest of Zimbabwe, 1884–1902*. Montreal: McGill/Queen's University Press, 1983.

Kimble, D. *A Political History of Ghana: The Rise of Gold Coast Nationalism 1850–1928*. Oxford: Clarendon Press, 1963.

Kruger, Rayne. *Good-Bye Dolly Gray*. New York: J. B. Lippincott Co., 1960.

Langer, William L. *European Alliances and Alignments*. 2nd edn, New York: Vintage, 1964.

Lloyd, Alan. *The Drums of Kumas*. London: Longmans, Green, 1964.

Lockhart, J. G and C. M. Woodhouse. *Cecil Rhodes: The Colossus of Southern Africa*. New York: Macmillan Co., 1963.

Lowe, C. J. *The Reluctant Imperialists*. London: Routledge & Kegan Paul, 1967.

Luvaas, Jay. *The Military Legacy of the Civil War*. Chicago: University of Chicago Press, 1959.

Luvaas, Jay. *The Education of an Army: British Military Thought, 1815–1940*. Chicago: University of Chicago Press, 1964.

Marlowe, John. *A History of Modern Egypt and Anglo-Egyptian Relations 1800–1953*. New York: Praeger, 1954.

Martin, F. *History of the Grenadier Guards*. Aldershot: Gale & Polden, 1951.

Maxwell, Leigh. *The Ashanti Ring*. London: Leo Cooper, 1985.

McElwee, William. *The Art of War: Waterloo to Mons*. Bloomington, IN: Indiana University Press, 1974.

Morris, James. *Pax Britannica*. New York: Harcourt, Brace & Jovanovich, 1968.

Oatts, L. B. *Proud Heritage*. London: Thomas Nelson & Sons, 1963.

Pakenham, Thomas. *The Boer War*. New York: Random House, 1979.

Pemberton, W. Baring. *Battles of the Boer War*. Philadelphia: Dufour Editions, 1964.

Porter, A. N. *The Origins of the South African War*. New York: St Martin's Press, 1980.

Pyrah, G. B. *Imperial Policy and South Africa 1902–1910*. Oxford: Clarendon Press, 1955.

Robinson, R. and J. Gallagher with A Denny. *Africa and the Victorians*. 2nd edn, London: Macmillan, 1981.

al-Sayyid, Afaf Lutfi. *Egypt and Cromer*. New York: Frederik A. Praeger Publishers, 1969.

Schölch, Alexander. *Egypt for the Egyptians*. London: Ithaca, 1981.

Selby, John. *The Boer War*. London: Arthur Barker, 1969.

Sheppard, Eric W. *A Short History of the British Army*. 4th edn, London: Constable, 1950.

Sheppard, Eric W. *Military History for the Staff College Entrance Examination*. Aldershot: Gale & Polden, n.d.

Shillington, Kevin, *The Colonization of the Southern Tswana 1870–1900*. Braamfontein, South Africa: Ravan Press, 1985.

Sillery, Anthony. *Founding a Protectorate*. The Hague: Mouton & Co., 1965.

Sixsmith, E. K. G. *British Generalship in the Twentieth Century*. London: Arms & Armour Press, 1970.

Skelley, Alan Ramsay. *The Victorian Army at Home: The Recruitment and Terms and Conditions of the British Regular, 1859–1899*. Montreal: McGill/Queen's University Press, 1977.

Spiers, Edward M. *The Army and Society, 1815–1914*. New York: Longman, 1980.

Spiers, Edward M. *The Late Victorian Army 1868–1902*. London: St Martin's Press, 1992.

Spies, S. B. *Methods of Barbarism?* Cape Town: Human & Rousseau, 1977.

Stone, Jay C. and Erwin A. Schmidl. *The Boer War and Military Reforms*. Lanham, MD: University Press of America, 1988.

Swartz, Marvin. *The Politics of British Foreign Policy in the Era of Disraeli and Gladstone*. New York: St Martin's Press, 1985.

Symons, Julian. *Buller's Campaign*. London: Cresset Press, 1963.

Thomas, Hugh. *The Story of Sandhurst*. London: Hutchinson, 1961.

Wallace, R. L. *The Australians at the Boer War*. Canberra: Australian Government Publishing Service, 1976.

Warwick, Peter (ed.). *The South African War*. Harlow: Longman, 1980.

Young, Peter and J. P. Lawford (eds). *History of the British Army*. New York: G. P. Putnam's Sons, 1970.

VII BIOGRAPHIES

Arthur, Sir George. *Life of Lord Kitchener*. London: Macmillan & Co., 1920.

Arthur, George (ed.). *The Letters of Lord and Lady Wolseley 1870–1911*. New York: Doubleday, Page & Co., 1922.

Baird, W. *General Wauchope*. Edinburgh: 1901; repr., Freeport, NY: Books for Libraries Press, 1972.

Barnes, John, David Nicholson (eds). *The Leo Amery Diaries*. London: Hutchinson, 1980.

Bonham-Carter, Victor. *Soldier True*. London: Muller, 1963.

Buckle, George E. (ed.). *The Letters of Queen Victoria*. London: John Murray, 1932.

Butler, Lewis. *Sir Redvers Buller*. London: Smith, Elder & Co., 1909.

Casser, George H. *The Tragedy of Sir John French*. Newark: University of Delaware Press, 1985.

Comaroff, John L. (ed.). *The Boer War Diary of Sol T. Plaatje*. Johannesburg: Macmillan, 1973.

Douglas, George. *The Life of Major-General Wauchope*. London: Hodder & Stoughton, 1904.

Dressler, Friedrich August. *Moltke in his Home*. London: John Murray, 1907.

Engelenburg, F. V. *General Louis Botha*. London: G. G. Harrap & Co. Ltd, 1929.

Forrest, George. *The Life of Lord Roberts*. New York: Cassell & Co., 1914.

French, Gerald. *The Life of Field Marshal Sir John French*. London: Cassell and Co., 1931.

Garvin, J. L. *The Life of Joseph Chamberlain*. London: Macmillan & Co., 1934.

Hamilton, Ian B. M. *The Happy Warrior: A Life of General Sir Ian Hamilton*. London: Cassell, 1966.

James, David. *Lord Roberts*. London: Hollis & Carter, 1954.

Low, Charles Rathbone. *A Memoir of Lieutenant-General Sir Garnet J. Wolseley*. London: Richard Bentley & Son, 1878.

Macnab, Roy. *The French Colonel: Villebois-Mareuil and the Boers 1899–1900*. London: Oxford University Press, 1975.

Maurice, Frederick Barton. *Haldane 1856–1915*. London: Faber & Faber, 1937.

Maurice, Frederick and George Arthur. *The Life of Lord Wolseley*. London: William Heinemann, 1924.

Meintjes, Johannes. *De la Rey*. Johannesburg: Hugh Keartland, 1966.

Powell, Geoffrey. *Buller: A Scapegoat?* London: Leo Cooper, 1994.

Rosenthal, Eric. *General De Wet*. Cape Town: Dassie Books, 1946.

Spies, S. B. (ed.). *A Soldier in South Africa: The Experiences of Eustace Abadie*. Houghton, South Africa: Brenthust Press, 1989.

Taffs, Winifred. *Ambassador to Bismarck: Lord Odo Russell*. London: Frederick Muller, 1938.

Walter, Jerrold. *Sir Redvers Buller*. London: S. W. Partridge, 1900.

Walter, Jerrold. *Field Marshal Lord Roberts*. London: Hammond, 1914.

Walter, Jerrold. *Field Marshal John French*. London: Hammond, 1915.

Walter, Jerrold. *Earl Kitchener of Khartoum*. London: Hammond, 1915.

Williams, Charles. *Life of Sir H. E. Wood*. London: Sampson, 1892.

Williams, Watkin W. *The Life of General Sir Charles Warren*. Oxford: Basil Blackwell, 1941.

VIII MODERN JOURNALS

Bailes, Howard. 'Technology and Imperialism: A Case Study of the Victorian Army in Africa'. *Victorian Studies* 24 (1980): 83–104.

Bailes, Howard. 'Patterns of Thought in the Late Victorian Army'. *Journal of Strategic Studies* 4 (1981): 29–45.

Bailes, Howard. 'Technology and Tactics in the British Army, 1866–1900'. In *Men, Machines, and War*, eds Ronald Haycock and Keith Neilson, 21–48. Waterloo, Ontario: Wilfrid Laurier University Press, 1988.

Barnett, Corelli. 'The Education of Military Elites'. *Journal of Contemporary History* 2 (1967): 15–35.

Beckett, Ian F. W. 'Early Historians and the South African War'. *Sandhurst Journal of Military Studies* 1 (1990): 15–32.

Chamberlain, M. E. 'The Alexandria Massacre of 11 June 1982 and the British Occupation of Egypt'. *Middle Eastern Studies* 13 (1977): 14–39.

Cook, Hugh. 'The Ballard Letters: The Boer War Writings of C. R. Ballard'. *Quarterly Bulletin of the South African Library* 45 (1991): 145–58.

Davey, Arthur. 'Milner/Forestier-Walker Letters'. *Quarterly Bulletin of the South African Library* 41 (1987): 115–18.

Galbraith, John S. and Afaf Lutfi al-Sayyid-Marsot. 'The British Occupation of Egypt: Another View'. *International Journal of Middle East Studies* 9 (1978): 471–88.

Hall, Darrel D. 'Guns in South Africa, 1899–1902'. *South African Military History Journal* 2 (June 1971): 7–15; (Dec. 1971): 41–6; (June 1972): 82–7.

Marks, Shula and Stanley Trapido. 'Lord Milner and the South African State'. *History Workshop* 8 (1979): 50–77.

Miller, Stephen M. 'Lord Methuen and the British Advance to Modder River'. *Military History Journal* 10 (1996): 121–36.

Morris, Roy, Jr 'Surfeit of Commanders'. *Military History* 6 (1990): 38–45.

Porter, Andrew. 'The South African War (1899–1902): Context and Motive Reconsidered'. *Journal of African History* 31 (1980): 43–57.

Preston, A. W. 'British Military Thought, 1856–90'. *Army Quarterly and Defence Journal* 89 (1964): 57–74.

Schölch, Alexander. 'Men on the Spot'. *Historical Journal* 19 (1976): 773–85.

Travers, T. H. E. 'Technology, Tactics, and Morale: Jean de Bloch, the Boer War, and British Military Theory, 1900–1914'. *Journal of Modern History* 51 (1979): 264–86.

Tucker, Albert. 'Army and Society in England 1870–1900: A Reassessment of the Cardwell Reforms'. *Journal of British Studies* 2 (1963): 110–41.

Tucker, Albert. 'The Issue of Army Reform in the Unionist Government, 1903–5'. *Historical Journal* 9 (1966): 90–100.

IX NEWSPAPERS

New York Times. New York. 1932
The Times. London. 1899–1902.

X UNPUBLISHED MATERIAL

Scales, Robert H. 'Artillery in Small Wars: The Evolution of British Artillery
    Doctrine, 1860– 1914'. PhD thesis, Duke University, 1976.
Stone, Jay C. 'The Boer War and its Effects on British Military Reform'. PhD
    thesis, City University of New York, 1985.
Thomas, James B. 'Sir Redvers Buller in the post-Cardwellian Army: A Study
of the Rise and Fall of a Military Reputation'. PhD thesis, Texas A&M
University, 1993.

Index